JFK JR.

JFK JR.

An Intimate Oral Biography

ROSEMARIE TERENZIO
and LIZ McNEIL

Edited by KIM HUBBARD

GALLERY BOOKS

New York   London   Toronto   Sydney   New Delhi

G

Gallery Books
An Imprint of Simon & Schuster, LLC
1230 Avenue of the Americas
New York, NY 10020

First Gallery Books hardcover edition July 2024

GALLERY BOOKS and colophon are registered trademarks
of Simon & Schuster, LLC

Simon & Schuster: Celebrating 100 Years of Publishing in 2024

For information about special discounts for bulk purchases,
please contact Simon & Schuster Special Sales at 1-866-506-1949
or business@simonandschuster.com.

The Simon & Schuster Speakers Bureau can bring authors
to your live event. For more information or to book an event,
contact the Simon & Schuster Speakers Bureau at 1-866-248-3049
or visit our website at www.simonspeakers.com.

Interior design by Jaime Putorti

Manufactured in the United States of America

10 9 8 7 6 5 4 3

Library of Congress Cataloging-in-Publication Data is available.

ISBN 978-1-6680-1851-4
ISBN 978-1-6680-1853-8 (ebook)

Rose
For my husband, Dave Mazzella. I love you madly.

Liz
For my husband, Michael Thomas, and our son,
Maxwell, with love.

Some people have asked, why talk after all these years? You've shut up for so long. And I think—it's for him. John wasn't interested in the VIP section—he didn't want to be behind the ropes, he wanted to be on the dance floor, in the middle of it. He would love some of these stories to be told, because we had fun.

—JACK MERRILL, FRIEND

Contents

Prologue

Sasha Chermayeff, friend from Andover

One time in the early '90s, John and I were walking in the East Village. I had my son Phineas with me—Phin was a little boy, almost exactly three years old. I remember we were crossing Avenue A, and I said, "My God, John, this is how old you were when your father was killed. If Phin's dad was taken away from him now, it would be a gigantic . . . it would color his entire life." John was just nodding and he said, "Yeah, you never get over it."

Ed Hill, friend from Andover

You wanna talk about the weight of legacy. . . . Not only is John Kennedy the only son of a revered martyred president, he's the son of a man who was publicly murdered. I mean, talk about a clusterfuck. He had to define himself— he had to invent himself—out of that.

Robbie Littell, friend from Brown

He brought it up, that we both didn't have our fathers. We didn't really talk about it. I didn't want to either—that's the third, fourth, and fifth rail. It's just: jump right over that.

The father thing happened too young for both of us. There really wasn't anything to talk about.

Narendra Taneja, friend from India

Look, he was a bit of a wounded seeker of truth. You could always sense that he was very hurt by what had happened to him, to his family—that was very clear. One can easily understand: wherever you go, you are recognized thanks to your father, and yet he's not there, you don't remember. And when you needed him most, when you were young, he was not there. But your very identity is immediately, instantly linked to him. . . . Just imagine that.

RoseMarie Terenzio, executive assistant and friend

I remember seeing that movie *The Truman Show* and getting very emotional. It was like, oh my God, there are all these people watching John, like he's some *thing* that's playing out. People all over the world have this emotion invested in him—they know nothing about him, and they think they do. I thought, *Just like this guy Truman, John has all these people tuning in.*

He gave an interview once where he said, "I can get in my plane and just fly away. . . ." No cameras, no people wondering what you're doing or why.

If he was an actor, he could stop acting. If he was a singer, he could stop singing. But it was his birthright—he couldn't choose not to be John F. Kennedy Jr.

When Jackie Met Jack

In 1951, journalist Charlie Bartlett and his wife, Martha Bartlett, introduced twenty-one-year-old Jacqueline Bouvier, a socialite and columnist for the Washington Times-Herald, *to Congressman Jack Kennedy, thirty-three, Charlie's good friend. A year later, after another dinner at the Bartletts', Jack and Jackie's courtship commenced and JFK began his run for the Massachusetts Senate. In 1953, Martha was a bridesmaid in the couple's wedding. Eventually, she and Charlie would be godparents to the couple's son, his father's namesake—John Fitzgerald Kennedy Jr.*

Martha Bartlett

My husband really loved Jack, and he always wanted Jack and Jackie to meet. They both were of a certain age and things were starting to get thinned out as far as who was available. Poor Jack was always making advances. Half the time they were not accepted. He thought he was a great Don Juan. And most women didn't think of him as a great Don Juan.

So the first thing Charlie and I did as soon as we got married was to have them for dinner. I had an extra woman, as I remember, in case Jack didn't enjoy Jackie. He could look very disinterested. But he was interested. Jackie was pretty, and he was interested. He followed her out to her car.

She had a boyfriend waiting for her in the car, and she was on to her next date. But after that she had me call Jack Kennedy all the time and really keep after that relationship. I did a lot of finagling.

Maybe he would've called her, but I think she did the pursuing. There was only a certain number of people with a certain amount of money and a certain wherewithal in Washington, if you were ambitious. There was nobody here. It's not as if you were living in New York.

We had something called the Dancing Class; you could ask whoever you wanted. So, Jackie said, "I think it'd be a fun time to have Jack Kennedy." So we asked him to the Dancing Class. Then the next thing that happened was he ran for the Senate. Well, he didn't have time to be squiring somebody around when he's running for the Senate, so he didn't call. But once he was senator and he had the time, he resumed the courtship.

To be honest, most people who would be sane and sensible would not marry Jack Kennedy. Because of his womanizing, even back then. It was laughable. It was really almost a disease. But if you have a father that's doing the same thing, like Jackie's did, you're not going to find it that peculiar. Jackie's father was bad—I knew him. Jackie was used to philandering. It's all about what you're used to. You connect it with love.

Were Jackie and Jack in love at the beginning? No, I think that's expecting a lot. They didn't know each other.

I think the first years in the White House were pretty deadly. Jackie complained a lot. She'd allude to Jack's infidelities once in a while; she could make fun of it. She could even joke about it to him—she was incredible. He didn't pay any attention. You know, you'd have to be insensitive to do the things that he did.

I do think Jack and Jackie had a wonderful relationship by the time he died. I think over time he began to appreciate her more. But it couldn't have been easy to be married to someone like that. You know, she was one of the world's best actors.

CHAPTER 1

A Son and an Heir

"He was elated it was a boy"

Two years after Jack and Jackie married, Jackie had a miscarriage. In 1956, she had a stillborn daughter, Arabella. Caroline Bouvier Kennedy was born in November 1957, and John came along on November 25, 1960, two weeks after his father was elected president of the United States. Born premature, John had trouble breathing and spent his first hours in an incubator.

Clint Hill, Jackie Kennedy's Secret Service agent

John's birth was a surprise. He wasn't due until December 15. On Thanksgiving Day, November 24, the president flew to Washington from Florida, where he was working on the transition and selection of his cabinet and staff, to spend the day with Caroline and Mrs. Kennedy. After dinner, the president flew back to Florida.

Everything seemed to be going okay and then, all of a sudden, she's having labor pains. My phone rang around 11:30 p.m. and it was my boss and he said, "Mrs. Kennedy has been taken to Georgetown Hospital by ambulance. Get there as quick as you can."

It was a caesarean. I paced up and down like an expectant father because there was nobody, no family member, there.

Shortly after midnight, the nurse came out and said, "Mrs. Kennedy has delivered a baby boy. She and the baby are fine but we're going to take some precautions and put him in an incubator for a while." John had some difficulty breathing.

Then another nurse came out carrying John in his swaddling clothes. I was the first person, other than the medical staff and Mrs. Kennedy, to see John. I saw him before his father did.

The president flew back in the middle of the night. He was elated it was a boy, his first son—a magical moment. They were just happy that it was a live birth because Mrs. Kennedy had had a difficult time carrying a baby to full term. Finally, they had a fourth member of their family.

Mrs. Kennedy was worn out. She and John remained in Georgetown Hospital for almost two weeks. Well, naturally the press was going crazy. We had an agent posted there around the clock, a guy named Ed Tucker. At one point she told the nurse that she wanted to see Ed. He went in: "May I help you, Mrs. Kennedy?" And she said, "Could you loan me twenty dollars so I can pay the hairdresser?" She wanted her hair done. She never carried money. I don't remember how it looked afterwards. We were agents—we didn't notice that stuff.

After spending time with Mrs. Kennedy and John, the president flew back to Florida and took Caroline with him. John was getting better and stronger every day. On December 9, when Mrs. Kennedy and John were released from Georgetown Hospital, I accompanied them to their N Street address, where Mrs. Kennedy changed clothes to meet Mrs. Eisenhower and tour the White House living quarters. Later that afternoon we flew to Florida on the *Caroline,* the family plane, with John and his nurse, Luella Hennessey. We went to stay with the president's parents at the ambassador's residence in Palm Beach.

In January, Mrs. Kennedy and the president flew back to Washington for the inauguration. They left John and Caroline in Florida. John was only an infant. If the children had been in Washington, the public would've demanded that they be a part of the inaugural ceremony, watching the parade, all that stuff. This way the president and Mrs. Kennedy didn't have to worry about that. . . . They left them with Secret Service agents and nannies. John was left behind a lot as a child.

John's birth was an historic event. He was the first child born to a president-elect. They made a special nursery for him. And Mrs. Kennedy had a school in the White House for Caroline, and she had a playground built near the Oval Office on the lawn.

Preston Bruce, White House doorman, interviewed for the John F. Kennedy Presidential Library Oral History in 1964

[The president] was—marvelous. I just wish I could have been the father to my children that he was. . . . It was always rather comical when John-John would holler to his dad [as he left for the office every morning]. "Don't leave me," he said. "We've got to go to work." The president would call back and tell him, "Come on, let's go to work." And John-John would come down in his pajamas and bathrobe and of course, I'd come out to the door. I'd follow them to the office, to bring him back. That was a lot of fun.

Clint Hill

Mrs. Kennedy was very insistent that Caroline and John grow up like normal kids. I always said to her, "That's impossible." She tried her damnedest. She insisted that if they fall down, let them get themselves up. If they make mistakes, let them. They had to be respectful of anybody they came into contact with. I remember her teaching John how to bow, all that stuff, because he would be meeting heads of state, kings and queens. I always thought, *They're the children of the president of the United States, they're never going to be like other children.*

Tom Wells, Secret Service agent

I thought John and Caroline both were very intelligent for their age. A lot of it had to be the fact that they weren't just with children all the time. They were around people that took time with them. And even being around the agents a lot—the five of us. I think that probably enhanced some of their communication skills. I would like to believe that it did.

At the White House school, they would have a recess in the mornings. There was a jungle gym. Their nanny, Miss Shaw, would usually take John out so he could have some time running outside. And it was not unusual that the president would come out of the office if he was not tied up with something. He'd come out and clap his hands and visit with the children a little bit and go back in.

One day he came out and the children ran over and greeted him. He looked around and said, "Where is John today?" And I said, "Well, Miss Shaw has taken him to the doctor's office—he fell and knocked out a tooth." The president thought for a minute and said, "That is a baby tooth, isn't it?" And I said, "Yes, sir." And he said, "Well, he'll grow another one. That'll be all right."

Martha Bartlett

I remember Jack said something to my husband, Charlie, once—John had had a slight accident—and Jack more or less implied that he was worried about him because he was so accident-prone.

Maud Shaw, nanny to Caroline and John, interviewed for the John F. Kennedy Presidential Library Oral History in 1965

John was one hundred percent boy. He [was] very intelligent and very inquiring, and the president began to be very proud of him because he was a little man to take around. . . . He had very good manners.

The very best of the times was after the president had finished up all of his duties and the office was closed, and we would go along with him to the swimming pool. He would swim and John would be like a little eel in the water. He gave his father great pleasure.

JFK Jr. to Larry King on September 28, 1995

We had a dog who was named Pushinka, who was given to my father by the premier of Russia, was it the Soviet Union at that time? . . . But I don't think it was actually from Khrushchev, I think it was the head of the Parliament. And it was the daughter of the first dog in space.

We trained it to slide down the slide that we had in the back of the White House. . . . Sliding the dog down the slide is probably my [first memory].

Clint Hill

If we were up at Cape Cod or down in Florida and out on a boat, the president loved to have the kids join and swim in the ocean.

Once I picked up John on the yacht to take him back to shore on the speedboat. There was this plume of water shooting out from behind. I said, "John, you have to see how this boat operates." And I tipped him over so he could watch it. He was laughing like crazy. Good thing I didn't drop him.

John loved to sail. He took after his dad in many respects, whereas Caroline took after her mother; she loved to ride horses.

When Mrs. Kennedy and I would go to New York for her to see friends or shop, and the children would be left back at the White House, the president would take advantage because he knew that Mrs. Kennedy never liked to have the children photographed. She wanted to maintain their privacy, but he knew pictures of the children made for good publicity. So, when she was gone, he'd arrange for photos to be taken in the Oval Office. This is where you see the famous picture of John crawling out from underneath the desk in that little opening in the bottom. The media would go crazy for those photos.

Gustavo Paredes, friend, son of Jackie's personal assistant, Providencia Paredes

I remember going in his room at the White House—he had lots of aviation stuff there. He would have models of planes and he'd always run around with them. He liked to go to airports. I remember watching helicopters take off from the White House lawn. He loved flying in the helicopters.

Clint Hill

John loved anytime there was something going on in the south grounds where the military were involved. And Mrs. Kennedy kind of fed into that. If there was a head of state coming to visit, she would bring John down. She wanted him to understand what his father was doing. She didn't want the press to see that he was there. We would go out a little side door and hide behind some bushes so that she could show John without anybody knowing about it. He loved all that pageantry.

John loved helicopters, loved airplanes, anything military. When we were out in the country, he'd find a stick and play like it was a gun and march. I can see him right now at Wexford, their place in Virginia, running in the woods, gun over his shoulder, marching, with boots on and a helmet. And his nanny, Miss Shaw, pretending to be his army nurse. He got her to put up a tent. She was his playmate, or the dogs. It was like "Well, John, you go play with the nanny." Whereas Caroline had all these friends.

The agents were a little concerned about John. We tried to broaden his horizons. We never thought he'd be very smart, because he just had a tunnel vision. It was the damn airplanes and the military uniforms and all that stuff—that seemed to be the only thing he liked. They put in a bouncy plane at Wexford for him so he could pretend to be a pilot. Mrs. Kennedy said that he would end up being a pilot someday.

We never envisioned he would grow up to be the fine young man that he did.

Pat Manocchia, friend and fraternity brother at Brown

The only real conversations I ever had with him about his memories of his father . . . He was so little, he didn't remember too many things. Just some imagery, running to the helicopter. Getting picked up, hearing the blades, and going inside. He said he had a very clear vision of that.

On August 7, 1963, Jackie gave birth to Patrick Bouvier, Caroline and John's younger brother. Born three weeks premature, he died on August 9, from hyaline membrane disease, now called Respiratory Distress Syndrome.

Clint Hill

The situation with Patrick all happened so fast. Baby is born, the realization that he was in trouble. I don't think Mrs. Kennedy even got to hold him before they rushed him away.

It was the third child she had lost. More than any woman should have to bear.

Richard Cardinal Cushing, archbishop of Boston, interviewed for *The Death of a President* by William Manchester in 1964

The funeral of Patrick was the first time I ever saw Jack cry. At the end of the mass of the angels . . . he and I were left alone. He was so sorrowful he tried to carry the casket out—it was such a little coffin he could get his arm around it, and he did—but it was in a marble vault, and I said, "Jack, you better get along. Death is not the end of all, but the beginning."

Clint Hill

Before Patrick died, the president and Mrs. Kennedy would never hold hands in public or embrace or anything like that. Afterwards, it was commonplace that the president and Mrs. Kennedy would embrace when they met, hold hands if they're walking somewhere. I think they were just both more attentive to each other from that point on.

Mrs. Kennedy spent that summer in Hyannis Port with the children. She seemed to become more and more depressed. For the most part she was secluded in her room.

The president visited as often as he could. I noticed he seemed more attentive to Caroline and John as well.

Martha Bartlett

I was visiting at Hyannis Port that summer. One night the phone rang, and it was Jackie's sister Lee. And she said, "Ari's got the yacht, and he wants you to come and rest because Patrick is dead, and you need a vacation." So Jackie came back to tell Jack that she planned to go on Aristotle Onassis's yacht. And Jack, even though he had a bad back, I'll never forget it—he tried to get down on one knee to be playful. And at the same time, he was dead serious. He said, "You can't go. He was indicted for past taxation on something, and his reputation is just too bad." And as you know, she went.

Clint Hill

I knew she wouldn't go on a trip like this without her husband's permission. He must have thought she was so depressed that she needed something to look forward to. But his staff was concerned—Onassis had long-standing legal issues with the U.S. government and a reputation as a womanizer and opportunist who couldn't be trusted. There had always been concern about Lee's friendship with him. But the president insisted Mrs. Kennedy should be allowed to go.

Jackie's spirits really improved after the trip to Greece. When we came back, she told me the president really wanted her to go with him on a trip to Texas in November. She hadn't thought she would feel ready, but now she thought she might go. She was coming back to the way she had been prior to Patrick's birth. And she was very interested in this election that was going to be held in '64. She wanted to do whatever she could to help him.

Martha Bartlett

That's the sadness of it. I think that for the first time, they were on the same page. It wasn't just Patrick dying. It was the whole thing, the fact that she went on the trip and was willing to be political, I think it meant a lot to him. I thought he couldn't be in love with anybody. . . . I'm not so sure he didn't love her at the end.

Clint Hill

By that fall, whenever the president was flying to or from Andrews Air Force Base, he would have John go with him. And usually at the end, if the president was leaving the country or something, John had to stay in the helicopter, and he would raise a hissy fit because he couldn't go on the plane. He wasn't always permitted on Air Force One. On November 21, 1963, we had flown to Andrews AFB from the White House in a helicopter. John realized when we got to Andrews it was the end of the line. The president told John that he couldn't go along to Texas. Mrs. Kennedy explained that his birthday was coming up in a few days and they'd be back and would have a nice big party. "Don't worry, we'll be back soon."

Then, when the president started to leave the aircraft, he turned to Agent Bob Foster, who was with John, and said, "Agent Foster, will you take care of John for me, please?" That was rather unusual. I'd never heard the president say it before. Bob answered, "Yes, sir, I will."

John was really crying. When the president got to the stairway of Air Force One, he turned and waved.

CHAPTER 2

November 22, 1963

"As bad as it can get"

Clint Hill

In the motorcade in Dallas, I was on the left front portion of the running board on the car immediately behind the president's car. I was scanning to my left and ahead, when all of a sudden, I heard an explosive noise over my right shoulder. It came from the right rear. I saw the president grab at his throat and move to his left. I knew that something had happened to him. So I jumped from my position and began running to try and get on the back of the presidential vehicle and get on top of the rear and form a barrier or shield behind Mrs. Kennedy, so that no more damage could be done.

They told me later that there was a second shot that I didn't even hear. Just as I approached the car there was a third shot that hit the president in the back of his head and exploded out the right side of his head. It was a massive enough wound that blood and brain matter and bone fragments came out of the wound over the back of the car and sprayed on myself and Mrs. Kennedy.

As I started getting up on the car, Mrs. Kennedy came up on the trunk and she was trying to grab some of that material that came out of the president's head and she didn't even realize I was there. When I got her back into the seat, the president's body fell to the left and into her lap and the right side of his face was up. I could see that his eyes were fixed and there was a hole in the rear upper-right side of his head. I could see into that hole that the brain matter in that area of the head was missing. It was gone.

I assumed it had been a fatal wound, so I turned around and gave thumbs-down to the agents in the follow-up car, to let them know our situation was dire.

When we got to Parkland Hospital, the agent in the lead car, Winston Lawson, jumped out and ran into the emergency room. We were about to try and help the president, but Mrs. Kennedy wouldn't let go of him. I finally pleaded with her and said, "Please, Mrs. Kennedy, let us help the president." I realized she just didn't want anyone to see the horrible condition he was in. I took off my suit coat and I covered up his head and upper back. He was lying on her lap. She let go, so we lifted him up and put him on a gurney and rushed him to Trauma Room 1. I assumed he was dead.

Doctors started to arrive. One after another. At one point I think there were fifteen doctors, all trying to do what they could to revive him.

I had been asked by my supervisor to get an open phone line to the White House. They put me through, and the operator cut in and said, "Mr. Hill, the attorney general wants to talk to you." That was Mr. Robert Kennedy, the president's brother. He got on the phone and asked, "Clint, what's going on down there? How bad is it?" I did not want to tell him that his brother was dead, so I just said, "It's as bad as it can get."

At 1:00 p.m., the president was pronounced dead. We brought Mrs. Kennedy out and we were going to put her in the car behind the hearse, but she said no, she wanted to ride in the back of the hearse with the casket.

Mrs. Kennedy didn't say anything. She was in shock. We got to the airport. She sat in the back of the aircraft with the casket. We couldn't leave because Vice President Johnson had to be sworn in on the plane before we could take off.

At some point earlier in the evening I had called and suggested to the agents with John and Caroline that they take them to Mrs. Kennedy's mother's house in Georgetown so they wouldn't be at the White House when we returned. I knew when we got back to Washington with the president's body, President Johnson was going to go by helicopter straight to the White House and John would hear the helicopter and get all excited because Mommy and Daddy were coming home. Well, Mommy and Daddy weren't going to be on that helicopter coming home, and I didn't want him there.

After Lyndon Johnson was sworn in on board, Air Force One took off for Washington. The plane landed at Andrews AFB at 5:58 p.m., and Mrs. Kennedy accompanied the president's body to Bethesda Naval Hospital for the autopsy. At 2:45 a.m., Hill was summoned to the autopsy room as an additional witness.

Clint Hill

Agent Roy Kellerman, my boss, wanted somebody to be knowledgeable of the president's condition in the event Mrs. Kennedy ever raised a question. I thought she never would, and she never did, not to me anyway. I came down as they finished the autopsy to have the doctors explain to me the bullet wounds and the condition of the body.

It was very emotional to see him lying there. I wondered, *Why isn't it me under the sheet?*

When we were at the hospital, Mrs. Kennedy found out Caroline and John were not at the White House and wanted them immediately brought back, which they were. They still had not been told that their father had been killed. They were told, as I understand it, by their nanny, Miss Shaw.

Tony Bradlee, wife of *Washington Post* editor Ben Bradlee, interviewed for *The Death of a President*

Nancy [Tuckerman, the White House social secretary] had asked us to come to the White House because she thought Jackie was going to come here. The children were running around. Miss Shaw said, "I haven't the heart to tell them." The helicopters were eerie; they were hovering around, and in the past their sound had always been a sound of joy.

Ben Bradlee, interviewed for *The Death of a President*

I played with the children. Only a few days ago I had been roughhousing with John-John. I told him stories—you know, the kind in which you tell the story about the little boy and imitate what he himself had been doing. Also I marched my finger up and down him.

There was one moment when I said to Nancy, "I'm going to tell those children." Nancy, the Secret Service, Miss Shaw weren't going to . . . And someone had to help Jackie over that task. Tony told me it was not a decision for me to make. Caroline was quiet, but then, she has been quieter.

That afternoon Caroline played across the room by herself—across the hall in her own room. But each time a helicopter came, the children would come running and crying, "There's Daddy." "Daddy's coming later," I would say desperately.

The evening got progressively worse. The great brown wasps of helicopters were making terrible noises outside, the bloody great choppers doing their business with the cabinet out there.

At first, the children and Miss Shaw were to go to [Jackie's mother and stepfather] the Auchinclosses'. Miss Shaw herself was in tears and went to pack for the children. I had a discussion with her. She said she didn't know how to tell them.

Tony Bradlee

I think we must have been at the White House about an hour and a half and then we went to [the hospital in] Bethesda about 6:30 or 7:00 p.m.—anyhow, it was before Jackie got there.

It was like a dream. Jackie came into the long part of the room, with her suit covered with blood.

Ben Bradlee

Jackie walked in looking as though she had been burned alive with that god-awful dress with blood on it. Everyone rose. . . . She came right into my arms and started to sob. . . . I held her as tight as I could, trying to crush her, and I said, "Don't be too brave—cry." She was sobbing, but there were few tears.

She gave me a brief version of Dallas. She said she saw the whole front of his head jump out, "and with that instinctive grace of his he reached for it and it wasn't there."

Janet Lee Bouvier Auchincloss, Jackie's mother, interviewed for the John F. Kennedy Presidential Library Oral History in 1964

I asked Jackie that night . . . whether she wanted me or Miss Shaw or anyone to tell the children about their father's death. She thought for a minute and then she said, "I think Miss Shaw should do exactly what she feels she should do. She will have to judge how much the children have seen or heard or whether they are wondering. . . ." I told Miss Shaw this. . . . I told her that Mrs. Kennedy had said that she should use her own judgment. I told her that I was going to sleep at the White House with Mr. Auchincloss, and that Jackie had told me that she wanted us to sleep in the president's room.

Miss Shaw—I found out very late that night, I suppose it must have been very late, that she had told Caroline before she went to bed. John, of course, wouldn't understand at all what death meant, and Caroline not very much more, but Miss Shaw told me that she had told her. I don't remember her words, but she had said that her father had gone to heaven and talked a little bit with her, and that Caroline had cried a good deal.

Maud Shaw

It certainly was a very difficult time, a very sad one. I actually didn't particularly want to tell the children the sad news about their father's death. I didn't tell John too much because I felt that he was too little to take in too much, but Caroline of course had been so dear to her father and so close to him and she was old enough to understand. . . . Caroline realized what had happened and what was going on and it was a very sad time for her. But she was such a comfort to her mother. She knew what her mother was going through, this very bad strain, and poor little John said, "My poor mommy's crying. She's crying because my daddy's gone away."

Janet Lee Bouvier Auchincloss

The next morning, shortly after seven o'clock, Caroline came into the president's room, where Hugh and I had rested, I think perhaps only for an hour. I don't think we laid down until six in the morning. She came in a little after seven and she had her big giraffe with her, which I think her father had given her. She knew we were there; Miss Shaw had certainly told her. She walked over to the bed after she had pushed the giraffe ahead of her, which was sort of to ease her entrance, and John came in pulling some toy. She came over to the bed and pointed to the picture of her father, which covered the front page of the newspaper, and said, "Who is that?" I said, "Oh, Caroline, you know that's your daddy." And she said to me, "He's dead, isn't he? A man shot him, didn't he?" And her little face was so extraordinary. It's hard for Caroline to—she's a very, very affectionate little girl and she's a very thoughtful child. And I think that the behavior of both the children through the next days was a remarkable tribute to the way the president and Jackie had brought them up.

Clint Hill

The funeral at St. Matthew's Cathedral was the same day as John's third birthday, November 25. When Mrs. Kennedy went to get the president's body from the Capitol, the children did not go with her. Her brothers-in-law, Robert and Ted Kennedy, accompanied her.

When they got back to the White House, we had John and Caroline in another car in the motorcade so that they could follow from the White House to St. Matthew's. At one point, the window in the car was open and Bob Foster, the agent assigned to Caroline, was walking beside the car and she reached out and held his hand.

At St. Matthew's, I was seated immediately behind Mrs. Kennedy and the children. At one point I gave Mrs. Kennedy a handkerchief I carried in my pocket. She was crying. John became a little rambunctious. She gave me the sign that she would like to have him taken out. The agents took him to a room off the sanctuary to keep him occupied. They thought they'd work on his salute.

Mrs. Kennedy had asked us earlier that month to show him how to salute because he was going to attend a ceremony at Arlington National Cemetery, where his father was speaking. She wanted him to learn to salute so he could be just like a member of the military.

Bob Foster took him over to a little anteroom off where the casket was. The agents thought they'd just have him rehearse. And John was saluting with his left hand. There was a marine colonel standing in the doorway. He said, "John, this is how you salute." With his right hand.

As the president's body was taken out of St. Matthew's Cathedral, Mrs. Kennedy and the children and other members of the family stood on the front steps of the cathedral. As the body was being placed on the caisson to go to Arlington National Cemetery, all the military personnel came to a salute. Mrs. Kennedy bent over and whispered in John's ear. I didn't hear what she said. But immediately he turned around to face his father's casket and threw his shoulders back and saluted with his right hand. I mean, I couldn't believe it, but it was right there in front of me. And you could see on the faces of generals and everybody else, there was this little bit of water coming down the side of their noses. Everybody choked up. And me included.

Philip M. Hannan, auxiliary bishop of the Archdiocese of Washington, interviewed for *The Death of a President*

I saw John Jr. salute. I was standing by him. I thought, *This is the picture that will live.* I saw the reaction of the people across the street. It was an instantaneous reaction; they broke down, especially the women. . . . I had heard Mrs. Kennedy say, "John, salute." I knew then that this was probably the most poignant picture of the century.

Clint Hill

It was almost too much to bear. We had been with them through the entire pregnancy, and the loss with his little brother, Patrick, who died just a few months before that. And now this. And he had been such a good little trouper.

Neal Gabler, journalist and Edward M. Kennedy biographer

Virtually every single human being in America was sitting in front of his or her television set for those days. We'd never had an experience like that and I'm not sure that there's been anything comparable to it later. I remember very clearly my parents and my brother and I, we never left the television set for those three days until my parents sent me to bed—we were just watching in stunned silence, almost as if you were in temple or a church. There was a sacred element to it that brought everybody together. The loss was so vast.

And then this little boy who's lost his father, who is too young to process it—when he does that salute, that's the crystallizing moment. His loss, our loss. They become conjoined.

Clint Hill

Mrs. Kennedy had arranged for a small party in the White House to celebrate John's birthday that same day. There was a reception and receiving line for all the heads of state to give their condolences to Mrs. Kennedy. I was not present, but I was told how Mrs. Kennedy met with a few dignitaries in private, including Emperor Haile Selassie of Ethiopia. John and Caroline came into the room and John sat in the emperor's lap, admiring all of the colorful medals pinned to his chest. Selassie told John, "You will be a brave warrior. Like your father."

Immediately after the meeting ended Mrs. Kennedy went up to the second floor and had the party. The military aides had put it together. They each had their own designated gift to give to him, an army this, a Marine Corps that, a navy this.

Imagine: they had just laid his father to rest, saddest day in the world, and now they're supposed to have a birthday celebration. It was just he, Caroline, a few cousins and members of the family, and David Powers, the president's special assistant, trying to keep it light and singing songs. Everybody was doing their best to lighten the mood. Thank goodness, it didn't last long.

Tom Wells

The public was sending in all kinds of stuffed toys to the children. We took the children over to pick one stuffed animal or toy. The rest were being sent to Children's Hospital. John had a big golden stuffed bear.

Clint Hill

Mrs. Kennedy indicated that she wanted to take the children and go to Hyannis Port and spend Thanksgiving with the president's father. On the way to the airport, we stopped at Arlington National Cemetery, and she and the children paid their respects to President Kennedy at his grave site. And that was the first time the children had been there.

On November 29, Jackie summoned Theodore White from Life *magazine to the family home in Hyannis for an interview. There she mentioned that she and her husband had often played the soundtrack record from the movie* Camelot *before going to bed. "The lines he loved to hear were 'Don't let it be forgot, that once there was a spot, for one brief shining moment that was known as Camelot.'"*

Martha Bartlett

She thought that all up. She tried to romanticize the whole thing—she wanted to have that image. That's something I have never understood, the business of making sure it was carved into the mantel. What does that do to kids, to be brought up with a father of extraordinary myth? She fantasized things . . . but underneath it all, she was pretty pragmatic. Tough as nails—a survivor.

CHAPTER 3

Aftermath

"Why are you taking my picture? My daddy is dead."

Tom Wells

We were all suffering from a traumatic experience. Mrs. Kennedy wanted the children to be engaged in the same routines as they would normally be. That message was clear. One day after we came back from Hyannis Port that Thanksgiving, we were at a park in Georgetown. There was a photographer. And we were trying to keep him at a distance so that he wouldn't be close to the children. Well, John wanted a drink of water. One of the agents, Bob Foster, was holding him up so he could get a drink out of the fountain. Just as he lifted him up, the photographer creeped in a little closer. John looked at him and said, "Why are you taking my picture? My daddy is dead."

The agents were shocked, and so was the photographer. That was almost earthshaking, for a kid that age to say that.

Gustavo Paredes

John knew his father was no longer around, but in the early days he did not know how he died, for sure. That was kept from him for quite a bit of time until he got older.

Clint Hill

Mrs. Kennedy and the children spent that Christmas in Palm Beach. The happiness was not there anymore. I mean, it was Christmas, sure, the kids were kind of happy when they got their gifts. But there wasn't this jubilation. Everything had changed. There was always a lot of activity when the president was there, comings and goings. Heads of state, members of the cabinet. Now none of that existed. And Mrs. Kennedy didn't like going out places because everybody was trying to console her wherever she went. She and the children used to go to the ice cream store. They didn't do that in December of '63.

Every day when I went to work what I saw was two kids without a father and a widow who no longer had a smile on her face. Six-year-old Caroline would wrap her arms around her mother's neck and try to console her, while John, at three, was too young to understand. The president, who we had the responsibility to protect, was dead.

Mrs. Kennedy and I didn't talk about what happened in Dallas. Never. The next year she was in Georgetown, and then the house across the street was up for sale and she bought that and moved across the street. She requested that the president's close aide, Dave Powers, stop by as often as possible to talk to the kids, specifically John, so he would come by almost every day. He was Irish, and he had all kinds of stories. He could make John laugh.

I was more involved with Mrs. Kennedy, trying to get her to go on a picnic down on the Potomac River or something, anything just to change the mood, trying to lighten the attitude. It was really hard.

After Christmas the kids went with Ethel and Bobby's kids to Stowe, Vermont. Mrs. Kennedy went to Antigua with Bunny Mellon, her good friend. I went with her. She was a lot stronger, but still very depressed.

Martha Bartlett

I think she learned to clam up. She just—it all shut down. She didn't like the situation, it shut down until she figured out the next play.

I would go over to the house in Georgetown. She was planning already to go to New York—she just always went on to the next thing.

Clint Hill

She was starting to make sure people were remembering the president. She was thinking about the legacy, about a library or something in his honor. She was always thinking ahead.

Among the people Jackie turned to for support was her brother-in-law Robert F. Kennedy. In the dark months after the assassination, she made frequent visits to Bobby's Virginia home, Hickory Hill, both with her children and on her own.

Thomas Maier, author of *The Kennedys: America's Emerald Kings*

Bobby had enlisted Father Richard McSorley, a Jesuit priest who taught theology and coached tennis at Georgetown, to tutor and teach tennis to his older children. When I interviewed McSorley I asked him, "Father, did the children ever ask you, if there's a loving God, how could these awful things happen in their lives?" And McSorley, who was about eighty years old, took a long pause, then said, "Well, they didn't, but Jackie did."

And then he began to tell me the story of how after the assassination Jackie was essentially suicidal, and how Bobby was so concerned about Jackie's frame of mind that he asked McSorley to set up counseling sessions under the guise of "tennis lessons" in his backyard.

"It's so hard to bear," Jackie told McSorley. She talked about her regrets that she hadn't been able to save her husband. "I would have been able to pull him down, or throw myself in front of him, or do something, if only I had known. . . . I feel as though I am going out of my mind at times. . . . Do you think God would separate me from my husband if I killed myself?"

Jackie's question left McSorley dumbfounded.

"Do you think I will ever see him again?" she asked. "It's so lonely. . . . Will you pray that I die?"

McSorley said that he tried to dissuade her from thoughts of suicide, but not from wanting to die. "It's not wrong to pray to die."

According to McSorley, Jackie no longer felt adequate even as a mother.

"The children would be better off here [at Ethel and Bobby's] anyhow. I'm no good to them. I'm bleeding inside."

"They wouldn't be better off here," he said he told her. "Nobody can do for them except you."

Just before what would have been Jack's forty-seventh birthday—May 29, 1964—the subject of suicide came up again. McSorley tried to talk her out of it, and she responded, "I know I'll never do it. I know it's wrong. It's just a way out. It's so hard to think about facing every day, the many days ahead."

When you think about the way Jackie was portrayed in the press, she was put in a very noble but kind of one-dimensional box: as the widow behind the black veil. Stoic and strong. And she did keep the country together in this awful moment. But the reality also was a person who had been shattered by what she had seen before her own eyes. I always saw both families, JFK's and Bobby's, for what they were: crime victims.

Clint Hill

By the spring of '64, the tourist situation had really started to get bad in Georgetown. There was a company in D.C. that began running tourist tours down the street where Mrs. Kennedy and the children lived. They refused to stop. The house sits back from the street somewhat, so people couldn't take pictures through the windows, but they were right across the street. And it just got worse and worse. Mrs. Kennedy and the children couldn't even go out and get in the car without everybody screaming, hollering, taking pictures. It was scary for the kids.

She finally decided that she'd had enough. We went to look in New York, where she grew up, and she found this place at 1040 Fifth Avenue. They moved in, in September of 1964.

And in New York, it's a world of difference. New Yorkers are so busy going about their own business. They don't pay attention to who's walking on the street in front of them. I noticed right away: I thought, *Geez, they don't realize who this is*. And so it got to be a lot easier.

One of the first things Mrs. Kennedy wanted to do was take the kids on a rowboat ride out in Central Park. And so we went. I rented a rowboat and she and the kids got in the rowboat, went out in the middle. Going around having a good time.

I stayed with her until after the election in 1964. We agents never discussed Dallas amongst ourselves. It's just one of those things you didn't want to talk about. We just wanted to make sure we got the job done—we didn't want anything else to happen.

CHAPTER 4

Starting Over

"After the terrible thing"

Joe Armstrong, *Rolling Stone* publisher and Jackie's friend

She never talked about the assassination. She would just say "after the terrible thing happened." The terrible thing: that's how she referred to it.

Kathy McKeon, live-in housekeeper and occasional nanny for Caroline and John

John was the first up every morning, by seven. He was always looking for his breakfast. And he loved the kitchen. He loved to cook. Making pancakes. Oh, what a mess. He'd put on a cook's apron and a big chef's hat. And he'd stand up on a chair because he couldn't reach the table, and he'd be mixing away and putting it in the pan.

My friend Bridey Sullivan worked for Jean Kennedy Smith. She had the son, William. Me and Bridey would meet in Central Park for the two of them to play. John was very small, and William was a big, tall kid. He was much taller than John, but they were almost the same age. And I used to say to Bridey, "William is too fat." She said, "John's a little squirt, a little mouse." We argued, you know. I loved telling her years later, "See, look what John turned out to be. Who's the most handsome now?"

John would go into his mother's room in the morning before he went to school, and he said, "Good morning, Mummy." And off we go. And then at night, he'd come with his little white robe on, and the belt tied around and his pajamas on, and he'd go and maybe bring his book with him. And Madam would read him a story. And if she was home and she wasn't going out, she'd always have dinner with John and Caroline. I would leave the dining room table and she would say, "No, Kathy, you can stay." They were very, very warm. You're actually part of the family when you are there.

Caroline and John were sometimes very friendly with each other, but sometimes John would do something and she'd get very upset. Caroline had a beautiful bed with pillows and everything, and her favorite doll was a Raggedy Ann. She was very neat and tidy. And John would go *pshhhh* right across the bed and knock everything off—he couldn't stay quiet for a minute. He was hyperactive, not that bad. Madam was strict. She'd go in and say, "John, this room is a mess." She didn't just let them do whatever they wanted.

I would go to Caroline's room at night. She would say a prayer to her dad. Then I would finish and John is at the door. He wants to come in and she won't let him in, and I would go to John and he would do the opposite—he would want me to march around the room and put on "The Ballad of the Green Berets." He had a little record of that. He played it all the time. He loved that song. He taught me how to salute, and I would salute with the wrong hand. He said, "Kath, no! The other hand!"

Thomas Maier

After Jackie moved to Manhattan, Father McSorley was still a big part of her life for some time. . . . All the horror was still fresh.

There was an attempt by Jackie to have McSorley as a role model for John—I don't know if as a father figure, but kind of that. I think she was very aware that her son was not going to have any type of male role models. McSorley took John to the newly opened World's Fair in Queens in 1964. They also went to the Central Park Zoo. That evening, Jackie asked the priest to say a few prayers with her son, which he did. Then she asked McSorley to sing "Danny Boy," which "John's daddy used to sing." Afterwards Jackie kissed John good night, but John wasn't ready for sleep—he insisted that his mother sing to him as well.

"I don't have a very good voice, John," Jackie told him. "What do you want me to sing?"

" 'America the Beautiful,' " he said.

As she sang for her son, McSorley noticed that Caroline was standing in the doorway.

America, America, God shed his grace on thee. . . . McSorley said he never forgot it.

During a subsequent visit, Jackie asked the priest for what he called an especially "difficult favor." She teared up as she said, "Maybe, sometime, you will get the chance to answer the question that comes to John: 'Why did they kill him?' "

Sasha Chermayeff

I don't remember John talking to me about his mom being depressed or anything like that; I remember him saying she could be strict or even angry: "We can't," or "Don't bother her" kind of thing.

Because emotionally, look at what she went through. She's in the car and her husband's skull is broken open in her lap, and she's scared to death that she's going to be next. A child can't help but absorb the stresses and the absence of somebody who's gone through a serious trauma. And her trauma was first-class capital *T*. John was absorbing not only losing his dad but having a mom who all of a sudden is afraid. The trauma he went through is complete character formation. His father's taken away, but also his mother becomes available, unavailable, available, unavailable.

He did not share a lot of his mom's feelings with me. A lot of privacy in that family—they had a special feeling of protecting each other's private lives.

In May 1964, Jackie began dating the architect John Warnecke, who designed JFK's memorial at Arlington National Cemetery.

Fred Warnecke, John Warnecke's son

Jackie was an amazing woman—my dad was very excited to be with her. He wanted her to try to get away from New York and Washington and have some time in Hawaii. He rented a house on Diamond Head. He convinced her to take that summer off and we went around to the different islands with Caroline and John. I was eleven.

One morning the phone rang early at the Diamond Head house. Hazel, the cook, said it was a very important call for my father, and I should go and wake him up. I ran over to the garage apartment, knocked on the door, but no one answered. Finally, I cracked the door open, and inside was Jackie and my father and she sat up and said, "Ohh" and lifted the sheet above her head. I turned around and ran back downstairs and told Hazel.

Once when Jackie and my father had to go to a party, they couldn't get a babysitter. Jackie suggested me, and Dad said, "That's a great idea." So I was the babysitter for the night. I just remember it was John and Caroline's bedtime and they were both upset, crying and wondering about their dad and asking who was *my* dad? Who was this new man in their mother's life, I guess. They were both crying and said they missed their dad. I didn't know what to say.

Jim Hart, friend of Jackie's

It was not long after the assassination, I guess, that Jackie and Mike Nichols were dating—I don't know, '64 or '65. Mike rarely spoke about dating her, but I remember talking about it with him and his response was "It was too heavy."

Rose Styron, friend of Jackie's

Jackie came to stay with me on the Vineyard for a while in the summer—it was maybe a year and a half after the assassination. She brought Caroline and John-John, and John's rabbit. I woke up the second morning—the two children were in the two beds in the guest room—and I could hear all these squeals. I walked in and Jackie was on the floor between the beds with her arm down a hole in the floor! Which I didn't know was there. She said, "John-John's new rabbit just disappeared down this hole."

We had three Secret Service men there, of course, with Jackie and the children. So Jackie got the Secret Service men organized at what we thought were the three entrances in the ground, you know under the house, where the rabbit might reappear. They were there for hours on their bellies or sitting, and the rabbit reappeared in the afternoon. Jackie was thrilled. Then she said, "Where's John-John?" They hadn't paid any attention to where he was. He'd been gone apparently for at least a couple of hours while they were looking for the rabbit. Of course, Jackie was beside herself.

We happened to have someone up visiting, a wonderful guy who was our caretaker in Connecticut. He went up the beach and found him—John-John had walked up the beach and he found people who were having some kind of a marshmallow roast, and he sat with them and they were really sweet to him and gave him marshmallows. They didn't know who he was—he was just a little boy who wandered up. It was quite a ways up the beach. Our caretaker found him, the Secret Service did not! But all was well.

John was absolutely adorable. He followed his big sister around—not his mom, but his big sister. They were very close. I remember my son, Tom, who was a year older, was very impressed by and jealous of this little boy who kept diving off our dock and swimming around, which my son didn't do for another year, I think. John was a daredevil when he was growing up, and that's what got him into so much trouble.

Cabot McMullen, friend and Hyannis Port neighbor

John and I were both third-generation Cape Codders whose families spent summers in Hyannis Port, a small town where everyone knew each other since childhood. A place where no one locked their doors and people dried their sails out on their lawns. Every Friday at dusk the entire town would run up the hill to the golf club to watch the president fly in for the weekend from

D.C. in the marine helicopter and land at the Summer White House out on Squaw Island.

I was five years older than John. I ran around with John's older cousins Bobby Kennedy Jr., David Kennedy, Bobby Shriver, and Chris Lawford, so John was usually somewhere in the mix. We'd play all day, and then everybody would go home and have dinner, and then we'd get together at night again. We'd go to the beach and play capture the flag, or we'd go ride our bikes around. We were the older boys who always got in trouble and so John's mother wisely got him involved in activities at places far away from his wild cousins. John was just a sweet, wonderful kid—when I think about him, I think of sunshine. Of course, he was incredibly beautiful just physically, but also his spirit and his soul and everything. Even from when he was just a little kid.

My brother, also named John, was the same age, same haircut—for a few summers, the two Johns were close friends and so identical in appearance that they would pull a switch on the Secret Service and be able to slip John away from the compound using my brother as a decoy. That way, John Jr. could enjoy a normal afternoon romp in our orchard playing with our big cat, Margaret. A boy just wanting to be a boy without all the noise and scrutiny.

After the president was gone, RFK was now the patriarch, the head of the family and the center of gravity—everything just kind of swirled around him. He was a father figure for many, including John, and I think it was so important to have him right next door.

Kathy McKeon

When their uncle Bobby would come to visit in New York, Caroline and John would run right on top of him and he would put John across his shoulders and with his head hanging down his back. They were so happy to see him. He helped Madam an awful lot with the kids, bringing them skiing and coming to see them all the time. He was like a second father.

Chris Oberbeck, friend and housemate from Brown

John told me that Bobby was trying to sort of fill in as the role of dad and, you know, would roughhouse with him and kind of "make a young man of him" kind of thing. They were sitting around one time and John was playing with an Easy-Bake Oven he'd gotten for Christmas. Bobby goes to John, in front of his mother and sister, "What do you wanna be when you grow up, John?" And John looks at him and says, "A chef." He said Bobby's face was like *Are you kidding me?* It was just such an outrageous thing to want to be, as a Kennedy. John laughed so hard about that.

Kathy McKeon

On June 5, 1968, it was my day off. I didn't have a telephone, so the Secret Service man came over to my apartment. He came to tell me that Bobby Kennedy had been shot. I said, "You're fooling me. Come on. You're playing a game with me." He said, "I'm not kidding." I had to come back to work.

I think John did understand what had happened. He knew that his uncle Bobby was gone. I think he knew he got killed, and probably he knew it was the same way, like his father. He was upset.

On June 8, Kathy was with John and Caroline on the train that carried Bobby's coffin from New York to Washington, D.C., for his burial at Arlington. Thousands of mourners lined the tracks.

Kathy McKeon

It was a very sad and emotional trip to Washington. Very sad to see those people along the tracks. It was an awful long ride—took almost twelve hours. We had one whole car for the family. Every station they came through, they held up the coffin with the American flag on it. I saw it through the window on the way down there: poor neighborhoods, tents and homeless people. Philadelphia, Baltimore, people waving and crying.

John had a few little toys with him, and he was playing on the floor with his cousin Anthony Radziwill. When it was time to get off the train, his pants were all dirty and a good job that I had a change for him. He was a mess.

I remember a big wreath hit the window. With red roses on it. John said to me, "What is that?" And I said, "It's okay, John. There's nothing." And he said, "Are they coming to get us, too?" He meant were they going to shoot us. I said, "It's okay. Don't worry about it."

Joe Armstrong

Jackie had a deep respect for Bobby. She said to me out of the blue one day in the early nineties, when we were having lunch in her little den—there was a picture of Bobby—and she said with real sadness on her face, "We helped each other out of the well. And then he's murdered in cold blood." She once famously said they're going to shoot all the Kennedys. She was so protective of her children that I think she just thought, *I can't have something happen to them.*

She knew Aristotle Onassis for many years and found him intriguing. She said he was a fascinating man, the kind of guy who would just charge up a mountain. She loved that he had a salon, that he always had interesting people around. And he had this island, and he had his own airline, Olympic Airways. Think how vulnerable she would have felt—the two people she was closest to are murdered in cold blood. He could give her security and comfort.

Fred Warnecke

Jackie was very fond of my father, I think, but not fond enough to not go off with Aristotle. And go for the money—I think she understood that architects are kind of poor. I think that hurt him a little bit, but he did stay in touch with her all through her life. They understood that they had had their time.

Martha Bartlett

Jackie's friend Bunny Mellon, I understand, told her she needed the protection of a really rich man. I think she took Mrs. Mellon at her word: marry somebody that can make it possible for you not to get hurt again. Money helps.

CHAPTER 5

Enter Ari

"I didn't like the guy, period"

Clint Hill

In 1968, when it was revealed that Mrs. Kennedy was going to marry Onassis, I got a call from Jack Walsh, who was the agent in charge of the Kennedy protective unit at the time, for Mrs. Kennedy and the children, asking me if I would come to New York because he thought I could persuade her not to go through with it. I said, "Look, she's got a brother-in-law, Teddy Kennedy. He's as close to her as anybody's ever going to get. And if he can't persuade her, nobody can."

Well, I didn't like Onassis. I had been around him in '63 when we were on his yacht, the *Christina*. I didn't think he would be good for Mrs. Kennedy and I didn't like the guy, period. Because he was all out for himself, and because he still had an ongoing relationship with Maria Callas.

I really didn't know, but I didn't think Mrs. Kennedy was in love with him. I have a feeling it was all because Bobby got killed and she no longer had any confidence in the safety for the children and herself. Even though we had Secret Service with her, I don't think she felt like she was in control enough. Onassis had residences in New York City, in Paris, besides Greece. She wanted to be away from the crowds. 'Sixty-eight was just a tumultuous year in the U.S.—it was terrible. She saw that.

Kiki Feroudi Moutsatsos, Aristotle Onassis's private secretary

The wedding on Skorpios on October 20, 1968, was a little bit sad because Alexandros and Christina [Onassis's son and daughter, then twenty and seventeen] didn't want to go. They didn't like Jackie at all. Not because they had something personally against her, but because they were always hoping that one day their father would remarry their mother.

But finally, they went to the wedding and they were with John-John and Caroline. Jackie's kids loved Christina and Alexandros.

John-John and Caroline were happy that day, running all around. It was raining, and everybody was with umbrellas. And there were so many paparazzi, you cannot imagine. They were swimming to arrive to the island. But Jackie was very happy. I think many people say that she was not in love with Onassis. That is not true.

From the very beginning, I couldn't insist that it was from love, real love. But little by little, Jackie realized that Aristo was not only a husband but was a father to her children. She married him for everything. Yes, for security, love, protection, and to be a father for her children.

Onassis was not an easy person. He would yell, he would make her cry. Although she was not a Greek woman, she found the way to approach him. When he was yelling at her, a lot of bad words, she never spoke. She was not fighting. Never. She would wait to find the right moment, when Onassis would be calm and happy, to speak to him.

Onassis adored Caroline and John-John. He wanted to show them Greek life, Greek food. He took care to bring them everything that could make them happy. He was buying everything for them, a hundred toys, different animals. I remember that he had ordered some ponies on the island, and they were so happy.

He was always teaching them to protect themselves, to be close to their mom, to be close to the people who were working on the boat, the *Christina*. Everywhere they were, there were people around them taking care of them. He was scared that something would happen. And maybe he was scared if somebody would take them and, after, ask for money. Onassis had never had security around him, but for the children, yes.

He never spoke to them about their dad. About the president. Because he didn't want to make them feel uncomfortable.

Kathryn Childers, Secret Service agent
for John and Caroline Kennedy in the early 1970s

One day Mr. Hill called and said, "I'm going to put you on the Kennedy detail because they're going to Greece, and Mrs. Kennedy would appreciate having a woman with Caroline when she travels."

Having a woman on the detail, particularly with women and kids, was an advantage because you could do things where agents stuck out like a sore thumb, and Mr. Hill said to me that the important thing was an agent needed to disappear. If they're riding horses, be able to ride a horse; if they're playing tennis, be able to hit a ball back. Don't just stand there with your hands crossed and your aviator glasses. I was a downhill racer and a marksman. I heard they first interviewed me because I could shoot cans off a post. John was really something as a little kid. Cute as a bug and always popping jokes, always being silly, but very engaging with the agents. He was one of those protectees, I think—even as a little kid—that seemed to appreciate your being there and was gracious about the fact that we could limit public access a little bit. I think he genuinely realized that protection would always be part of his life.

Jackie—and the children—wanted a normal life, and yet our even being there wasn't normal. I was called to that big dandy boat called the *Christina* on a number of occasions to meet with Mrs. Onassis to plan her schedule. It was a yacht that had been a navy frigate that Mr. Onassis had redone—it was incredible. There was a swimming pool on the back, and there was a little red speedboat called the *John* that I never saw him on, and a little sailing boat they named the *Caroline*. They certainly had lovely playthings.

Bob Cramer, childhood friend

I spent eight or nine days on Skorpios with John and Willie Smith, his cousin. We were about eleven years old. We spent our time hanging out with the crew on the *Christina*. We would shine the brass and have coffee with the crew members, and we jumped off the boat and went swimming. We went waterskiing. Mrs. Onassis and Ari Onassis were there the whole time, and they were incredibly friendly. I remember before we went to bed every night, we would say good night to Ari and Jackie, and they would both give us kisses on the cheek. I remember them sitting on a balcony in a beautiful setting.

Gustavo Paredes

John had had conversations with his mother, so he understood that Aristotle Onassis would never replace his father. I think he looked at Onassis as a companion to his mother, that his mother needed someone there. And Mr. Onassis, he was always very generous with John and Caroline, and me. A couple times he came to the Cape, and I remember he had a lot of bags when he traveled. It was interesting because the scale of everything was so much smaller in Hyannis Port—because the *Christina*, that boat is as big as that whole little part of the Kennedy compound.

Steve Gillon, teacher at Brown, friend, and later author of *The Reluctant Prince*

When I visited John at 1040 Fifth Ave after he graduated from Brown, there was a big piece of plexiglass with all of the family photos and many of them were from Greece. John on the boat. John fishing with Ari. He said those years in Greece were magical. He said he had loved Ari. It was his family. His cousin Tina Radziwill told me that they had the whole island of Skorpios to themselves. Nobody was staring at him. It was a place he could explore.

Kiki Feroudi Moutsatsos

Whenever John was on Skorpios, he was next to Onassis. I remember once he and John were walking down the street, and he's teaching John how to be a good businessman. He was telling him that we must take care of the women because we are men. Greek men are always thinking like that: *We must protect the women and we must succeed.* He was giving John instructions.

Onassis's son Aléxandros loved to be with John-John, maybe because he loved machines like Aléxandros did. They loved the cars, the planes. John-

John was listening carefully to what he was telling him, teaching him about the plane. Aléxandros was flying little planes, and he started taking John-John on board. And that was a huge problem for Jackie. She was asking me all the time to speak with Aléxandros, that she was scared and she didn't like John-John to be on board. I didn't succeed because Onassis loved Aléxandros to be with John-John.

I tried to persuade her that Aléxandros was an expert pilot—he was. But it could be very dangerous because of the weather. She told me, "I'm scared, Kiki, if John one day will become a pilot, because he likes planes, and he will try to do the same, like Aléxandros." She was very very scared. And she was right, finally. They had the same bad fortune.

On January 22, 1974, Aléxandros was a passenger in his own plane, where he was instructing another pilot, when it crashed at Ellinikon International Airport in Athens a few seconds after takeoff. He died on January 23. He was twenty-four.

Kiki Feroudi Moutsatsos

The day the accident took place, Aléxandros left the office at three thirty. Half an hour, three-quarters of an hour later, they called me from the airport. "Aléxandros went down with his plane. He had a terrible accident." For a moment, I lost my senses. Then I began the impossible task of telling the family. When the doctors said there was no hope, Onassis said take him off every life-support machine and let him pass away in peace. "I have lost my boy," he said. But he never wanted to show to the children that he was suffering. He didn't want anyone to feel pity.

Caroline and John went to Skorpios and were seated at the funeral with their nanny. Even now I don't want to remember those moments. They were crying. They knew what was happening. Jackie was saying that if Aléxandros wasn't so risky . . .

Forty days after his son's accident, Aristo's hair was becoming white. Immediately white. He was so sad.

CHAPTER 6

Collegiate Kid

"Like a Labrador puppy"

In 1968, John left St. David's School and entered third grade at Collegiate, an elite, all-boys prep school on Manhattan's Upper West Side. The almost-eight-year-old took the crosstown bus from Fifth Avenue; Secret Service agents would follow in an unmarked car.

Massimo Maglione, John's ninth-grade history teacher

Collegiate had a very good reputation as being academic and a strong school, and we had a strong scholarship program. The culture of the school was inviting to scholarship students—you could come from the projects or from Fifth Avenue, that's what I liked about it. I imagine Mrs. Onassis knew all that and wanted to send John to an elite school, but one that didn't have attitude. Collegiate did not have a luxurious look to it—it was old and drafty.

David Duchovny, friend

There was more money at Collegiate than I knew existed, but because we had uniforms you didn't really know. You couldn't tell who was wealthy, and the kids didn't care about it. That was nice.

David Clarke, friend

John showed up in third grade, when I was in fifth. One day the summer before he came, my father says, "Hey, Dave, look at the newspaper. They say John Kennedy Jr. is going to go to Collegiate starting in the fall." And there's a photo of Jackie and John. John's carrying, like, a briefcase. It's almost a third of the size he is.

When he first arrived, because everybody loved President Kennedy and the assassination wasn't that long ago, just to see him walk by was shocking a little bit. John was America's kid, who lost his dad, who was this great president.

He had this big mop of hair. You'd see him wandering around the halls, his shirttails hanging out, his tie ripped off to one side, his hair a mess. He was known for losing blazers.

Before he started, the phone company came and they ran wires all over the building and put in these emergency buttons. There was one in Colin Reed's office—the head of the lower and middle schools—hidden under his desk. And there was one down by the kitchen. If something's happening to John, you were going to push the button and the Secret Service would come running.

Jason Beghe, friend

John was clumsy, kind of like a Labrador puppy tripping over his feet. I just teased him because I was the alpha guy, and we had a lot of fucking fun. We had a very comfortable, fun kind of bromance from the get-go.

We had forty kids in the class. A lot of kids, perhaps through their parents, were pawing at him, wanting to be his friend. I didn't care one way or another who he was. I was kind of unaware.

Geoffrey Worrell, friend

Teachers were much more aware of who he was than we were. John was pretty normal, and if he wasn't, he wouldn't have gotten along with the kids at Collegiate. You throw a football and you hit the sons of three famous people.

The son of Jason Robards and Lauren Bacall, Sam Robards; the son of the choreographer Jacques d'Amboise . . .

There were these two middle-aged women who lived in my building who used to wait for me when I got home and ask me, "How is John-John?" I said, "Nobody calls him John-John and I think he's fine, thank you for asking." I got so annoyed. But, my mother said, "Be polite. Don't get an attitude."

Massimo Maglione

John was strikingly good-looking as a kid. However, he had an awkward look, too. He would sometimes freeze up when called upon in class. I would see him play ball with the kids and he wasn't the most natural athlete.

Joe D'Angelo, teacher

I had John as a student in fifth grade for English and sixth grade for social studies. I also started teaching a karate program, and John was part of that program for all the years he was there.

Kids at that age, they're growing, and everything is all thumbs—they're clumsy. I think that's part of what appealed to John, that karate was a way for him to learn physical control. And the self-defense aspect of it was interesting to him, too, because much of his life was sheltered. He always had security around him. I think at some level that made him cautious, afraid, as it would any kid. And he'd been mugged riding his bicycle through Central Park. They'd stolen his bike.

At that time the West Side of Manhattan was kind of like the Wild West. The boys would take the crosstown bus and a bunch of my boys got mugged, it would happen all the time. It got to the point where I was walking onto the bus to make sure nobody bothered them. I remember John had some fear about that happening to him. He wanted to know what he should do in that situation.

Hans Hageman, friend

He was kind of goofy and he was funny—he was popular. He would come with Secret Service protection, and his agents would sit in the lunchroom, drinking coffee. Kids were aware of it, but it wasn't that big a deal. All those kids at Collegiate were pretty elite themselves.

Geoffrey Worrell

Because of John, we got covered by *Cosmopolitan* magazine and some others. They reported that we had tea and biscuits at three o'clock—but we had juice and cookies in little disposable cups. Ever since I was a kid, they got it wrong about John. There was just such a big to-do around him.

Massimo Maglione

The Secret Service guys were not petite—they were two big, big men. They were noticeable. They didn't come to class. But it was a little eerie. Mrs. Kennedy was extremely concerned about John's safety. I heard things she said—she wanted to make sure he was very safe. She would talk to the headmaster about it. She didn't want a repeat of Dallas.

Geoffrey Worrell

John misbehaved a little bit in school. His father and his uncle had just gotten shot. *Perhaps they ought to give him a break*, I thought. If someone is acting out, talk to him and find out why. Collegiate had no counselors, it's the teachers or nothing. Teachers didn't necessarily see it as their role to do a whole lot of counseling.

John got into food fights from time to time. Once, he threw ice cream at somebody. Some of it hit me and I turned and glared at him. And then he said, "Wait a minute." And he took some ice cream and just put it on his head, completely defusing the situation and making everybody laugh. That's the type of person he was. Very self-effacing, down-to-earth.

I once hurt my knee playing basketball in the gym. The school called my uncle to pick me up—Tollie Caution, he was a minister and he'd been to the Kennedy White House for a state dinner at one point. He comes to take me to the hospital. John had stayed with me in the school infirmary until he came, and John said, "I'll just have the Secret Service drive you down to the hospital." As if it were a taxi. My uncle says, "John, you can't do that!"

David Clarke

John was definitely one of the "cool kids," but totally unpretentious and quite nice. He did everything everyone else did. Like all of us, he had a bus pass and rode the 79th Street crosstown bus. Many mornings his cousin William Kennedy Smith would travel with him. Sometimes he would stop at Carvel and get an ice cream. I don't recall strangers ever recognizing him or speaking to him on the bus. He was kind of hiding in plain sight.

He liked to make prank phone calls with us. It would be this kind of thing: "Is there a Mr. Richard Hurtz there? No? There's no Dick Hurtz?"

But there were these moments when you'd be standing in line and John was there and you couldn't help but think back to John standing there saluting in 1963. And it never went away. There was always this feeling that you were standing with a piece of history.

And then of course there was the fun part, which is where you're in American history and they're talking about the Bay of Pigs and Joe D'Angelo, our teacher, says, "And John, your dad said . . ." That was intense.

Geoffrey Worrell

John was good in history. Not so good in math. He was really good at discussing politics.

Massimo Maglione

He was a solid student in my ninth-grade world history class. I could see he liked reading the books. He did not raise his hand that much, but when he did, he knew the material. I'm not sure how hard he worked, but he did work.

He had a distracted look sometimes. As a teacher, you look at people's faces, so I'm good at that. I can't tell you all the psychological ramifications, but I could see there was something he held in for himself that was not easily shared by others. This guy had a lot on his shoulders. He had a bit of sadness to him. He was a more complicated person than people think.

Joe D'Angelo

I'm going to be honest: John was not a great student. He was not. He was kind of distracted and perhaps a little bit more immature than the other kids. And I'm not sure Collegiate was the best place for him because the intellectual rigor was almost unimaginable. Thirty-six kids in a class and when they graduate, thirty-two of them will go to Ivy League schools. It was a pressure cooker, honestly.

He was forgetful about things, constantly leaving things places. The security guys were always picking up after him. "Where's your bag, John?" He'd go and play in the courtyard, a favorite thing to do, and he'd leave his stuff there.

Kids are always leaving pens around. What pen do you think he left around? A Montblanc. What kid leaves a Montblanc? There's no cap. Just the pen. That's how he was.

David Clarke

One day I'm sitting on the black bench, which is where you got sent if you were bad. I have my Nikon camera because back then, we all thought we were photographers. John comes up and he's like, "Whoa, nice lens. You wanna trade?" And he takes off his watch and hands it to me, and I take the lens off and I hand it to him, and I slip the watch on my wrist and snap it.

It's a stainless-steel Rolex Daytona wristwatch. On the back it says "To John from Ari and Alex 10/20/1968." Alex is Aristotle Onassis's son. Ari gave it to John when Jackie and Ari got married. I'd never heard of Rolex.

That watch and I were friends for two years. I asked Rolex how much it would be to change the back because it gave me the creeps that it was engraved to somebody else. And they said thirty dollars. And I was like, eh, I can't afford that.

Anyway, so then I'm sitting on the black bench again and I'm in tenth grade, John's probably in eighth. He comes up and he goes, "Hey, do you still have the watch? My mom says I have to get it back, only because it was a gift from my stepfather." Okay, I said, and I took it off and handed it to him and he handed me the lens.

Well, since then I found out that that model watch is a huge collector's item, even without John, and with John it might be the second or the most valuable Rolex Daytona on the planet. That model was nicknamed "the Paul Newman" because Paul Newman had one. Do you know how much Paul's sold for in 2017? It was auctioned off for $17.8 million. The single most expensive wristwatch ever sold!

About three years ago, I wrote Caroline a letter and I told her the story and I said, "Do you know about this?" You've probably got $15 million in your underwear drawer clanking around, or your mom's sewing box or something. And she wrote back, "I didn't know about it or ever see it. He probably lost it. He lost everything." A nice letter.

Hans Hageman

John really disliked the media coverage. I remember reporters being outside of school, trying to get in his face. There were occasions where students would try to interfere or try to block the lens. I recall feeling, *Wow, that must really be annoying after a while, every day.* How do you deal with that?

Joe D'Angelo

I remember when John was in eighth grade, John and Mr. Onassis and Jackie were coming out of the Dutch East Reform Church, the church that Collegiate was attached to, for Christmas services. I was behind them, and we all ended up in a heap on the bottom of the stairs because the Secret Service pushed us down. A guy in a Santa Claus outfit had reached into his bag and they didn't know if it was an attack, so they were on him in an instant. It turned out to be Ron Galella, the paparazzo who famously followed Jackie, dressed in a Santa outfit. The stuff he had done was so absurd that he couldn't legally get within twenty-five to thirty feet of Mrs. Onassis and her children.

What I'm saying is, you have a kid growing up in this environment where he's trying to be a regular kid and he knows he's not a regular kid. There's that struggle going on. We were watching out for him all the time.

Wilson McCray, friend

He and I both played football for Collegiate. We were practicing and somebody threw the ball pretty hard at John and it got him in the gut. He got pretty winded and was sort of down on his knees, and I remember everyone being really worried, like, is he ok? That was the moment when everyone kind of realized that John was special—John couldn't get hurt at school.

David Clarke

In Film Club, we made a movie the first year he came called *The Young Art*. They were doing the first edit of it, and there's a part where the kids in John's class were taking Magic Markers and making little cartoon animations. There's a beautiful close-up of John, right smack-bang on his face. So cute. And everybody's like *Oh, it's a beautiful picture*. And then Colin Reed—he used to smoke a pipe and he's sitting there puffing—he rolled that back and played it again. And he goes, "Cut that out. That kid lives in a circus and we don't need to contribute to it." So they cut it out.

Geoffrey Worrell

For the first year or two he was there we had bomb threats. The kids would file into the courtyard. They told us nothing, but we thought it was related to John being there—John comes, we get bomb threats. When John's not there, we don't have any bomb threats.

We weren't frightened. We made it a big joke. We should have been frightened.

David Clarke

Any time there was a fire drill, we'd all go running down the stairs and outside. But every once in a while, John would get escorted out, thrown in the back of the Secret Service car, and driven away, lying down on the back seat.

Everybody knew it was not a fire drill. It was something else. It was a fire drill and something weird with John.

Massimo Maglione

There was one bomb scare that very clearly was linked to John's being there—there was a note saying that. Think about when a kid has to feel he's responsible for that—it was him, and him alone. I was twenty-four or twenty-five at the time and I remember when I told my mother, she was hysterical. And if *my* mother was hysterical . . . When Mrs. Onassis came in to talk to the headmaster after a bomb scare, you could see the fear in her face.

She was continuously concerned and that's why she ultimately pulled him out of the school—that filtered down to us.

"Definitely a white school"

Joe D'Angelo

Collegiate was ahead of the curve, honestly, because they were making a concerted effort to seek out kids who were Black and Hispanic, especially Black. And I remember John thriving in that kind of environment. I remember it being free and easy for him to mingle. John was just an accepting kid. I think mostly he was looking to have fun.

Not all the boys were like that. Some of them were sort of out of sorts because they came from very privileged backgrounds and did not have friends who were of other races. Most of the people they encountered of other races, from what I could tell, were people who worked for them.

Hans Hageman

John and I would eat together sometimes in the lunchroom. I was in fifth grade, and he was in third. I have a *McCall's* magazine article that covered our relationship from 1969. It was so far back then that I was referred to as "John's Negro friend." That was pretty interesting.

Geoffrey Worrell

Collegiate was definitely a white school. My parents sent me with full knowledge that I was gonna be the only Black kid in the class for a while. I got a scholarship. There weren't that many Black kids. John was very friendly to me as soon as he came into the class.

At Collegiate there wasn't racism as in hostility. Lots of kids said stupid things because they didn't know any better, you know, but I didn't sense any hostility. Like in eighth grade, where somebody said, "I want a brown pencil," and they said, "Use your finger." That sort of thing. Or you're studying slavery, and everybody turns to the Black kid to hear what they have to say. What the hell is that about?

When we had Parents Night, Mrs. Onassis came and sat with my mom and me to eat that cafeteria spaghetti instead of sitting with the other big donors at the school. She must have pissed people off by doing that because I was a scholarship kid. But they knew each other. My mother was raised Catholic and so was she and they would yak and yak.

Many of John's friends and the people he looked up to were Black. That probably has more to do with Rosey Grier than anybody else. Rosey Grier, the football player, came for father-son night. I believe it was in sixth grade. He was John's father at father-son night. Wow. John and I were talking in the stairwell and I said, "It's really cool that Rosey Grier came to be your father." And he said, "He's not my father, though."

John really missed the idea that his father wasn't there for him. But Rosey Grier was.

Rosey Grier, NFL star and former bodyguard
for Robert F. Kennedy

The first time I met John, a group of us were out playing football on the grounds of Hyannis Port. This little boy kept running around onto the field where we were playing. I asked [decathlete and actor] Rafer Johnson who was the little boy. Rafer told me that it was John Kennedy Jr. and that his mom was standing over on the sideline watching.

After the game I went over and started talking to Jackie and said, "I don't have anybody here with me, so you and I are going to be friends."

So, Jackie and I went into Ethel Kennedy's house and sat down and started talking. That was the beginning of a lifelong friendship with Jackie and John Kennedy Jr.

Joe D'Angelo

I was the substitute dad for another kid on Father's Night the year Rosey Grier came with John. The boys are all excited: *We want to do a tug-of-war between Dr. D'Angelo and Rosey Grier!* There were all these different contests on Father's Night. Now, Rosey Grier was huge. And at first, you know, he's trying to be nice to me, but inexorably I get pulled across the line. And the kids of course go nuts because it's Dr. D'Angelo who's the martial arts expert who's now been defeated.

But Rosey was such a nice, nice guy. He was very fond of John. Here's this giant man, and he comes in and he puts his arm around this kid—it's almost like that TV commercial where the football player, Mean Joe Greene, gives the little kid a jersey in exchange for a Coke. It was just beautiful to see them together. They were friends.

But I think John set me up that day. I really do.

Cabot McMullen

We used to play touch football with Rosey Grier and Rafer Johnson in Hyannis Port. I mean, Rosey Grier was seven feet tall, and instead of doing a kickoff, he would throw the ball underarm; we'd all look up and it wouldn't come down for five minutes. Rosey, he was very protective of John, very sweet.

There was a connection there. I just remember when Rosey walked up, literally, I was in the shadow. The sun was blocked, and he was just that big. He was larger than life, but a gentle giant.

David Duchovny

I came to Collegiate in ninth grade. I had applied in second grade—my mother had targeted it as this school that was gonna lift me out of whatever she thought we were in. I didn't get in and Kennedy got in for the same grade, and my mother had a hard-on for Kennedy forever. It was like *He took your spot.* So when I got to Collegiate in ninth grade, I was like, I don't like Kennedy because Kennedy took my spot!

But I became friendly with John. He was very sweet, a very innocent, very sheltered kid at fourteen. Very kind and kind of gentle and not very worldly.

The school paired me up to room with him for a trip to D.C. that year—which, thinking back, it was very odd to send John there. But we went and spent one night, and we visited the White House. I remember the person giving us the tour had maybe gotten a tip that one of the boys was JFK Jr. He kept trying to figure out which kid was John. He was saying to the group, "Oh, John, you should remember this because there's that famous picture of you under the desk here." We were all like, "Who are you talking to?" Kind of denying John was there. "We don't know what you're talking about." We all felt kind of protective of him.

Joe D'Angelo

We went on the subway once on a field trip, I believe to the Metropolitan Museum of Art. John had never been on the subway before. Back then they had these latched windows you pushed down from the top. So, if you stand on the seat, you can stick your body through the window. I turned around for a minute and then I look and John's hanging out of the subway car as it's going past the pillars. The other boys are screaming and he's screaming, too. I was horrified. I'm pulling kids back in, imagining them on the tracks!

Every kid rides the subway, but that was special for John. He talked about it at school the next couple of days. "It was a roller-coaster ride." That's what he kept saying. "But better, it's better. The noise is incredible!" He liked that.

Jason Beghe

My mother would always have a heart attack when John came over to our place. Not because she gave a shit about his fame, but because invariably he would break something. I remember once the house had just been painted and he sat on one of the windowsills and got upset because his pants and sweater were ruined. My mother was upset because the paint was ruined. Another time he broke the chandelier with his tennis racket. Every time he came over there was something. John was an accident waiting to happen.

"Jackie was on it"

Jason Beghe

Mrs. O did an amazing job with Caroline and John, and that's a big responsibility to have two of the most famous children on the planet. They just had a sense of who they were and were able to deal with it comfortably from the time I met them, which was nine or ten years old.

Massimo Maglione

You could tell when Mrs. Onassis came in that John was a big focus of her life, which is not always true. Sometimes the children, the parents love them but they're kind of ancillary. John was not ancillary to her.

When she came in you really were impressed by not just her beauty—she was stunning, most photographs didn't do her justice—but her grace and style. It just was, nothing affected. Certain parents try to put on airs. She never had to put on airs.

Here's a funny story: In those days, the parent had to write a note if a student was absent. So she wrote a note about John's absence, and it was the famous perfumed blue stationery that she would send out. My last name is Maglione—but she called me Mr. Zabaglione, which is an Italian dessert! Apparently, it was her favorite dessert. I could not stop laughing. And then when I saw her afterwards, I said, "Thank you, Mrs. Kennedy. My name has never sounded more delicious." She laughed.

Joe D'Angelo

Jackie was *on it*. I have to say, in all my experience . . . We dealt with many different kinds of parents there. High-powered parents, many sons of actors and actresses. The kids would say, "Oh, did you see my mom on Johnny Carson last night?" That kind of thing. But lots of times you were dealing with nannies or babysitters or the administrative assistants. You weren't dealing with parents. Whereas Jackie was hands-on. I'm telling you, she adored her kids, and I don't use that phrase lightly. They were her life. John and Caroline had a great mom.

One time, when he was in about fifth grade, I got a ship-to-shore call from the *Christina*, Onassis's yacht. I don't know where Jackie was, but she wasn't in New York, I knew that. We didn't have his homework and had sent a note home and her secretary told her that we were asking for his homework. She said she was sorry, which I was flabbergasted by because this was one of our first interactions. And she said, "I'm sorry. I assure you you'll have his homework tomorrow." So I said, okay, you know, and she thanked me and said, "Well, if there's ever any problem, just don't be afraid to call me and let me know." And that proved to be true.

I met Jackie and John for lunch several times. It was very nice, mostly small talk about John. She was worried at that point. John was not doing terribly well at Collegiate. And she was very, very realistic about his abilities. It's not that he wasn't bright, I just think he was distracted by so many other things. But the intellectual powerhouse in that family was Caroline. She's just so smart.

Gustavo Paredes

In the early days, Caroline did tease John. I mean, they were very close. But always at the lunch and dinner table, she was like, "Oh my God, you're a mess"—because he was just sloppy when eating.

He would wear unpressed pants and sort of wrinkled shirts. He wanted to be comfortable. Sometimes his mother had to say, "No, no, no. You are wearing something that's pressed." There were just certain lines that she didn't allow him to cross. . . . I would always look [at what he was wearing] and say, "That's really mismatched." He didn't really listen. He was exerting his personality.

Geoffrey Worrell

I went to the apartment at 1040 Fifth just a few times. Mrs. Onassis would call my mother to arrange for me to come over. In middle or upper school, John's mother conducted these dinners that were prepared for us, and everyone spoke in French, which was very close to her heart. We had to speak French, or we weren't going to get any food. Jesus, pass the legumes—or nothing! John was not, to his mother's dismay, so good in French. She was patient with us. But still nothing unless you could speak French. Caroline was there. Her French was very good.

Mrs. Onassis had a lot of breakable stuff in that house. Ming vases. We went outside and played because we wanted to throw around the ball. At that point, neither Jackie Kennedy nor my mother made houses childproof. That was not a concept. The child didn't throw the damn ball in the house.

Jason Beghe

Mostly when John and I got together we'd either go to the park or hang out at 1040 Fifth. 1040 was huge. There was an elevator that came right up to the apartment. You opened the door and there was an entrance hall, and to your right was this huge living room with several different seating areas. I think George Washington's desk was there. And there were all kinds of little tchotchkes—like figurines of delicate birds. Very expensive and fancy.

Ari Onassis had his own butler there, a Chinese guy named Chan, and we were scared of Chan. Chan didn't mess around. Maybe we were hungry, we'd go into the kitchen, of course we'd probably make a mess, and he just gave us dirty looks. One time John and I were coming up in the elevator and even before the elevator door opened, we could hear this racket of yelling and screaming and crashing. We came through the vestibule like, "Jesus Christ, what's going on?" We hear Mrs. Onassis going, "Chan! Chan! Chan!" He was taking the figurines and throwing them and yelling, "Fuck you, big lady! Fuck you, big lady!" We never knew what it was about—but that was Chan.

Ari was cool and he was kind. He once came to see us in a play at school that John and I were singing in. He was a petite guy, but he was a force. John always told me he loved going to Greece.

Jason Beghe

Ari was very regimented. He always had the same bottle of wine at the same chair and table at the same time. Every night, at exactly five o'clock, he would open a bottle of wine. One of his idiosyncrasies was that he wore fairly baggy pants and he would put his socks and garters and shoes on before he put his pants on. I would see him walking around in socks and shoes and underwear and a shirt and tie and jacket and no pants sometimes, because he always put his pants on last. He was getting sick at the time with myasthenia gravis, and one day when we were in ninth grade Mrs. Onassis was trying to convince him to come skiing in Switzerland with us because she thought the mountain air would be good for him. She had invited me and this other kid, Wilson McCray, to ski in Switzerland for Christmas break. Ari didn't want to go because he never skied and didn't want to learn. Finally, she got him to consider it and he called a fancy store on Fifth Avenue and had some ski clothing sent over. When he couldn't get the ski pants on over the shoes (since he always put his pants on last), he said, "Fuck it, I'm not going!"

Massimo Maglione

I remember Aristotle as this lumbering, taciturn figure. He never really participated. Mrs. Onassis would do all the talking, she would engage the people around her, and he was just quiet. There was one time there was a show that we put on, and I was right behind her and Onassis in the audience. I noticed they'd hardly ever talk to one another. Whereas other couples, they were just chatting away.

Geoffrey Worrell

I remember John telling me that Mrs. Onassis told Mr. Onassis, "Don't give my son presents that will kill him." Like a plane. Or a motorcycle. You gotta think in terms of what Onassis could afford. That's what she was concerned with.

David Clarke

John used to tell me Ari's son Alex would take him flying in a helicopter over Skorpios. And I was like, "Wow, your mother lets you do that?"

Kiki Feroudi Moutsatsos

After Onassis's death, the children never came back to Greece.

"Girls would line up to speak to him"

Jason Beghe

After we got older, John and I wanted to sneak off and smoke pot, and there was the Secret Service guy, Jack Walsh. But they understood and I think they looked the other way.

We used to go to this one bar a lot called Malkan's. This is 1975, John and I were fifteen. It was all underage kids, run by this shady guy. All the private school kids used to go and get drunk and hook up. We heard about it from a guy named Willie Wu, who graduated from Collegiate. We saw Willie at Mrs. Onassis's Christmas party that year and he gave us cocaine at the party and that was the first time either of us ever did coke.

Wilson McCray

John and I constantly got caught smoking cigarettes. One of my favorite stories is one of his aunts took us aside to show us how to smoke a cigarette without letting anybody see that you're smoking. She was giving us this secret technique. It was fantastic.

David Clarke

You weren't allowed to smoke on the block that Collegiate was on. So you would go across the street, and there was this stoop there. I can visualize Jason sitting there smoking a butt and all of us hanging out. Sometimes John would smoke cigarettes with the rest of the bunch. While smoking was far from considered healthy then, it was not like it is now. Many of the teachers smoked.

Collegiate, being an all-boys school, meant there was no posturing during school to impress the girls. There were plenty of after-school activities and siblings of classmates where a nice Collegiate boy could meet girls. They would most likely be from Brearley, Spence, Nightingale-Bamford, Chapin, Sacred Heart. . . . There were school dances, movie nights, school plays, etc. John did very favorably with girls, which is probably not a big surprise.

Geoffrey Worrell

I went with John once to an Irish bar, the type of place where somebody would get up and sing "Danny Boy." He wanted to take me. Everybody wondered why this guy was in there with this Black kid, you know? In 1976 or '77, interracial anything freaked people out. Made people look twice. Not everybody had a Black friend, even though everybody *said* I have a Black friend. And not a lot of Blacks ventured into Irish bars.

I think he kind of enjoyed it. Being the center of attention for something other than being John Kennedy.

After tenth grade, John transferred to Andover, an exclusive boarding school in Andover, Massachusetts.

Joe D'Angelo

I'm not entirely sure why he left Collegiate for Andover, but I think a boarding school can give more educational support than a day school can. And when you're in trouble, there's people there to help. Being in a school in the middle of the city is much more difficult to manage. I think the bomb scares played into his leaving, too. Questions about his safety certainly must have weighed on his mom, and a boarding school is a safer and more circumscribed environment.

Geoffrey Worrell

When the boarding schools had break, we made sure the boarding school kids knew about our parties. So when John was at Andover, he would go to those. Girls would line up to speak to him. One night he and I were having a relatively long conversation and these girls were, like, sitting there tapping their feet: When are you gonna get through so *I* can meet this guy?

John will forever be "the hunk" for many people, but if you see pictures of the two of us as really skinny kids, you can't understand why he was a heartthrob. Those skinny pictures, that's who he was. We both had to grow up.

David Clarke

John was happy during his Collegiate years. Just one of the boys running down the hall with his shirttail out, that mop of hair, laughing, yelling, and free. We loved him and we loved each other. He turned from a little boy into a young man. Smoked cigs, smoked pot, met girls. It was so normal, as normal as it could be. It can still make me cry.

CHAPTER 7

Bong Hits and the Brothers Johnson

Sasha Chermayeff

I first saw John at a party in New York City, probably ninth grade. Everybody was saying, "That's John Kennedy Jr." I just saw him sitting on a couch and I was thinking, *No big deal. Not my type.* He was gawky. His hair was really big. He was not Mr. Gorgeous.

And then at Andover we were both new in eleventh grade, which is unusual. If you're new in eleventh grade, you're not used to that level of academic pressure. It ended up that he stayed for three years. His mom and the folks at Andover all decided he needed to stay another year, so he didn't graduate until '79.

I met him at orientation, and he seemed like this really nice, sweet guy. I went to my first class and there he was again. And then I went to the next class and there was John. We started just walking from class to class, then going to eat lunch together. By the time two weeks had gone by, we were constantly together every day and studying. Both of us being what we called math cripples. It was fucking algebra. That's when it gets hard.

We just had this affectionate beginning. Part of it really was, I was not in love with him. I was not gaga. I was all about other guys.

William Cohan, Andover friend

The day that he was arriving, I remember going to the room of the guy across the hall, and we were looking out the window, which looked down on the path coming to the dorm. Everybody was just starstruck. John and Jackie were unbelievable stars.

But soon enough he was just a regular kid, like the rest of us, trying to figure it all out, make friends, get through the academics, have fun.

Rachel Horovitz, Andover friend

My first impression of John was that he was a wild combination of jock, freak, preppy, and drama nerd who was also incredibly conversant in politics and history. And as macho as he was, he had a gentleness—a feminine side.

Sasha Chermayeff

John dated Meg Azzoni when we were in eleventh grade. Meg was a senior. John was sixteen and Meg was seventeen. She had a superhot body. It was that kind of body that was so perfect at that moment in time, which was super athletic, very slender hips, big boobs. Like a lot of models. And John, he went for a certain type.

He then dated Lydia Hatton, another super-busty girl. I think he was exploring giant breasts—I think giant breasts were the criteria. Maybe that's life at sixteen. Kind of was for him anyway. Plus, he had come from an all-boys school. . . . And then Jenny Christian. She was my best friend. Jenny and John and Ed Hill were my closest friends from Andover. And we all stayed pretty darn close.

Jenny and John dated the whole senior year. She was not a part of the hipster cool crowd, just in her own little world. John had lots of girls going after him, but Jenny was the first love of his life, no doubt. . . . Up until that point, he was just exploring the fact that he could basically sleep with any girl he wanted. And then with Jenny, I felt like this is a relationship where it's not just about sex, to be blunt. He was impressed by her. Because she was so intelligent. And funny.

And I think Jenny was someone who was a challenge because she was reclusive by nature. She wasn't outgoing and extroverted the way that John was. I always think about the way he protected people that he loved. He had a way of making sure that you weren't being left out or you didn't feel like you weren't included. He was sensitive if you felt awkward.

Jenny got into Harvard. I was dumbfounded by how smart she was—she would sit there and, last minute, type in an essay, just boom. "Oh fuck, I have to write a five-page paper on Lenin and Trotsky before the Revolution," and then she'd sit there for forty-five minutes, smoking Larks, and then she'd say, "Okay. Done." And she would get an A+ and they would say, "Can I keep this essay to show future students?" That was Jenny. Sharp as a tack. And John was super attracted to that, too. He was a little bit more like me, a little clumsier, bad at math.

I had one tiny little moment of romance when John and I were studying together. We were so tired in the library, we decided that we needed to take a nap. So we just took all the books off a metal shelf, enough space so we could just get on the shelf and lie down and no one would see us. Then we climbed onto the shelf and the two of us snuggled and took a nap. And I remember having mild confusion, *Do I like him now?* And then the next day, he and I were like, *Oh no, that's not what we wanted. I think we're good the way we are. Let's not cross that Rubicon, because here we are, and we love each other.*

And then I told Jenny about it, and she was like, "Thank God. Because I love him. I'm in love with him." And I was thinking, *Oh, trust me, this is going to be big news.* Because he liked her, but she didn't know that he liked her that much. So then John and Jenny were going out. She was my best friend, and he was my best friend. And then they were in love with each other.

So that was the beginning, and then going back and forth to New York together. Ed Hill lived in Tuckahoe, New York. Eddie was a scholarship kid, just a brainiac. Jenny came from an upper-middle-class family in New Jersey. And I came from a New York family of artists. The four of us became really involved.

Chris Leggett, friend

I first bumped into John walking out of our dorm heading to dinner at the campus cafeteria. We started a conversation and had a great time and our relationship took off from there.

He loved sports and had a great athletic body—I mean, anybody with two eyes could see that. He had great coordination. Whether it was skateboarding, football, soccer, basketball, dancing, or whatever, he wanted to do well at it. He was only an average basketball player. I was like, dude, there's not a chance you're ever going to beat me at this game. We could play all day if you want and it's never going to happen. John's retort was "Let's play another one, let's play another one."

We both liked sports, loved the ladies, were friendly and knew that we were appealing. John's father died at 46 and mine died at 40. So we talked often about our moms.

We had family weekend every year, when parents came to campus. I wanted him to meet my mother and he wanted me to meet his. Before his mother arrived, John came to meet my mother, but I never got to meet his that weekend. Part of it was that I felt a little anxious meeting this enormously famous woman. When my mother asked if I met John's mom, I said no and explained why. She said I should meet his mother because he requested I do so as his friend and you must put all the rest aside—he didn't ask to be born the son of a president any more than I asked to be born the son of a Baptist preacher.

When I finally met his mom, she was very gracious and kind. She was not one of those parents with a whole list of questions trying to figure out whether you should be hanging out with her son.

Sasha Chermayeff

That first Christmas break, '76 going into '77, that was when I went to the first Christmas party at 1040. His mom's Christmas party. Got to know his sister a little bit. Had fun sneaking around seeing all the celebrities. Chic people of that time: Cheryl Tiegs, Peter Beard, and George Plimpton. Basically, obligatory meetings. *We have to go meet George Plimpton*, and then sneaking back and smoking weed in John's bedroom.

It took me a long time to get to know her. I wasn't allowed to call her Jackie O—John didn't like that. He just felt it was this kind of slang thing. I called her "Mrs. Onassis," but even if she said, "Call me Jackie," I couldn't do it. It was a long time before she recognized me as somebody who was in his life. I had met her for the first time in 1976, John's birthday party, and the Christmas party of '76, and every year after that. I got five solid years of every time I went into 1040 she would put her hand out, she would say, "Is that Sasha?" Five years. Yes, still Sasha. . . .

Rachel Horovitz

I remember so many parties at 1040. One year John gave Caroline a bottle of Geritol for her birthday as a joke. In his characteristic clumsiness, he spilled this disgusting liquid all over the furniture. Caroline was not amused. Jackie was definitely not amused.

Ed Hill

Mrs. Onassis, what I know of her as a mother, deserves a ton of credit. I can't speak to how much she was around; what I can tell you is she was wise. The way she moved her kids through the world with a recognition of what was expected of them and ways in which they were vulnerable. But also, in the advice she would give—things she would say to John about how to conduct his life.

John once told me that she cautioned him to be very careful about people's feelings because people who got close to him would have difficulty emotionally managing the situation, since it was just so extraordinary. She told him, "Do your best to find personal time for your friends. Don't hang around with four of them at one time, because that's inevitably going to inspire jealousy. It's going to create hurt. You need to be attentive to your friends individually to avoid all that."

I saw that play out. I could see people sort of getting cloying. I witnessed how he compartmentalized his relationships—he was good at it. One of the reasons that he was able to pull it off without bruising a lot of egos was because he could be very attentive. I mean, within the scope of his

John Kennedy distraction disorder, whatever the hell it was—talk about not being able to walk and chew gum at the same time. But he really did feel very present. And he would also do great things, like call you up out of the blue and say, "How would you like to hang out backstage at a Sly and the Family Stone concert?" He would give you these episodes of extraordinary entrée that would make you feel incredibly special.

Chris Leggett

One memorable thing that John and I did together was watch the *Roots* miniseries. It was based on Alex Haley's 1976 novel about the slave trade and slavery in America. I remember us scraping up five dollars and going to this place called My Brother's Place and getting a Brother's sub before the show. We'd split the sub and eat it on the way back to our dorm to be ready to watch *Roots*. We watched that together every night in complete silence. Other kids would come and go, but we sat there and took all it in. There were probably only fifteen or twenty people of color on a campus of 1,200 to 1,300 students. When I say he was gentle and comforting, I use words like that because those were real. He knew how to be quiet when it was time to be quiet, and he expressed compassion and empathy for the lives of the slaves.

Ed Hill

John was one of the first wealthy elite white people I knew who had reverence for African American culture. At Andover there were certain recording artists who set the standard for our musical aesthetic. Among the girls, the standard-bearers were Bonnie Raitt and Joni Mitchell. Among the boys, it was the Grateful Dead, the Allman Brothers, and the Band. And somewhere in the middle, Jackson Browne and James Taylor. And yet in comes Kennedy with these records—he had the impertinence to assault us with the records of Sly and the Family Stone and the Brothers Johnson and Earth, Wind & Fire.

We would do bong hits and John would throw on a record by the Brothers Johnson and crank it, and he'd start boogying around his room and playing air guitar to these funk riffs. And right away I knew. The bull comes through the door of the china shop, just kicking over all our literary *High Plains Drifter* pretenses with fucking Sly and the Family Stone.

Kennedy's aesthetic was much more inclusive and much more visceral. It really set him apart, and it was reflected in so many things. His hairstyle, his clothing style. But where the rubber really hit the road was in his ability to interact with the African American students, who did not have an easy row to hoe in that era, in the late seventies.

When you're young—I'm talking fourth grade, fifth, sixth—it's easy not to be hung up on race because you're just a kid. There are nice people, there are not nice people. It's a very unsullied view of the world. The way John could interact with Chris Leggett and Greg Moten—it reminded me of myself in, like, sixth grade. He had to make no fucking effort. How does he do it? He's John Kennedy, what does he know about the son of a single mom with eleven kids from Cleveland? But his embrace of African American individuals and African American culture was completely authentic. It was an outstanding part of him.

Chris Leggett

One day we ended up walking into town looking for a place for me to get a haircut. I had a big Afro, you know, a lot of hair. John and I walked into the only barbershop in downtown Andover. As the barber puts me in a chair and places a drape on me, he fesses up that he has never cut an Afro or had a Black customer before. He says, "Okay, what do I do next?" I say to him, "What you do next is just take this drape off me and allow me to get out of this chair and I'm good. You won't be cutting my hair today." John and I left the barbershop laughing hysterically as we walk down the street. I said, "I'm going to take you to a barbershop in Roxbury with Black barbers." John was all in.

Roxbury was a one hundred percent Black neighborhood in the center of Boston. In 1977, busing riots had taken over Roxbury and South Boston—the idea of desegregating schools was met with severe resistance. We were innocently walking into the middle of it all for a haircut.

John looked at me and said, "I'll just be outside skateboarding while you're getting your hair cut." If you know John, he always had his skateboard with him. He skateboarded up and down the sidewalks of Roxbury without his shirt on—he didn't have a shred of concern for his safety. When we got back to campus, I said, "Now you see how I feel as one of the few Black students surrounded by white students. Today you were the only white boy in Roxbury. How did that make you feel?" He said, "Man, I'm good. I was raised to treat all people with dignity and respect regardless of color." Few other kids from Andover would have even gotten off the train at the Roxbury stop.

Our little journey probably drove the Secret Service crazy.

William Cohan

My father was an accountant. So John figured, *Okay, well I never have any money—I can barely ever find my wallet—so if I need money, I'll borrow money from Bill.* So first he borrows twenty dollars. These are 1976 dollars. And then he borrows another twenty dollars. He owes me forty dollars. To me, forty dollars was real money.

On principle, I just didn't think it was right that a guy with this kind of obvious wealth never had any money and was borrowing it from me, and without paying it back. So one weekend, he invites me down to 1040 Fifth Avenue. I walk in and it's mind-boggling. I remember there was a very large scrapbook with a huge presidential seal embossed on the front. I really wanted to go through that, but I never got the chance. . . . And his mother's there. *Say hello to my mother. Say hello to Bill.* You know I'm taking all these mental notes because of course I have to report it back to my mother.

And then John goes into his room and decides he wants to get high, takes out the bong, smokes a bowl, pours the bong water out onto Fifth Avenue from his bathroom. I thought, *Okay, well, this is a good moment for me to ask about my forty dollars,* like, *Can you pay me back? You know, New York's expensive.* So, I asked John for the forty dollars, and of course he didn't have it. So, he went out and asked his mother, who was in another wing of the apartment. I could hear him say, "I owe Bill forty dollars." And she gave him the money, and then she said—now bear in mind, he's seventeen years old—and she says to him in her inimitable voice, "John, tomorrow we talk about money."

Chris Leggett

John and I never carried around any extra money. But all he had to do was call home or go to the bank to get some cash, whereas I was poor and on scholarship. One time after he said to me, "Legs, you got five bucks?" I said, "Do you see the irony in asking me for five dollars?" We both started laughing uncontrollably. We were just hungry teenagers with no shame in scrounging up enough to buy a sandwich any way we could.

Sasha Chermayeff

He had a lot of freedom, way more than most. Kids going in and out of his room, smoking weed and experimentation with drugs, and rock and roll, and sex, and all of the stuff we loved so much in the seventies. John was never shy and standing back, he was a part of the crowd pretty quick. He had no fear of breaking the rules. I mean, we were breaking the rules constantly, running around at night, just like normal kids.

And for John, now that the Secret Service had stopped protecting him, I think that was pretty much the first time in his life that he didn't have protection in the background. So, he had some kind of capacity to mix in with all the crowd of the rest of the kids, without being this one that stuck out. He acclimated himself—*I can be a part of a community here. I'm not alone.*

I was just at my Andover reunion and a guy told me a story: He had bought a bottle of alcohol for John's birthday, like a bottle of rum. And then when he got caught with it, he didn't get in trouble for having an unopened bottle of alcohol, he got in trouble for getting John in more trouble. Because John was already in so much trouble, a combination of academic and disciplinary probation, that the idea that somebody else would get John in more trouble was a bigger deal than him bringing the alcohol.

He got in trouble for a little rule breaking. Being out too late. It was all of the standard things. If you overslept, you weren't allowed to miss classes, no excuses, unless you were in the infirmary. So, you have a kid like John, who's losing stuff or not knowing where his keys are, or leaving his books, or being late, or getting caught smoking a cigarette somewhere that you're not supposed to. We, believe it or not, were allowed to smoke cigarettes if we had parental permission. There was a pub at Andover, back then the drinking age was eighteen. Sneaking into the pub, we had to sneak John out if somebody was coming because he isn't eighteen yet.

We were in a really kind of a wild era. There was marijuana, cigarettes, and alcohol. But there was also post-sixties stuff coming through. Psilocybin . . . There was experimenting with psychedelic drugs, and John was definitely not averse to experimenting. We did mushrooms together and went skiing. Oh my God. It was a great day.

We took mushrooms with Billy Way. Billy was one year younger, he was in tenth grade. Really sweet guy. I just remember getting to the bottom after one run and getting ready to go onto the chairlift and then seeing John, who had torn his pants. And he wasn't wearing long underwear, he was wearing a pair of khaki pants that had this giant tear across his whole thigh. I was looking at him thinking, *We're on a mountain, we're on mushrooms. It's winter, and your leg is just completely uncovered.* And I just thought, *He may be on mushrooms, but he is not having a hard time skiing, despite the fact that he's numb clearly to any kind of sensation in his legs.*

William Cohan

We went into Boston together and somehow ended up at the Black Rose bar in the North End. We were both underage, but it didn't matter because he was John. You go in the Black Rose and the bar was filled with photographs of his father and his family. We managed to have whatever beverages we wanted, and as much of them as we wanted, before catching the last bus back to Andover.

He certainly liked to smoke pot, and he smoked a lot of pot. He loved his pot, loved his cigarettes. I'm sure there were other kinds of substances that he liked, too. He wasn't shy about any of that.

Another time, he turned to me and asked me if I thought his father was a good president. I mean, I was seventeen. For me, to be friends with him, for him to ask me questions like that, it was almost overwhelming. Surreal. I said I thought he'd been a good president because that's what I had always heard about him.

Any number of things that he did from academic inadequacies to busting of the rules would've merited him getting kicked out had he not been

John Kennedy Jr. As an eleventh grader, he did not know how to divide. . . . I taught him how to divide! But John, if he wasn't interested, he didn't make any effort. He had a very short attention span—for the things he wasn't interested in. If he was interested, he did have an attention span. It just sort of happened that what he was interested in really wasn't academics. He was interested in partying and hanging out with his friends and going to Boston.

But I don't think anybody wanted to kick him out because (a) of who he was, and (b) he was, like, such a good fellow, which of course is subjective, and therefore not the way you can run a disciplinary program. But that kept John from getting kicked out of Andover.

"Definitely a good time to get him out of the house"

Sasha Chermayeff

Back home in New York, John would bring friends to Studio 54. I wouldn't go if I wasn't with John, there would be no point, I would just be waiting outside. It was filled with people like Jerry Hall and Mick Jagger, or Bianca Jagger, Bryan Ferry, Rachel Ward. . . . Andy Warhol was there a lot. All of the chic people. And this sort of elite old New York society, like Cornelia Guest, who was a debutante type.

With John, even if there was a gigantic crowd outside, they immediately pulled us in. . . . We would be ushered up to Steve Rubell's office to do coke—yes, John would do that sometimes. There was a lot of coke at Studio 54. I used to brag that I've never done bad coke, because I've never done coke except with John Kennedy. And I'm assuming that Steve Rubell and John Kennedy have access to decent cocaine. We would dance like crazy. It was a riot.

John was not an angel in that way at all. He just winged it, assuming that it would work out. When we were young, like seventeen, eighteen, going to Studio 54, I guess it's so corny, but people fucking loved him. Did everyone try to dance with John? Yes. Did gay men love John? Yes. Did young women love John? Yes. He wasn't as recognizable and famous as he would ultimately become. But New York knew.

I just remember the way that even the famous, Jerry Hall, Patti Hansen—that famous and beautiful model who married Keith Richards—everybody, no matter how big a star they are, they all wanted his attention. Everybody wanted to chat him up. And they would stampede over Caroline to get to John. It never made any sense. It was just like, "Okay, he's just this star. He just is."

I remember Cornelia Guest just falling all over him and him having no interest, but being as polite as you could possibly be to someone who you wanted to ditch. There were a few of those ditching-people nights. . . .

John Perry Barlow, Wyoming rancher and friend, from interviews with *People* magazine

John was like . . . a giant puppy—he just needed a lot more space to run in. He had been doing stuff like mixing wallpaper paste with flour and pouring it down the mail chute at 1040 Fifth Avenue. It was definitely a good time to get him out of the house.

In the summer of '77, John had been sent off—basically kicked out of the nest—to Yellowstone, Wyoming, with the Youth Conservation Corps and it wasn't working out. He was way too vulnerable.

So, I am sitting at my desk and it is relatively late at night and I get a phone call saying, "Hi, this is Jacqueline Onassis." And I said, "In the highly unlikely event that this is not some kind of a joke, what can I do for you?" Three days later, John was working on my ranch. We became very close friends.

Amelia Barlow, one of John Perry Barlow's three daughters

Jackie had called Dick Cheney to say, "Hey, Dick, John is being really dangerous. He's gotta get outta the media. Where do we put him? Is there a place in Wyoming we can put him?" He was a rambunctious teen, you know—drugs, alcohol, and girls. Dick said, "Yeah, put him at the Barlows'. That's where all the crazy people go."

There were all these people who were super dedicated to ensuring that the Kennedy legacy was intact and John's young-buck-ness wasn't gonna really mess that up. There was no one really to call him out. My dad kind of did it, but then he was simultaneously handing him a bottle of Wild Turkey. Putting him with my dad wasn't necessarily the best way to reduce the danger, but it certainly was an interesting story. So that was how John was, full of youth and wanting to sort of break out of the places that he had been put in, these ivory towers. I really think that he exercised a lot of his irresponsible masculine element with my dad on the ranch.

John Perry Barlow

That fall, Jackie invited me and my wife to come out and spend Thanksgiving in Peapack, New Jersey. She had a horse farm there. I was astonished at how good she was at making people get over the virtual her that they were carrying around in their heads and deal with her directly as a human being like everybody else. John was very good at this, too.

When I had been there a day or so, I said, "My God, what is it like to be so famous?" It was John's eighteenth birthday and Caroline's twenty-first birthday and it was also right in the middle of the anniversary of the assassination, the fifteenth. She said, "Well, at first it was very difficult because you can see I am a bit shy and I didn't like being exposed, but I could see Jack was going to become very famous and I wanted to be with him, so that was the price of admission. Then for a while I became obsessed with it and tried to control the way I appeared. Then I realized that it wasn't actually about me at all. It was this other weird cartoon strip about somebody who had my name and looked like me and did some of the things that I did, but it was a completely separate reality from my own. And I read the cartoon strip avidly for a while and then I just quit reading it." Which is about the most intelligent way I have ever heard about dealing with celebrity.

She tried to be as incidentally aware of it as possible. She also had a fierce awareness of what it could do if it got ugly.

Caroline was very sweet, but John was rambunctious. At John's eighteenth birthday party there was a brawl out on the street. After the party, there was Ron Galella outside. And one of John's friends who was a big-headed enthusiastic jock was drunk enough that he took a swing at Galella. He hit him. There was a whole bunch of guys out there, and some other photographers got some pictures of John trying to pull people out of it.

Jackie was very displeased the next day. She was like, "God, you really ought to know better." She thought the incident itself was funny, but she was really unhappy that John had been . . . unconscious enough to get himself where he was—right in the frame. It wasn't a matter of keeping up appearances, she had a legacy that she wanted to provide stewardship for. But aside from that, I think she gave those kids quite a great deal of latitude. I mean, sending him to some ranch in Wyoming of some guy she didn't know on his first real foray out of the house—I thought she showed quite a lot of faith.

Gustavo Paredes

I do remember after John's eighteenth birthday party—the scuffle. Of course, we were all drunk, because that's quote, unquote the legal age where you could drink. I remember finally when we got back to the apartment, 1040, Caroline was there and asking John, "Are you okay?" Then I remember she said, "Oh man, Mummy's going to be so upset." She said, "But don't worry, I'll be there for you to support you." I also remember at that time she was breaking up with someone and John says, "Yeah, you didn't need to be with him. That guy wasn't good enough for you." So he was buttering her up that same night. She left a little early, which . . . Was she *really* concerned about how hard her mother was going to come down on John when she got home?

Joe Armstrong

Jackie once told me that she said to John and Caroline when they were teenagers, "You're gonna hear a lot of stories about your dad, but I want you to have lunch with two, maybe three people who knew all sides of him. And I want them to tell you about your dad."

She picked Abe Ribicoff, who was the senator from Connecticut who sat next to JFK in the Senate. He became one of the most trusted members of Jack Kennedy's cabinet. I remember asking Abe about it and he said, "My first sentence to John and Caroline was 'Your dad played hardball,' meaning he was a lot tougher than people are gonna tell you."

You have to remember that John and Caroline probably had only seen their dad from film clips of speeches he made or from his press conferences where he was so much fun and made brilliant, witty comments. We'd never had a president who did live televised press conferences before. And here he followed America's grandfather, who was Eisenhower. So here's this young, vibrant, handsome guy who's solid in his answers and very articulate, but also warm and fun, witty. So Abe was like, he plays hardball, meaning he can be tough: serious, rigid, maybe cold. Like with political opponents or anybody who got in his way. If somebody came out against him, they better run for the hills.

Sasha Chermayeff

By the spring of 1978 it became clear that John was not going to be graduating with us; he was going to be staying for another year. John was failing out of Math 30, the class that you have to pass in order to graduate, right before calculus. Jenny got into Harvard. I went to University of Vermont. And John was staying, which was kind of weird.

John and Jenny were really in love. John had gone off to Cora, Wyoming, with John Perry Barlow, and was writing her love letters that summer. He wrote her a letter a day.

By fall of '78, John's back at Andover, which is not that great because he just spent two years thinking he was part of this other class and they're all gone. And Jenny's at Harvard. And John could come on the weekends, but had to go back to school on Sunday night. And she had lots of guys after her.

I think it was harder on John than it was on Jenny. And it was more Jenny's idea than it was John's—Jenny felt they needed to break up, because she was in college now, and he was still in high school. With a lot of rules. And she didn't want to be responsible for getting him kicked out, either.

John was her first boyfriend. Serious first boyfriend. John, it was his first love, but he had been with a lot of women. And I think it really did hurt John. Because, usually, it was him breaking up with people—Jen was the first time someone had broken up with him, and he had a lot of conflict about it.

He got a new girlfriend, Sally Munro, at Brown, and there were always lots of women wanting to be with him constantly. And so he and Jenny kind of fell apart from each other, but not in a bad way. I used to love getting them back together. I was constantly trying to matchmake moments where they would have a reunion.

Judge Paul Heffernan, former Juvenile Court probation officer who oversaw John's independent study internship in 1979

I was a politician type around Boston and became an advance man for Robert Kennedy and also Teddy. Years later, the faculty advisor at Andover asked if I would be willing, at the request of the family, to assume responsibility for John's winter internship.

A wonderful kid. Very pleasant and almost breezy, like his father. He had that air about him that indicated that he wasn't particularly concerned with anything that was going on except his own interests. I remember going through that period, don't you?

My charges were kids on probation in the area of the Boston Juvenile Court. I would go out and supervise their homes and make an initial investigation and John would accompany me.

He had a very interesting ability to reach into the thing to say, "Mr. Heffernan, why did you ask him about whether or not he's still smoking? And did you notice that he didn't have any shoes?" These kids, many of them were neglected children as opposed to delinquent children. I was impressed by John and I'm not so easily impressed.

I sent his mother a little note telling her that he had done a good job. I heard back from her. As we say in South Boston Irish talk, "She writes a lovely feast." That's what the nuns called it when they were teaching penmanship. This is from May 23, 1979.

> *. . . What one hopes most for a boy, especially one without a father, is that he will find mentors who will motivate him to the finest.*
> *He found that in you. . . . Thank you with all my heart. . . .*

Of all the people in the Kennedy family of that generation that I came in contact with, and there were many of them, this kid was obviously a star. He wasn't running around saying, "Look, I'm a Kennedy. My old man got shot by some bum and I expect to be taken care of anytime that I demand it." Not even close. Who knows what the kid could have become?

Rachel Horovitz

The night before Andover graduation was an emotional night. We were lying on his bed while a party raged in the next room. He was showing me his father's watch which his mother had just given him. Maybe at dinner that night. Then "Sympathy for the Devil" began playing on the other side of the wall and the line about the Kennedys came on. We just squeezed hands. I don't think we said anything.

Paul Kirby, Hyannis Port friend

When he graduated from Andover, John had a party with all his class-mates, two hundred kids on the front lawn. It was really around that time that he became kind of his own man, had his own sort of posse and his own persona—when he was a little kid, he wasn't really a ringleader; he'd catch up to the group.

So there were two hundred kids on the front lawn, and he had a huge stereo system. It started raining, and John all of a sudden said, "Move the party into the pool." The pool had this covering on it, a plexiglass covering. It was in the early spring, so it wasn't full. So they brought in the stereo.

It was just like one of the coolest things—people dancing up there, and then there's people ten feet below you dancing in the bottom of the pool.

Lou Awodey, director of the ten-week National Outdoor Leadership School (NOLS) course John took in Kenya, summer 1979

He was a very considerate young man. Always concerned about the family. When we were on safari looking at wildlife, he said, "I need to call my mother. It's her birthday. She's kind of sensitive about that." It might have been her fiftieth. And so I took him into a lodge in the Serengeti, and he called her.

He had some idiosyncrasies. A few days into the mountaineering course, we started referring to him as Dirty Johnny. He just couldn't keep himself clean—he always had dirt on his hands and his face and everything else. And I said, "Come on, you gotta wash your hands, keep yourself clean a little bit more." He said, "My mom's always harping on me for that."

He didn't have any girlfriends at that point. He always had his eye on some of the nicer-looking gals on the course. They sort of kept him at arm's length. One of the things I do remember, he always pushed the limits a bit. He didn't always listen to what we said. Of course, that's a young person, too. Sometimes they would take warnings as challenges.

One time he couldn't find a good flat spot to sleep in the campground. And he went down and found a sandbar in a creek bottom and slept on that. I taught him, "You stay in your tents. Leopards and other predators hunt the river bottoms, looking for prey at night, and you don't wanna do that." He just didn't listen to it.

I mean, not out of the ordinary, but there were things that could get him in trouble. Like smoking pot or buying marijuana from the locals could have landed him in jail. We didn't want that to happen to any of the students.

The Africa courses were semesters in outdoor education, ten weeks long. We spent about three and a half weeks up on Mount Kenya doing a mountaineering course. They would spend another week or two hiking on their own in small groups of four to six people through the Rift Valley area. They had their own dehydrated food, but they didn't have an instructor. Sixty-two miles through the Maasai territory. And that's basically where four or five kids, including John, got lost.

Somehow, they got disoriented and didn't show up when they were supposed to come out to pick up provisions. They're walking on Maasai trails or game trails. So they just didn't read their maps properly. The Rift Valley's huge. Goes from Egypt all the way down to South Africa. You're going through really dense vegetation and it's tough going.

I panicked a little bit. I wasn't gonna wait around two or three days and find out something had happened. I had to get a plane to do a search on the second day they were gone. And when we took off out of the Serengeti area, we saw the group coming into camp. It was one of the only groups that ever got lost the time I was over there—I've never, ever lost another student, and then I lose him. How does that look?

Sasha Chermayeff

He wrote me a long letter after they got back to base camp. He said, "You won't fucking believe what just happened to me," and then told me how he and his group got lost in the mountains filled with rhinos and lions and elephants, ran out of food, and were finally rescued by a Maasai scouting unit.

> *Four teams of rangers were already out looking for us, as well as a helicopter and an airplane. The American Embassy had been notified and everyone was preparing to get in touch with our parents. There were about 50 people all-told looking for us. We finally straggled into camp very dirty, exhausted, and hungry.*

He ended it so abruptly:

> *Sasha, man, you can't believe what it's like to be lost nowhere near civilization and not know if you're going to make it out. I said many prayers. Now it's off to the Indian Ocean coast for fun in the sun and recuperation. . . .*

Now when I look back, I wonder if perhaps that moment was so intense— that feeling of being lost and maybe I won't make it, and feeling a deep connection with some kind of prayer, "If you help me live through this. . . ." Maybe the profound nature of that experience was something he wanted to feel again. Not the fear as much as the depth of sensation, and that would be something you would seek. Maybe this Kenyan trip set the bar high in terms of intense experiences in nature. This deep need to feel part of something else.

John wanted to feel part of the living, pulsing river of life. Not just be this famous celebrity, having people take my picture. He connected viscerally to risk.

CHAPTER 8

The JK Factor

"It was always good to be John"

Seamus McKeon, husband of Jackie's former assistant Kathy McKeon

We probably hadn't seen him for five years. He had gone away to boarding school and had just finished, and we met him again when he went to college. He was like the statue of David! He had grown up so quick; he was older with curls. He'd been a scrawny little kid and sickly, a little weakling, really—and God, we were shocked. I said what the hell happened to you? I remember saying, "Oh, you've been juicing," you know. John said, "No, Seamus, this is all natural."

Steve Gillon

From my research, John never should have been admitted to Brown. There's no way with his grades, after being left behind at Andover, that he would've been admitted. When I spoke to the admissions director, I eventually got him to admit that of course they admitted John because of who he was. Brown was sort of in the basement of the Ivy Leagues, and they were losing money. And they realized that they need to admit the children of wealthy people in the hopes of getting donations. Brown's strategy was to admit celebrities knowing that celebrities would bring attention to the university. John was the guy who led it off. Brown went, in the years that John was there, from being the second-tier Ivy League school to being the most popular university in America. They admitted a guy who was the biggest celebrity on the planet. Then Jane Fonda sent her kids there. I used to call it the day care center for the Democratic Party because you had Billy Mondale, Geraldine Ferraro, Jimmy Carter's kid [Amy]. John transformed Brown University. Brown would never admit that, but there's no doubt.

Santina Goodman, friend; quotes from her 2018 book proposal

From the moment I arrived at Brown, the campus was abuzz about its resident celebrity. John was all people talked about. . . . I'd worked damn hard to get there, so as much as possible, I tried to tune out all the Kennedy talk.

My sophomore year, I took an acting class, and lo and behold, guess who's in it. My first introduction to John was as the kid who was perpetually late. For the first three weeks, John was at least ten minutes late for class. It didn't really bother me until I noticed that the professor seemed to repeat himself after John arrived, as if to say, *Oh hello, John, let me tell you what we talked about now that you're here.* Five weeks in, John was still coming in late. One day, I sat on the fourth tier and John sat on the third tier right in front of me. Again, the professor was repeating the lecture. I tapped John on the shoulder. When he turned around, I said, "Do you think you can get your ass here on time, so I don't have to hear this shit twice?"

John waited a few seconds, then turned back around and gave me this weird look. I waited a few seconds and tapped him on the shoulder again. When he turned around the second time, I said, "And yes, I know who you are."

Again, John waited a few seconds, turned back around, and gave me what I would come to know and love as his "shit-ass grin." I would love to say that John never came in late again, but of course he did. Each time, though, he would look at me and mouth, "Sorry." I would just reply with a nod.

Gary Ginsberg

I met John in the second-to-last row of a history class. It was the first day of class. We were both back-benching that day.

Before the class started, the professor, a really learned scholar not known for congeniality, walked down the aisle to favorably comment on a shirt John was wearing. They had never spoken before, and I was just gobsmacked. I could've been wearing a clown suit and the professor wouldn't have taken note of it. But the prof actually walked all the way down to compliment John on his shirt. I turned to John and said, "That is ridiculous."

Then we just got to be friendly. We studied together. One day, I forget who it was, Kant, some philosopher—neither of us had any clue what was really going on in the class. John had to give an answer, and it was so inane, and it was so clear that he had no idea what he was talking about, nor did I. But after he finished his two-minute response, the professor's nodding vigorously. "John, that was so insightful." I just couldn't believe it. That's when I realized it was what John always referred to as "the JK Factor." That it was always good to be John.

We used to laugh—you'd see it everywhere. We'd go to a tennis club and they'd say no, we're booked . . . and then the person would go into an office and suddenly it's like, well, we found a court for you. JK Factor. There's no table in a restaurant? Then one appears. He'd always look at me with that shit-eating grin and go, "JK Factor." That was our shorthand for life was always a little easier when you're John.

The professor took a crazy interest in him in that class. I didn't get the time of day. We were completely aligned with our relative lack of any understanding of the content, and yet he sailed through and I struggled over the finish line.

Steve Gillon

At the time, I saw John as your typical B student, nothing exceptional, but reasonably bright. John was never book-smart—he didn't have the attention span. What John had was emotional intelligence that was off the charts.

"An eclectic bunch"

Robbie Littell

Our thing was pretty raw. It started at Brown orientation, on a beach in Newport. Just two guys who were pretty full of themselves, frankly. Who found a good place to joust, if anything. And that was always the thing. There was a competitive element, whether it was racquetball or school. He had his advantages and I had my advantages—his mainly were follicle numbers. You'd say, that's the dumbest outfit I've ever seen. And he'd go, "Yeah, yeah, this is going to be in *GQ*. This is gonna be what everyone's wearing in six months, you idiot."

Pat Manocchia

We met the first week of freshman year, on a bus to Newport. Somebody had a football, and someone else had a Frisbee, and John kept trying to get the Frisbee and the football. Like, *Dude, calm down, you're on a bus.* I think he threw something at me. I thought, *Okay, I like this guy.* Then we'd see each other around campus, and we would chat, and it would inevitably be about when can we play some game somewhere. There's a game . . . be there in an hour. We both joined the same frat. Phi Psi. Very social.

John liked borrowing things. If something would be gone from the room, you'd know where it would be. *Where's my towel?* He would frequently try and borrow money. *You're borrowing money—from me?* He goes, *Come on, man. I'll write you a check. I need thirty dollars.* He wrote me a check for thirty dollars, and then I sold the check for one hundred dollars to someone, one of these people coming down the hallway trying to see him. "He's not here, but I have a check with his name on it." He was furious. I'm like, *It's a fee, man.*

People would show up looking for him and knock on our door because we lived next door. That's when the idea of being protective started, which anyone who knew him well eventually became. There was a level of fandom that was going across the line of being friendly. You go into someone's dorm and knock on a door when you're coming from another school, that's a pretty aggressive move. It was mostly women. . . . I would just say, "You're in the wrong spot." I think he got upset about that once or twice, but I said, "Trust me, this is not somebody that [you want to meet]. . . ."

Brown was a small enough school where everybody kind of knew everyone—I never really saw anybody give him any real grief. Except for me, when he lost my towel. I just borrowed his crate of records.

Robbie Littell

Phi Psi was just a nuthouse. We were not a national fraternity—it was a bunch of free spirits that didn't want a lot to do with that. We didn't do secret handshakes or anything. . . . We had the basement with kegs flowing all the time. It was just a big party. John and I lived there sophomore year, and by the end of that year you were like, *Wow. I'll never do that again.*

Christiane Amanpour, friend

I was at the University of Rhode Island, and for a number of reasons, John thought that it would be a good idea to have me as one of five people sharing a house his junior year. I was slightly older, and I had every English boarding school view of how you run a group house. So I think I was a little bit den mother there. I knew this house would be a complete and utter frat house mess unless we were able to have at least some kind of order. So I made rosters for cleaning, including the toilets, and cooking. They all knuckled down. We used to have such funny chats when it was John's time to do the toilet. . . . His cooking was usually burgers. So my early connections with him showed he did not stand on ceremony.

I remember once having to go and get lemons for somebody's, I don't know, garnish. John lent me his car to rush up to the supermarket on the corner. And for some idiot reason, he had the biggest, heaviest key ring, which was on some kind of a spring. As I was parking the car, I pulled the key out and it went right into my mouth and it broke my front tooth. But I still bought the lemons, came back. I was hysterical. The reason being I wanted to be a television journalist. And I thought, this is just not good. When I came back to the house I was crying, and I had this, you know, chipped-off tooth, and John said, "Well, Kissy, there goes your career as a television correspondent." Oh my God. I don't know whether he thought it was gonna make me laugh, but I cried even harder.

Anyway, then they got together, and they figured out where to send me to a local dentist to get my tooth fixed. So he and the rest of the housemates rallied around.

Cordelia Richards, housemate and friend

I met John through Billy Way, who lived in my dorm freshman year and became my boyfriend for the better part of those years. John and I did silly things together. We had talked about getting our ears pierced. We looked up places in the phone book and found this seedy tattoo parlor in East Providence. I remember hopping into his little silver hatchback and laughing the whole way there. I got both ears pierced and he got one. John ended up with a little gold stud earring. We laughed about it all on the way home. John's laugh was explosive.

We shared a house with three other friends, and when we'd make dinner together, there would always be a debate. The conversations got loud. It was always about politics or something in the news. John was interested in what was happening in Africa with apartheid.

He would stand at the head of the table, debating and accentuating each word with a jab of his finger. He was in his element, in one of his jaunty hats—or a dashiki and his telltale retractable key chain looped across pleated baggy pants. You were *not* going to win a debate with him!

Friends of friends sometimes came through and would be starstruck— they would get quiet and their eyes would get big. When you're living with him day in and day out, you would forget that part. He would always break the ice by asking the person a distracting question.

When I didn't get into Yale drama school, John got the mail and saw the letter and the thin envelope. He knew I didn't get in. Instead of rushing up the stairs to give it to me, he put the letter between his legs and hopped up each step. He didn't want to give it to me. He didn't want me to feel bad about it.

John and Billy had gone to Andover together and they were close, and it seemed that if you got one of them, you got the other. Billy was a charming and handsome guy. He was funny and he was a playboy. They were playfully competitive, each confident in their own prowess. Billy could hold his own when he and John were in a room full of fawning women, which I imagine was not easy to do.

Robbie Littell

Billy and John both went to that orphanage in the north, Andover. Same fraternity at Brown, both ladies' men—very competitive on that level, actually. It was something that Billy could beat John with. Old green eyes: five minutes at a cocktail party and you'd go, *Where'd Billy go?* And he'd come out of a room like with some girl he just met. Minutes later, I swear to God—the guy was magic on that. Billy had talked up every hottie since the age of five.

He and John bonded well on multiple levels, a lot of competition going on with sports and girls and they're both good-looking, too. But just for fun.

John played rugby, which is the last of the sports—that's like, if you haven't ever done anything before with a ball or a stick and you've grown up, they ask you to play rugby. So it was pretty eye-opening for him. The ruggedness, and it was actually a pretty hard, physical game. We always joked that he improved a lot physically—his capacity. I used to joke that he could barely walk downstairs when I first met him because he was kind of fumbly and gangly and skinny. And then all of a sudden, he started going to the gym regularly. He started lifting weights. As long as he didn't gain weight he was gonna have a hot-looking body by *GQ* and *Esquire* terms. He wasn't the first one to see it. It was pointed out to him, and he ran with that.

Ed Hill

John played rugby at Brown and was surrounded by jocks both at Andover and Brown. He was educated in that milieu—in that New England Ivy League world there's a real premium placed on athletic bravado. When I visited him at Brown one weekend—it was a big rugby weekend—John's squad won. So everyone was very excited. I remember us trying to enter the Brown dining hall with a keg. . . . Someone put a stop to that. But there was this one monster—one of these enormous boarding school jocks you can't believe is capable of putting two sentences together, much less get themselves admitted to a school like Brown—at one point this guy walks over to this beverage service glass recirculator with, like, juice circulating up the sides. We were already throwing food all over the place. This guy literally picked up this thing and dropped it on the floor.

Smash! And of course, John thought it was just as hilarious as I did. But remember that most of the dudes we were with in this escapade lived in that world almost exclusively—as frat brothers, as rugby players, etc. And they probably still do—they probably all still belong to the same golf clubs. Of course, John could handle that world.

But I needed John not to be a douchebag if I really was his friend. There had to be more to him than his commanding physique and the fact that he could keep up with those dudes. I always felt like his mom made it pretty clear that she preferred it when he kept the company of men who weren't exercising an all-out effort to prove themselves on the playing field. I felt that she liked writers, she liked thinkers, she liked nerds. When you think about the men in her life after the president, they were, generally speaking, a very intellectually powerful group of men. They weren't Kennedys.

She encouraged John to encounter something very different from the jocks, and he did that, very authentically. I credit his mom . . . because it would've been so easy for him just to remain in the world of touch football and sailboats.

Gary Ginsberg

He picked friends because he found something interesting or worthwhile or fun in them. And he didn't give a shit what the world thought of the friends he kept. You look at John's group of friends, they were an eclectic bunch.

Santina Goodman

Usually, John hung out with the "beautiful people," friends he either went to prep school with or who grew up with him on the Upper East Side. But he was no snob. He was friendly and at ease with people.

One day, as I'm eating my lunch on the green, John plopped down next to me. "Hi, Santina," he said. Immediately, I was aware that people were staring at us. I just wanted to eat my lunch in peace. We made small talk about our acting class, then out of nowhere John asked, "What are you?"

People often asked me about my heritage, usually something like "What's your background?" or "Santina, that's a pretty name." But the way John asked the question threw me off a little. I wasn't sure what he meant. So I figured I'd throw him off, too. I looked down at my chest and I said, "The last time I looked, I was a woman."

He gave me a little chuckle, but I could tell that the question was sincere. I explained that my mother was Italian and my father was Black.

"So how did you get the last name Goodman?"

"Well, John," I said. "I guess the Jews must have had slaves."

I don't think it's a stretch to say that our friendship took root in sarcasm. . . . But for the longest time I was fascinated by why he was fascinated with me. Eventually I decided, why wouldn't he be fascinated with me? I didn't fawn all over him and I wasn't the norm.

I explained . . . to John [that I had been a flight attendant after high school and gone to Hunter College before Brown], and finally he just stared at me and said, "How old are you?" When I said I was twenty-seven, he said, "Holy shit . . . You don't look so bad for an old girl."

I can't explain how or why John and I became so close. Maybe it was because we were both Sagittarians. I always tried to push him away. . . . But it seemed like the more I pushed him away, the closer he wanted to get.

John invited me and some friends to Oktoberfest in Providence. On the way home, John was in the front passenger seat, and I ended up on his lap. Suddenly I felt his hand rubbing against the side of my breast. I turned around, we looked at each other, and it was as if we were both thinking, *Naw!* We laughed. We knew that if anything romantic happened between us, it would ruin the friendship. (Years later, there was an item about us in the *New York Post*'s Page Six implying that we were in a relationship, and I told John, "If we're fucking, I didn't feel a thing.")

Back then, John and I used to smoke when we drank. One time while sitting around, I realized the book of matches we were using had a picture of his father on it. It was an ad selling John F. Kennedy stamps. I said, "Does it bother you when you see this?" He quickly shook his head and smiled. "No, I'm used to it."

Chris Oberbeck

He had these lifelong brother-sister relationships. . . . I think he really had this longing for a big family. He didn't have that growing up because he had the Secret Service and then he was in Greece with Onassis, and it was isolating. I think when he got to Brown, he really could sort of capture the youth he never had. It was like a neighborhood, and he loved it.

Sasha Chermayeff

John really connected to people who felt either abandoned or betrayed by their dad. My father wasn't an abusive or deadbeat dad, but he was emotionally really difficult. Robbie's father killed himself. Santina was abandoned by her father. John wanted to give that fatherly sense of security to his friends— probably because it meant so much for him to lose it. He became a father figure. It's a big part of who he was and the way we all felt so loyal to him, and so soothed. He understood everybody's dark shadow sides. He understood when people were in pain.

"He liked being able to disappear into a role"

John Emigh, Professor Emeritus, Theater, Brown

My first encounter with John was in the tryouts for Ben Jonson's *Volpone* in his freshman year. I was looking for someone who could be a dashing hero— he played Bonario. There was one time where he rescues poor Celia from the clutches of the lecherous Volpone. So, the woman playing Celia, John hauled her out of the bed and said something dashing and gallant about rescuing her. And at the same time, he put his hand on the hilt of his sword and the sword went up under her dress, and she squealed. Everyone collapsed with laughter. So we kept it as a part of the play.

Acting was a release for John—becoming a "you" that isn't ordinarily presented to the world. And the wonderful surprise was that he had a great sense of humor about himself.

Santina Goodman

When the audition flyers [for the play she was directing, David Rabe's *In the Boom Boom Room*] went up on campus, John asked if there was a part for him. "Well, the only way you'll know if there's a part for you is if you read the play."

As I walked away, I was thinking, *Shit... There's a perfect part for him, but I'm not going to tell him....* Honestly, there was a part of me that didn't want to cast him because I didn't want people to come see the play just because John Kennedy was in it. But that would not be fair to John.

On the second day, five minutes before the end of auditions, John came bouncing in with the play in his hand. He wanted to read for the part of Big Al, exactly the part I'd had in mind. Big Al Royce was a nasty, foulmouthed, abusive, racist, lowlife guy. John read the part perfectly.

The play tells the story about a go-go dancer who works at a sleazy night-club. John took [his] part seriously from the get-go. At the time, he had long curly hair. I told him to put some gel in his hair and comb it back.... The next day John walked into rehearsal wearing a wool knit cap. Underneath, his luscious curls had been reduced to a severe crew cut.... I would never have asked an actor to do that, but it was perfect for his character. Just before he left rehearsal that day I said, "Big Al, I like the hair!" He just put the knit cap on, nodded his head to me, and walked out.

He used to drive his girlfriend, Sally Munro, crazy because he'd go around acting like Big Al all the time. She'd meet up with him after rehearsal and moan to me, "When is this play going to be over?" But I think he liked being able to disappear into a role.

The production rehearsal schedule cut into the Thanksgiving break, as well as John's birthday, which was November 25. I mentioned that my birth-day was December 1. He was planning a party on the weekend of the break. I never had a birthday party because growing up we always celebrated it at Christmas. When I mentioned that to John, he was incredulous. He insisted that I come to his party at his mother's home, at 1040 Fifth Avenue. "From now on," he said, "we'll always celebrate our birthdays together."

When I arrived at 1040 Fifth Avenue, John greeted me with a hug. "Happy birthday, T." He ushered me into the apartment and told me to make myself at home. . . . When it came time to sit, I headed for a place at the end of one of the side tables. John came over and steered me to the head table, saying, "You're sitting next to me."

He pulled out my chair, then settled into the seat beside me, all the while wearing that "shit-ass grin." On my plate were tarot cards, which I had never seen before. I opened the box and was flipping through the cards, when I looked up and saw, off to the side of the room, Mrs. Jacqueline Kennedy Onassis. My first thought was *Oh my, is that who I think it is?*

During dinner, John kept putting his arm around me, talking real close and whispering in my ear. From time to time, I'd see Mrs. Onassis staring at me. "John, cut this shit out! You're making your mom crazy," I whispered. He smirked. "I know!"

When we finished dinner, John got up to talk to other guests. A moment later, Mrs. Onassis took a seat beside me. In that lovely, breathy voice of hers, she said, "I see you have the tarot cards. That's my favorite gift."

I introduced myself, then said, "You know, your son was trying to make you crazy. Would you like to get him back?" She smiled and nodded. I took her hand, and she patted mine, and every time we'd look at John we'd laugh. Sometimes I whispered in her ear, and she would laugh like it was the funniest thing in the world. All this time John was watching us. He finally walked over, put his arms around us, and said, "What are my two favorite girls talking about?" Mrs. Onassis got up and simply said, "Santina, it was a pleasure to meet you."

"Mrs. Onassis, thank you for a fun talk." John couldn't stand it.

Later a cake was brought out, and for the second time that night, John walked over to me, grabbed my hand, and made me stand next to him in front of everyone in the room. When I looked down at the cake, I realized it read "Happy Birthday, John & Santina." We both blew out the one candle. It took all my strength to hold back my tears. At this moment, I had no idea that John would keep his promise to celebrate our birthdays together, which we did for eighteen years.

Sasha Chermayeff

Santina was incredibly loving and warm. Being that she was older, it had that nice maternal feeling toward John, like super protective. She was funny and beautiful and I could totally get why he loved her.

You gotta be pretty brave to be a single Black woman going to college when you're in your late twenties with a bunch of privileged white people who are eighteen. I think that their connection, a lot of it had to do with warmth and kindness. John needed to have some people—a lot of his good friends fall into this category—who didn't need anything from him, other than friendship. It's not opportunistic. Santina was somebody you couldn't really get confused with false motivation.

One time, I was talking to John's cousin Ted—Ted Kennedy Jr.—and he said how hard it was to know if your friends were really your true friends because so many people are constantly trying to get close to you because you're a Kennedy or you have something that they think you could give to them. And he said that he was always amazed because John didn't seem to have that problem. John didn't seem to struggle with who were real friends and who were fake friends and who was using him or who wasn't. He just had his real friends. That was it.

Brooke Shields

When I was looking at colleges in 1982, I wanted to tour Brown. Somehow it was set up that John would give me a tour of the campus. We went to the sandwich shop, and they named a sandwich after me, and they had a sandwich named after him—they just named all their sandwiches after people.

We had the best day. He took me to parties, showed me classes. I met all of his roommates. He had an off-campus apartment at that point. When I accepted Princeton and I didn't accept Brown, he sent me these sweet flowers and a note, and said, "Rumor has it, we lost you to Princeton, but I won't hold it against you. Stay in touch."

He loved how he could just walk around, bike around. Nobody bothered him. Nobody bugged him. The people of the town protected him, and he was free to be himself. I loved the school, but it was too much of a city for me. I wanted gates and campus, and the environment of Princeton was what I coveted. And he liked the city aspect of being able to just bike around, know the pub guy by name, the sandwich shop guy. He said, "You could totally disappear here." I know it's a cliché, but he was so down-to-earth that I think people were refreshed. Because you build him up and then he just only wears shorts and T-shirts, like, in your face, *I'm going to be rollerblading. I'm going to be on my bike.* And if you do it enough, it works. It's what I did in college, and it changed the whole trajectory of my life. You have to fight for it. But then people, they're not going to be that interested after freshman year. Not a novelty anymore. They'll get over it.

I think there was a kinship for us in that because of the magnitude, because that was the eighties. That was the height of a lot of [the fame] for both of us. And I joked, "Well, we each have a sandwich named after us." I said, "Yours is probably ham, right?" He's like, "Damn, you beat me to it."

"Real women and real relationships"

Chris Oberbeck

I introduced John to Sally Munro. I was a year ahead at Brown so I kind of knew all these people. Sally was from Marblehead, Massachusetts. She was her own kind of girl. . . . Sally wore the jeans and the sneakers, not the pleated skirts from New York City. She didn't comb her hair—it was kind of knotted, just pushed back. She was attractive, but she wasn't like a chick, you know? She was a New England–attractive, intelligent girl who came from a big family. She wasn't trying to be like everybody else.

Sally's roommate and best friend had been killed in a car crash while they were at Brown—it was a deep tragedy. There was definitely a sort of death-sadness about Sally. I don't know if that was part of her and John's connection.

One thing I always liked about John, which I thought differentiated him, not only from the Kennedys, but just from other people: He could go out any night and have one-night stands if he wanted to, but he didn't believe in that. He wanted real women and real relationships.

Paul Eckstein, friend

He'd walk in to play rehearsals with Polaroids of naked women, which were sent to him every day. Me and the other guys would be like, "Dude, why don't you just go get some of these women? Why are you so shy? What's this thing that you are always with one person? You're fucking John Kennedy, how are you not a player?" I always sort of felt this thing from him where he just couldn't. I knew guys who were rich, powerful, famous, and good-looking and they could just be killers with women, and John was so not a killer. He was surprisingly shy and unable to be a dog. That surprised me.

He enjoyed getting shit from a bunch of brothers on a daily basis and giving it right back. That's when I realized this dude must be kind of special. He's the president's son. His pops was killed, got Jackie O as his mom. That's a lot of pressure, and yet he's so chill and such a regular idiot. I mean, we're all idiots as twenty-year-old men. And he was so right there.

Robbie Littell

John and I would wake up together when we were roommates and I'd pretend I was him. I'd look over and I'd pull my waistband open, look down into my underwear area, and go, "So what should we do today?" That was me mocking him. But he was actually pretty much a serial monogamist.

Sasha Chermayeff

Sally was down-to-earth, I really liked her. I have my favorites of all of them, my least favorites. And Sally, she had a really nice heart. Very wholesome. And she did kind of look like Caroline, which was kind of weird—she reminded everybody physically of his sister. But it's not surprising. Who made him feel comfortable, and where did he feel safe? Somebody who looks like his sister.

The summer after John's first year there was a weekend that Sally and Eddie and me and John spent together on the Vineyard. Eddie and I were dating at that point. We did the whole cover-ourselves-in-clay thing, nude, and then went walking on the cliffs of Gay Head. Then we'd jump in the water and clean off. Sally was unpretentious, fun-loving. I remember we were walking in front of John and Eddie, so they were, like, watching our booties. And I remember John saying, "Wow, this is a fine day. What do you say, Eddie? This is a pretty fine view right here."

Anyway, I remember liking Sally and thinking she was genuine. But I also knew that John, at that point in his life, wasn't ready for reality. Sally seemed grounded in a kind of earthy way. I had this strange feeling at the time that it wasn't gonna be challenging enough for John. It was exploratory and he landed on someone really healthy. But I also think it left part of him wanting something more provocative.

Chris Oberbeck

He always managed to have the hard relationships with women. He could've had the easy ones, but he didn't. He's like, it's gotta be complicated, I gotta have a lot of heartache and turmoil. It just can't be a smooth ride. It can't be like a rental car, you know, just put it back—it's gotta be something that goes on and on. The relationships never completely ended—it wasn't like, okay it's over and they never saw each other again.

"I read this about my dad . . ."

Charles Neu, History Professor Emeritus, Brown

I think it was 1980 when I gave my seminar on the Vietnam War for the first time. John was a freshman. A friend of mine in political science, who was advising John, wanted me to let him into my seminar. I must have had seventy or eighty students apply for fifteen places. I did let John in. I just remember his performance, which was pathetic. I don't think he did any work at all. We sat at a round table—I can see it now. He was as far away from me as possible.

We sat there for two and a half hours talking about the books we read. And you can't fake it. You've got to know what you're talking about. He spent half of each seminar just looking out the window. I don't think he participated at all, except for once I said something critical of Robert McNamara [who was secretary of defense under John's father and then LBJ]. And he did challenge me a little bit on that, asking me what I meant. I think McNamara was important in John's life, right?

I don't think we were especially critical of JFK in that class because no one was really certain what he would've done [regarding escalation of the war in Vietnam] had he lived. But I *was* critical of Robert McNamara. In 1965, McNamara had decided that the U.S. could not win the war, but he kept that to himself until many years later, and the war lasted until 1975. So, some people on the left accused him of a crime of omission. John asked me what would I have done in McNamara's situation. That was the only time in the whole semester that he seemed engaged.

He never made an appointment to come in to talk about his final paper. And then, it must have been toward the very end of the term, the papers were due, and I happened to see him walking on the green. He said, "Oh, I need to come in and see you about my Vietnam paper." And by this time, I was very annoyed with him and his lack of performance. I just said, "Forget it." Now, most undergraduates, if I had said that, would argue with me, right? They would've given me some very good reasons for why the paper was late. Could they have more time? He didn't do a thing. I walked away and he walked away. And I never saw him again.

He failed my class. He failed the discussion part, then he failed the written part—there was no way to get around that. He didn't know how to participate in a discussion. He obviously didn't know how to read books, evaluate them. He didn't know how to write a research paper. And I got the impression he thought it was all kind of a lark—not a serious inquiry. Not what you would expect from someone coming out of an elite school. I don't know what he did at Andover, but not much, is my guess.

Steve Gillon

There weren't that many classes at Brown that covered modern American politics, and John took the two that would've dealt with his father's presidency. One was Neu's class, and the other was the class that I was a teaching assistant for, 20th Century American Political History. I gave the first lecture, which was on JFK and civil rights. I pointed out the obstacles that President Kennedy encountered in trying to deal with civil rights and how he was slow to address it. But then, in the summer of 1963, on national TV, JFK becomes the first president to say that civil rights is a moral issue.

As a student, John could be focused and engaged, or he could be living on another planet. When he showed up to class, which he didn't always do, you could tell when he did the reading. John, when he was prepared, would talk a lot and have interesting things to say. When he hadn't done the reading, he would just be really quiet. He did a research paper on Paul Goodman, an early sort of hippie, who wrote *Growing Up Absurd*. I gave him a B because it was sloppy, and he wasn't happy. He said he'd like to set up a time to talk to me about the paper. He never did.

John and I started playing racquetball. We'd go to Wendy's afterwards. He'd say, "Stevie, I was reading this about my dad. . . ." If they were critical of the Cuban Missile Crisis, he'd ask, "What do you think?" That was an ongoing conversation. "Stevie, I read this about my dad, but I don't believe it. . . ." Then after ten minutes, we'd change the topic and move on, or he'd make fun of something I said.

We talked about civil rights. People criticized his father, and he wanted it to be recognized that his father was in a tough situation and ultimately had the courage to do the right thing. That and Vietnam were the two main topics that were central to our conversations over an eighteen-year period.

We had a conversation about whether his father would've pulled troops out of Vietnam. I said I thought his father, whether he wanted to send troops to Vietnam or not, would have been politically forced to. He called me the next morning and said, "Stevie, I talked to Bob McNamara last night and he said you're dead wrong."

He was a guy who knew the literature about his father and his presidency. John was not his father's son defending him—he was trying to reach his own point of view. But he was influenced by members of the administration who remained very close to him and his family, Robert McNamara being chief among them. John felt a sense of personal loyalty to him.

John had said to his advisor, "I want to take Charles Neu's course on the Vietnam War because I want to see if my dad was responsible for the war." Neu thinks John was unengaged in the class because he was lazy. I think he was unengaged because he was completely turned off by criticism of Robert McNamara. For John, it was more than a course on American history. It was also the story of his father and his legacy.

Chris Oberbeck

John didn't talk about his dad a lot. But I remember, one time, I walked into his room, and he was reading this book and he said, "Obs, look at this." I think it was a book on the first one hundred days of his father's presidency. He was like, "I mean, can you believe that he did all this stuff in a hundred days?" You know, he was in awe. He was just sitting there by himself and just amazed. Like Michael Jordan scoring seventy points in a basketball game or something.

He had his father's chair that had been in the Oval Office—the chair he sat in as president, and John had it in his dorm room. He would always joke around like, "What if I'm president? Who would be in my cabinet?" He's leaning back in that chair, and he goes, "Who do I have in my cabinet? This person would be secretary of state, this one would be secretary of the treasury." And he goes, "Obers, I think you'd be an aide," and he just started laughing so hard. He always had that ribbing thing—he was good at it.

Charlie King, friend

I was the Kennedy for President organizer on campus in 1980, and I was tasked with asking if John would speak at an event for Teddy at Providence College. At this point, John hadn't spoken publicly anywhere. The people on the Kennedy campaign told me, look, he is just gonna speak to a few volunteers for a couple of minutes, and it was not gonna be that big a deal. He said, I'd be happy to do anything for my uncle.

He says, "How do you think I should dress?" I said, "I'm going to be really casual." So he's in jeans. As we're getting there, the first giveaway was these television news trucks. As we get out of the car, John gives me this look. . . . We're hurried onto the stage and there's two hundred people there. He's ushered up to the podium to give remarks. And the next day the *Providence Journal* compares his comments to his father and says, you know, he's not his father. He doesn't speak like his father, all this sort of stuff.

After it was over, John doesn't say anything to me about the experience. Fast-forward six or seven years, we're eating pizza after playing football in Central Park and everybody's going around talking about the most horrifying experiences in one's life. And he piped up, "Well, Charlie, I think one of the worst experiences I ever had was when you got me to speak at Providence College. That was pretty terrifying."

Oh, God. But, you know, he was pretty gracious at the time—I never would have known it was so terrible for him.

John Perry Barlow

John had been giving this matter a lot of thought—I think he was a junior at Brown: trying to study the literature of a good man. There is no literature on good men. You can find stuff about courage and leadership and valor and war and tragedy . . . but if you want to find out what constitutes a good man and has throughout human history, you are not going to have much to read.

I remember John saying, "It seems to me as I read these biographies of *great* men, they were not particularly great at home. Even Gandhi hit his wife. They were kind of nasty at home." He said, "Even my dad could have been a lot nicer, from the sounds of things."

I think he was talking about infidelity. How his father had been kind of a ladies' man, which, despite widespread belief, John never really was. He was kind of a one-woman guy. Sometimes the turnover was a little high. . . . But he had a natural instinct for not hurting people's hearts.

He said, "Everybody expects me to be a great man. . . . I think it would be a much more interesting challenge if we found the good man under the circumstances that I am fortunate to be in." A good man was someone like Paul Newman, who John had a very quiet admiration for. A good man just does good stuff and doesn't give a goddamn who notices. A good man shields other people. A good man has a circle of empathy that includes others beyond his immediate friends and family. He knows when it hurts, and not just when it hurts him.

I said, "I can't think of anything that would make me happier. . . .
Surprise them all: set out to be a good man."

"Kennedy, get your ass over here"

Barry Clifford, diver and underwater explorer, friend

I had my dive shop on Martha's Vineyard, and John and I had been diving
for a couple of years. He'd come over from Hyannis one day and asked if he
could work with me, so I brought him on board. Then in the summer of '83,
I put a team together to look for the *Whydah*, a pirate ship that sank off Cape
Cod in 1717. At first everybody was like, "What the hell's Kennedy doing
here?" So I gave him the hardest, dirtiest jobs on the boat, like cleaning the
bilge out. He never complained. I never called him John, I always called him
Kennedy. *Kennedy, get your ass over here.*

Todd Murphy, diver, Army/Special Forces, friend

We had fifteen of us living in a three-bedroom house on the Cape. We called
it the barracks. John lived in—we called it the Florida Room. It was a deck
with an enclosed porch.

John Beyer, diver and friend

There were no rooms left and that's how John and I ended up in the Florida
Room, everything else was taken. John would ride a bike from Orleans to
Provincetown to go to work. That's a pretty long ride, twenty miles. So he'd
leave the house at six in the morning.

Todd Murphy

Being the younger guys on the crew, John and I did all the cruddy diving
when it was cold and miserable and boring. It was always John and I in the
water. It can be fifty degrees out—this is not tropical bathwater you're diving
in. You'd run the engines and it would shoot water straight down and blow a

hole in the sand and then you'd dive down to see if anything was there. Hours just back and forth, we'd call it "mowing the lawn." Boring as all heck.

At the end of the day, everybody would leave and it was just us out hanging on the boat. We used to blast Jimi Hendrix, "All Along the Watch Tower." I used to go up in the bow and do some knife work with John, the music blaring, the sun setting. I got some dates with a number of girls that summer. I knew they didn't care anything about me, they figured they'd end up meeting John. I used to tell John, "Hope you don't mind, but I'm taking advantage of it." John wasn't out womanizing. Sally Munro was his girlfriend and he was faithful to her. Sally was his main squeeze.

Barry Clifford

We didn't find the *Whydah* that summer, we found it in the summer of '84. But we found a lot of pieces of different shipwrecks.

We would dive off of West Chop, off Martha's Vineyard, which used to be a long dock in the 1800s. People back then would take their trash out to the end and throw it into the ocean. So, we found all of these incredible old bottles, at least a hundred feet offshore, and Jackie had her whole living room just packed with things that John and I had found. Old bottles and all sorts of things. That was Jackie's treasure.

Todd Murphy

I was not aware that John's family had what they referred to as "the compound" in Hyannis. One time, John said, "Come pick me up and we'll go out and have some beers because the weather is bad." So we drove down to Hyannis, and he pulled into a driveway, and he says, "Let's go get some beer," and he looked in this refrigerator. No beers. And then we walk over to this other house, and he just whips open the refrigerator door and still no beers here. And we go in another house. And I go, "John, with all your neighbors, you just walk in their house and look for beer? Where are we at, Johnny?" He said, "My grandmother's."

She had a beautiful home—the big one right on the water there. There's tons of pictures. His dad, Bobby, something you'd see if you went to the museum. And it's two o'clock in the morning, we're drinking beers on her sunporch, and we go, "Whoa, Rose. Dude, are we going to wake her up?"

John Beyer

John said, "She's half deaf." But we moved. You know John, he had good manners.

It was kind of confusing—you didn't realize how many houses the Kennedys had. If we ran out of beer, we would just go over to Ted's refrigerator, which was huge. I mean, it was restaurant capacity.

Another time, I was at a party at his mother's apartment and I'm roaming around, looking at the photographs on the wall, and I'm just enthralled. Caroline came over and said, "You're not supposed to be in this part of the house." She was polite about it. I mean, I looked like a fisherman or an old hippie. I had long hair and a scraggly beard. So I went to the other end of the apartment with John and his dive buddies. Arnie was there, too, Arnie Schwarzenegger.

Todd Murphy

I'm in Special Forces, the Green Berets. And John was going to law school after college. I had been joking, "You've got to join Special Forces. You'd be respected." And he goes, "I was thinking about it because I know it's really good for a political career."

We didn't make money [that summer], we actually ended up losing money. We had free food, and we used to get T-shirts. You weren't there for money—you're there because it's adventure. I think the following year, it was: okay, it's time for all of us to grow up. John might have had some family pressures—he alluded to that. You're out looking for treasure on Cape Cod, but it's time to get serious. He wasn't sure whether his mom, his family, kind of appreciated it. If it was more like, *Okay, John, go sow your oats. . . .*

Barry Clifford

I've recently been going through my papers and found this diary entry that I wrote [that summer]. John had lost the metal detector.

> *They spent an hour or two looking . . . no luck. John was embarrassed, almost to tears. He felt terrible. . . .*
>
> *I feel very responsible for him. He's almost defenseless at times. I'd like to see him toughen up a little. I'm afraid people will take advantage of him. . . .*

When I think of him now, I see him on the boat, covered in grease, and just one of the guys.

Charles Neu

John very nearly didn't graduate [in 1983]. It came down to passing one course at the end of his senior year. One of my former colleagues, I think, was the unfortunate professor who had to pass him at the last moment.

Looking back, it was all kind of sad. He wasn't ready for Brown. I understand the reason why Brown took him, but once it took him, I don't think we did a very good job of advising him. When I read Steve Gillon's book, I was struck by the demands on JFK Jr., just because he was such an incredible celebrity. It took a lot of energy, and I would think a lot of time, to deal with all of that. I didn't appreciate that enough at the time.

Roberto DiPelesi, friend of Santina Goodman

Santina told me that on graduation day, nobody from her family was there. She was in her room crying. John called her and said, "Where are you?" And she said, "I'm not going to graduation." He said, "Why aren't you going?" She said, "Because nobody's here for me." He said, "Then you're with us. And if you don't come, my mother said she's going to get security to come and get you." She adored John. That was her brother.

Gary Ginsberg

John and I both ended up staying on campus that summer, studying for the LSAT. We'd walk down the hill every morning for the Stanley Kaplan test prep class, then play sports in the afternoon and study. It was a lot of fun. He was getting ready to go to India and he wanted to knock off the LSAT first.

They'd have these logic games where they're like, "If you can't sit next to me, and I can sit next to that waiter, and the waiter can only sit two seats down from the cook, can the cook sit next to you?" John would be like, "What the F is this?" We used to drive ourselves nuts trying to figure out how to figure it out.

Did John have ADHD? We didn't know what ADHD was back then. But did he have a problem sitting down and focusing? Yeah, sometimes. But then again, he had a lot of external stimuli coming at him from more directions than the rest of us did. The thing about John that most intrigued me was how intellectually imaginative he was. He was a really good writer, was quick on his feet with a quip, always willing to try things even if they didn't naturally come easy to him. He did things that interested him with a lot of gusto and it served him really well.

CHAPTER 9

Postgrad

"A wounded son, seeking answers"

Narendra Taneja, friend

I was in my twenties and wanting to do big things in life. I had a friend who was a junior diplomat in Delhi, and he invited me to [a gathering at] the home of an Irish diplomat [in 1984]. This apartment was not very lavish. There were not enough chairs. There were quite a few of us sitting on the floor and enjoying our drink and some sandwiches. The guy sitting next to me, we had a great conversation. There was a discussion on American politics and the Soviet Union. Almost two hours. He said, "My name is John," and I said my name was Narendra. I said, "So where are you staying?" He pointed to a corner of the same room. I said, "You mean on the floor?" He said, "Yes, he is kind enough to give me someplace. He doesn't have enough beds. So, I'm an honored guest." I said, "Look, you can stay with me as long as you want." It was eleven in the night. We took this three-wheeler [tuk-tuk] and he put his rucksack in, and we just moved to my place.

I said, "Would you like to have some whiskey?" And he said, "That sounds like a good idea."

He came down into the living area, just a few chairs and an old sofa. After we were about one hour into conversation, he took out a diary. We were talking about our families. Then he started making some notes and he asked for some spelling of my name. I noticed there were some pictures as he was flipping through the pages. And so I said, "What is this picture doing in your own notebook?" He said, "This is my mom and dad."

That was President Kennedy. And there was a photo of him as a little boy. I said, "You mean you are John Kennedy?" Then I discovered that the man in my house is President Kennedy's son.

In the morning he made a few phone calls and then said, "Oh, we gotta meet a guy." At a small café, this guy turned up who worked with the American embassy. He said, "Take care of him. Don't tell anybody that he is Kennedy. He is a friend staying with you."

Three or four days later, I said, "I'm going to my hometown." I explained my hometown is a very little town near Agra, the city where Taj Mahal is situated, about two hundred kilometers east of New Delhi. I said, "So you want to come along?" He said, " I *am* coming with you." I said, "Very basic accommodation." He said, "Oh, don't worry about these things."

The train took about four and a half hours. Hardly a place to stand, forget about having a place to sit. We were traveling in the third class, the lowest category.

We stayed there about five days. In that small town, being a foreigner was good enough to be treated like a VIP. My friends—they were extremely warm to him, fighting with each other to invite him over to the house for tea, coffee, dinner. They knew nothing about him. Everybody just called him John.

There were six family members in the house. Eight of us in about five hundred square feet, two tiny rooms. No running water. I said, "Look, this is how it is." He said, "Don't worry, I'll manage."

One evening, he said, "India is well-known for people who tell your future." We call them palmists. So, he said, "Do you know anyone who can tell me my future?" And I said, "John, we know your future. You're going to be president." He said, "No, no, nobody knows. I'm not interested in politics." I said, "But you discuss politics all the time." He said, "Well, you don't have to be *in* politics to discuss politics. In any case, I'm not interested in electoral politics."

I started trying to find out who was the best person to read hands. I discovered that there is a Jain temple—Jain is a tiny religion in India. The chief priest was also a very respected palmist. So, one morning after breakfast, we went to the palmist. He gave a small cushion and said his small prayer. Then he asked to read the hand of John for the first ten minutes. And then he looked at me. He said, "Who is he?"

I said, "He's a friend. He's visiting India." He said, "No, no, no, but who *is* he?" I said, "What are you trying to say?" He said, "He's not an ordinary man. Tell me, who is he?" I said, "He's an ordinary man, well-educated and from the United States, that's all, and he's trying to discover India." He said, "No, you're hiding something from me." And then he said, "His hand says that he's got to be the son of a king."

"King" is an expression that means the ruler, not king in the same way as England and all that. Just to make the priest comfortable, I turned to John and said, "Is your father a king somewhere?" He just laughed. But he kept returning to this and the palmist said, "He's not an ordinary man."

John asked him, is he going to have a healthy life. And he said there is no serious threat to your health as such, but you need to take care. And he said, "Stay away from alcohol and tobacco." All priests will tell you the same. And he said, otherwise you'll have a healthy life. You'll find love in life. He said, "You are blessed with good health. But you should be always careful."

John asked, "Careful in what sense?" He said, "You see, you have a long life, but there is a risk. So, you should be careful." He didn't elaborate. John was always returning to this point: "What do you mean by risk to my life?" John wanted to know if he would have a normal life. So, he said, "If by normal, you mean that you'll get a job and settle down with kids, then go with a family on vacation, all that. Probably not. That's not your destiny."

I could sense that John was anxious about his future. How's life going to unfold? And when we were leaving, the priest told me in Hindi, in our language, "You are hiding. This guy is not an ordinary guy."

The next morning, John wanted to go back. This time without me. He spent two or three hours with the priest.

I used to tease him. "John, whatever you may say, you are going to run for the White House." And he said, " I'm interested in other things. I'm interested in philosophy, and I'm interested in history. I'm interested in people." And so, I said, "Well, if you're interested in philosophy and history and people, that's what makes a very good politician." He said, "Not at this stage, but the future, I don't know, it's too early." He said, "You are pushing me." But I said, "Maybe there is something that's holding you back."

In India, we say the father is like the shield in your life. Mother is love, affection, care. But father is the shield, someone who protects you. I could see that whenever he talked about his father that he missed him, though he didn't remember anything of him. [He spoke] about his sister. And you could hear this love in his voice for her. Only time I saw a kind of glow in his face and happiness, that was when he talked about his sister.

I think he stayed with me ten days and then a few days in my hometown. We used to have discussions: philosophy, history. Women, of course—we were both in our twenties. I asked him, "Do you have a girlfriend back in America?" Then he laughed and said, "I'm young and I think I'm reasonably good-looking. So, what do you expect?" I said, "Any kind of relationship you're deep into?" He said, "I don't know."

There was a small gathering of professors. It was a friend of mine whose father was a professor of international relations and diplomacy at a university in Delhi—he recognized John. He asked him, "Are you President Kennedy's son?" Then asked some questions about his father. Then John came to me and said, "Let's go."

He talked about what a great presidency his father had, and he was happy to talk about that. Not about the tragic part. But he would never talk about his father at length. He missed him. That was very obvious. But he also had this raw thing. This raw emotion. *Why his father? Why did this happen to him?* He was like a wounded son, seeking answers.

I could see that he had big dreams. The fact that in India he met the prime minister, and he was meeting the top editors. . . . He said, "No, those meetings are being arranged." He didn't look like someone who was hungry for a profile. John was conscious of one thing: those who treated him differently because he was President Kennedy's son, he didn't like that. He would immediately make a distance.

What he enjoyed most was talking with ordinary people. He was a people's man. He said, "I'm basically just trying to understand life, the world." He was very interested in ancient Indian cities. One of them was Varanasi, one of the holy cities in India, seven thousand years old. I put him on the train to Varanasi. He didn't want to have a reservation.

We met again when he came back to Delhi. He was not staying in those expensive hotels, that's for sure. He wanted to live as ordinary as possible.

He heard about India from his mother. And so he decided to come. In India, we think that "If you cannot be interested in India, you're not interested in life." We are the oldest surviving civilization or culture in the world. He did tell me that he's learning much more in India than he could in any university.

He was basically trying to find answers to these questions: What is life, what is death? But the void was there. He had everything, but there was something that he wanted and that was not there. He was extremely touchy about anybody asking questions about his father's assassination. He just didn't want to discuss it at all.

I found him a very serious person. We would always enjoy a drink, have happy conversation. But then within ten minutes, the same John would be very serious. He talked about poverty in America. And we would also talk about this discrimination of Black people in America. At that time, there was no internet, so I didn't know much. He said, "You don't know the problems we have in my country. Look at the way people treat Blacks in America. Look at their contribution and the way some people treat them." He was disgusted with such people. He had this golden heart. He cared for people. I mean, he couldn't speak the language. Yet he was able to connect with them. But India is that kind of place once you visit, stay a longer time, like five, six months, which he did, you're never the same person again. You can leave India, but India never leaves you.

He went back to the palmist the second day [and it] had more to do with this aspect. On the one hand he knew he was recognized, even celebrated for that because he was President Kennedy's son. But at the same time, John Kennedy was his father he didn't have. The first time when I said, "What is this picture?" you had to see his expression. There was silence. There was this void. And then he said, "My dad." And then there was silence from my side. And he was reminded of that every day. Very complicated. I could see that void. And the loneliness because of it.

Gustavo Paredes

One of the reasons John traveled was because his father traveled all over the world. I think John would do his own kind of Peace Corps—he would search out how people lived around the world, get a sense of their struggles. India made a tremendous mark on him.

Pat Manocchia

After John had come back from India and I had just come back from Spain, I came to do interviews in New York, and I stayed at 1040 and slept in Caroline's room. Very sweet, the mom. As a hockey player, you learn not to be intimidated by people, but she was without question the most intimidating person I've ever met. The three of us are sitting down to dinner, the first thing she said was "I want to let you know how grateful I am that you have remained friends and that he was able to go to someone's house and have a meal." I'm from Providence and John came to my house for Sunday dinners a few times when we were at Brown. And she said, "Tonight, we're going to have the spaghetti and meatballs for you." And John went, "You can't do that." She goes, "John, what are you talking about. . . . " John says, "His mother made the best meatballs on the planet. You can't make meatballs for this guy." And I said, "Calm down, man. I'm a meatball guy. I'm all right."

Then she said, "I didn't realize how much you two had in common. You both chose Brown. You both lost your fathers at a fairly early age. You both decided to go out of the country after school. And now you're both looking for jobs and you understand how difficult that is." I said, "Excuse me, Mrs. O. He's having a hard time finding a job?" She just looked up and looked at me and said, "It's not really that simple."

I'm like, *I'm such an idiot.* Of course no one wants to hire him for his ability to work—they want to hire him to leverage who he is and take advantage of him. So, I'm thinking, *Oof, should stick to what I know.* She asks, "How was Spain?" I said, "Spain's a really interesting place post-Franco." She says, "Yeah, he was an interesting guy." I'm like, *Oh, shit, she knew the guy, so maybe we should talk hockey here, because you just know more about everything than I know, except maybe meatballs.*

Gary Ginsberg

When he got back from India, I went over to his house at 1040, and we watched the movie *The Right Stuff*. There's a scene where John Glenn presents the flag that he took up to the moon to his father in the Rose Garden. We're watching and John's like, "That flag is in my bedroom." And there it was. It was in a frame.

Robbie Littell

John and I shared an apartment on West 86th for a while. We had a great time. I don't know what he was doing for work, but he wasn't doing much. It was just kind of party time those couple of years. I remember his mother saying to me, "You guys can't live together anymore because he's gotta buckle down."

We had a party once to watch the Giants game and the Mets were playing the Red Sox in the World Series at the same time. John had everything turned on at once. The VCR cranked up, the TV cranked up. All at once this [porn] video called *Bun Busters* came on. We pointed at each other right away and his face turned redder than mine. So everyone knew that *he'd* left it in there. I think he pulled the plug outta the wall.

Sasha Chermayeff

I was studying painting at the New York Studio School of Drawing, Painting and Sculpture and lived in a downtown apartment on the first floor just above street level. There were bars on the window. But you could tap on my window and that was right next to where I had my bed. There were many nights where I would hear this little *tap, tap, tap* on the window. I'd wake up and look out and it would be John—he had locked himself out again from his apartment. It was two in the morning. And he would sleep with me in my bed, crash out for a night.

Gary Ginsberg

We hung out the summer of '84, or '85, we were both working in Washington. I was at a law firm. He was working for Bradford Reynolds at the Civil Rights Division at the Reagan White House—Civil Rights Division of the Justice Department. He was a really right-wing guy, Brad Reynolds. And the epitome of the anti–civil rights ethos of the Reagan era. This was another example of how John was always so unpredictable—hard to pin down. He was willing to explore viewpoints that weren't necessarily natural to him. He was always a bit of a contrarian intellectually, ideologically, and was willing to explore far beyond traditional Democratic orthodoxy. Part of it was to play against type, part of it was genuine intellectual curiosity. We used to have really forceful debates because he was always defending the Reagan presidency. I remember being in a car after playing racquetball in my sophomore or junior year at Brown and we kind of went at it, arguing whether Ronald Reagan was an effective president or a national embarrassment. He really defended him, saying how well he used the bully pulpit of the presidency to push his agenda. I was kind of stunned, but also amused that this scion of one of the great Democratic families of our time was defending a president that pretty much everyone at Brown despised. But later, when I knew him much better, that really was John. Never really wanted to play to type, and never changed.

He was just impressed with how effective Reagan was as a communicator, how clear he was in staking out his positions and restoring the majesty of the presidency. It was really the strength that he projected that I think John found so attractive. We didn't get into, well, what about race-baiting? What about warmongering? Cutting entitlements?

Fred Ryan, Ronald Reagan's appointment secretary

I got word that President Reagan had agreed to meet with John and Caroline Kennedy and to set it up in the Oval Office. They had a very nice meeting. So they then said, "We need to raise"—I think it was $8 million—"for the Kennedy Library." Unlike other presidential libraries, President Kennedy was not alive to raise money for it. President Reagan said yes on the spot.

John saw his father's desk, the *Resolute* desk. I remember how they were happy to see it there and there was some conversation about the little door panel, which had been put in when Franklin Roosevelt was president because of him being in a wheelchair. They called it a modesty panel so people wouldn't see his feet, which created this little door that John could open and crawl through.

Afterwards Ted Kennedy hosted an event at his house in McLean, Virginia. The whole Kennedy clan was there, John and Caroline and Jacqueline Kennedy and various cousins. Tip O'Neill was there and President and Mrs. Reagan. Everyone was embracing, even though the party affiliations were different. I think they were aligned on the importance of the presidency and of history and mutual respect. Those days don't happen anymore.

John Emigh

A few years after John got out of Brown, he and his friend Christina Haag did a show by Brian Friel called *Winners* at the Irish Arts Center. John and Christina were beautiful in it, but it got treated as "Here's our prince, and he's off just fiddling around with the theater." And it became evident to John that this just wasn't something he could do. Certainly not just out of college, unless he proved himself in some other way.

Paul Eckstein

God, that was a boring play. I was asleep in the second act, but it was clear even then how good he was. In some ways, the curse of his life is that he is a Kennedy, because if he wasn't, he could have been an actor and he probably would've been a freaking movie star because he was that good. He was able to access what it is to be a regular person. He didn't have a regular life from day one, so to be able to act so fucking regular means you're acting.

Steve Gillon

I had people tell me such contradictory things about his mother and her expectations for John. A lot of it had to do with acting. But John knew he couldn't go into acting. He didn't need his mother to tell him.

**Jack Merrill, friend, co-founder of Naked Angels
theater company**

Everybody always said he wanted to be an actor. If he really wanted to be an actor, I think he would've become an actor.

Janno Lieber, colleague

John and I ended up sharing an office [when we both worked at] the Office of Economic Development for the City of New York [in the mid-eighties]. I don't remember much except that he was a prodigious eater. He would exercise like crazy. In those days, before fitness became such a big part of life, John would show up in the office after rollerblading and then have a three-course meal.

Barbara Vaughn, friend

One sunny Saturday, John and I met in Central Park to catch up. He had been running, and I was rollerblading. We were sitting on the side of the road, talking and watching bikers and joggers go by, and he asked about my Rollerblades. They were fairly rare in NYC, still somewhat of a novelty. "Tell me about those things," he said. I explained that for me they were a form of transportation and exercise similar to a bike, but less likely to get stolen. They were particularly efficient for distances that were a bit too long to walk, and too short for a taxi. His eyes lit up. "This is such a cool idea! My mom keeps asking what I want for Christmas, and I'm telling her Rollerblades."

Mike Tyson, friend

The first time I met John he almost hit me with his bike. It was in New York. And I was like, "Hey, what's up, man? Be careful." And we were talking and he was explaining. I knew who he was. No doubt I knew who he was.

How do you *not* know who he is? In the eighties, they paraded him around television—you know what I'm talking about. But I was just very uneasy that he was alone. And he's running into guys like me. I said, "What are you doing out here? Are you with somebody?" He said, "No, they're in my way. It's just too much."

And listen, it was nighttime too. I'm out with a wild party crowd, this guy is by himself. What was the deal? Why was he always by himself? He just rode his bike, stopped, talked to people, took pictures. You know, he didn't make a big thing.

In my opinion, he was just too normal. You got to realize this is not a good world—you know, it's kind of bad. And he just never protected himself. He was always open and vulnerable. Physically vulnerable. So vulnerable, man.

He said sometimes he's in a situation where there's too many people to, you know, navigate. I said, "That's why you have to have somebody with you all the time." I was saying, "Listen, I'm Mike Tyson, I have a bodyguard. I have to have people to navigate my situation." He said, "That's just too much excitement for me. I just can't handle the bodyguard." That's his words. Too much excitement.

He was that kind of person. He didn't wanna live big.

Kerry Kennedy, cousin

John wore his fame lightly. Hounded by photographers, he hardly allowed them to interfere with his skateboarding, his dancing in clubs with his cousins, his inquisitiveness about the world. His breeziness was reflected in [one] of his favorite stories. [One] time John was campaigning for David Dinkins at a primary school in Harlem, in front of an assembly hall full of kids sitting cross-legged . . . and then a second layer of fancy people, politicians and hangers-on. When John got up to speak, he noticed a little boy making very

odd faces at him. So, after the muckety-mucks and press left, John made his
way over to the child. Here's their exchange:

Kid: What's your name?

John: John.

Kid: What's your last name?

John: Kennedy.

Kid (totally screwing up his face with curiosity and disbelief, in a very
challenging interrogation): What is your middle initial?

John: F.

Kid: Do you know you were named after an airport?

Julia Roberts, actor

He came across as wildly accessible. For him to be out on the streets of New
York . . . he would come out of the chaos into a restaurant or somewhere and
it seemed like he was very good at leaving that fluster behind. I don't know
how you walk through the world like that with so much grace. He didn't take
up a lot of space, and he really could have.

We met through mutual friends, back in the good old New York days. For
sure he had that radiance—like a shiny penny—but I found him to be very
down-to-earth and nice and kind of goofy. A little bit absent-minded—
and I say that with love, especially because he had so much going on all the
time. I remember once, a bunch of us were going to meet for dinner and
first he was going to be late, and then he was not going to be able to come
because he had his bike lock chain around his waist and he couldn't find
the key so he had to go and deal with that . . . and you're thinking, *what?*

"The guy couldn't catch a balloon"

Gary Ginsberg

We started playing football I think in '85. Touch football during the weekends, that was a big part of our friendship. We spent more time organizing
these games . . . because you couldn't do it by email back then, you had to do
it by phone. But we were religious about it.

We'd play for a couple of hours, in Central Park, early afternoon, almost any weekend that we were in town. It went on for years. We'd ride our bikes up there or he would drive and then park anywhere, whether he got a ticket or not. His back seat was like a repository for those orange fines they'd stick on your windshield. Never really occurred to him that he actually had to pay them. One time, he came back and his car was booted because he was such a scofflaw.

It was very social, but also we got our ya-yas out playing competitive touch football. There were shitty fields back then on the Great Lawn, which was anything but a lawn—it was basically a dirt pit. But we loved it.

Paul Eckstein

We came to learn, don't throw the ball to John because he's got the worst freaking hands in the world. It was like he had clubs for hands. For someone who was such an exceptional athlete, the guy couldn't catch a balloon. It was so hysterical. We'd be like, "Nice move, John."

But you can't give John too much shit because he's John and you love him.

Nick Chinlund, friend from Brown

It was like, *Really? Wow, dude, you couldn't catch that one?*

The touch football games in Central Park were all driven by John, put together by him. That was important to him—to bring his friends together.

Pat Manocchia

He never had a shirt on. I asked him, unless he was trying to catch skin cancer, what are you doing? Do you not wash your clothes?

Joanna Molloy, New York *Daily News* gossip columnist

Concentric circles of people would just be standing there watching him in the park. Men and women. He was gorgeous, he was chiseled. And he was not conceited—that added to his appeal.

Frédéric Fekkai, hairstylist

I was the owner of the salon at Bergdorf Goodman, and he was one of my clients. Listen, he had a head of hair for two people. So much thick hair, and it was a signature style—brushed back and short on the side and a little bit long on the top. Because his hair is very thick, it needs to be tamed. I usually cut it in a way that plays with the thickness and the volume of the hair, so that it's almost like a sculpture, you know—architecture.

He was coming frequently because his hair was growing fast. I would say that every four weeks I had to reshape his hair. And don't forget, he was always biking. So he needed to make sure that the hair was not going to be all over the place.

I have to tell you, when he was coming, people were just glued to the window, to just look at him.

Robbie Littell

Many times, he was like, "Hey, block me." You know, "Tell that guy to get out of the bushes"—paparazzi or whatever. You'd yell, "Hey, you've got to get out of the bushes. He'd much prefer a close-up!"

I think he absolutely loved attention and was so skilled at it. He was well-groomed by his mother. He had great facility in the arena of the media of the time and enjoyed it immensely. Yeah, I've always liked to think that the day the paparazzi didn't show up would've been a real bad day. He thrived on it. He came out of *Life* magazine, for crying out loud. That was the original OG.

Cabot McMullen

We'd always all come back to Hyannis Labor Day weekend. We'd have these incredible football games. And, of course, the first thing to come off was John's shirt. He would just be standing there—and he was like Adonis, he was the most beautiful man you'd ever seen. And he'd always pick the perfect lighting—he'd stand there just as the sun was going down and we'd all just kind of stand there for a moment and look and go, "Oh my God." I think that was sort of the actor in him, the theatrical side of him. He knew exactly what he was doing, but it was all in good fun.

At the same time, he was a little bit serious about it, that Kennedy thing. *See what I've got? You don't have this.* I look back and he just always carried himself with this sort of air of destiny. He didn't let it go to his head. I think he figured out that it was his superpower, but he could put it to good use.

Sasha Chermayeff

I don't think he was more of an exhibitionist than anybody else—I don't think he took his shirt off more than most people do at the beach or playing football in the park. . . . It just so happens that he was being photographed. He was comfortable with his physicality. He was gorgeous and he was comfortable.

I mean, why shouldn't he? He said it himself when he answered a media question [one time]: "People can say a lot worse things about you than you look good in a bathing suit." Like a gorgeous woman wanting to wear a beautiful outfit: Why not? He had a lot of self-confidence, but he was not riddled with vanity.

Steve Gillon

The one thing in his life that John could control was his body. He spent a lot of time at the gym building up his body, not just out of vanity, but because he could control it—he could decide how big his body was going to get. I think that's one of the reasons he took great pride in it. It was all through hard work that he had put in.

That was one side. But there was this whole other side. John had a softness, a gentleness to him. He had all the physical attributes of a bodybuilder, but he was a really sensitive, caring person inside.

Radu Teodorescu, owner of Radu's Physical Culture gym

Sometime in the summer of '83 or '84, he came to my gym at 41 West 57th Street. Some things in life, you remember—I vividly see him coming in the gym. The elevator opened and this guy comes inside: a sinewy, athletic-looking guy with Rollerblades over his right shoulder and sunglasses on top of his curly hair.

New York magazine called me the toughest trainer in town. Everybody wanted to come to my gym because it was the most challenging class. I had all the movie stars, models coming. . . . Halston was one of my first students. Ellen Barkin, Candice Bergen, Matthew Broderick, Sarah Jessica Parker, Alec Baldwin. Bianca Jagger, Jennifer Lopez, Marla Maples, Raquel Welch.

John had a great magnetism. But my gym had absolutely no personality cult. Everybody was a personality, in '83, '84. Really, nobody cared who he was.

The class was very challenging. I told those macho guys—scuba divers, track people, basketball players, you name it—I said, "Listen, don't try to keep up with these regulars because this class is demanding different qualities and you'll have a very negative reaction. You'll go to the bathroom and throw up." But John, he right away jumped into the class. After the class, I said, "Listen, you did very well. I'm really very surprised you didn't throw up." "Really? People throw up?" "Yeah, but you didn't. Congratulations."

He didn't have an ounce of fat on him—was a very, very good-looking boy.

John was not a bodybuilder. I mean, he did biceps, triceps, pecs. He was playing football, a lot of biking. He was kayaking, running, he was throwing the Frisbee. He was sinewy, very muscular, but not bulky—a beautiful body. He was proud of his body. Yeah, absolutely, he knew it.

Brian Steel, friend and fellow assistant DA

John and I were at Radu. It was all sorts of calisthenics, push-ups, chin-ups, and nonstop activity, which John loved. The music was really loud and John was next to me and there were maybe twenty people in the class and John whispers something to me and I can't hear him so I'm like, "What? What?" All of a sudden he says, at the exact moment that the music goes off, he screams, "Do you see Cindy Crawford?" Everyone turned to look. He was so mad at me and embarrassed.

"Incoming, incoming"

Brooke Shields

I was in a wedding in Aspen. His grandmother Rose had invited me over to the house they were staying in for a cocktail party. We had to get from the cocktail party to a pub, wherever people were going, and John was like, "Come with us." I went, but I had to sit in the hatchback of the car because there wasn't enough room and John was like, "Just get in the trunk." His uncle Ted was there at the pub with all the cousins in this back room.

I honestly just thought he was babysitting me—he was going to take care of me that night because I was by myself. And his uncle was frisky. I was pretty guarded and not very experienced. He was so lovely. But he kept saying I looked like his mother. And I was thinking, *Okay, is that weird?* He said, "God, you have that scarf on your head. You remind me so much of my mom." And he reminded me of my dad when my dad was younger.

Also—it's a little crazy—when I was two and John was a bit older, my mom would show me a picture of him and she'd say, "See that boy, that's going to be your husband one day," which, I mean, is pretty insane to say to a two-year-old. My mom revered his mom. She came from Newark, New Jersey, and to her, his mom was just the epitome of class and beauty, style and intelligence.

John and I went outside. He was a delicious kisser. He tasted like . . . pillow lips. Very sweet. They were just like, oh, they fit perfectly. . . . The lips were just ridiculous. Just full, beautiful—so edible. I was nineteen or twenty. But I was still a virgin, so I literally was like, "You *so* do not want me to lose my virginity to you—because in my world, that means we're married. So do yourself a favor, back off."

I was brutally honest. He was just like, "Oh, come on." And I was like, "No, I'm telling you, I'm not trying to play games here." I said, "You do not want to be saddled with this. It's, like, I'm America's sweetheart. You do not want to have that on your head. You might not even care, but I will make your life miserable." I mean, he was kinda like, "Jesus Christ. All right." He's like, "This has never happened to me before." And I said, "I would love to, but I'll just cry. And then, you might not talk to me the next day, and then I'll really cry. It's easier for all of us if you just let me go." Verbatim. I was brutally, stupidly honest. And I think he really realized how crazy I was—that I meant all of that. He's like, "You've done a lot of therapy." I said, "Yes."

He also was probably pretty shocked that I wouldn't sleep with him. He didn't say that. But I said, "I'm not trying to prove a point. You really don't want to deal with me if I fall in love with you. And I'm just going to get hurt."

I think he was just like, "It's okay. It's okay if you don't want to sleep with me." And I literally was like, "If I sleep with you, I will fall madly in love with you, and you do not want that."

I think he was just a little insulted. Because he's a guy and guys are just dopey. I think he got his feelings hurt a little bit, but I was like, "Please don't take this personally. . . . I think I need to go home." So he called me a cab and sent me home.

He wanted to be a gentleman about it. And it was not a case where I was like, *Oh, I'm all that, and I'm turning you down because everybody wants to get in my* . . . I just knew my heart was going to get broken. I had built him up so much in my mind from the time I was a baby that it was just too much. I was just so scared. I would've been much better as a really good friend rather than a romantic interest.

The next day, he ignored me on the slopes. And then we got snowed in and he had to come and stay at the chalet where I was staying. We all hunkered down because all the flights were canceled. He was like, "I'm going to sleep on the couch." All of his family had left, and it was just him, it was me, and it was my mother. It was like, *This is fucking surreal.* . . .

He said, "This is a weird situation for me." And I said, "I've got a ways to go. I have growing up to do." It was a very sweet, honest conversation at eleven o'clock at night. I was sitting on the floor, and he was on the couch. And he's like, "I get it, Brooke. I get it." We went to New York. We got off the plane and we dropped him off at his mom's. That was the last time I saw him.

I think he wanted me to meet his mom and then he changed his mind at the last minute. On the way to the apartment, he said, "Well, why don't you come up with me?" And then he just got out of the car and went inside and didn't invite me in. I always wanted to meet her because, as an adult, I was like, "She's going to like me. I know I'm not like actresses and all those other people." I think maybe he just thought better of it or didn't want to spring me on his mom.

I had to literally get him out of my system and let it all go. I mean, everybody was like, "You're perfect together. You're American royalty." People were so hell-bent that it was just too much pressure, and I was just too naive.

He was tender—and he was funny. He was wry. Because we're both recognized everywhere we go. We'd see somebody recognize us and I'd go, "Incoming, incoming, incoming, beep, beep." And it was just like, there aren't that many people that can understand. It made it like, *Okay, we're not alone in the world.*

I mean, girls would go berserk over him. To me—they wouldn't go berserk over me, but sometimes they'd cry. You want to be flattered, but it's also just really strange. I even said to him, "But you didn't do anything to get that. You were born and you saluted at your dad's funeral. I sort of can at least hide behind performing." He goes, "Yeah, you never get used to it—just is what it is."

He had that sweetness. And he fought so hard to be just like everybody else, normal. And I think he knew that in me, too. I think we both felt really relieved to just be with each other because I didn't want anything from him.

He wasn't cocky. He was really like a little boy, that's what surprised me. It was probably an arrested development in a way. He wanted to play. He wanted to laugh.

I think there was a kinship. Because I was a little flustered, too. I had such a crush on him—I wasn't exactly being confident. It was just too much for me to take in. I like to preserve this whole experience for just what it was. He was lovely. I think probably I understood him more than he knew.

Robbie Littell

While we were living together on 86th Street, John found out that Christina Haag, who was in our class at Brown, had broken up with her boyfriend. John ran to the window and yelled out the window—we only had an alley view of the bricks—"She's free, the girl I'm gonna marry!" Later he said in front of me and Pat Manocchia, "My wife is now available!"

The timing was off—at twenty, twenty-three? That's awfully young to settle down. Especially for two very attractive and beautiful people, particularly Junior.

Christina, how shall I say—she had a certain esprit de corps. A sophistication. I think John did see some of his mother's elements in Christina. She wasn't going for that, she just happened to have a certain look and feel and New York sophistication. There was a veil of intrigue as well. Veil of mystique she held over herself as a thespian.

Gustavo Paredes

Christina was very kind. She understood John—they were simpatico. She was striving to make it as an actress—he liked that she knew what she wanted to do in life. He was serious about her. That's when he started to look at relationships as long-term, leading to the serious step of marriage.

Sasha Chermayeff

I think the relationship with Sally Munro was just a casualty of John's world getting bigger, faster, and more complex. And she wasn't going to be able to compete with what was coming, all the swirl around him. Going into his twenties, it was just the kind of temptation—the kinds of women coming after him, people have no clue. None, zilch, the kind of attention that John was dealing with. Always. Everywhere.

Chris Oberbeck

The relationships he had with Jenny, Sally, Christina . . . These were heavy, deep relationships. Relationships that were hard to end. Each ran their course, but they hit a level of intensity that you never forget—they were really in love with each other. And then the sadness of falling out of love.

Sasha Chermayeff

Because I was John's friend, I had to sort of navigate some of his girlfriends, some of the more jealous or competitive issues with our closeness. With

Christina, it was a little bit more rocky. Sally was more let it all hang out; easy come, easy go. Christina was not like that. I remember thinking she was trying too hard. I felt like, with Christina, John was a little bit more . . . He was not exactly himself. He was more compartmentalized. Because she was more possessive and more frustrated, I think, with John.

So we didn't end up hanging out that much when he was with her. And because of that, he probably didn't go on about her so much. But he did say to me one time that they just had amazing sex. She was a sex kitten for him. He was having his first really adult sexual dynamic with Christina—that was my take on it.

Sometime in the early eighties, he sent me a postcard. He wrote, "You are the koolest, least fucked-up girl I know. And I love you for it." I don't know what was motivating him at that time, other than fucked-up girls in general. People could be so neurotic around him . . . and not just women. People were always trying to impress him.

Sometimes I think, *How come I was such good friends with him? How come our whole life?* I think the fact that we both had depth, but we seemed very childlike or happy. I cared more about how he felt than what he was gonna do—I loved John for who he was. Who he was had a lot of meanings out there in the world, but the living, breathing John was interested in understanding his personal history, his conflicts. Even though we were kids, maybe you can sense that in another: a genuine need to grow into something that was purposeful and meaningful, even though at times it might seem like he was lost, or looking.

I think we shared an awareness of loss, pain, death. I think his mother didn't want to approach the losses directly—that was something you just didn't talk about. And Caroline, his sister, also seemed very closed off. She seemed emotionally shut down, not in any way going to share deep emotional content with anybody, let alone somebody outside of her immediate close circle.

"A bit of a competitive thing"

Chris Oberbeck

The first time I met Caroline was for her birthday at Jackie's apartment. Caroline was in her early twenties. She was a little more distant; John was super warm. She was his big sister forever, you know? Caroline knew who his real friends were and who were the hangers-on.

I had the sense that she was always advising him—she was a really important confidante. She was kind of a "less is more" person. She was super non-publicity seeking. She had no desire for anything to be known by anybody more than the absolute core people involved. Like, at parties, she wasn't reaching out, trying to meet more and more people. Where John was always expanding the circle, she was more deliberate.

They were a team, a super-close brother and sister. His mom and his sister were really the most important people in his life. They sort of kept him from the other Kennedys. John was different than the others, and sensitive. He could have been such a horrible, spoiled princeling. But he wasn't, and the question is, why wasn't he? Who did he spend most of his time with? He spent most of his time with them—Caroline and his mom—and they were programming his operating system. Who else did it? Nobody.

Robbie Littell

He had a certain reverence for Caroline. He loved her to death. He was the bad boy, she was the good girl a little bit, and lorded it over him to a certain extent—what all siblings will do. She had a real power over him, being the living mother and father figure for five more years after their mom died.

Sasha Chermayeff

His relationship to his mother and his relationship to Caroline were like these sacred spaces. You can never overestimate how important it was. Inside that little triad, there's a loyalty, and nobody's going to break it.

John and Caroline really only had each other, in a certain way—they had this tragic shared experience that nobody else could really understand. When they were little, John was the apple of everybody's eye, and that's not Caroline's personality or her temperament. He was a very different person, much more extroverted. In photos of them together, you see her expressing joy around him—John made her laugh. He had a super talent for breaking people's guards down, breaking down the veneers. And he admired her because she was independent and strong.

They had differences and she made fun of him, for being a slob or for the way food would spill off his plate. John was considered the little brother with the goofy friends who you kind of boss around—exactly like a six-year-old girl and a three-year-old boy. Other people in his family treated him that way, too. Up in Hyannis, when playing tennis, it was always "You missed, that was an easy one. . . ." Just jabs. The stoner jokes, the clumsy one. I saw that in his family, they weren't going to respect him fully. Even Ethel said something disparaging about John that had to do with flying the plane because there was a lot of commentary about, should John really be flying a plane? Because he's distractible.

He did look like a movie star. If John had looked like Wally Shawn, things would have been different. The male cousins who had been his really good friends, Timmy Shriver, William Kennedy Smith, they were not exactly getting attention. Timmy was fine, but nobody was chasing him around to find out what he was doing.

They're all attractive people. I'm not saying that the Kennedys are unattractive, I'm just saying that John was like his mother, the gorgeous one. Period. And America loves beauty.

I always felt like Caroline resented not being in any way the darling girl. She just wasn't. I felt she had a chip on her shoulder, like a lot of people around John. *How come he's getting all the attention?* The same with Anthony Radziwill—Anthony being a first cousin and not a Kennedy, but still, not the special one. There was a bit of a competitive thing. John was sort of like *I can't help it. I'm just me.*

We used to make fun of Caroline and her friends when we would overhear their conversations. Once, they were all in the living room on Martha's Vineyard. We were sneaking by in the hallway, and they were talking, and John turned to me just when we walked by and said, with a false pretentious tone, "No, it's not. That wasn't the Strachey translation of Freud. It was a different translator."

I was friends with John for twenty-three years. There was never a time where we would say, "Caroline's gonna come up to the Vineyard this weekend with her friends and we're all gonna hang out together." We did not overlap with Caroline almost ever, unless I was having dinner with their family or going to the theater. My contact was always with John and his mother, or John and his mother and Maurice Tempelsman. We didn't form that kind of relationship, she and I, but I knew that John's relationship with her was intense and tight. I witnessed them as close siblings. But I also witnessed him not wanting to hang out with her friends. Later on I saw them not getting along a lot.

Gustavo Paredes

They had a great appreciation and respect for each other, and they would spend a tremendous amount of time together. It's only after Caroline got married [to Ed Schlossberg] that they spent less time together, simply because you are in a relationship.

Robbie Littell

If John had any issues, it was with Ed, not Caroline.

One day early on, when we would see each other at some cocktail party, Ed was going, *Yeah, I'm designing fifteen different things, and I just completed my book about a conversation between Einstein and Beckett.* I was like, that's the most pretentious thing I've ever heard . . . Buckaroo Ed. I called him Buckaroo Ed. That movie *Buckaroo Banzai* was out at the time, about a physicist, a neurosurgeon, a rock star—you know. . . .

Once, John and I had a two-day crossover with Caroline and Ed at the house in Palm Beach. Granddad's house. Beautiful house. Which was haunted, by the way—you walk around at night and there'd be giant oil paintings of people that had passed on many years ago; it felt like there were ghosts. It was a house shared with all the cousins—I think Caroline had two weeks, John had two weeks. It was a cool place. Tennis courts, right? We were there for two days with John and with Ed, and they started sort of mocking each other. Every encounter was just making fun of the other guy—you go through the kitchen and try and get the other one's goat. I remember Ed said, "Oh, we're heading out for the day." I'm like, "Where you going?" And he said, "I'm engaging in a collaboration with Rauschenberg." I was like, *God*, but he was dead serious. He was going to go see Robert Rauschenberg and then whatever they did was going to be either put on the wall or put in the patio area of MoMA. I was like, who's Rauschenberg?

"You might get mauled"

Sasha Chermayeff

The RFKs were another whole group. I was essentially afraid of Bobby Jr., and when John and I were together, we hid from him sometimes when we were younger. He was a little scary to us because he was so intense. I got to know him and I liked him a lot, but he's not an easygoing person.

He was six years older. If I was hanging out in the Vineyard or Hyannis when I was younger, say eighteen-to-twenty-five era, he was already in a much heavier drug scene. I remember playing pool with him and his little brother David one time and liking David. And Joe, who was at least eight years older, was a tank that walked around.

All of the RFKs were more intense, more competitive. Super competitive. You felt like you were going to get killed if you were running around at night playing capture the flag. You might get mauled.

Cabot McMullen

Being at the compound during the summer was like a season of *Survivor*. Everybody was super competitive, but John had what I'll call the immunity card. Everybody gave him a pass because he was John, and everybody knew that he was going to get the first crack at whatever chance anybody had at being successful in a political sense. He was the family's best shot.

Sasha Chermayeff

The RFK cousins never were invited to the Vineyard when I was there. I saw Senator Kennedy and he came by boat, and Arnold Schwarzenegger and Maria came to the Vineyard. This is while John's mother was still alive, back in the early eighties, but I never saw any of the RFKs. They were never part of it in those days.

John and Bobby became friends later, in our thirties, and that's when I got to know him because he and John became closer. There was a lot of compassion. Bobby was a full-blown functional heroin addict for over a decade, and during that time, he and John were not really close. And Bobby's brother David OD'd and died in 1984. John told me all this stuff later. David had had the hardest time. David had been the one that was with his father out in California when he was assassinated. He was alone upstairs in the hotel room watching it on TV. There was this soft feeling that Bobby had toward David—and then he overdosed.

Cabot McMullen

David, like John, was not your typical Kennedy—he was a very sensitive, artistic, gentle person. And whether that's who you were or not, it was an environment where you had to kind of put on your big-boy pants and be, not macho per se, but you had to really kind of hold your own. I was raised in a military family, and you weren't supposed to show your emotions at all—boys don't cry, that kind of thing—and it was very much that way there, too.

I'll never forget, I think it was the year or maybe a year and a half after the senator was gone, one of the networks did a TV special about the '68 campaign. It was this documentary that was kind of a celebration of what RFK had achieved. Right up to the end. I was in Ethel's living room with the entire family watching this. And as soon as the assassination came on, Joe got up, he started kicking furniture, people started throwing things. It was just like this outburst of emotion. And I realized, *Oh my God, everybody's just still so devastated. Nobody's dealt with this yet.*

Sasha Chermayeff

By the time we were in our early thirties, John and Bobby had created a thick bond. When we were young, it was always Timmy Shriver and Will Smith and sometimes Ted Jr., but not as much. And then Willie went through all the shit he went through, the rape trial in 1991. And Timmy has a very different personality from John, much more straightlaced and conventional. John didn't go to church and all that. Bobby became the number one closest cousin.

John liked his cousin Maria, and he liked Arnold Schwarzenegger. He told me they were all together at some family event, before Arnold and Maria were married. And they're all just drinking and playing pool. Then in the morning everybody's totally hungover. John was asleep on the couch and other bodies were strewn around this house. Arnold was up at 6:00 a.m. and walked through, saw all these slovenly, hungover young people, and just looked at the group and went, "You looooos-ahs." John said he was naked. He had a little towel around him, and he was like, "You bunch of looooo-sahs." John being among the "looooo-sahs" lying there. And then he walked out, threw the towel down, and dove in the pool to do fifty laps.

Gary Ginsberg

Law school was the obvious thing for John to do next. Think about it: His uncles went to law school. His sister went to law school. . . . It was a credential that you wanted to have.

He went to the DA's office right afterward, but he wasn't thinking about a long-term career in the law. The DA's office confirmed that for him. Being a full-time lawyer didn't seem like it would give him the gratification he was looking for.

I don't remember having any long conversations about the law, but then again, I wasn't terribly interested, either. It's not like he and I spent a lot of time arguing the nuances of collateral estoppel.

Randy Hertz, NYU Law School professor

In John's final year of law school, he was in my juvenile defender clinic, which was called the Juvenile Rights Clinic. Back then it was not a graduation requirement; he chose to do this. He was very interested in the rights of children and in getting some practice experience. The students represent young people accused of crimes, like car thefts or armed robberies, and charged in family court proceedings. John represented kids accused of crimes. Everybody—the bailiffs, the judges, the lawyers, the courtroom clerks—made a point of treating him just like any other student and it was clear that's what he wanted.

I remember him caring deeply about the kids and wanting to do everything he possibly could for them. On a few occasions going with John to court or coming out, somebody would stop him on the street. Usually an elderly person, and they would talk about his dad and how much his dad meant to them. John dropped everything and always said that it meant so much to him that they remembered his father.

CHAPTER 10

A Star Is Born

"That indefinable quality of heat"

Jim Seymore, *People* magazine executive editor

Going into 1988 there just didn't seem an obvious candidate for Sexiest Man Alive. *People*'s Sexiest Man covers had started in 1985. Mel Gibson was the first one, then Mark Harmon, then Harry Hamlin. The choice was determined by that indefinable quality of heat, or just something in the air—whoever was really hot at that particular moment, and in the public consciousness.

Jim Gaines, the managing editor, asked me and another editor, Carol Wallace, to get a group together and discuss it. Finally, the conversation turned to John, who had been photographed in Central Park without a shirt. Carol and I locked eyes. At the same time we said, "The Sexiest Man Alive."

It wasn't like John did anything much to make himself prominent, except to play sports without a shirt on, but women were gaga over him. And men also, certainly with some degree of jealousy. We had some discussion later, because he was the first person—I think the only person in the history of the Sexiest Man Alive—who was not in entertainment, either a movie star or a TV person. Except for the occasional paparazzi photo, he'd been somewhat out of the public eye for many years. But he had developed into a very handsome young man. By the time he got to New York, he was a presence. We decided he was a well-known figure and therefore somebody we could write about.

Victoria Balfour, *People* reporter

Right after Thanksgiving in 1987, Jim Seymore called me in and said, "We want you to do John Kennedy Jr., Sexiest Man Alive." My heart's saying, *Oh, no. He's not going to talk, so what am I going to do?* But I was a freelance reporter and I wanted [to get hired]. I realized I would have to do what they call a write-around—that meant we interviewed friends, probably the second-tier friends. People who really knew him weren't going to talk.

They didn't have the story scheduled. So between November '87 and September '88, I got little bits and pieces on John, but it was half a teaspoon here and there. . . . I had a friend whose boyfriend had gone to Brown and he knew someone who had been in John's dorm. I found out that John had a pet pig. . . . It was slim pickings. It was just me in my dark studio apartment making cold calls, desperately asking friends, "Did you go to Brown? Did you know John?"

I was told to keep it totally under wraps—no one was to know. So whoever I called, I didn't tell them I was working on Sexiest Man Alive, just that I'm doing a story on John Kennedy Jr. I remember talking to some model who had dated him a few times and she asked me, "Oh, is he single again?" And I said, "No, I don't think so."

I asked a Kennedy family friend to ask Bobby Kennedy Jr. if he would be interviewed, but I didn't say it was for Sexiest Man—he would have told John. I went to see Bobby, out to Brooklyn—it was a skating party for one of his sons. He must have known it wasn't going to be a *Wall Street Journal* or a *New Republic* story—he just said, "John is really good with the cousins, he remembers all their birthdays."

John wasn't big then, he was just schlubbing around. He always seemed to have a freedom in New York. Two years earlier, he showed up at my book party—I did a book about women marrying rock stars—at the club Area. I looked over and there's John Kennedy dancing with some girl, boogying away. He had on some stupid hat. I'm thinking, *How did he get here? What the hell?*

On Christmas Day 1987, I was walking down Central Park West, probably eight thirty in the morning. I was the only person on the block. A cab stopped in front of me and out pops John, who lived nearby at the time. He's got his suit in a dry-cleaning bag—he's probably on his way to Jackie's to Christmas dinner across the park. The cab had a flat. John looks straight at me—he was talking to his driver but looking at me—and he said, "You got a flat, I don't believe it." He seemed a little goofy.

There was no way I was going to say anything to him—we were keeping the story top secret. I thought, *John, if you only knew what we were up to.*

It was exciting to be underground for almost a year on that story. It's not like it was Watergate, like I was getting Deep Throat. It was just a reporter trying to get crumbs. I needed a job. I needed therapy. New York is expensive.

I kept bugging the editors to schedule the story, and then in July 1988 he made a big splash at the Democratic convention and they said, "Let's do it."

At the 1988 Democratic National Convention in Atlanta, where Massachusetts governor Michael Dukakis was nominated as the party's presidential candidate, John made his political debut, introducing his uncle Ted, and receiving a two-minute standing ovation.

Michael Sheehan, speechwriter and media trainer who worked with John

He came into the media training room with Senator Kennedy—it was like the senator was dropping his kid off at school for his first day. He was somewhere between shy and being asked by your parents to play the piano in front of company. I remember making one slight joke: *Look, all you have to do is keep your head up and they'll scream*—the audience isn't going to care about anything else. It's John-John, dammit.

This was his first time up at bat in the major leagues. For him not to be nervous and awkward would have been nuts. He had been putting this kind of thing off for so long. *I'll do it next time, next time, next time.* Well, now it's next time. He was 80 percent surprised and 20 percent embarrassed by the ovation and the response.

After that speech, on the Republican side of the Hill the reaction was: if this guy ever runs, we have a problem. On the Democrat side, most would have loved it. For some Democrats who had their own ambitions for a House or Senate seat, there would have been a sense of resignation—because nobody would have taken him on.

Jeffrey A. Sachs, health-care consultant and friend

Before the speech, Andrew Cuomo and I went up to meet John in his suite at the Omni Hotel. We were hanging out in his room and Andrew coached him—John got behind the couch as if he were giving the speech and we were going over it. John was supposed to get a haircut that day. After practicing the speech, we went up on the hotel roof and there was a running track up there. It was one hundred degrees and Andrew and John decide they're going to have a race around the track. So, they're running on the roof, and . . . John just keeps running and running and running. He ran so long that he didn't have time to go get a haircut. And that's why you look at all those pictures and his hair is so long.

When he said, "Over a quarter century ago, my father stood before you to accept the nomination for the presidency of the United States . . ." the place went crazy. Berserk.

Bob Shrum, political consultant and speechwriter for Senator Ted Kennedy

I helped write John's remarks for that speech. It's very interesting what he does: he acknowledges his heritage, his father, but then he gives it to the convention. He says, *You are his living legacy*, and then he segues to introducing Teddy.

John and Teddy were very close. And Teddy was very proud of him. He did hope—I mean, he didn't push him at all—but he did hope that someday he would go into politics. He said, "He's a natural politician. He's got all the gifts his father had."

The feeling in the room when John was introduced was electric. We were looking at maybe the future of the Democratic Party.

Cheryl Gould, friend and executive producer of NBC News

Everybody was blown away. I was the senior producer of *Nightly News* with Tom Brokaw. Because John and I were friends already, he asked, "Would you show me around?" after the speech. I brought him through the newsroom, and he asked for a cup of water. Two female junior staffers went diving into the garbage pail to pick up the cup he drank from. The whole newsroom was looking. We were walking the halls of the convention and the crowd was pushing, and I thought, *Holy shit, I've gotta protect him.* People just wanting to paw at him and I'm becoming his bodyguard.

One woman fainted, I swear. I have friends who will verify this story. She had to be taken to the infirmary. John said we've gotta make sure she's okay. We get to the infirmary. The woman just began to come to, saw that he was there, and fainted again. He was just flustered—he was embarrassed. I think at that moment, he realized what an impact he had.

Hilli Pitzer, *People* magazine art director

It was very easy to find sexy photos for our cover story—John was just so photogenic. The photographers who would come visit us with their photos, we'd say, "Oh, you got so close." John was so friendly, even to the paparazzi that used to follow him.

There were hundreds, if not thousands, of photos—every image that came in was better than the one before. The only one who equaled him in number of pictures was Princess Diana. The huge table in the layout room was packed with images of John-John. There was one shirtless one where everyone said, "Okay, this is it." That was the opener for the story—a unanimous agreement. Who looks like that? And the look for the cover image was that side glance. I would've argued for the shirtless one to be on the cover.

Let me tell you—he was not retouched. I remember Barbra Streisand, she demanded a lot of retouching. But none of these photos were. With John it was very natural.

Jim Gaines, *People* magazine managing editor

It wasn't shocking that it sold like crazy. I think part of it is that people were buying the memory of John's father, in a sense. And they were buying the little boy who saluted. You couldn't think of him as a shallow celebrity because of the way you first met him on TV, when the funeral cortege was going by, the horses. Everybody felt for him. And the fact that he was also gorgeous made it easy.

Jim Seymore

This was just a slam dunk. It was maybe the bestselling issue of that year, and he was probably the most popular Sexiest Man Alive ever. It put him on the map. It was a sensation—papers just about everywhere covered it.

Victoria Balfour

Bobby Kennedy wrote a letter to the magazine saying something like "I'm very disappointed in *People* for doing this story." He was mad enough to write that letter. But I met him several times after that, and he didn't even seem to remember.

After the story came out, I got hired. And thereafter John always seemed to be known as "John Kennedy, Sexiest Man Alive." Somehow that stayed with him.

Jim Seymore

We did hear that he was kind of embarrassed by it. But how would you not also be secretly pleased?

Gary Ginsberg

He was thoroughly amused by it—thoroughly amused. We gave him a merciless ribbing, and he reveled in it. We thought of John as a lot of things, but the Sexiest Men Alive was not something that we actually attached to him. . . . So it was a source of constant amusement.

The paparazzi became even more intense as a result, that was for sure. You could see it in Central Park. You could see it everywhere he went.

Robbie Littell

He didn't legitimately ever complain about paparazzi. He didn't want to be chased around or anything, like his mother getting a restraining order against that guy Ron Galella. But he loved the attention. So the idea of being Sexiest Man Alive was like: "Yeah, exactly. Unfortunately, they're gonna pick another one someday."

No question his fame changed—his Q rating definitely shot up. But he wasn't done; he was grooming himself. And his mother was grooming him, too. I always like to think that about her, in a good way: she was always preparing him for the big stage. And I think he enjoyed it—that was his acting thing. He enjoyed that stage and he trained for it; he looked the part, and he had the wit for the part. So you know, to me it was where he wanted to be.

Sasha Chermayeff

There was a very noticeable shift after that cover, all the fanfare—it made his face so mainstream that it was harder for him. John was one of those people who was always the center of attention—it was very familiar for him to go to a restaurant, have everybody look at him, go to a party and have everybody look at him. . . . So it wasn't like this big shock. But all of a sudden it was more intense. *Everyone* recognized him. And whereas before, they mostly left him alone, now they were approaching him.

It didn't bother him so much. He still took the subway, but city travel was harder. He got more into rollerblading and biking everywhere, which he did anyway, because he was John.

Brian Steel

John took the subway all of the time. You can't imagine the most famous person in the world doing that today. He had this attitude, "I'm a New Yorker and I belong here."

As a friend, you got into a rhythm with him. If you went to a game with John and the plan was to meet him at the game, John would always get there five minutes or ten minutes later than you had said. Not because he was not timely, but because standing there by himself could be a little uncomfortable. . . . Imagine Derek Jeter going to a Knicks game and waiting out front for fifteen minutes.

Sasha Chermayeff

He told me how hard it was for him to be in an airport. Once he got to the gate, he was kind of trapped in an enclosed space until the plane boarded. It was like being an author who's sitting there with a line of people who want their books personalized—there was just not going to be any peace. It became a dreaded experience—to be trapped in public places.

Jeffrey A. Sachs

We were out at dinner one night and the owner comes up and goes, "Jeffrey, can you guys move to the bar?" Because the whole second seating was waiting at the bar to come in—nobody would leave while John was there! We leave the restaurant and there's a homeless guy. And he goes, "Hey, man, you got any money?" So John pulls out a dollar. And the guy goes, "Hey, I know you, you're John-John." He said, "My name is John Kennedy. What's your name?" And the guy said his last name was Green. John shook his hand and said, "It's very nice to meet you, Mr. Green." Then the guy said, "Can I have your autograph?" John says, "No, no autograph." [But] how many people would stop and shake hands and introduce themselves?

Pat Manocchia

We climbed Mount Rainier together in 1989. It was fun, even though we didn't get to the summit, because we got turned around in the summit ridge—the wind kicked up to about seventy-five degrees. John was pissed about that.

That trip was loaded with interesting shenanigans. We were hiking down and there was a young girl just sitting on a rock about halfway up, waiting for him to come down. Somehow, she found out he was on the mountain. He just starts chatting with her. And I just kept walking and I'm like, *Get me outta here.*

There was an even crazier story on the plane home the next day. Somebody who worked for the airline ends up flying back with us because she knew he was on the flight. He was of course the last one onto the plane. A woman came on and was looking where he should have been and was freaking out—he wasn't there. He came on and sat in a window seat, and the woman went over and sat in the empty seat next to him. Half an hour later, he calls me to the back of the plane. He goes, "You gotta get me outta here, man. This person flew here to be on the plane with me. When she saw I switched seats, she followed me." I said, "Well, you shouldn't have been late getting in your seat, dude. I dunno what to tell you." He had no choice but to sit there. We ended up getting some headphones, but she talked to him the whole time.

"The attention could be difficult for Christina"

Jack Merrill

When I first met them, I thought they were gonna get married because they seemed to be in love. They looked great together and were able to create enough space for each other.

In the summer of 1988, we all went to L.A. for six weeks or something to put on some one-act plays that we had done in New York with Naked Angels, and we all hung out. We had a really fun summer. John and Christina had rented a house in Venice. Their relationship that summer did seem idyllic. They had this great house with a porch and he was busy with his internship at the law firm and she was busy with her play, but they had a really good time.

I also remember being in Boston with Christina for some reason, I don't know when this happened, and I said, "You're gonna marry him?" And she wouldn't answer me. I said, so you don't want to marry him? I was confused.

I think the attention could be difficult for Christina. Because it's not only the attention that comes with dating him, there's a lot of judgment that comes with it.

When John and I went to clubs or went out dancing, Christina wasn't there. She didn't want to do that stuff. Christina liked the Met Gala, and she took him. . . . I think he was an unexpected guest, and he was miserable. There are pictures—she looks beautiful. We would joke about it: Christina made me go to the Met Ball. . . . That's the kind of thing he didn't wanna do.

Sasha Chermayeff

During the beginning when everybody's dreamy and in love, you don't really talk to your best friend—you start hearing about it when the shit starts getting more complicated. With all the girlfriends, when the relationships got really complex, that's when I started to hear about what wasn't working.

I saw John and Christina in their play together, and there were some nice times in the city, but I felt as if they were playing a couple—playing a New York City couple or something. And then the fact that they had great sex to me was just like, okay, in your twenties you can understand, you know. Why not? You're exploring the world. He never said, "I'm gonna marry her," or "I want to marry her." Not to my knowledge.

Pat Manocchia

One day I was running with Madonna—I was working with her as a trainer—and John came by on a bike. I'm like, "Hey, what's going on?" He pulled over and I say, "John, this is Madonna. Madonna, this is John." He says, "Good, so you're out for a little run. You guys are running slow. . . ." I told him, "You're biking pretty hard, too. Hit the road, dude. Get out of here." I don't know if they had met before or not. . . .

Robbie Littell

Madonna was totally a fling. Nothing more. Barely a fling at that.

A friend

She came on to him and it was flattery—she was at the top of her game. All about physical attraction, it wasn't going to be anything beyond that. She sort of made the first approach because she was married to Sean Penn, even if they were no longer together, so she became more forward about it. But when you get this chemistry, who's going to say it first? It doesn't matter.

They got together on a few occasions. The bottom line is they never had sex. On one occasion when she was on tour, they didn't have the proper protection measures and she was very on top of HIV prevention. . . . They had fun in other ways. He said she had one of the most beautiful bodies he had ever seen.

RoseMarie Terenzio

I don't remember how it came up—I think there was like a note or something from Madonna's close friend Ingrid Casares and I'm like, "Oh, it's so funny—they call her M." John was like, "I'm the one who started that. I started calling her M."

Sasha Chermayeff

Madonna was incredibly alluring. That's what happens when you're the most famous, handsomest guy in the world. You can go out with any woman in the world. You can go out with Helena Christensen one night. You can go to Milan, you're going to meet Linda Evangelista for dinner. Models and movie stars were all around him all the time. Is he going to dabble? I mean, why shouldn't he? And he was better-looking than all those movie stars, who when you meet them, they're small, skinny, and they have a big head—John was better-looking than any of those guys.

Robbie Littell

He wasn't really into the celebrity thing. I do remember going to Cindy Crawford's twenty-first birthday. But that didn't nourish him—he didn't need to go to the twenty-second or the twenty-third. . . .

I think that was one of the things he cherished about himself, that psychologically he was on the ground. He did feel pressure to succeed—he had to grind it out. But he also had an observation post that he always watched himself from. He was an observer, a spectator of his own life.

Part of that was, you know, having a bunch of pretty normal friends. We would go to a party at the Styrons' in the Vineyard, and it would be Michael Mailer and all the famous kids. But he didn't gravitate to that. It gravitated towards him. He was polite, but that's not where his heart lay. He loved the regular man. He had some great friends. And that he stuck with through time—he didn't discard people. His relationships were not shallow.

Ed Hill

Something that he once said to Sasha when he was becoming more of a public figure . . . She expressed some insecurity like, "Wow, John, now you're such a big deal. I'm afraid it's gonna become much harder to feel close to you with all your new friends." And John looked at her with complete bewilderment and said, "Sasha, I don't make new friends."

Rachel Horovitz

His life became bigger on such a massive scale, it kind of crushed me. I saw it as a loss. I had the sense that what was being asked of him was expanding exponentially. Whether it was Kennedy family expecations or moving into more public realms, he had this other life that felt like it was imposed on him. I felt like, *Who are you and what have you done to my friend John?* In certain settings he had started "acting" like an adult. I thought it was wild how he could turn it on and off.

Sasha Chermayeff

He was learning how he had to use his fame. . . . Not just that he had to use it for good, because that was understood. But in his twenties, it was his mom's favorite causes—the New York Municipal Art Society—and then it became *I've got to figure out what* I'm *doing*. The amplified fame catalyzed some changes, some maturity.

"I'm not here to talk about whether I'm the marrying kind"

Jack Merrill

Naked Angels was coming together in 1986 and I got a board of directors together. I didn't wanna be *that* guy. So I just told John, "Look, don't do it if you don't want to do it. But if you come on our board, it would be amazing." He immediately said yes. He gave me so much confidence, knowing he was behind me. He was my "get-out-of-jail-free card." The secret thing I kept in my back pocket, but I just knew it was there.

Dr. William Ebenstein, executive director of Reaching Up

John formed Reaching Up in 1989. Eunice Shriver headed up the Kennedy Foundation and part of the mission was to support individuals with developmental disabilities. Eunice held a competition amongst the younger Kennedys to submit a proposal for a nonprofit program that would help these individuals, and the winner would get $50,000 to fund the project. John wanted to enter the competition.

His friend Jeffrey A. Sachs, who worked for Mario Cuomo, started taking him to meet with prominent people in the disability field to discuss ideas, including Michael Goldfarb, who was the head of what was then called the Association for Help of Retarded Children, a very large agency that serves people with developmental disabilities. He presented John with the idea of supporting higher education and career advancement for these high-turnover, frontline direct-care workers. It instantly appealed to John.

A number of the cousins submitted proposals and John won. His angle was unique.

John opened up a whole avenue because it created all sorts of better-paying jobs for low-wage workers in home care and childcare. It touched on something that was a systemic problem: How can you provide a good life for people who are in need, including people with developmental disabilities, if you don't have a strong workforce to support them? John had to apply every year again to renew the funding for up to three years. We got it for all three years. It wasn't just a giveaway. You had to prove that you were making progress.

We visited so many of the schools that held classes—classes John was directly responsible for—for direct-care workers who were working during the day and going to school at night. These workers are undervalued, and this hero was coming—I'm using that term because that's what he was to them.

Peter Kiernan, board member and later chairman of the Robin Hood Foundation

We'd have the Robin Hood Heroes Breakfast every year [to honor those who have overcome adversity and gone on to help their communities]. I remember one year—it was after he'd failed his bar exam—he was introducing this woman at the breakfast, Victoria Bjorklund, who was a lawyer and very well regarded. He ad-libs, "I'm sure she passed the bar exam the first time. Every time. In every state." He got a huge laugh.

We allowed the press into the breakfasts to ask questions of the board. I'll never forget this woman at one of them—she was with one of the TV shows. She said, "I have a question for John. Are you the marrying kind?" Everyone in the room groans. He said, "I'm not here to talk about whether I'm the marrying kind. I'm here to talk about whether I can help the poor kids in New York who are desperate." He didn't get mad. He just staked his claim.

Hans Hageman

At some point I said, "John, I got this idea. Me and my brother, Ivan, we're putting together this new school in the place where we grew up, and I know it's a big ask, but I'd love it if you would consider becoming a board member." He said, "I've got this other thing that I've been asked to do. It's the Robin Hood Foundation. What I can do though is, I will make your school my first pitch to the board."

He kept his word. We got our first funding from the Robin Hood Foundation through John's advocacy. Over the course of a few years, because we were new and the Robin Hood Foundation was figuring out who they wanted to fund, anytime there was a question about the East Harlem School at Exodus House, John would say, "This has to get done." That was important to us in terms of our survival, literally, those first few years.

CHAPTER 11

"John Jr.'s in the building"

At the Manhattan District Attorney's office, John worked under DA Robert Morgenthau as an assistant DA in the Investigation Division. During the four years he spent there, between 1989 and 1993, he tried six cases and won them all.

Michael Cherkasky, chief of the Investigation Division, DA's office

I ran the Investigation Division. I had the office right next to Robert Morgenthau. I knew that Morgenthau was close to the Kennedys, and I knew that Mrs. Kennedy had come in and asked him to kind of look after John. There are three units in the Investigation Division: rackets, frauds, and special prosecution. John went into special prosecutions.

Leroy Frazer, deputy bureau chief of the Special Prosecutions Bureau, DA's office

Special prosecutions did short-term investigations, wiretaps, things like that. The secretaries loved John, even the cleaning ladies. I had to tell our cleaning lady, "You clean my office first, not his." Jokingly, of course. But his office would always be clean, now that I think back on it.

John liked to talk to people. I used to tease him and say, "You're not gonna be a good prosecutor because you like to believe what people tell you. If we are interviewing a defendant, you're gonna be looking for the good in them, and we can't always do that, you know." I'd say, "You believe everybody you talk to, so I can't let the defendant be the last person you talked to." He chuckled.

Michael Cherkasky

The DA's office was a place that did not suffer fools—you better be good. And John was fine. No airs. I'm not gonna tell you he was a superstar, but he was smart and he did his work. . . . John wanted to be treated normally. There was no special stuff.

Andrew Kandel, assistant district attorney

I thought John was very smart. I don't know if his passion was being a prosecutor. I always found that he was way more interested in history and literature.

Brian Steel

We spent eight hours a day in a small office. We had to split the office. He just stuck out his hand and said, "Hi, I'm John." He wasn't one to sit there and not talk. And that's how it started. A few days later, I get a call. "Hey, we're playing Frisbee, you want to come play?" I said, "I think I'll get too sweaty." He said, "Well there's a shower here in the building." It was not luxurious. . . . I remember after we played, we took a shower and I was like, *Look at that, he's got a tattoo on his back.* A shamrock.

Leroy Frazer

The first case I did with John, he did second seat, meaning he could assist and sit at the table with the ADA who's trying the case. Prep witnesses, take notes, and consult with me on the case. He couldn't speak to the court because he had not been admitted to the bar yet. There was a conviction, and after the case, a few of the jurors approached me. The first question—I'm not making this up—was "Why didn't you let him talk?"

He ended up trying a burglary case. There was a case where the burglar, in the course of the burglary, stole pills and took them and fell asleep in the bed. I teased him because it was what we call a "rock crusher." Meaning the case is very strong. I don't remember what the defense could've been. . . .

He would get letters, cards, pictures from all over the world, professing love. One secretary had to open all his mail. I remember at one point, some young lady whose dad owned a pineapple plantation sent a crate of pineapples along with her picture lying by the pool. He said, "Leroy, I think this is a keeper."

Bob Viteretti, acting bureau chief of the Organized Crime Unit, DA's office

We had an off-site conference on Long Island. That evening, we had our choice of different sports and I wound up in a foursome with John playing racquetball. Now, this was a private event. We're playing and I'm looking up above us at who's watching—when we started there was no one. Now there's a few women. I said to someone at one of the breaks, "What's going on with this crowd of women upstairs?" And somebody told me there's two other conferences going on, mostly women, and I'm quoting: "Word got out that John Jr.'s in the building."

So we finish up and shower and meet for dinner. The dinner was to be followed by drinks, where we'd be interacting with the other two convention groups. I said to John, "We gotta hang out after dinner because there's all these women who wanna meet you. And I'm good at talking." He was almost—I don't know if shy is the right word—but he definitely was not interested in hanging out in a big bar. So I said, "Well, if you're not gonna go, how about you give me your name tag?"

And he did—he was totally cool with that. I had a lot of hair like he did, but that's about where the resemblance broke down. I was three inches shorter. I was thin and a decent-looking guy, and I'm a trial lawyer, so I was able to pull it off for a few seconds—maybe a minute or two. I wasn't trying to impersonate John, I was just doing it as an intro. Actually, I didn't have to initiate conversation—women were initiating conversation with me! At breakfast the next day John just said something like, "I hope you had fun last night."

The other thing I remember—he was dating Daryl Hannah at the time. And there were many times she would walk into the office. You go around the side to 1 Hogan Place and it's not even like a lobby—it's a very tiny area, just big enough for two cops to sit behind the desk and two elevators. John would come in with Daryl. He would make out with her before saying goodbye for the day. And any number of us would try and get a glimpse of him and Daryl Hannah making out in this tiny little lobby before he got on the elevator. And then the rest of us would get on the elevator and go about our day.

Leroy Frazer

There were times when young ladies would come by the offices because they wanted to just see John, and security would turn them away downstairs. So we had a code name for Mrs. O—this was before cell phones—and the secretaries would know to put her through because of the code name. One time we had this security guard on the desk downstairs who just wasn't having it. Mrs. O came in and she says, "I'd like to go up to see John." And he goes, "I'm sorry, who are you?" "I'm his mother," she says. And he says, "Yeah, sure lady, and I'm the king of England." The most recognizable woman in the world!

I couldn't believe it. They once mistakenly let up a guy wearing a pot for a hat—we had to drag him away. And this guard wasn't letting Mrs. O up. She went and called John. I went downstairs and said, "Eddie, what's the matter? Are you crazy?" He said, "I didn't recognize her. She had these dark glasses on." And I say, "Of course she did!"

Some trouble with the law

Jack Merrill

When he flunked his bar exam for the first time—there was a newsstand on every corner in the city back in 1989, and the *New York Post* cover was "The

Hunk Flunks." I was having dinner with him at his girlfriend Christina's family's apartment. He wasn't there yet, so it was me, the girlfriend, and her mom and dad waiting. It was awkward because no one knew what to say. John comes in late, and we don't say anything. I'm thinking, *Oh God, he's just ridden through the streets, and his photo and "The Hunk Flunks" is on every single corner*. His persona was woven right into the fabric of New York City. We sit down at dinner and her father turns to him and goes, "So, you flunked." He just said, "Yeah, I flunked." We all laughed. He was beaten up in the press. Any bump in the road was magnified when it came to him.

Michael Cherkasky

At the DA's office the photographers are all out front, waiting to get pictures of John. Your heart goes out to anybody, certainly to this young man. Everyone in the office felt bad.

And by the way, some of the smartest people in the world failed the bar. It's a stupid test.

Joe Armstrong

The biggest misconception about John was that he wasn't that bright. And I think it's because (a) he was so handsome, but (b) it was mainly because he failed the bar several times and it was on the front page of the papers. I remember Jackie said to me, "The first time, he forgot to study. He just didn't even study for it. He just went and took it." The second time, Jackie said he was having romantic problems and he failed. The third time, he finally studied and passed with flying colors.

Brian Steel

A few years later, I was getting negative press when I was running for a congressional seat in New York and John was like, "Buddy, you have no idea what negative press is like until you fail the bar and it's on the front page of the *New York Post*."

Jim Hart

On the day he flunked the bar exam, we were going to the Rolling Stones concert at Shea Stadium—we had extra tickets and we'd asked if John wanted to go. He called that morning and he said, "I can't go. Have you seen the front page of the *New York Post*?"

He said, "Jim, I can't go. I can't bear it." I told Carly [Simon, his then-wife]. Carly called him right back, and she said, "You're going." Carly was a friend of his mom's and kind of auntlike. She said, "I don't want to hear this. This is not going to define who you are. You have a life to live. Get busy. You'll meet me at six o'clock," or whatever it was. She had a bit of sway with him.

We went to Shea Stadium. John was ecstatic—he was so happy he had gone. I said something like "Oh, I know a million people that have flunked the bar exam." And he said, "Yeah, but are they all on the front page of the *Post*?" I said, "Ah, you got a point there." He had a good ironic sense of who he was.

Gary Ginsberg

We played racquetball the night before his second bar exam. Because he was really nervous, we stopped playing at one point and just sat down on the court and talked. I could feel his tension. The first time he flunked, the *Post* made it the headline of the paper: "The Hunk Flunks." He laughed, but he was also resolved he wasn't going to give them the pleasure of a second headline like that. So we sat there and I was just trying to calm his nerves and get his head in the right place. One of the reasons he liked to play racquetball was it was a way to relieve stress, but he was so stressed that night he couldn't sweat it out.

When he ended up failing it a second time, it was hard. But John had an amazing ability to dust it off and carry on without a care—at least to the outside world. He made some great quip. "I'm clearly not a legal genius. . . ." But he knew he had to pass it the third time or he was going to lose his job at the DA.

Robbie Littell

When he failed the second bar exam, it hurt him bad. I don't think he could be with anybody. He literally got a twelve-year-old bottle of Macallan's, which was not his style—he wasn't a big drinker at all. He got in the car and drove to a hotel in upstate New York. He was really sad, but his was the only shoulder to cry on, at that point. His sister would've been angry with him. He was just ashamed. Sheer embarrassment.

He was hungover for a week after, which helped him cope with it, the mental side. That was a grim, grim, grim thing. He wasn't sure he'd ever pass it at that point. But the main thing was just, he didn't want that to be part of the story. You get mad and you get mad at yourself, too. Part of it is you don't wanna be looked at as a victim, felt sorry for. You wanna be seen as Captain America. So if you can't be seen as Captain America, it hurts.

I hardly ever saw him drunk. I always thought it was a control thing; he didn't want to be seen out of control or feel out of control. Particularly "seen." Once, up at the Vineyard, we got up there after a fifteen-hour journey through Providence to go to a Brown reunion and then go to Martha's Vineyard by ferry. I made margaritas and he had two margaritas on an empty stomach and it was hilarious. He let go, which was pretty rare. He was making fun of people and mimicking them. He went on a five-minute roll and then collapsed and went to bed.

Sasha Chermayeff

It was hard to be the "Hunk Flunks." That was painful—it was mean. John took it with kind of a graceful attitude, which just added to why everybody liked him. He wasn't the best student. But America loves triumph over adversity, and that's kind of what he symbolized with that bar.

Leroy Frazer

I think it was the second time, when the paper came out with that headline ["The Hunk Flunks . . . Again"], anybody else wouldn't even have come in that day. He came straight to work.

At the end of the day, it sounded like he just wanted to shoot off some steam. So he and his office mate and I went over—I think it was called the East River Bar on Hudson Street. We were just having a couple of beers, shooting pool. It started to get dark, John was getting ready to leave. He had put his Rollerblades on. He takes another few shots of pool and this young guy leans in next to me and he says, "Hey, that looks just like JFK Jr." And I sort of waved him off and said, "He hears that everywhere he goes." And he says, "Yeah. You know—the dumb guy who flunked the bar."

I see John rolling toward us, pool stick in hand. He wasn't threatening the guy, but he just looked so menacing because he's tall with the Rollerblades. He said, "What did you say? What did you say? What did you say?" The poor guy—and I say poor guy because he's almost in tears. "I'm so sorry. I apologize. My father came to this country because of your father. We love you." And John said, "Well, you see, you gotta be careful what you say about people." That's the most upset I've ever seen John. He says, "I'm outta here. I'll see you guys later." And the poor guy is crying. He said, "You told me he wasn't here!" I said, "I didn't say that, I said that he hears that everywhere." It was a culmination of everything John had gone through that day—everything came to a head. But to his credit, he didn't stay home. The bottom line is he hung in there. Took it again.

Victoria Balfour

It was in May 1990 and I got called into my editor Jim Seymore's office at *People.* He said, "What are you doing this weekend?" I said, "I might be doing something...." He goes, "No, you're not. You're going to be following John Kennedy Jr. to see if he's studying for the bar exam again, because he told reporters he's going to be studying for the bar."

So on Thursday, knocking on doors between 85th and 91st Streets, and the stores on Columbus, I would go in and say, "I hear he bought some flowers here—or groceries." Most people didn't know what I was talking about. But this dry cleaner on 90th and Columbus goes, "Yeah, he does his dry cleaning here and he lives on 91st." It was a quiet street and there was a guy playing dominoes. I said, "I hear John Kennedy lives on this street." He goes, "Yeah, he lives there," and pointed to a building. I walk in. There's no doorman, and there's a "John Kennedy Jr." engraved over the mailbox. Bingo.

I told Jim Seymore I needed another reporter. And he said, "We'll give you a town car and a driver to follow him around." So we got this guy who was a fact-checker, Khoi Nguyen. Friday night, Khoi went down to the DA's office and staked him out there and he would call me. He reported that John went to the health club and worked out Friday night and then Khoi followed him with the town car back to his place.

Since I lived on 85th, I took John duty early in the morning . . . and got in the town car and waited. Khoi probably came around 7:00 or 8:00. We got bored. John didn't emerge until about 10:00 or 11:00 in the morning. He walks to Food Emporium. I remember him inside reading the *National Enquirer* and he's sampling free strawberries and buying English muffins.

He locked eyes with me. Usually celebrities, they don't make eye contact. For the second time in my life I thought, *John, if you only knew. . . .* I wrote down whatever he had bought. I remember the editor wrote in the margins on the copy, something funny like "Pulitzer Prize reporting."

He went back home. We waited another couple of hours. He comes out with his girlfriend, Christina Haag. They had a tiff in front of his apartment. He rollerbladed into the park and we followed him in the car. But we lost him.

I got a call at about 10:00 at night. Khoi had followed Christina and John to a movie theater at Columbus Circle and it was an Alec Baldwin movie, I believe with Jennifer Jason Leigh—I think it was *Miami Blues*. Khoi was standing with a photographer and he overheard John say to Christina, "That movie really sucked." So we put that in the story. Alec Baldwin later told the *New York Post*, "What is John Kennedy doing going to a movie on Saturday night when he should be studying?"

That weekend, I saw a more complex side of him. He wasn't strutting around like "I'm a stud." He seemed anxious, like a kid. Maybe I felt a little motherly towards him.

The Hunk Finally Does It
—*NEW YORK POST* HEADLINE

Steve Gillon

John's friend Michael Berman, who sometimes worked as his sort of PR person, got the New York State Board to give John a private room to take the exam the third time—the other times there were paparazzi peering in the windows. This time he passed.

Leroy Fraser

I was just so happy for him. I know that the night before, his mother had sent a masseuse over to him to make sure that he's loosened up for the bar.

Sasha Chermayeff

I remember being so relieved. Oh God. How much he wanted that.

The press wanting to portray him as this kind of hunk flunks eternally got on my nerves. One time, there was a *Spy* magazine joke. . . . They did a kind of a comic strip of John. And the little bubble was "John F. Kennedy Jr. Putting the Cute in Prosecute." It was condescending. I thought it was kind of funny, too. . . . And I remember saying to him, "But at least that part's funny, putting the cute in prosecute." He got angry that I loved it. And I was like, "Come on, it's not insulting. It's just that you *do* put the cute in prosecuting. Nobody thinks about prosecuting attorneys as being gorgeous until they think about you."

He said, "It's not funny—not if you want to be looked at as somebody who actually has meaning in what they're doing and is not just walking in being dumb and cute." He was always in that position, in his own family and then by the media—kind of the dummy. He was so not the dummy.

Kerry Kennedy, cousin

I never met anyone who read so voraciously or constantly. When John slept over, one of his best friends . . . lined up cereal boxes on the breakfast table so that John, once he finished consuming three morning papers, would have something to read. He was so thirsty for knowledge, we joked he was completely indiscriminate about what he read, as long as he was reading. . . . If I had one word to describe John, it would be "curious."

"Not a Grey Poupon affair"

Greg Boyer, trombonist with the Chuck Brown Band

John finally passed the bar exam, and he was turning thirty. He had become a fan of go-go music. Go-go is Pentecostal, it's tribal, it's about as funky as it gets. It was the brainchild of Chuck Brown—the godfather of go-go. John insisted on having Chuck Brown play at his party that year. "Look, if I'm going to get a go-go band, I'm going straight to the epicenter."

Sasha Chermayeff

John's birthdays, he always wanted to really have fun. The thing is, every year he had to think about the fact that his father's assassination was the twenty-second of November, and his birthday is the twenty-fifth. I don't think we directly talked about it so much, but I feel like it was always present—a number of times we talked about feelings of emptiness, or existential dread, around timing. It's a birthday that kind of had this other stuff going on. So it did follow that he always wanted to make the most of it.

Santina Goodman, from book proposal

1990—JOHN—
30TH BIRTHDAY CELEBRATION AT *"TOWER"*

- John calls for a "birthday meeting" to plan his "BIG 30"
- He had the party planned like a "military operation"
- Frozen daiquiris tasting to make sure they weren't too sweet
- Reviewed DJ play list to make sure it had all his favorite music

- DJ must have *George Clinton—Atomic Dog* (John's favorite song)
- Favorites: *Rolling Stones, Prince, Jackson 5, Michael Jackson*
- John's request to me to have "hanging mannequin parts"
- "John, where the hell am I going to find mannequin parts?"
- "T, you can do it, you can do anything" (with that shit-ass grin)
- To this very day, I'm not sure how I did it, but I found the "parts"
- "Bernstein & Sons" in Long Island City makes mannequins
- When I go to request parts, they give me a surgical mask and gloves. They slide open this huge warehouse door and there's a room filled with just parts. "Just take what you need"! I could not believe my eyes (heads, arms, legs, torsos). I go through selecting parts. For every "white" part, I selected a "black" part.
- For the entrance, I hung a white head with blond hair and a black head with an afro. Using my lighting design skills, I hung the parts over the dance floor so that they cast shadows on the walls.
- John was so thrilled, he couldn't stop laughing ("T, you're my girl")
- John wore a handmade 1940s "zoot suit" with "zoot suit hat"
- John told me we were having "Go-Go" music. I'm thinking '60s go-go music. He takes me into this room and I see around eight black guys. John introduces me to "*Chuck Brown*" who is famous for this music style called "*Go-Go*" which I never heard of. John says, "This lovely lady is also celebrating her birthday with me and she'll take very good care of you." As we walk away I whisper, "John, are you pimping me out?"

Karen "Duff" Duffy, MTV VJ

He was a one-man conga line on the dance floor. He had this current of electricity that ran through him.

Greg Boyer

It was a star-studded event. Three of the people I remember seeing were his mom, Jackie Kennedy Onassis; Sally Jessy Raphael with her unmistakable red frames; and Patrick Swayze. There's no telling who else was there.

John Mosley, friend

There was a table with his mom and George Plimpton. . . . I talked to them the whole night. She told me to call her Mrs. O.

Greg Boyer

It was at a small club in Manhattan, and we cranked out some of the best go-go possible. They call it go-go because it doesn't stop. It's a very percussive, driving style.

John would rollerblade down the middle of the street in New York—none of that "I don't want to be seen" stuff. He was very much a people person, and it was on full display that night. He was a huge funk fan. That was very much street-level funk.

Oh yeah, he was dancing. HE. CUT. UP. I mean, I wouldn't have picked him to come down the line on *Soul Train*, but he was very much enjoying himself. And it was nothing spastic, à la Elaine on *Seinfeld*, the way he was dancing. He had on a pair of high-waisted slacks and a regular cotton button-down shirt and a tie. I was like, *There's no way in the world I could pull off those high-waisted pants.*

I don't remember the body-part decorations. . . . For ambiance? Like "Welcome home Jeffrey Dahmer" or something?

I remember the party was still going when we left—he had a live band and a DJ also. He was so much not the son of the president, but just the guy that wanted to have some really good music. He's not standing on top of a mountain with the wind blowing his hair back, saying stuff like "Truth, justice, and the American way." I don't think there was anyone that had a tuxedo—it was a sweating dance party. It was not a Grey Poupon affair, at all.

Barbara Vaughn

In the fall of 1991, John was dating Julie Baker, my upstairs neighbor and friend. We had all been invited to a Halloween party with an unusual theme—*Come as your favorite artist or work of art.* John did not shy away from unusual attire, but my curiosity was piqued when he called saying, "Julie and I will come down and pick you up on our way to the party. You're going to be very impressed!"

I dressed as Annie Leibovitz's portrait of Keith Haring. My date decides to go as [Michelangelo's] *David*, sporting a white bodysuit and six-pack muscle definition drawn on with a Sharpie pen. The doorbell rings and my jaw drops when I see John. He, too, was dressed as the *David* in a white unitard, but instead of the Sharpie six-pack it was the real deal, and a strategically placed fig leaf below. We arrive at the party, and as we're chuckling about the duo of *David*s, we encounter yet another. No one could believe that three guys dressed up as the same work of art—and that one of them was John, who far outshone Michelangelo's masterpiece.

CHAPTER 12

"With every girl . . . it was one more notch up"

Sasha Chermayeff

John met Daryl Hannah for the first time in the late seventies. He and Jenny Christian were on vacation in St. Martin and John met Daryl on the beach. Even though Daryl was in the movies, she had a very ephemeral, almost reclusive personality. John was really intrigued by these women—they were almost innocent. Jenny was a bit like that, too.

Robbie Littell

He got introduced to Daryl again around 1989 by her stepdad, who was in touch with somebody at the law firm John worked at out on the West Coast one summer and set up a date. Daryl was pretty funny. She was irreverent and playful—she was a little bit like a kitten. I remember we would talk for ten minutes about cereal. Our favorite cereal, favorite cartoons, you know.

Sasha Chermayeff

Daryl was a very interesting mix of sophistication, education, culture, and a kind of naivete. A strange mix. She was the first woman John was with who had her own public life—she had her own thing going. She knew some of the issues of public/private that John knew. But she didn't have ego problems that some Hollywood people have—no self-absorbed, it's-all-about-me thing.

She was really good at snowboarding, so she could keep up with him in that way. Not quite as gung ho an athlete as John was, but they had fun. When we spent a few weekends together on the Vineyard, because my husband, Philip, and I were both artists, she wanted to look through our drawings and show us what she had drawn. There's this kindness to her.

John had been protected and had a very insular home life in certain ways. But his mom was not overprotective, and he had traveled the world. Daryl still had this childlike quality. I remember him telling me, "She's so innocent when it comes to her sexuality." And I was like, "That's sort of funny, coming from a Hollywood glamourous Helmut Newton model and sex symbol." We were, like, thirty, not fourteen. He was like, "No, she's so innocent." He said she'd never heard the expression "going down on someone." I remember him saying, "I was incredulous." John and his vocabulary . . .

He went from vixen into innocence—that was what happened with the Christina-into-Daryl transition.

Jack Merrill

I don't know exactly what happened with Christina, but I think it had something to do with Daryl. I did know John and Christina were taking some time off, and Daryl's name would come up in relation to him. . . .

RoseMarie Terenzio

I think in the beginning Daryl was still technically living in L.A. and still seeing Jackson Browne—from what I remember John and Jackson had some overlap. A friend of John's told me that once or twice, John and Daryl had an argument and she would just pick up and head back to L.A. without telling him. She was seeing Jackson when she went out there and John wasn't happy about it.

Carole Radziwill, Anthony Radziwill's wife

In 1991, the first summer Anthony and I were dating, we shared a house in Sagaponack. John came out Memorial Day weekend with a girl he had recently started dating—her name was Carolyn Bessette.

The following weekend John came back to the beach house, this time with Daryl, who he had been off and on with for a couple of years. He said he needed to try one last time to see if their relationship could work. I believe Daryl had agreed to move to New York to live together. I guess being long distance wasn't working.

They stayed together for several more years and seemed happy. Anthony and I didn't spend much time with them as a couple. Although there were many times I saw John and he'd ask me about Carolyn because we stayed in touch a bit and I just knew he still had a longing for her.

Amelia Barlow

Daryl was awesome. I remember we went to their apartment in Manhattan and she put a toucan on my head and it made a nest out of my hair. It was just like, who are these hyper-noble, dignified people that are also very weird and funny and quirky and strange, just like me? Daryl and I ended up forming a very deep relationship.

I can only tell you what their relationship felt like to me—it felt fantastical, adventurous. It felt somewhat young and a little bit maybe naive or immature compared to his relationship with Carolyn. There was a little bit more, like, fire—and fight.

Sasha Chermayeff

When he and Daryl were dating, John sought out Kuala Lumpur. I'd never heard of Kuala Lumpur. I asked him, "What are you going to do there? You're going with Daryl, so I know you're not going to be jumping out of an airplane to land on a desert island by yourself." He said, "We need to go somewhere where there's no one. No one."

And then someone at the travel agency or somewhere alerted the press.

There were over a hundred people waiting when they got out in the fucking middle of nowhere in Malaysia. Not only paparazzi, but people wanting to see the Hollywood celebrity and the handsome American prince. It wasn't that bad until that time—and then it started. Got harder.

Joanna Molloy

You have this gorgeous son of the president that is going out with a movie star. It was a double whammy—we'd always make them the lead of the gossip column. John wasn't an actor, but he was a star. He had it all. I think I wrote about the fact—that was when Princess Di said, "I hope my sons grow up to be just like him." He was even bigger than a Hollywood star, because Hollywood actors have a shelf life. Especially back then.

Laura Raposa, columnist for the *Boston Herald*'s "Inside Track"

We were at Teddy Jr.'s wedding on Block Island [in 1993]. And John had Daryl Hannah with him. I think it was so stupid. They ran through the media line—I mean, there's a bunch of cameras and, trust me, nobody's there for Teddy and Kiki. They knew that John was gonna be there with Daryl. It's like, W*hat do you expect? Of course they're gonna run after you.* . . . That's why we were there.

Gayle Fee, columnist for the *Boston Herald*'s "Inside Track"

That turned into a big paparazzi, you know, shit show. And I think that was one of the first times that the paparazzi started really focusing in on him. That and when he kept flunking the bar exam.

There was a pack of photographers. Back then there were the tabloid TV shows like *Hard Copy* and *Inside Edition*. I remember him and Daryl trying to run through this mob of press and he's dragging her by the hand into the church. They were a top get for the paparazzi. He and Princess Diana were the two top celebrity paparazzi targets.

All summer, we had photographers—they would just hang out at the Hyannis Port compound and wait for John to go swimming and we'd get the shirtless photo and slap it in the paper. We used to call him the "hunk of tutti hunks." I don't know if there's anybody I could even name now—maybe like a Beyoncé type of fame, worldwide fame. He's as handsome as can be and the whole tragic backstory and the heroic family saga—he was the whole package.

His sister had none of the allure that he did. He was the star of the *Track* for years until Tom Brady came along.

Laura Raposa

He was huge. It's like Prince William, you know what I mean? Speaking to him was a big friggin' deal. He was like our big white whale. He knew what we wrote—he read it. See, back then there weren't aggregators, or we knew how many hits we're getting on the website—it was all before that. He always sold papers. Anytime he showed up at the Kennedy School [of Government at Harvard] it was always a must-see. You drop everything.

Gayle Fee

When Mitt Romney was running against Ted Kennedy for the Senate, Mitt, he had these two sons who were very good-looking. So his press people were always pushing those two kids on us. I think to kind of balance the scales, whoever was Ted Kennedy's press person called up and was like, "Would one of you like to interview John?" We're like, *Oh yes, we really would.* Laura drew that assignment. . . .

Laura Raposa

He was campaigning for Teddy in East Boston. And I got to ride around in the car with John's cousin Michael Kennedy, God rest his soul, and Michael Skakel at the wheel—my God, I can't believe I got out of there alive—and John. A lot of old ladies came out for him in East Boston. They were talking about his mother and mostly his father. Granted, he wasn't a politician, but he knew what to do. And of course he was gracious to old ladies because his mother would've killed him if he wasn't. He was a regular guy just driving around in a car with his cousins and eating potato chips, and there was me. I was supposed to go to Woodstock that weekend with Aerosmith, but John took precedence. Yeah, that was a good call.

Joe Armstrong

In the summer of 1993 I spent a week with Jackie at the Vineyard, just the two of us. We would watch the news every night. That's when he was in a big romance with Daryl Hannah, and it was on *ET* every night. *John Kennedy in love with movie star.*

We'd gone out sailing and were walking around Menemsha one day. We walked into a little country store for a scoop of ice cream and she went right over to the magazine racks and saw John on the cover. She just made a huge sigh and shook her head and said, "They're gonna do to him what they did to me."

The paparazzi and celebrity journalism meant that his having a quieter life was over—this has gone to another level. Because she'd had to come to terms with how to live with the paparazzi. She told me she would go away on November 22 every year—didn't want to be seen going to Mass that day, didn't want a feeding frenzy. She just quietly went to Virginia and rode her horse—she removed herself. I think now she just thought, *They're gonna follow him around like they did me.* And she didn't know how he would handle it.

We had dinner that night and right above her dining table was this mobile, like an Alexander Calder mobile. And it was bones. I thought, "What an unusual art piece." She said, "Oh, John did that." They were animal bones he found in Alaska, and he had designed this hanging sculpture above the dining table. She got a kick out of it because it was him.

Jackie built him a silo next to her house on the Vineyard—he had his own little tower. He could look out and just have these panoramic views, and he could be separated. She was always making life really good for him, I thought. We went up there and she said, "Look how fun this is." And she just plopped down on the bed and said, "Get in here." We just lay there and laughed and talked and looked up to the ceiling and looked out at the views. Because only if you were in bed could you see the view. For a young guy, that'd be a paradise, to have your own tower. Like having a little castle with views of the ocean and the ponds.

Carly Simon, singer and friend of Jackie's

John visited my Vineyard house when it was built, updated from a quirky farmy/hippie cabin . . . to a slightly more middle-class, quirky, one-of-a-kind cabin, at the center of which stood a forty-five-foot four-story tower. John loved the tower and wondered if it (or its concept) would appeal to Jackie.

Jackie was a combination of the conservative and the bohemian all wrapped up in elegant and designer styles, as well as her own personally designed creations. Her taste in people was drawn to laughter, but her silliness was modified by sophistication. She allowed a lot, but didn't tolerate too much. All in all, people who knew her well were drawn to her sense of humor, her charm and style. In turn she appreciated these things in her son. She loved the loony outgoing messages John left on his answering machine. . . . Of his girlfriends, she loved John's girlfriend from Brown, Christina.

Jim Hart

Carly and Jackie were very close—I think Jackie loved that Carly could be free in a way that Jackie never, ever could be. . . . Also, I think she loved having a rock-and-roll pal.

I went to a dinner with Carly and Jackie and Mike Nichols and Caroline and John, and it was absolutely beyond delightful. I didn't know John very well. He was strikingly handsome and charismatic and engaged. There was always a sense that John got the joke or was about to tell the joke himself. He had a very fine wit and a fun mind. He would've been very appealing if he had been the shoemaker's son.

Carly would get the download on Daryl Hannah when he was dating her. Jackie was not a fan of that relationship. It wasn't like she hated Daryl at all, she just didn't want her son marrying an actress—it kind of was that simple. There was no great animosity, but she was always talking about "What do you think of Daryl? Do you think that's right for John?" And those kinds of things. But again, it wasn't arch or creepy or anything. It was just her trying to look out for her boy.

He clearly loved his mom. They loved one another. In a way that seemed like *Wow, these are well-adjusted people*. Well-adjusted may be an impossible

166 ROSEMARIE TERENZIO *and* LIZ McNEIL

thing to say about both of them because of their bizarre lives. But it wasn't
like he had a mommy hang-up or something. It seemed very right. She would
light up when she talked about them—she was very proud of both of her kids.

Rose Styron

John was courting a girl, I don't remember her name—I think it was Daryl
Hannah, but it may have been someone else. I was having lunch with Jackie
at their house on the Vineyard up at Red Gate Farm, and John came in and
sat down and his girlfriend came and sat on his lap. And Jackie looked very
disapproving. But she didn't say anything.

Sasha Chermayeff

I never felt that John was kowtowing to his mother's wishes—I didn't feel
like she put that pressure on him, or influenced who he loved or who he
didn't love, or what he did or didn't do. I don't believe that she didn't like
Daryl because she didn't want him to be with a movie star. I see that as a
tabloid version and not the way she actually was.

Julie Baker, girlfriend

I met John in Palm Springs in 1989. I was there for some holiday, staying
with a friend whose parents had a house there, and we ran into my friend
Billy Way and John one night. We ended up going to a bar and no one was
in there. There were six of us and it was like our own little private bar where
we were just dancing like crazy and being dorky. I think John loved hanging
out with Billy because John wasn't into names or famous people. He liked to
hang out with people that didn't care who he was. . . . He felt safe.

That night they invited us to John's house for the next day. We were all
throwing the football around in the front yard. And then, of course, John
was reading his newspaper for a lot of it. He loved to read his newspaper. I
thought he didn't really want us there. We had fun but it was a bit awkward,
truth be told.

I had no idea he even liked me or noticed me. And less than a week later he called me up. . . . I was actually surprised to hear from him—I guess Billy gave him my number. He asked if I wanted to go to a poetry reading. And I was like, no. You know, to me that sounded so boring. It didn't matter that it was John. I said no thank you. He called back like a couple days later and said, "I have tickets to the Andrew Dice Clay show. Would you like to go to that with me?" And I was like, "Yeah, sounds good." We went and we had a blast. And then we went out to P.J. Clarke's or somewhere and I ordered a chili cheeseburger and he was just like, *What the hell?* And he said that's when he knew that he liked me—when I ordered a chili cheeseburger.

On our third date, he cooked dinner at his apartment, which was romantic. We started dating consistently, but not exclusively the first year. We went to Utah skiing, we went to Aspen. He took me to Hyannis to see his uncle Ted and his grandmother Rose. We even went duck and pheasant hunting. There were not a lot of dull moments with John.

I think it was Mount Washington—we went ice climbing up there with a couple other people, and it was like really far up and really far down and I was kind of miserable . . . because that was not my thing. Straight up a wall of ice and we had to dig in with crampons. There was an instructor with us, but I did not make it up very far. I was so over it by that point. I told him I had frostbite before from skiing a long time ago. I told him my feet get so cold, but I tried it. John was like, *All right, go wait in the car with the heat on.* He wasn't bummed, because *he* got to ice climb.

One time he brought me these little earrings and they were like daggers. He was mad at me, maybe because I didn't want to get together or something. I was probably mad at him. So he dropped them off with my doorman with a note. He would do things like that all the time—drop off notes and letters to me. He would write a three-page letter on the yellow long legal paper, notes, stuff like that. He liked to write notes. He was a great writer. The letters always had a bit of teasing—he was always teasing me. But when I was upset at something going on in my life, John would do his best to turn my mood around with humor. I will always remember his laugh.

He loved animals. I don't know if people knew that he loved animals. Anytime he would pass an animal, a dog on the street, usually he'd stop, and he would always say the same thing. *Who is a bad, bad dog? Well, who is a bad, bad dog?* As he's petting them.

He would do it to my cat. *Who is a bad, bad cat?* It was really cute. That was an endearing thing.

The second year we dated more seriously. We agreed we were soulmates at one point, but ultimately I thought it would be better to be friends. I knew we would be close for a long, long time.

Sasha Chermayeff

Julie was kind of a floater. She was sometimes overlapping with Daryl—I remember meeting Julie, and Daryl was definitely still his girlfriend, and John and Julie were definitely having some nights together.

John's relationships were not clean. I mean, most people I know who go from one girlfriend to the other or one boyfriend to the other, it's not a clean transaction. We just assumed . . . they were all overlapping.

Lisa Shields, girlfriend

John and I met between 1988 and '89 when I was attending Columbia School of Journalism. We had a lovely, brief dalliance but lost touch when I graduated. We reconnected in 1991 after I ran into him one evening when we were both dining at Mezzaluna. I was a tousled mess because I'd been painting my apartment in overalls and a torn T-shirt, so I tried to hide behind my menu. He bounded over and teased me for pretending not to notice him, and we embarked on an enduring and often intense friendship. We could talk endlessly about world politics and the arts, and shared a mutual respect that went beyond the whirlwind of our (mostly his) dating lives. I adored him, of course, but was under no illusion that I was the only woman in his life.

A friend

There could never be a news story that said "John and his girlfriend broke up"—he could never appear to be on the market because of what would've been unleashed. Everyone, including crown princes of Europe, wanted to introduce him to their daughters. People who were in his father's administration in the White House would call about a granddaughter who would love to meet him. So there was always a transition from the known girlfriend who was onstage. When he realized that things were not maybe for the long haul, he would've been on some dates with some other long-legged possibilities.

Sasha Chermayeff

Bruce Springsteen's wife, Julianne Phillips—after her relationship with Bruce ended, she was calling John and leaving messages saying, "I want to meet you, John. Why haven't you called me back, you bad boy." I don't know if he ever called her back. She was hitting on him. You end it with the biggest rock-and-roll star in the world and then, seconds later, you're leaving messages on his voicemail. *Bad John, Naughty John* . . . That's how it was for him.

Julie Baker was a woman that he was attracted to, and they had a sexual relationship. So when you say, what was he attracted to, my answer is gonna be her body. She was a lingerie model. She was nice and friendly. She looked like his mother in a way. He liked that sometimes, but his dream was his kind of Daryl-Carolyn moment; you know, he had a preference for the tall blond stunner. I remember it being something that people talked about, including John.

Robbie Littell

He dated *Sports Illustrated* model Ashley Richardson for a while. Once she showed up in nothing but a big fur coat. *Welcome back, honey.* I think it was in public—like getting out of the car when he got home, coming outta the doorman building or something. I remember this being pretty dramatic. She was a giant, too. They met at a club through Billy Way. They didn't date very long.

RoseMarie Terenzio

There were actually a few times when a woman showed up at John's apartment in only a fur coat—he never told me who it was. One of his friends used to tease him—"That's getting old . . . enough of those." And I remember John said to me, "The first time it's sexy and cute but after a while it's kind of a cliche." I thought, *There is not a man on the entire earth that would get tired of that.*

Jeremy Spiegel, *A Current Affair* intern

I started as an intern at *A Current Affair* at Fox. I used to go through the newspapers—remember those?—to find stories. In 1992 I found this story about Xuxa, a Brazilian superstar. She was a kid's TV host. She was very beautiful, blond. She wore these little short shorts, and she had this massive following. I pitched it as a story. So we interview her manager, and in the course of the interview we ask, "Is Xuxa single?"

 She goes, "Well, she's single. But her secret crush is JFK Jr. She keeps a picture of him in her compact." So blame this on the naivete and the enthusiasm of a twenty-year-old intern. I'm like, "Well, why don't we try and introduce her to JFK Jr.?" And the manager goes, "She would love it."

So I write a letter to JFK Jr., who was working in the Manhattan DA's office. On *Current Affair* letterhead. I mail him a letter with a picture of her and wrote, "Mr. Kennedy, I work at *A Current Affair*. I just interviewed this woman. I don't know if you're familiar with her, but she has a crush on you and would love to meet you.... Let me know if you want me to connect you."

A week or two passes. I'm in my newsroom. Reception goes, "Jeremy, there's a call for you." I pick up the phone.

"Hello? Is this Jeremy?"

"Yeah."

"Hey, it's John Kennedy."

Hey, it's John Kennedy, just like that. *Oh hey, what's up, John?* I first thought someone was playing a joke. He says, "Yeah, it's John Kennedy. I got that letter you sent me." I recognized the voice, and next thing you know, he goes, "Yeah, I'd really love to meet her. I would appreciate if you could connect us."

We wound up connecting them and they went to lunch at the Tribeca Grill. We shot video of them. Honestly, he probably was not aware we were doing it. We definitely didn't announce it. First they had lunch, then they walked around the neighborhood and they were holding hands. Afterwards we interviewed her, and she was bright red in the face, so excited. She was very shy and said, "He was very romantic."

It was our lead story on Valentine's Day that year. I think the headline of the story was "My Hunky Valentine" or something.

Back then, John was constantly in the *New York Post*. Even bicycling to work at the Manhattan DA's office. Every girl he went out with was a story. People loved him—it was never mean. They worshipped him, especially in New York.

Lisa Shields

The summer of 1992 he went on a kayaking trip with a group of his male friends in the Baltic Sea between Sweden and Finland. He called me as soon as he returned and left a sweet message, joking that he was "tanned and fit" and that he was eager to see me.

He told me he was writing his first article for the *New York Times* about his trip. He asked me to help him edit it. The story was engaging, amusing, and, like him, always self-deprecating. He was a beautiful and skilled writer. Given the embarrassing publicity he'd endured from the New York press about his failing the bar, I felt protective of him and wanted the editors at the *Times* to see his true intelligence and wit. But the piece needed to be reorganized for flow and readability. He asked me to move into his Tribeca loft for a while so that we could work on it together. We would take the computer up on the roof because he had trouble sitting still and was constantly in motion. I sent him rollerblading or to pick up lunch to keep him from pacing around and distracting me while I was working. He was always more focused after he blew off some steam.

After the piece was published, he gave me a leather-bound thesaurus and dictionary, with a funny postcard of people diving off a ship in Turku, Finland. He wrote: "Boating in the weathered port city of Turku. The erratic coastline ain't nothing compared to the erotic editor. Discipline was never so much fun. Thanks, xo, John."

Joanna Molloy

I went to a Bob Dylan show at the Beacon Theatre. This is before Carolyn. And he was there with a brunette gal, which actually was kind of unusual for him. I don't know who it was. I went up to him and I said, "Hi. So should I get a great scoop here, or should I let you have a life?" He put his arm around my shoulder and said, "Please let me have a life." And so I did.

I was bursting to cover it, but I just felt like he and his sister had been through so much already and he was so cool about everything. He didn't ride around in limos and hide. He was just living on North Moore Street with no doorman. He used to go jogging and would put the key under the stoop.

He never made us feel low or anything like that. I think he felt like we were doing our jobs and people liked to read that stuff and he was nice about it, you know?

This is another thing about him. There were all these fancy espresso places down in Tribeca. Bubby's was right on the corner. Fred and Mary's magazine place was right next door to where Robert De Niro lived. But John would just go to the Greek coffee shop, Socrates, kitty-corner. Like here was De Niro's building, here was Nobu, here was Bubby's, and here was Socrates coffee shop, from the old days. That's where John would go to get his coffee.

One day, this girl I knew is getting her coffee and she feels a tap on her shoulder. She worked down in Tribeca. She turns around and it's him, it's John. He said, "Excuse me but I believe that you may have my coffee. Do you take your coffee black? I take mine regular (as we say in New York). I believe this is yours." So she hypnotically exchanges it. And she went back to the office and built an altar on her desk and put the coffee cup on top. And said, "John-John touched my coffee cup." She had it there for a year.

Jack Merrill

Years ago in the Hamptons, a certain actress spent some time with John, and first thing Monday morning, there it was on Page Six—it was like somebody sent out a flare or got a pigeon to fly the news back to Manhattan. John called me up and said, "Wow, that was quick. Can you believe she got it out that fast?" "She's an ambitious actress first and foremost," I told him.

As far as I knew, he never spent another moment alone with her, but that weekend sure has grown with each of her re-tellings. She wasn't the only one who did things like that.

Sasha Chermayeff

I saw Sarah Jessica Parker saying on some TV show that she dated John for six months, and I thought, *John did not consider you someone he was dating for six months. He considered you someone that he went out on a date with, was not interested in, wanted to have a kind of nice working dynamic since you were a part of the same theater company, Naked Angels. It was just not a relationship.* Those moments, Sarah Jessica Parker and Madonna, were just John seeing what it's like to check them out and changing his mind, essentially. I don't know how they saw it, but it wasn't like he brought them around.

It was just weird to see her talking about it. She was asked, "Did you run your fingers through his hair?" I was looking as she answered and I was thinking, *Not as many times as I did.* I used to do it all the time, sitting in his lap and hugging him and putting our arms around each other. We really had such a nice affection, and it was so physically comfortable.

I felt like the women that he went for, after Sally Munro, just with every girl and how gorgeous they were, it was one more notch up, one more notch up. I never felt like I needed to compete—he would always make me feel okay in the presence of some of the world's most beautiful women. I always felt fully seen and acknowledged by him. He always told me that I was beautiful, that I looked pretty. I never felt, *This is depressing, I never get to be the center of attention.*

Everybody always sort of thought that any woman that was hanging around John was in love with John. And I don't think I was in love with John. I just really loved John—it was different. I loved him like a brother, as they say. And I think that's why I was able to make friends with all of his girlfriends.

Once at his apartment on North Moore Street—probably in 1993, before I knew Carolyn—John made a comment about how I looked, alluding to the fact that I was attractive, which was kind of weird for us. I was not a wallflower—I got a lot of male attention, but John and I didn't do that very much with each other. He said, "Wow, you're looking really sexy." And I remember looking at him and being like, "Oh, gross." I was wearing some really sexy outfit and not taking the compliment properly, being sort of mean to him, and then realizing that I'd hurt his feelings by saying, "Don't talk about my body" when he was complimenting me. It's the classic woman thing. A guy says, "You look really good, you really look slender," and your response is "You mean I looked fat last time?" I gave him a little bit of *I'm not pretty enough for you normally, now I look good? Oh great.*

Now it's all so silly. But there was something about my dynamic with him that if the innuendo had a particularly sexual side to it, it kind of rubbed up against our friendship taboo, which was, we are not sexually attracted to each other—we're platonic buddies. We survived a long time as friends because we never were lovers.

Steve Gillon

John would do things to try to capture your attention. He and I used to play racquetball at the New York Athletic Club. After racquetball we'd go for a sauna/steam. They had an ice dip, and John jumps in and he roars, "Ah, that feels great." Then he looks at me and says, "Stevie, your turn." I had no interest, but he insisted. He wrestled me into the plunge. Thank God they didn't have iPhones back then.

R. Couri Hay, publicist and gossip columnist

I had the good fortune to see John naked all the time because he was a major exhibitionist. . . . I want to just preface it by saying I loved him. I respected him. And then I was a major gossip columnist—at one point I had 28 million readers a week [at the *National Enquirer*]. It was a professional acquaintanceship. I knew Jackie, I knew Lee Radziwill. So he couldn't avoid me. But John never failed, ever, to smile and say, "Hello, Couri," and it drove everybody crazy when he would do that, because it was like the Camelot seal of approval.

The truth was, he had a love-hate relationship with celebrity, and I think it was more love than hate. He knew he was beautiful. He spent hours and hours at the gym. I never saw him take a shower with the curtain closed. I would see him at the New York Sports Club and then when he was in Aspen at the Aspen Sports Club.

He knew exactly who I was. I'm in the shower across, and John's taking a shower and lathering all up and totally naked and totally comfortable. He could have been a nudist. But the stories—like at a party in Hyannis Port is one of my famous stories I got from a source. Before a big party there, he went skinny-dipping in front of all the gay waitstaff. John was very proud of his body, and I can close my eyes and see every inch of him. The guy was stacked, he had all the right muscles. And there was no shyness about him. He knew I was there. He saw me. He smiled at me.

So in the Aspen Club, he would work out, strip down, no towel, go to the shower. I will tell you that the showers in those days were small. It wasn't pleasant to close yourself in this little shower with a cheap plastic curtain, so it may have been partly convenience. But it was a deliberate move not to close the curtain and one I much appreciated. He was very flirtatious, definitely metrosexual, in touch with all sides of himself. He knew that he was adored and fantasized over.

He used to love to embarrass me. We're in Aspen, at Bonnie's restaurant. He's with all the Kennedys. I go downstairs to go to the bathroom. John Kennedy Jr. walks up to the urinal next to me, whips out his apparatus, and proceeds to do what men do. I looked at him, he looked at me. I mean, I was so startled. And John looked at me, seeing my embarrassment and everything, and what did he do? He laughed. I think I peed on myself, it was so startling. So he laughed at me, went back upstairs, and then he said, "Let's take a run." And so we went up in the gondola. John had no idea that I could ski. So he picked the most dangerous, the most insane thing. And you know what? I was right behind him. I think he gave me a measure of respect that day. We just had that one run. He went off, I went off, and that was it.

"Ultimately, they didn't see eye to eye on much"

Jack Merrill

There was a club on Fifth Avenue. It was a supper club and there was some party they invited John to. He liked to go out and Daryl didn't like to go out as much. We went to this club and she was there with a couple of friends and they sat us in this booth up front and the craziest club kids and drag queens are seated all around us. Daryl stared at me and said, "Why did you bring us here?" John said to her, "Why wouldn't you want to come here? This is fun."

It was very New York, and she just looked at us like, *What's the matter with you guys?* Rolling her eyes, that's how I remember Daryl—that encapsulates my experience with her.

I remember him saying, "Will you explain it to her, please? Will you explain why this is fun?" The more uncomfortable she got with all these crazy people, the more we laughed.

Charlie King

I think it was the thirtieth anniversary of his father's assassination and we were eating lunch and just talking, and he was not really engaged. He was saying, "I'm having a fight with my girlfriend," which was Daryl Hannah. He goes, "Because she's not getting along with my mother, and so I'm living in the basement of one of my friend's places now. And I can't watch television because everything that's on TV has to do with the anniversary of my father's death." And he goes, "So it's like I'm in the middle of hell right now." I began to sort of give him advice about his relationship with Daryl Hannah, which I just thought was ironic because here's supposedly the Sexiest Man Alive and I'm giving him advice about his romantic life.

I don't remember exactly what it was—just that Daryl and his mother were not getting along, and it was causing discord between him and Daryl. It felt like they were, like, estranged at the time. They seemed to be happy when they were together. . . . And the thing with John, you know, he was kind of oblivious to the hubbub around them.

Brian Steel

Daryl was a sweetheart. John loved her, but I think she was needy, and he wasn't great with that.

Barry Stott, Air New England pilot

For about twelve years I was running Air New England, a charter aviation company up there on the Vineyard. One time, we were picking John and Daryl Hannah up in Boston at Logan. He got to the flight on time and her flight was late or something like that. He said, "Oh, the heck with her, let's just go." I said, "John, are you sure you wanna leave your date behind?" And he said, "Well, damn it, if she's late, she's late." I said, "Well, geez, I don't think we should. . . ." We taxied out and we're about halfway to the runway and the ground control came on and said, "Maybe you should come back to the terminal. There's a passenger who's quite upset." And so we turned around and picked her up and she had gotten in and sort of had a scene there. It was just a funny thing. But it surprised me a little that he would leave without her. Anyway, we picked her up and flew back to the Vineyard.

They had a big argument in the back of the plane while we were flying back. Just that she was pissed that he left her, and she was sort of berating him for having to make her get the plane to come back.

Robbie Littell

We went to the Vineyard for a couple years, and I can only tell about those experiences. Over dinners John and Daryl had a good time, but there was never really a spark. You never saw them look each other in the eye, you know, lovingly. Ultimately, they didn't see eye to eye on much.

Sasha Chermayeff

I think he felt that she wasn't going to be up for the task, essentially. He'd felt that way before. . . . I mean it's such a big deal taking on him. Even though he was great in lots of ways, any woman would have to be like, *Okay, your life is going to be consumed a lot of the time.* It was weighing on him that she was not going to be able to handle the pressure. Sorry, that sounds kind of harsh. But John was going to need a really strong person with a lot of independence. They were also going to have to sacrifice a lot to survive the tsunami of being a Kennedy wife.

CHAPTER 13

Weight of History

"The easiest path to sanity was
to accept the Warren Commission"

In 1991, Oliver Stone's JFK *was released in theaters. Leaning into long-standing conspiracy theories about the assassination, the film made news and sparked controversy.*

Michael Sheehan

In 1992, John was going to do his first national TV interview—on ABC's *Primetime Live*—to promote the Profile in Courage Award for the JFK Library. We met at his friend and advisor Michael Berman's house and spent almost the entire weekend going over questions. John did not want to have to answer inevitable questions about his personal life. But he knew he had to do it. We went over the on-camera dos and don'ts, about eye contact, animation, smile. We had to come up with an immense list of questions that no one had ever had the chance to ask him. He had been named *People* magazine's Sexiest Man Alive a few years before, so I asked, how do you feel about it? He said, "Well, it beats the headline I got the day after I failed the bar exam: 'The Hunk Flunks.'" That was his line, and it was a great one.

It was not long after *JFK* had come out, so I said, "Did you see the movie? What did you think of it?" He said, "I didn't see the movie." I said,

"Come on, you must have seen or are curious about the movie." I pushed him. "But look, your father had immense curiosity and read everything positive or negative. So why wouldn't you consider seeing the film?" He looked at me and said, "That's not entertainment to me." I said that's great—if you give that answer, that will change the subject.

We looked at clips they might show John when interviewing him. I showed the clip of him saluting. I just looked at him there as an adult and looked at him then as a boy . . . and I burst into tears. He looked at me with this quizzical look. *Really, I just don't get it.* People came up to him every day for his entire life to say, *Your family was so important to me.* I think he was struck by the potency of these memories and the fact that he could trigger it. He said at one point, "People think Caroline and I walked around the house singing *Camelot.*"

I told him, "They're going to show the picture of you saluting at the funeral procession." He said, "I have no memory of that. I just don't remember it. The one I do remember is the famous picture of me hiding underneath the desk." I said, "How could you remember that and not remember the funeral?" He said, "My mother didn't allow us to chew gum, but if I snuck into the Oval Office and hid underneath the desk, my dad would give me a piece of gum." I thought, *Oh my God, he was a kid.*

Sasha Chermayeff

I remember him saying to me, "This is not something that I can take lightly— *Oh, let's go to the movies.*"

Steve Gillon

I do think he went and saw it—a friend told me he did. He put on his wool hat and watched it. John was open and he wanted to learn, and he wanted to see what people were thinking so he could understand it and deal with it.

The assassination was a topic that John did not discuss. I would have conversations with him about his father and his presidency and his legacy, but that topic—the assassination—was absolutely off-limits. He never talked about the Warren Commission.

The only time we came close was years earlier at Brown. We were driving to the gym, and we were talking about Bobby, and I told him I saw the train go by with his uncle's casket. And in that twenty-minute car ride, he opened up to me more than the rest of our twenty years as friends. He was telling me Bobby was a surrogate father to him. And he was volunteering all this stuff he had never mentioned before. Then he paused and said, "Bobby knew everything."

You'd think as a historian I'd want to follow up, but I knew it was a sensitive topic. I knew it hurt him. I always had that boundary with John—he could share with me what he wanted, but I was not going to probe.

Bobby was always skeptical that Lee Harvey Oswald had killed his brother. The first question on November 22, when he first finds out his brother has been assassinated, the CIA director John McCone comes to his place in Hickory Hill, and Bobby goes right into his face and says, "Did you do this?" He's asking the head of the CIA if they assassinated his brother.

He also blamed himself—he thought that the mob may have been involved because of his efforts to go after the mob. I don't think he ever believed the Warren Commission. So it was not surprising that John thought that Bobby knew more than anybody else.

Sasha Chermayeff

Our friend Ed was always probing. *What did you know?* One time Ed said to me that he thinks John knows stuff that he will not discuss—Eddie thought John had classified information that left him satisfied that he didn't need to investigate the assassination.

John Perry Barlow

John and I talked about the assassination at one point and John said that he really felt that the easiest path to sanity . . . was to accept the Warren Commission report and not get sucked into anything else. We talked about the fact that it was weird to know one's father only as he could be reconstructed from other people's accounts and through general mythology.

John on the *Honey Fitz* yacht off Hyannis Port, Massachusetts,
August 21, 1963.

With JFK at the White House in 1963.

John with his parents, his sister, Caroline, and their Connemara pony, Leprechaun—a gift from the president of Ireland—on the South Lawn of the White House, September 30, 1963.

Jackie and John in Palm Beach, Florida.

Father and son in Hyannis Port, August 31, 1963. JFK's yellow trousers later became a part of John's wardrobe.

The salute: John with his uncles Ted and Robert Kennedy, his mother, and Caroline at John F. Kennedy's funeral in Washington, D.C., November 25, 1963.

John at his third birthday party, held hours after his father's funeral, wearing the Marine costume his grandmother Janet Auchincloss gave him.

Jackie, John, White House butler Eugene Allen (far right), and other guests at the birthday party, November 25, 1963.

9

John with his Radziwill
cousins Anthony (left)
and Tina (behind),
on a trip to London,
May 13, 1965.

10

Senator-elect Robert Kennedy giving his
nephew some skiing tips, December 31,
1964, in Aspen, Colorado.

11

John and Caroline (front)
photographed in Virginia for the
cover of *Life* magazine with their
uncle Bobby and cousins, 1964.

12

John and Jackie at a snack
shack in Central Park in the
late '60s.

Aristotle Onassis and John outside
Trader Vic's Polynesian tiki bar in the
Plaza Hotel, New York City, 1969.

13

Duchovny

J Kennedy

14

Ninth graders David Duchovny
and John in the Collegiate
school yearbook, 1975.

Eighteen-year-old
John in Hyannis Port,
September 5, 1979.

With girlfriend
Meg Azzoni and
friend Gustavo
Paredes in 1977 in
New York City.

Before there were Rollerblades: John on
skates in New York City in the mid-'70s.

With girlfriend Jenny Christian at his June 7, 1979, graduation from Andover.

John as a freshman at Brown University in 1980.

With friends including Dan Samson (front right), Benjamin Warnke (leaning over), and cousin Mark Shriver (behind Benjamin) at the Kennedy compound in Hyannis Port, Labor Day weekend, 1980.

John at his Brown graduation with friends Julie Smith (left), Billy Way, and Cordelia Richards, June 6, 1983.

Barbara Vaughn

In the early days of my photography career, John allowed me to take some formal portraits for my portfolio. The date he chose for this surprised me—November 22, the anniversary of his father's death. He said, "I'll be coming from a church with my family, let's meet at the Kennedy Enterprises offices on Fifth Ave." He was more contemplative and subdued than usual, but very warm, gracious, and "happy for the distraction." He said, "It's a difficult day for me every year." One could read many emotions in his eyes that day, but the most poignant was his vulnerability.

Gustavo Paredes

I remember in conversations with my mom, John always wanted to get the sense of the kind of person his father was—when he relaxed, simple things like how he greeted people. My mother provided grounding for John. She was kind of a second mother—she gave him a sense of comfort. Plus, my mother could cook very well. He would ask about little things like how his father combed his hair. How would he eat? Of course my mother said, "Well, certainly he didn't eat like you!" John was very sloppy. She always said he loved John, loved him dearly.

My mother always had a little crush on the president—she would say he was always a natty dresser. Even when he relaxed, he had a great sense of style. Unlike his brothers—they were more Brooks Brothers—the president liked Brooks Brothers with a French cut. I mean, cashmere sweaters . . . He really had exquisite taste in clothing.

I always told John that, at the Cape, just like at the White House, there were a whole lot of people around, touch football games on the lawn. . . . [I was six years older, so I remembered things he didn't.] His father always made sure everybody was comfortable, found a common thread, or brought people together with jokes—understanding that he was the center of the spokes of a bicycle. John, he was very much like his father in that way—he ended up inheriting or inhabiting many of the qualities of his father. Although John was a good speaker, I said, "You're not as smooth as your father, though. Nothing you can do about that. . . . Your dad was smooth."

Steve Gillon

In 1995, around the time of the Oliver Stone movie *Nixon*, John was about to go to L.A. to meet with Stone for a possible feature for his magazine *George*. The question was, what if Stone brings up your father's death? John said Michael Berman set it up so that Stone was not allowed to ask the question. Sometime beforehand, we were walking to lunch, and we were on 50th Street and were talking about the meeting. He said, "I don't understand why people are so fascinated by my father's death."

RoseMarie Terenzio

My understanding was they had dinner and all went fine and the deal was— if Stone asked about the assassination, John would excuse himself, Michael would say goodbye and leave. And towards the end, Stone brought it up, John excused himself, and Michael paid the bill and they left. Michael was more annoyed about it for John than John was.

Oliver Stone, director

The dinner that I remember was very friendly, and I was impressed with John. He was very polite, aristocratic, educated, handsome, tall, proud of his pilot ability. I was very respectful of him. I admired his father greatly.

There was no talk about the assassination—I knew it was sensitive to him. Of course. Your father was killed. I'm not going to go there.

I assumed that he did not agree with us at all. You're Prince Hamlet in this situation—you know Hamlet's story? He knew that his father was killed because the ghost comes to him in the first scene. . . . If what we were saying [about the U.S. government's involvement in JFK's assassination] is true, then it becomes John's obligation, as in *Hamlet*, to do something. And what could he do? He didn't have the power to open it up, investigate. He had to accept the orthodoxy in order to exist.

He seemed like a good man. He wasn't questioning the things I'm questioning, but he was a good man who could be perhaps persuaded to rethink some things.

Steve Gillon

A couple of years later, when Seymour Hersh wrote *The Dark Side of Camelot*, John asked me, "This Seymour Hersh, what do you think? Is this going to damage my dad's reputation?" He was always concerned about that—how the public would remember his father.

The book was a scathing critique—you would think JFK was having sex all the time. But it was more than the affairs. He made a compelling case that he was morally and politically a failure and a fraud. The Hersh book was the first time I saw an emotional response in John.

John worried later generations would remember his father more for the salacious details than for his ability to inspire the nation. That's one of the reasons why they set up the Profile in Courage Award—to keep their father's memory alive for future generations.

John believed his dad should be judged based on his actions as president and not his private life. But he had a completely different attitude when it came to what his father had done to his mother. I think he deeply resented that, and he was determined not to do the same thing.

Martin Luther King III

I was invited to meet with John at the Kennedy School at Harvard, and in the latter years, I met with him at his office at *George*. I don't remember the specific conversations. When you're young, you think you will remember everything. . . . There was something unique and special about this young man. Most people could not live under his circumstances, where everything you do is scrutinized: school, law school, passing the bar. I mean there are great lawyers, and no one knows they took the bar seven or eight times.

When you live in the shadows of amazing parents, and I'm saying parents as opposed to parent, and when you carry the name of one, it is often considered a burden. But I've always tried to look at it as a blessing. We have to utilize the legacies we have . . . for the good of humanity.

We've been connected to the Kennedy family over the years because of the tragedies that have befallen our families. Also to Medgar Evers and his family, and to Malcolm X and his. No one wants to be in the club of losing a parent to an assassin's bullet. We share that experience. Tragedies that no one should have to experience.

On the night that my dad was killed, April 4, 1968, I was ten years old. I remember Dexter, Yolanda, and I (my youngest sister, Bernice, was asleep) waiting to get a message from Mom. She told us, "Your dad has gone home to live with God. When you see him, he will be as if he is sleeping and will not be able to hug and embrace you. But one day, we will see him again." Initially, I went into beyond shock. I didn't know what to feel, other than emotionally destroyed or devastated. I saw my mother, who did the best she could to prop her children up.

Two months after Dad was killed, Robert Kennedy was killed. Mom went to the funeral. I remember my father saying back in the late sixties that America is a sick nation. I think he was referring to the assassinations of President Kennedy and Medgar Evers and Malcolm X. I don't know what he would say today.

I had a tremendous amount of admiration for John because of his humility. He had a unique charisma. He had the looks, the ability to make people feel at ease, everything that we want to see in a really great politician. After the meeting at *George*, I remember hoping that one day he's going to run for office.

Jeffrey A. Sachs

In 1993, I brought John down to Washington to be interviewed by the Clinton administration. There was no specific job—we went down to meet with Mark Gearan, who was President Clinton's deputy chief of staff, to explore what opportunities there could be in the administration. Mark brings us into the Oval Office and it's President Kennedy's desk. We were standing around the desk, and I suggested to John that he pose for a picture underneath the desk, and he told me to go fuck myself. And so, John starts playing around with the desk and the drawer. He wasn't sad, he was interested. Mark takes us out to the Rose Garden and President Clinton's having a press conference with all these foreign leaders. John Kennedy is standing in the Rose Garden watching a press conference at the White House and nobody knew he was there. And I'm thinking, *They're missing the story—it's right here*, but nobody sees it.

I think this was John's third visit. He went to the White House when Richard Nixon was president, and he spilled his milk on the table.

"One of his best young buddies"

In 1991, John's cousin William Kennedy Smith was accused of rape by a young woman named Patricia Bowman, who said the assault had taken place in Palm Beach, Florida, after the two spent a night drinking with Smith's uncle Ted Kennedy and cousin Patrick Kennedy. During jury selection, John appeared in court to support Smith, who was ultimately acquitted.

Jack Merrill

One day when William Kennedy Smith was on trial, John and I are riding our bikes downtown and some truck driver rolls down his window, honks, and yells, "Hey, Kennedy! Ya cousin's going down!" I mean it was just the worst thing you could say, but John laughed.

Sasha Chermayeff

Willie had been one of his best young buddies. John's take was that no matter what had happened, he was just going to be a support to him.

Gary Ginsberg

In general, John never bought into conventional thinking about people who were controversial or in trouble. And when people would tell him to stay away to protect his own name or his own reputation by not getting involved, he would scoff at it. And if he thought somebody was wronged or thought somebody was innocent and needed support, he was always willing to do it. He did it all his life, and that's what he did with William.

Sasha Chermayeff

In 1998, when Bobby's cousin Michael Skakel was accused of murdering Martha Moxley with a golf club in 1975, Bobby was his big defender—he stood by his cousin and just stood there in court as if to say, *Look, no matter what happened, I've got your back* kind of thing. I remember talking to Bobby about the Skakel thing and he said to me, "They got the wrong guy." I thought to myself, *Very different from John's tack.* John's attitude with Willie in '91 was not *Let me tell you about how they got this wrong.* It was *Whatever happened, this is my cousin.* He was very tight-lipped. If he formed his own personal opinion . . . whatever his feelings are were kept to himself.

He and Willie stayed close after the trial, but I don't think I saw Willie again. . . . I think John showing up in the courtroom for him was like *This is me showing good faith in support of him. This is an obligation that I feel our long history merits.*

You can never overestimate how important that was to the Kennedys. There's a trust, there's a loyalty—nobody's going to break it.

RoseMarie Terenzio

Sometime around the Skakel accusations I got a call from the *New York Times*. I didn't know anything about Martha Moxley, and I had no idea that this guy was associated with the murder of this girl until it began to make news. John overheard me say, "Can you spell Skakel?" He just looked at me and took his hand as if to motion *Hang up the phone.* I took the message and that was it.

"I don't want to do what people expect me to do"

Steve Gillon

One of the things John said to me was that he was two people. That he was John, your typical privileged guy who grew up in New York. And then there was a role that he played—John F. Kennedy Jr.—and a lot of people knew John F. Kennedy Jr. They felt they knew him because it was the role that he played in public. He accepted that burden. It provided many opportunities for him, but it also placed upon him expectations that made his life complicated. I think the John part of that is what people don't know. They don't know how many challenges he had in his life and how he continued to struggle with his whole issue of identity.

Who is he separate from his late father? Who is he separate from his famous mom? Who is he separate from his powerful political family?

John spent most of his life trying to figure out who he was, separate from all of that.

Joe Armstrong

Sometime in the early nineties Jackie said to me, "Would you meet with John? He's down in the DA's office. Sometimes he has to prosecute somebody that stole a bag of potato chips, sometimes it's something more complicated. He doesn't really want to stay there, but he doesn't know what he wants to do." She was always secretly trying to make opportunities happen for him behind the scenes. She didn't want him to think she was trying to control anything; she just wanted to make sure he had interesting options. She removed her fingerprints.

Steve Gillon

His mother was very involved in his life. . . . She would arrange for John to have summer jobs or internships, but would do it in such a way that John wouldn't know—he thought he was just getting them on his own merits. Jackie was making phone calls behind the scenes and she was worried about him because he had a short attention span. She made clear to him that he was given lots of privileges and he had a responsibility to use his life with something of purpose. But she allowed him to find what that purpose was.

Joe Armstrong

So, we had our first lunch. An opportunity had come to him to head up an after-school program at the Labor Department. He was interested in the concept, but he said going to Washington and working in the Clinton administration, "that's what people would expect me to do. I don't want to do what people expect me to do." I think he and Michael Berman had talked about starting a company to manufacture kayaks. They both had desk jobs, but they wanted to try this kayak business.

About thirty minutes after I got back to the office from that lunch, Jackie called. She was just so wanting things to be good for him that she was just saying, casually, "How did the lunch go?" And I said, "Oh, it was great. He was so impressive." I told her the truth and that probably reassured her about him. She was obviously close to John. And it's not to say they didn't lock horns sometimes, because they were both strong-willed.

Chris Oberbeck

He invited me to dinner. He says, "Oberbeck, I'm thinking of going into business. Politics would be an easy and natural choice, but I'm gonna do something that's my own thing and prove I can make it there. I started this company. . . ." And then he said, "I now have a business card." He hands me his card and it says, "Random Ventures." And we both burst out laughing.

It's just so hysterically John, right? Random Ventures! That's not how you raise money for business—business is more like "Focus Ventures." Only John could pull that off—it was his personality. Like, *I'm going into business and all you business guys are so full of yourselves and all about focus and intensity so I'm gonna call it Random Ventures just to lampoon it.* There was nothing he disliked more in people than if they were overly puffed up.

RoseMarie Terenzio

John was friends with my boss, Michael Berman, who ran the company PR, NY. One day, I walked into my office and all of my stuff was in boxes. John was moving his things in. I was really pissed off that I was losing my space. I said, "Why do you need an office? Do you even have a job?" Michael said John was getting my office and I was getting a smaller one. John had to pass my office every morning and I ignored him for about a week. One day he stood in my doorway and said, "Good morning, Rose." I looked up and he gave me the finger. We both cracked up. About a month later, Michael told me they were starting a magazine.

CHAPTER 14

Death of an Icon, Birth of a Magazine

"You don't really grow up until both of your parents are dead"

Gary Ginsberg

John was fascinated by the '92 campaign. I'd worked on the campaign for Clinton, so he was constantly quizzing me about him, his use of the media, the celebrity that was surrounding him. He was fascinated with staffers like George Stephanopoulos and James Carville, and the celebrification of a campaign in a way that he only knew about from hearing about his dad's campaign in 1960. The 1960 convention was the first real joining of celebrity and politics, because the Rat Pack was there, and they were all ambassadors and surrogates for Kennedy. It added glamour and pizzazz and energy.

I think John saw a lot of the same forces at work thirty years later, and I think that's when the spark actually crystallizes, that there's a magazine that can be created from this phenomenon. He was also intrigued by the fact that his dad's first real job after leaving the navy was covering the opening of the UN for Hearst—that his father held the journalism profession in high esteem.

Joe Armstrong

John came back to me almost a year after we first talked and said, "Michael Berman and I are thinking about a magazine. Can we come and see you?" He thought a political magazine would be interesting because he could be involved in public affairs, but he wouldn't have to constantly be in the spotlight like you would with elected office.

He wanted privacy, but he's in Central Park with no shirt on.... I'm not a psychologist. There are just some contradictions.

The first thing I said was "Tell nobody. This has got to be the biggest secret ever." Media people would think, "Who are you? A young guy with movie star looks coming from a political and wealthy family, with no experience?" They will ridicule you and ask you questions that you don't have answers for yet, like "Who is your audience? What kind of articles are you gonna publish?" They're not gonna take you seriously and that's gonna make it really hard for you to get investors. I mean, he and Berman knew nothing about magazines except they wanted one.

John did not want [*Rolling Stone* publisher] Jann Wenner to know that he was working on this magazine—he told me he didn't trust him. At one point, Wenner was up in Boston and ran into John, who had been at the JFK Library. We'd already been working for about nine months secretly. And so Wenner had heard about it and says, "Hey, I'm going back to New York. Do you wanna ride on my private jet?" John took the ride, and on the plane Jann said, "What's this all about? Are you thinking of starting a magazine?" John said, "Well, we're just sort of looking into it." And Wenner said, "Were you gonna come talk to me about it?" John said, "No, I don't really think so." And he said, "You'll never make it. You're gonna fail because political magazines don't sell." Months later, John heard he'd been saying a lot of critical things about *George*. John wrote a letter confronting him. Wenner never responded, and that was the end of their relationship. John felt it was such a betrayal.

I told John, "We need to go to the Gridiron dinner." The Gridiron dinner is the power players of Washington—courts, executive, legislative, media. The heads of everything go to this dinner. Whoever was at the microphone that night said, "Ladies and gentlemen, we've got some honored guests here tonight. We have a man here that every woman in America would love to have dress her, Mr. Ralph Lauren." Ralph stands up and there's all this applause. Then the person says, "Ladies and gentlemen, we have a guest here tonight who every woman in America wishes would *undress* her, Mr. John Kennedy." It was maybe six hundred people, and a spotlight came right on John, and he sort of half stood up and held his hand up and half smiled. I said, "I'm so sorry about that." He said, "Oh, it's not a problem." And that was that. He was going to be a good sport.

He told me he'd come up with the name *George* for the magazine. Jackie just said to me, with a chuckle, "Well, it sounds like *Mad* magazine to me." She didn't know what to think of all this. But I could reassure her that John knew what he was doing, that he was going about this in a careful, thoughtful way.

Gary Ginsberg

We all got the sense from how he talked about his mom that she had very specific ideas of how John should live his life and make his living—and I didn't get the sense that she thought being a magazine editor was a high-enough lifetime goal. What I think he really wanted was a project that was entirely his own, one he created. If he could start a business that grew and succeeded, especially one that intrinsically interested him, he could prove to himself and to others that he was a serious person.

In 1992 his uncle Ted called after New York congressman Ted Weiss died and said he could get John his seat. John was thirty-two then and still at the DA, if I remember right. We talked about it and he said he didn't want to be handed it; he wanted to earn it. Starting something like *George*, in his mind, was a qualification he needed—the credibility for whatever he would do next in life.

John started talking about *George* to me in 1992 and he and Michael kept talking about it for the next two years. It's not coincidental that a year later, after his mom dies, he's able to start a magazine and not feel the slightest bit of doubt.

Steve Gillon

Jackie was diagnosed with non-Hodgkin's lymphoma in December 1993 and died in May. He always thought there would be more time. He was devastated.

The weekend before his mom died—no one knew that she was going to die so quickly—Daryl had a funeral in Los Angeles for her dog.

Sasha Chermayeff

The dog's death was John's fault. He'd been walking it in the city, in Central Park, and the dog got off the leash and got hit by a car and died. Daryl was devastated.

Carole Radziwill

It was a freak accident and John was obviously very upset about it.

Steve Gillon

John was supposed to bring the ashes out from New York. I think he put the ashes in a box that Daryl didn't approve of—I think she wanted something gold. So he goes out there to bury the dog. And while he's out there, his mom has a dramatic turn for the worse. He was deeply resentful that Daryl dragged him out there to attend a funeral for her dog when his mother was dying of cancer.

Carole Radziwill

I recall it was a Sunday night and we went to Sant Ambroeus on Madison for dinner. He was so upset and angry that he had to spend that weekend going to Daryl's dog funeral. In her defense, she truly was a great lover of animals. But John felt she was punishing him by insisting he fly to L.A. that weekend. It was just a terrible time and a bad omen. Things were not holding.

Sasha Chermayeff

I think there was something really difficult about Daryl and John's dynamic even when it was going right. She told him that she had never been so abused by anyone. It was so hard for me to believe that John was being verbally or emotionally abusive—I just didn't believe it.

Joe Armstrong

Sometime that spring, we were going to a meeting when I was introducing him to circulation experts, who could do tests to prove there was a market for the magazine. He always seemed to look down at the pavement as he walked. I remember him looking down at a newsstand and the headline just said "Pray for Jackie."

RoseMarie Terenzio

I remember John was feeling that Jackie's companion, Maurice, was kind of isolating her—he was being really tough about letting John see her. It was sort of like *Oh, I'm going to come by and see Mummy*. And Maurice was like, *Well, not today. She's not feeling great. I'll let you know when she's up to it*. And I think it was hard for John.

Joe Armstrong

Carly Simon and I had lunch with Jackie the day before she went to the hospital for the last time. That day was hard because she had no eyebrows, no eyelashes, and an ill-fitting wig, but she wanted to be upbeat. We had to act like it was a regular lunch, but my heart was just breaking inside because it was just, "Oh my gosh, she's so different." She said to me, "Four more weeks and I get my life back." And four more weeks and she was gone. She collapsed the next day, and she was taken to the hospital, and I never saw or heard from her again.

John and I were scheduled to have lunch the day she died. That morning he called and said, "Joe, I'm not gonna be able to have lunch today." I said, "How's Jackie doing?" He said, "Well, it's like a car speeding down the highway and parts are falling off." Carly Simon came over to my house because we'd spent time together with Jackie and we were praying, and I got a call from Marta [Sgubin], who was sort of the house guru, and she just said, "You might want to come over." Carly and I went over there, and Marta said, "I don't know if Jackie would want a man to see her like this." I said, "I'll just wait here in the living room."

I talked to John and he walked us to the door. He just said, "Mummy really loved you two." He had tears about to start rolling down his cheeks. I'd never seen him be emotional. He took it really hard. And now he had to go be composed and be the spokesman.

John F. Kennedy Jr., to the crowd outside his mother's apartment on May 20, 1994

Last night at around 10:15, my mother passed on. She was surrounded by her friends and her family and her books . . . the people and the things that she loved, and she did it in her own way, and in her own terms. . . . We all feel lucky for that, and now she's in God's hands.

Jim Hart

When Carly and I were leaving Jackie's wake at her apartment, John ran down the stairs after us, before we got out on the crazy street. . . . And he said, "I just want to talk to you two for a second. Do you mind?" He said, "My mother's life, I think, really began to get happy about seven years ago. And you two were a very, very important part of that happiness." And, of course, we were just all in tears.

Steve Gillon

John had dealt with so much death in his life. He'd written a letter to a mutual friend of ours, Charlie King, after Charlie's father had died, and it said, "You learn as much from death as you do from life. Don't run away from it. Accept it. Accept its challenges. . . ." I think that's how John learned to deal with it. He had dealt with so much death . . . but the death of his mom was by far the most painful.

Barry Clifford

Someone like John, who grew up with the world watching him, had a certain shield around him that he put up. But inside that shield was a very delicate, kind, sensitive person. He was devastated.

Clint Hill

After she died, I saw John make the announcement, and now he was speaking again at the grave site, at the service for Mrs. Kennedy at Arlington. I thought about how he had matured, mentally and physically—and I was impressed by how much he looked like his dad.

The last time I saw John was that day. I'd been told where to stand, but I decided that wouldn't be too good because I was a reminder [of Dallas], so I stood in the back. There's a photograph of me way in the back, behind Maria Shriver Schwarzenegger.

Julie Baker

John was really very touched when so many people came up to him on the street after his mom died to say how sorry they were and how much they loved her and his dad. Very touched by all of that.

Carole Radziwill

Daryl flew out for the funeral and I took her shopping to get a proper funeral dress. I could see it was over. John could barely look at her. I think she knew, too.

Sasha Chermayeff

The funeral mass was at St. Ignatius Loyola in Manhattan. John had told me ahead of time, "You're just going to come. I'm not going to be able to see you. I'm not going to be able to talk to you. We're going to be separated. They're going to be ushering me out and then I'm going to go to Arlington, and I am not going to cry in front of a million people. I just want you guys to be in Hyannis when I'm done. Just be there." And then John was gone.

My husband and I and our son drove to Hyannis and met him. His car pulled up. I remember looking through the kitchen window and seeing Daryl's face looking angular and sharp and I thought to myself, *Oh, not good.* He had already told me, "I'm dreading dealing with her."

I just remember him in the kitchen—he was so wrecked. He let down his guard. He was just like a ghost. I was thinking, *He's just so lost right now.* And then he and Daryl—there was this clash. Her dog was old and dying—this was *another* dog. It was the dog, the dog, the dog. I'm thinking, *Oh my God. I'm sorry that you have an old dog who's sick. But your partner—whatever it is right now—he's downstairs in the kitchen. His mother died. He's just been through a huge public performance and televised funeral that wasn't intimate and quiet where he could express his feelings.* He's sitting in the kitchen saying to me, "I just wish she hadn't died so young. I wasn't ready. I just didn't know she was going to die this soon." She was the age I am right now. Sixty-four. Daryl was upstairs crying over her dog. I remember Timmy Shriver, we were both like, "Oh my God, could somebody do something? Just stop."

Daryl was incapable of it. And I realized, *Oh, you have to leave her. . . . That's a big one. Your mom has died and your girlfriend is not able to see how to be supportive of you.* It was totally obvious that they were going to break up.

Carole Radziwill

John just couldn't face her after his mom died. Anthony had recently been diagnosed with a recurrence of his cancer and was recovering from a serious operation. It was just all too much. I believe they broke up for good shortly after the funeral, because three months later Anthony and I got married and John had quietly rekindled his romance with Carolyn.

Sasha Chermayeff

The weekend his mom died, it was sort of the John-Daryl demise weekend following the empowerment of "My mother died, and now I'm going to make decisions about what I need to do." You're broken, and you're empowered—the breaking down makes you see what is more important in your life. He talked about it. "You don't really grow up until both of your parents are dead."

The following summer, he was in his mom's master bedroom at the Vineyard house and he was changing her decor a little bit. The house was becoming his—Caroline didn't use it as much as John. And I thought, *He's sort of taking on this role.* . . . Now, instead of being the kid that left his bike on the beach who needs to be picked up, he was going to be the man of the house.

Gustavo Paredes

His mother's death was just devastating. But . . . How should I say this? He became an adult at that time. He didn't have his mom to kind of be his protector. So he got much more focused on life, his family's legacy, where he fit in the world, where he fit in the relationship between him and Caroline. . . .

Robbie Littell

He was a different person coming out of that. His wings came out.

You got the sense that his mom's hand was always there in the background on his shoulder, giving him guidance. But when she passed, he was the bird coming out of the old nest with his wings wide open. Before that, I think he was on someone else's track, doing what other people expected him to do—a groove of other people's making. And then he was able to shoot out of the groove into the air and fly on his own. I think that his intellect sharpened, his views of things sharpened, his confidence sharpened, his ability sharpened. He became a self-sufficient, potential juggernaut out there.

JFK Jr. on *Larry King Live*, September 28, 1995

Larry King: Would [your mother] have liked George?

John: I think that, when we first talked about the idea, she said, "Well, John, you're not gonna do the Mad *magazine of politics?" And I said, "Well, no." And*

I thought that was good advice to keep in the back of my mind, what direction we wanted to go. But I think that she would've appreciated the fact that people had always said that "you can't do a fun magazine about politics that combines the serious as well as the playful." Which is about personalities, because that's what public life is about.

And in the sense that we, I think, have flouted a lot of conventional wisdom, I think that that would have appealed to her. She had a good sense of humor. And I don't think she was a slave to conventional wisdom. And I think that, that there's a certain irony in the whole enterprise, and I think she would've appreciated it.

Larry King: She would've said, "This is a cute idea," right?

JFK Jr.: I think something more than "cute."

CHAPTER 15

Carolyn

"He was obsessed from the minute he met her"

Paul Eckstein

I remember John at one of our Naked Angels parties coming up and being like, "Yo, man, you gotta hook me up. Who is that girl? Introduce me." I was like, "John, I'm not going to introduce you to anybody. You're fucking John Kennedy. Go introduce yourself." We were doing a 1940s speakeasy theme for this party, and we were both dressed in cheesy 1940s outfits. I had a crush on Carolyn's sister Lauren. He was trying to get me to help introduce him to Carolyn and I wouldn't do it. Of course, he met her anyway.

RoseMarie Terenzio

The story I heard was that John and Carolyn first met at Calvin Klein. It was around 1991. He had gone to pick out some suits and she helped him—she was the handler for a lot of the VIPs. He asked for her number and they went out on a few dates. Carolyn was dating around and so was John—Daryl was still in the picture, but they seemed to be on and off. Carolyn wasn't sitting by the phone waiting for his call—it was the opposite. For the first time, he was getting a taste of his own medicine. And that intrigued him.

Sasha Chermayeff

John had taken me to this event. We were going to dinner, but he's like, "I've got to swing by this place first." I saw Carolyn from across the room and she was leaning on this post. And I said to myself, *That's the kind of woman that John is so attracted to. . . . That's so John's type right there.* We meandered around the party and we're working our way to the focal point of this party—that woman—and I realize we are not here for any other reason. I remember the way she looked at him and the way he looked at her and I was just like, *Okay,* this *is why I'm here.*

He was very casual. *We're just coming to say hi.* I didn't say anything. He was still with Daryl. It was private and I wasn't going to be like, *Oh my God, do you have the hots for her . . . and what about your relationship?* John never said anything to me, but he was overlapping with Carolyn while he was with Daryl—I'm convinced that there was quite a bit of overlap. I think he was obsessed with Carolyn from the minute he met her.

Then by the summer of '94 when he came up to visit me in Catskill, there was a feeling that there was something he had to get back to Manhattan for—something was pulling him back. I was saying, "What's the rush?" I thought, *Hmmmm.*

Brian Steel

We were running around Central Park West and we started walking, which was unusual because the guy just wanted to run forever. He said he was completely enchanted by this woman, Carolyn Bessette. And I was like, "What about Daryl?" because they were still together, and he is like, "I think we're going to break up. . . . I met her at Calvin Klein."

He went out on a date or two with Carolyn and he's like, "I want you to find out as much as you can about Carolyn—I know you know people, like, you know, nightclub people, restaurateurs. . . . I know you know people that went to college with her." And so I found out as much as I could about her and not all of it was good. I told him all of it. She was a club girl, and she dated a lot of people.

And then at his birthday party—he used to throw a birthday party at El

Teddy's, the Mexican restaurant in Tribeca—and that year there were about fifteen to twenty friends, and I was sitting directly across from Carolyn, and she had this way of making you feel like you were the only person in the room. She would touch your hands and the hair on the back of my head would go up. She was electric, dynamic. Much more than any photograph could ever capture. Midway through dinner, John pulled me aside and asked what I thought. He was so enthralled, like a kid in a candy shop. I said, "She's stunning. Enchanting." And he was like, "That is awesome. I knew you would love her." Then he said, "I told her everything you told me." And I said, "You are a moron. Why would you do that?" He was like, "No, no, she loves you." We did come to love each other.

RoseMarie Terenzio

I met Carolyn in Michael Berman's office. This was probably in the fall of '94—I'd been working for John since the beginning of that year. Carolyn and I had already been chatting on the phone before we met. I remember she was wearing this pencil skirt with a white button-down shirt. Very clean. It was kind of intimidating. But then as soon as you got a sense of her personality, she was really warm. I think it was Fashion Week. Her nails were robin's-egg blue, right when that trend started, and she's like, *Isn't this weird?* She was standing next to my desk waiting for him, laughing at how much the phone was ringing. She was like, *Oh my God, this is crazy.* . . .

She and John had been hanging out on and off—they were both dating other people, but they reconnected in 1994 and it was more serious. They had dinner at Provence downtown, and John gave her the impression he was no longer in a relationship with Daryl and he wanted to date her exclusively. Not long after, there was a picture in the *Daily News* of John and Daryl holding hands at a movie premiere. Carolyn saw it and cut off contact. Her mom sent her the clipping with a note that said, "Dear Carolyn, please get on with your life. Love, Mom," with a sad face.

John sent flowers to Carolyn's office at Calvin and told her it was just this once, that Daryl hadn't wanted to go to this event by herself, it was something they had planned to go to together, and he felt bad for her. He called several times and left messages, which Carolyn didn't return—she took her voice off of her answering machine, so there was no message, just a beep.

Then the morning after Jackie died, Carolyn saw the news and she called him back. Soon after his mom died, John officially ended the relationship with Daryl, and he and Carolyn got together for good. As they got more serious, I think he was disappointed that Carolyn never got to meet his mom.

Sometime after he and Daryl broke up, before the press knew about Carolyn, there was a *People* cover, "Is he a man with a plan or a dreamboat adrift?" I remember going to the office that day and I took the cover off and put it on his door. When he walked in that morning, he said, "Hey, Rosie." I said, "Hey, dreamboat," and he was like, "Shut up." Then he took it off his door and he put it on mine.

Robbie Littell

John was head over heels for Carolyn. . . . She was a bright, bright, shining light. She was obviously a star in the sky. . . . *Who is this? It's Calvin Klein's muse.* All right, that sounds good. . . .

George Kyriakos, hairstylist and Carolyn's friend

At Calvin, I mean, Carolyn was a grunt—it wasn't like she was a princess. She used to work her ass off.

I met John when we went over to their apartment for a football game. He was the nicest dude. He started to come to my apartment on Thompson Street for a haircut. He used to bring Chinese food for himself from Suzie's on Bleecker Street—it was his favorite Chinese food. He always had a newspaper; he was always reading the news. We would just talk about life and stuff. It seemed to me he wanted to be my friend because I was so close to Carolyn.

I've worked with celebrities for years and I always think of him. 'Cause when I meet a celebrity that has an attitude, I think, *I used to be friends and work with probably the most famous guy in the world. He didn't have an attitude. So I don't know why you do.*

Sasha Chermayeff

The first time we spent a weekend all together was '95 on the Vineyard. I was pregnant. And it was me and Robbie Littell and his wife, Fran. It was usually Robbie, Frannie, me, and my husband, Phil, and the kids—my son, Phineas, and Robbie's kids—and Santina. That was our little hub. That was the "John lovefest," as we used to call it.

We had that first time there together and it wasn't great. I think I was getting on Carolyn's nerves a little bit because I was too close to John. That was hard for her. She got used to me and we became really close. But we had to have an argument first.

We were all eating dinner. I was giving birth in three months. And I wanted that dinner and I was like, "Okay, I've got to put Phinnie to bed upstairs, but nobody take my dinner." Effie [Jackie's former butler Efigenio Pinheiro, who then worked for John] had made an amazing dinner.

I put Phinnie to bed and John's friend Kevin Ward had been sitting next to me. When I came back twenty minutes later, my plate was empty. I went into the kitchen and said, "Effie, they ate my dinner," and he said, "There's no more of the fish, can I make you something else?" I was sort of seething. Carolyn came in and asked, "What's going on?" I said to her, "I'm sorry, I just didn't want to make a big deal of it." She said, "You didn't want to make a big deal about it, but you did." I said, "Just wait. Because one day you'll under-stand what I'm going through right now and right now I'm talking to Effie because I'm pregnant and he's going to make me a fucking cheeseburger." She just said, "*God*," and huffed back to the table. And it just broke some barrier between us.

Later on that night, John was lying on the floor and he asked, "Sasha, will you walk on my back? Will you crack my back?" He was lying on the floor face down. I'm mushing my feet into his butt. She looked at him and she looked up at me and then she smiled. Like, *Okay, I get this.* We were friends after that.

She was that kind of girl. You had that kind of encounter with her in order to break in. She had to suss you out and get used to the fact that you were there for good. There's nothing she could really do about it.

Santina Goodman

We were hanging out at John's apartment. At 2:00 a.m., the doorbell rings and I asked John, "Who's that?" He replies, "Carolyn." I'm thinking, *Why is his sister visiting so late?* When Carolyn walks in, I make a comment to our friend George, "This must be a booty call!" The second time I saw Carolyn, John had invited me over for dinner. As soon as I walked in the door, Carolyn walks over to me and says, in a very nasty tone, "Are you the one who made the booty call joke?" It was clear to me that she was pissed and wanted to fight. I asked her, "Carolyn, where are you from?" Her reply, "Greenwich, Connecticut." I said, "When a woman comes to a guy's apartment at 2:00 a.m., where I come from it's called a booty call. And you better be nice to me because if you're not, I'll find John a beautiful Black woman who will cook for him and give him the best blow jobs he's ever had." That was the "first time" I saw that beautiful Carolyn smile.

Jack Merrill

We had dinner at the Odeon. John had been telling me about Carolyn—*This is my new girlfriend and I really like her and she's gonna come by*—and then the chair is empty. He was embarrassed and annoyed. I thought it was hysterical—I loved it from the minute the chair was empty. I just loved the fact that she was an hour late. . . . Most girls did not do that to John. She showed up and she sat next to me and we laughed from the minute I first looked at her.

George Rush, New York *Daily News* columnist

I was doing a column at the *Daily News* when I heard about this Carolyn Bessette, who nobody had really heard of. That she was the Calvin Klein shopper—and that she was juggling John and Michael Bergin, the model. The headline was "The Hunk Love Triangle." The *Daily News* gave that a lot of play. Anything concerning John would almost automatically go on the front page. However trivial.

This Hunk Love Triangle story came out, and the same day Joanna [Molloy, his colleague and later wife] and I were due to meet up with [then Calvin

Klein PR executive] Paul Wilmot and some people at Elaine's. We arrive at Elaine's and who do we find sitting at the table among our dinner companions, but Carolyn. Joanna thought that it would be too awkward to sit with her. She sat down at another table with Elaine Kaufman, the proprietor. I wanted to find out more about this Hunk Love Triangle, so I hopped back and forth between the two tables, trying to politely get to know Carolyn, who didn't talk a lot. Elaine told Joanna that she shouldn't worry about how Carolyn felt—because Carolyn can get over it. If she doesn't like attention, she should stay home. Frankly, Carolyn seemed kind of tickled by the situation, and according to people who knew her, was delighted by the article because it may have made John jealous.

Pat Manocchia

It was not casual from the beginning—this is someone who was not casual. She was very engaging, very much her own person and smart and funny. She had a job, she'd gone to college. She was strong—not a pushover. They were always physical and affectionate and engaged. It was vibrant.

Robbie Littell

She intrigued him more than anyone he'd met. I remember Christina Haag, when she'd broken up with some guy, he goes, "I'm going to marry her." But Carolyn I think was the most exotic thing he'd ever dealt with in terms of her own capacity, her own passions. She was pretty enigmatic in the sense of who is this wild person—a force of nature.

He said he wanted to marry her. He was adamant. But John and Carolyn—they were just children emotionally on a certain level. They hadn't had an opportunity to mature. She had her crazy family, too. Her sisters were fierce. The other was kind of cool, too, I liked her—the one that lives in Michigan now, Lisa. She was funny. And she was a very good spectator. Her mom was a force. She was ahead of her time—a Nancy Pelosi type.

Gustavo Paredes

After John met Carolyn, he became a dresser. Before, it was always some mishmash of stuff. He had absolutely no style—he had a style of no style. He would wear these kind of balloon pants, cotton with some odd stripes, faded T-shirts. He had a great attraction for color, and he spent a good amount of time in Kenya and Africa and India. He never did wear those Cape Cod, Brooks Brothers, prep-style clothing. But he had an idea of colors from these travels. He'd put African and Indian styles together, but better to do all of one or the other, you can't mesh. And he started getting better haircuts, too.

Karen "Duff" Duffy

The image I have of Carolyn was at a baby shower where she looked like she was wearing her uncle's golf pants. She'd hiked them with a belt and they were blue plaid. It looked like she was wearing John's blue sweater, and her eyes were the color of the bottom of the swimming pool. I loved that she was this fashion plate, but had a sense of humor about her clothes.

They were serving cocktails out of baby bottles. I was not going to drink a cocktail out of a baby bottle. I remember Carolyn saying, "Why are you making such a big deal. . . . You're drinking it." I liked the fact that she could take the mickey out of me, for me thinking I was too cool to drink out of a baby bottle.

She did have an incandescence that doesn't always come across in photos. When I saw her and John at big, glamorous events, it was almost like a hive of bees, all the bees follow the queen bee, and the lights and people would just kind of swarm them. . . .

Jack Merrill

Carolyn called the attention around John "the freak show." She came up with that term and I loved it. I used to say the room tilts—like we'd walk into a party and all of a sudden the room would tilt and everybody would start sliding in our direction. That was the way it felt. And Carolyn knew how to handle it—she knew how to go out. The funny thing is, both Christina and Daryl were not as adept at that sort of thing as Carolyn was. They came from . . . they could wear white gloves, both of them. If Carolyn ever wore white gloves, she took them off. She was able to get dirty. She and John understood that sometimes there has to be a little grime to have a good time.

RoseMarie Terenzio

She moved in with John in early '95, while he was staying at his mom's, at 1040, because the Tribeca place at 20 North Moore was being renovated. I remember Carolyn saying that she didn't want to move in with him unless she knew they were going to get married. Two months or so after she moved in, they got engaged. They had been dating seriously for a little over a year.

Chris Oberbeck

I'd only met her once, at his birthday. I was like, John, you know, you shouldn't be getting married this soon after your mother's passing. Too much of a life change. You're destabilized mentally over your mom's death and it's not a time to do something as dramatic as this. Live together, but don't get married. I was kind of negative about it and I think that may have contributed to why he didn't invite me to the wedding. I was not a supporter of him getting married right then.

I think also maybe what happened to him, too, a little bit with her, was he had lots and lots of friends, but a lot of his core friends were no longer present. People got married. . . . I was married, I didn't have much time to hang out. I had, at that time, three children and wasn't really in the day-to-day orbit anymore. He was making new friends. But you can't make old friends, right? So I think maybe he had a higher level of vulnerability. I don't think he had the kind of support, and there was a vacuum there. I think Carolyn stepped up and filled that vacuum.

"So kind and loving"

RoseMarie Terenzio

Carolyn would come up to the office maybe twice a week, sometimes to help Matt [*George* creative director Matt Berman] figure out what stylist to use. She'd look at the cover. She'd come to pick John up, sometimes to pick me up, and we'd go to dinner. She was always pretty casual, just jeans and a shirt, unless, in the beginning, when she was coming from Calvin Klein.

They were very affectionate together, holding hands or hugging or her sitting on his lap. They laughed a lot. He was very goofy around her—not relaxed at the beginning. They called each other Mousey and Mouse. I had told Carolyn about this woman, before I worked for John, who used to call her husband "Bunny lamb" and she was howling laughing. When she would call, she'd say, "Hi, Bunny lamb," and then she started calling me "Lamb."

They both loved animals. They took their dog, Friday, everywhere. John wasn't a big cat person, but he bought Carolyn a black cat, Ruby, because he always said she was like a cat. Ruby was Carolyn's buddy. Ruby would come in and jump on the bed at three in the morning and John would say, "Oh brother, there goes the neighborhood," because she'd keep them up all night.

Before they moved in together, Carolyn lived in this really cool brownstone in the West Village, the whole bottom floor. I think Kate Moss lived upstairs for a little while. She had two other roommates. It made me feel good, because it was a little messy—I was expecting this fancy, perfectly neat, decorated place, and it was more like a college dorm. There were clothes on the couch, and I was like, *Oh, thank God.* We smoked cigarettes and chilled.

We used to go to that restaurant all the time, Flea Market—a French bistro place in the East Village. We'd get a booth in the back and my friends would come by and then her friends and we'd have drinks and dinner. We'd sit there for hours, hanging out, smoking cigarettes, having wine. We used to go to Odeon. Me and her and her friend Jessica Weinstein, from Calvin Klein, and Gordon Henderson, a designer from Calvin. We would always sit at the bar and have a burger on a toasted English muffin. Always the bar, unless there were more than four of us. Instead of fries we would order the sautéed spinach. Carolyn drank vodka and white wine. I know she and John both did coke with their friends recreationally. But I never saw her use drugs, and I never saw her drunk.

Everybody kind of knew each other. And we'd go to Zutto, the sushi place in Tribeca, and sit at the bar because you could smoke cigarettes at the bar. Marlboro Lights and Parliament Lights—back when everybody smoked.

We talked about John, but honestly more about me—me complaining about whoever I was dating and asking her what to do. She told me to take my voice off of my answering machine, "Because that'll freak him out when he calls your house.... And don't call him back for three days." It worked. He called the office and said, "What the hell's going on?" Another time she told me to change my number—back when we had home phones. That freaked him out, too.

If I was going on a date, or just someplace fun or fancy, she'd say, "Come down to the apartment" after work. John would be at the gym or playing Frisbee and I'd go to the apartment, and she would say, "What are you gonna wear?" She'd have all these things out for me to try on. When I was going to London for a wedding, she gave me two pairs of jeans and a black jacket, a cool bomber. One pair of Levi's I couldn't wear, they were too long. She had another pair, a little cropped, so I could get away with those. I may still have those—orange tab Levi's. She'd say, "Okay, you're gonna wear this to the wedding, this the night before." She'd lay out my outfits and tell me, "You're gonna be the best-dressed person in London no matter what you wear."

Both Carolyn and John were so generous. Around Christmas of '95, the second year I worked for John, I go out to my desk and there's a pile of gifts. Carolyn gave me these Miu Miu pumps and a bag and a Loree Rodkin gold ring with carved crosses and skulls with diamond eyes. John got me Prada skis—I didn't even know Prada made skis—and a Moncler jacket. It was this weird color—shocking blue. I looked like a giant blueberry walking down the street. He loved colors. I actually got a lot of compliments on it.

For the White House Correspondents' Dinner in 1998, I couldn't find a dress, and nothing felt right. Carolyn said just get a long skirt and a black shirt, because it was black tie. She let me borrow this crazy necklace that Maurice Tempelsman had given her for Christmas—it had three rows of diamonds, and when you turned it over, it was this Indian enamel pattern, red and gold. You could wear it both ways. I said, "What if I lose it?" She said, "Look how big it is, you can't lose it."

We went shopping in L.A. when we were there for an event *George* was hosting and we stayed at the Chateau Marmont. At Neiman Marcus, there were these Versace boots that Liz Hurley had worn on the cover of *George* in 1997. She said, "You *have* to get them." I couldn't afford them. They were like $700. The next day, there was a knock on my door and there was this big box. No card or anything. She's like, "You work so hard, and you deserve them." She got herself a pair, too. Beyond buying you something you'd never buy, she had this way of making you feel like Cinderella.

She'd throw something on you and it's hers, so of course you feel like a million bucks—because look at her. She'd say, "Honey, that looks so much better on you." And you're like, *Nothing looks better on me than it does on you.* She let me borrow her black leather jacket, almost like a blazer. I think there's a picture of her in it. It was sick.

She was always pointing out your strengths, and not in a BS way. If I ever criticized myself or felt fat, she would say, "Please don't talk about yourself like that, it hurts my feelings."

For my birthday, we got a giant table at Pravda, that vodka bar on Lafayette. There were fifteen of us and it was me and my friend Frank and Gordon. She said, "It's Rosie's birthday. We have to take her somewhere special." John was away on some ice-climbing or camping trip with Brian Steel. She had a fancy white cake ordered with all these beautiful flowers on it. I have a picture of me blowing out the candles and she's sitting next to me.

Santina Goodman

Carolyn called [one day] and needed to talk with me about something. I thought I could hide the fact that I'd been crying, but the first thing Carolyn said to me was "Santina, what's wrong?" I said, "Nothing, nothing, I'm okay." The next thing I hear is "Santina, I'm coming over right now." Then she hangs up the phone.

The doorbell rings and there's Carolyn with a bottle of Ketel One vodka, tonic water, and limes. She throws this colorful scarf over my antique lamp that creates this beautiful glow in the room.

I suffered from depression. . . . We talked about my depression in such a funny way that I didn't feel uncomfortable letting her know. Then Carolyn went on about how John's friends were so normal and how she wished she had friends like his. . . . And did I need money? I said, "Carolyn, I might be depressed, but you're crazy. And I don't need your money."

A few days later, Carolyn calls to tell me she found a therapist near where I lived and made an appointment. Before I could yell at her, she said, "Please, just do it for me." The way she said that was so kind and loving. I said, "Okay." I go to the appointment to meet the therapist. I'm buzzed into the reception area and there's Carolyn sitting there. I'm not sure why, but all we could do was laugh. The therapist calls me in. After one hour, I walk out and there's Carolyn. She says, "Let's get something to eat." She didn't mention anything about the session. Before leaving, Carolyn handed me three books: *Depression: The Way Out of Your Prison*; *Prozac and the New Antidepressants*; *An Unquiet Mind: A Memoir of Moods and Madness*. This happened in 1995 and we never talked about it again.

RoseMarie Terenzio

Santina never realized her dreams of a career in the theater. She was floundering, working menial jobs. Carolyn was getting her out of the house more, more outings. John would try to create freelance opportunities for her—he asked her to send all the official thank-you notes after his mom's funeral, which took a week. He and Carolyn wanted to help Santina find her strength. Carolyn was a big proponent of therapy. She helped me find a therapist as well. She saw a therapist regularly and she took antidepressants. She told me, "Rosie, therapy is the best because you get to sit there and talk about yourself the whole time."

"John's fierce protector"

Gustavo Paredes

We would spend Thanksgiving together in Hyannis with my mom, because that was the connection to his mother and father. He would always bring somebody—he would meet people and bring them. John always wanted to have—like his cousins—a larger family. It was hard for him to have a good radar in terms of who really wanted to be his friend and who wanted to be there because he's John F. Kennedy Jr. Carolyn helped with that—she was a good judge of character. Sometimes they got knocked off the perch—she did a great job of shedding a whole lot of his friends, which always caused consternation among them. She and John could then become a unit. It became less of a need to have so many people around him all the time.

Sasha Chermayeff

John's friend Kevin Ward was using him to promote things that he wanted to promote in New York, and Carolyn knew that full well. Kevin could be a jerk. Early on, before I'd met Kevin, John wanted to meet at a fancy cocktail party. I came to this apartment and I was wandering around. It was a schmoozy crowd. And then I saw John from behind. I didn't want to interrupt, so I just stood there. Kevin Ward was like, "Excuse me, can I help you, what's your name? Are you standing here because you would like to meet John Kennedy?"

John put his arm around me and grabbed me, kissed me, and said, "This is Sasha. This is my BFF, man. She's my girl from way back." Kevin said, "Oh, sorry." And I was just thinking, *Is that what you do to the nice girls that want to meet him? Are you one of the assholes that make them feel like shit that they want to meet John Kennedy? Because John doesn't do that to those girls.*

It all culminated in Kevin inviting John to a gallery opening at the National Arts Club sometime in the nineties. Kevin told the paparazzi that John would be attending in order to bring attention to this show—and it's a feeding frenzy. John was pissed, but he felt, *Whatever, they follow me anyway.* Carolyn was furious, saying, *He can't do that to you.*

RoseMarie Terenzio

There was a circle of people that, I don't know how to put this—John was a commodity in that circle. They knew that their friendship with John kind of solidified their place in this circle. But they were not somebody he's going to pick up the phone and call when the shit hits the fan, or if he was having a really tough emotional time. There were only certain people he was going to call. Carolyn was protective of John, and she saw that he had a certain vulnerability.

On February 25, 1996, the couple had a fight while walking their dog in Washington Square Park, all captured by a photographer and a videographer. The film shows the two shouting at each other, then Carolyn pushing John. According to the New York Daily News, *he appeared to rip the engagement ring off her finger. Carolyn jumps on his back, their shouting continues and then abates before starting up again as they walk home, and finally ends with an embrace. On the* Howard Stern Show *a few months later, John calls it "a silly argument."*

RoseMarie Terenzio

The fight was about him being taken advantage of by his friends. They had gone to the wedding of a friend he'd gone to Brown with, Toni Kotite. Toni sat John and Carolyn at the first table—next to the *New York Times* reporter that was doing the Vows column on their wedding. John was really uncomfortable with that. Carolyn thought it was a bullshit thing to do to your friend.

Because of the video footage, their argument played out in the media a lot longer than it would have if it had been just photos. It became a three-day promo on *Hard Copy*, like, *More footage of the fight!* Michael Berman was furious. "How could you be so stupid to have a fight in the park? You're trying to do a political magazine and you're having a fight with your girlfriend in the park." Then there was a whole other argument from John's perspective—it's none of Michael's business. And then Michael said, "Well, it's my magazine, too."

John didn't think it was a big deal. Carolyn was upset because they were being followed by photographers—and now a videographer. I think on some level she felt like it was her fault, but she was also angry at John because she felt she was trying to protect him, not wanting him to be taken advantage of.

Gary Ginsberg

John's friends . . . He attracted many different types—people who were at the top of their game, people who were muddling along, and people who were down and in need of help. That was the fun of John—you just never knew. But the downside was it could also allow people to take advantage of him. A lot of people would ask him for things, from money to opening doors, recommendations, introductions. A constant barrage. He was pretty elegant. There's one friend who ended up losing a lot of money, and John would lend him money all the time. I'm like, "John, you're never going to get this money back." He didn't care, nor would it necessarily occur to him. I'm like, "John, what do you expect? He's broke." John embraced people of all stripes. But there was a downside, and it was going to get more and more complicated as life got more and more complicated for him. I used to say, "You need to have a little bit more guile," but that wasn't him.

Carolyn had all the discernment that John lacked. Like "Honey, he's playing you." Or "Honey, you don't need to do that." She was the eyes and ears that he sometimes didn't have. Part of John's charm was he would say yes to a lot of things. She brought a certain discipline to that.

Sasha Chermayeff

She became John's fierce protector. I don't think there was much love lost between her and Caroline—Carolyn felt it was high time that John be defended against this condescending older sister and her husband.

Carolyn was beautiful, intense, funny, smart, but if you could pick on her for one thing, it would be that she came from . . . what, a Connecticut upper-middle-class background that wasn't blue blood. It became clear to me that Caroline was not going to accept Carolyn until the very last minute, until she had no choice—until she was standing at the fucking altar and there's no doubt whatsoever, you're in the family.

Steve Gillon

Caroline did not think Carolyn was good enough for John—she and Ed just found her temperamental and selfish. And John despised Ed for a lot of reasons.

It was either Christmas or another holiday, John and Carolyn were going over to Ed and Caroline's apartment and Carolyn was so concerned, and she had all these gifts for them.

RoseMarie Terenzio

She was definitely a little intimidated by Caroline.

Steve Gillon

They go over and Caroline and Ed left within an hour to go to some sporting event or something. Carolyn thought that was so disrespectful. So there was a lot of tension there on both sides. One of the big issues in John's relationship with his sister was their spouses.

"Will you be my partner?"

RoseMarie Terenzio

Carolyn called me at the office after the Fourth of July weekend in 1995 and said, "Can you go to the pay phone?" We had this thing where if she wanted to tell me something privately, she'd call me first and I would go down to the pay phone on 51st and Broadway. So I went down and called her back and she said, "I have to tell you something. We got engaged! John proposed this weekend."

She said, "He took me out in the boat and he said, 'When you go fishing, it's always better with a partner. Will you be my partner?'" And—that's when I realized the ring was *the ring*.

A few weeks earlier, John had me pick up a ring from Maurice Tempelsman's office. Maurice was a diamond dealer—I think John told him what he wanted and Maurice had it made. He gave me a velvet bag, which he put in a brown paper bag. I didn't know what it was. He didn't say it was the engagement ring. I didn't look. I swear to God, I didn't open it. John said just put it in his desk. I put it in a Duane Reade pharmacy bag so that no one would open it up.

John gave Carolyn two rings. There was his mom's "swimming ring"— that was Jackie's name for the ring she wore when she didn't wear her wedding ring—designed by Jean Schlumberger. Bunny Mellon had it and had given it to John—he had called Bunny to tell her that he was getting engaged a month or two earlier.

Jackie's swimming ring was emeralds and sapphires. Carolyn's engagement ring from Maurice was in the same style as the swimming ring but with diamonds and sapphires around a band. She could wear it as her engagement ring because she wouldn't wear Jackie's swimming ring every day—I think she was afraid of losing it. It meant so much to John and to her.

At first, John and I didn't talk about the engagement. Carolyn is telling him, "Don't tell anybody!" They were living together, but she was not fully on the media's radar yet, and she felt once the news got out, she would be under a microscope. So John was trying really hard not to give it up. But then Carolyn told me. So I didn't want to give *her* up by telling John I knew.

The Friday before Labor Day weekend, the front page of the *New York Post* had a blowup photo of Carolyn's hand with the engagement ring and speculated that they were engaged. The press was all over it. John had never addressed his personal life in the media. Which is why he first thought ignoring it was the best response. But the *George* press conference was happening the following weekend. Michael and John were concerned that if it was out there that he was engaged and he didn't deny it, then the entire press conference would be about his engagement, and it would overshadow the launch of *George*.

They decided to issue a denial. John was very uncomfortable addressing his private life to the press. He was also concerned that it would hurt Carolyn's feelings. John and Michael discussed it behind closed doors for hours. When they finally came out, Michael had the statement written for the media and said it should come from me, as John's executive assistant and spokesperson for him and Carolyn. I was terrified, but it was a brilliant idea because it wasn't coming directly from John, and no one knew who I was. "Once again, John Kennedy seems to be bearing the brunt of a slow news day. The stories circulating regarding an engagement are untrue. He is not engaged."

I felt bad for Carolyn because she'd been trying to hide the ring. She was engaged and she was excited. I remember her saying to John, "I just want this to be our little secret for a little while, because once it gets out, it's not going to be ours anymore." And he was a little bit like, *Oh what do you care if people know we're engaged?* She just wanted to hold on to it a little bit. The privacy and the romance of it. She also felt that it would be impossible to plan a private wedding once the engagement was announced.

It was complicated because Carolyn wanted it to be a secret, but having him publicly deny that they had gotten engaged was a different story. To say nothing about it and just let it be was one thing, but to deny it was another. She didn't come to the *George* press conference. John and Michael thought her presence would be too distracting. She wasn't that upset about that, honestly—I don't think she wanted to go. But there was part of her that felt, *It's my fiancé and I'm left out of it.* That was tough.

It's like always being eclipsed. I think she was also hurt by the fact that there were people behind the scenes that were saying she is not to show up at that press conference. They thought it's going to be all about "John has a new girlfriend." I'm not saying they were wrong. But how do you think that felt?

Sasha Chermayeff

I remember thinking the public denial of the engagement bothered her so much. It would bother me, too. It was so hurtful, and it was like, *We can't talk about your hurt right now, we have big things that we're doing.* She is so not important compared to the man's career. That was the first sign of *Okay, this is what life with him is going to be about. It's going to be about whatever looks good for him and his world, and I just have whatever role I'm given.*

CHAPTER 16

Ladies and Gentlemen, Meet *George*

. . . We stuck with the idea even after the instructor in our two-day seminar called "Starting Your Own Magazine" told us, "You can successfully launch a magazine in just about anything except for religion and politics." . . . We believe that if we can make politics accessible by covering it in an entertaining and compelling way, popular interest and involvement in the process will follow. . . .

—John F. Kennedy Jr., editor's letter in the inaugural issue of
George magazine, September 1995

President Bill Clinton

When John told me about his idea for starting the magazine and asked whether I thought it could work, I told him I believed it would be hard, but he had a unique combination of star power, strong support, and a clear vision of the people he wanted to reach at a time when the walls between culture and politics were crumbling, with young people especially hungry for meaningful connections between the two. I encouraged him to give it his best effort, to bring us more intriguing information to blunt the rapidly rising "us vs. them" tribalism already prominent in our politics. I'm glad he did it, with all the heart and energy he could muster.

Jonathan Alter, political columnist

You had to admire the moxie—the balls it took. Political magazines in America don't make money. Full stop. John's reaction to that was—that just makes me more excited, I'm gonna prove the doubters wrong.

I was struck by his determination, but thought that he was a little naive. John was trying to create a new category for a political entertainment magazine—not just a new magazine, but a new category, and that ain't easy. To redefine what political journalism could be. But he was not to be underestimated. He had such charm that he might be right—that he could do something that nobody else could do.

Robbie Littell

He loved the idea of merging what he'd experienced in politics and celebrity. One of the oldest traditions of the human condition is gossip—you put fifteen nuclear scientists together, they'll talk about who's having an affair. He thought you could go into politicians' lives and discuss them—people did want to look in there.

Elizabeth "Biz" Mitchell, *George* executive editor

John really did believe that politicians were fascinating people, and that America should care more about these human beings who could change lives for the better—over Hollywood celebrity. But there was also a part that made you think, maybe he wants to bring out what is exciting about politics so that if he pursued that, it would be exciting enough for *him*.

Gary Ginsberg

We worked without a day off from March of '95 to when we sent the magazine to print. I don't think I'd ever worked that hard in my life. I don't think John ever had, either. But for all of us, it was a passionate experience—we started something from scratch, and we knew that it was going to get enormous attention. None of us knew where it was going to lead. It was tremendous pressure.

We used to go into the park and throw Frisbees around at lunch, just to break the pressure of it all. John and I would go to a ton of movies. We'd leave in the middle if we didn't like it. He couldn't take scary movies—he'd either sleep through them, leave halfway through, or cover his eyes.

Clearly, the pressure was wearing on John, but he was outwardly just so in charge, and as energized as the rest of us.

Matt Berman, *George* creative director

The first cover was Cindy Crawford dressed as George Washington. John said, "Come down to my apartment, I want you to meet Herb Ritts. He's a friend." I had a Vargas Girl idea—those iconic pinups from the World War II era in *Esquire*. John wanted George Washington. Then it was "Who's gonna pose for it?" I'm just the kid at the table. Carolyn said, "What about Cindy? She's perfect. She's apple pie. She's Midwestern. . . ." We all joked, let's do Cindy in drag dressed as George, not knowing that we had just come up with the most iconic magazine cover of the nineties.

Gary Ginsberg

There was a big party to celebrate closing the first issue in July of '95 at Elaine's. I remember how excited he was that we had delivered the magazine on time and that it was good, really good. And most of all that he had taken the kernel of an idea and built a business out of it, and if everything went right, it might really succeed. We walked in, past all these tables of publishing literati, and got to the back room where the party was. There was so much energy. And *George* had given jobs to, at that point, probably forty people. It was clear this first issue was going to be a big deal. People were saying it could be the most successful magazine launch in history. I think it all gave him great professional joy, unlike anything he'd ever experienced before.

Michael Sheehan

There was big prepping for the launch of *George*. I think [political consultant] Paul Begala is the one who wrote the riff "Let me just get all the questions I know you're gonna ask out of the way: Yes. No, we're just good friends. . . . I'll think about it. Maybe someday, but not in New Jersey." I mean, it was brilliant.

We went through a bunch of questions. John was prepared. And just cordial beyond fucking belief. I do remember his concern was "Is the press going to take *George* seriously? 'Does this mean you're going to run for president?'" He knew once he gave an indication, it would be like crossing the Rubicon. No turning back. The folks on the Hill were lighting candles hoping that he would agree, are you kidding?

Gary Ginsberg

It was me and Paul Begala at John's apartment on North Moore. Carolyn was there. Nothing was more fun because I knew that there was nothing I couldn't ask him. Paul was just slack-jawed because he's used to prepping a president of the United States and I'm prepping my buddy. I said, "John, you failed the bar twice. Were you lazy? Or just plain dumb?" And he roared.

Paul Begala, political consultant

Gary said, "Are you going to do investigative journalism with this magazine?" John said, "It's not really where I'm headed but I wouldn't rule anything out." Gary pressed the point and said, "Are you going to look into who killed your father?" And the air went out of the room. John changed—he wasn't quite as relaxed. He said, "No, I'm not. I've thought about this a lot. I could spend the rest of my life trying to chase down who killed my father and it wouldn't change the central fact of my life: I don't have a dad." Heartbreaking.

Matt Berman

The day of the launch, September 7, I just walked from where I was living down to Federal Hall, and blocks and blocks before I get there, I see all the trucks and stuff from news and TV stations. I had no freaking idea. I'm like, "What is going on?" I just didn't realize what a big deal it was. . . .

RoseMarie Terenzio

I'd never seen so much media in one place at one time.

Nancy Haberman, friend, publicist for *George*

Everybody wanted to be in *that* room with John. He was the face of it. Right before the press conference was the first time, the only time, I saw him look a little bit anxious.

Joe Armstrong

That was an electric event—there were people begging to go. We don't have any editors that are movie stars, and he's a movie star who wasn't really in a movie. . . . I don't know how else to put it. He could always get attention; he was a live person out of history. He got up and said, "Ladies and gentle-men," and he twirled a billboard around revealing the first cover and said, "Meet *George*."

"Is this normal in an office?"

RoseMarie Terenzio

On a typical day, John would get in to the Hachette building at 8:30 or 9:00. But there was no typical day. In the beginning I took messages, typed up let-ters, and kept John's calendar. The phone was nonstop, like a switchboard. One time he said to me, "Is this normal in an office?" I just said, "I'm sure it's a little more excessive here." . . .

He'd have me book a massage once or twice a week. And then his shrink, I remember, was at 9:00 on Thursdays. So I always knew I could kind of get away with coming in a little later on Thursdays. One time he didn't go, and I walked into the office a little late, at like quarter to ten. And he goes, "Well, if it isn't Rip Van Winkle."

We got to be like brother and sister. One day he came in clean-shaven—he looked like he just walked out of the showroom. He must have not ridden his bike to work that day. The crisp, clean white shirt with this navy-blue, thin pin-striped suit, a red tie. His shoes were polished. Impeccable. It wasn't his usual khakis and a shirt. He was coming down the hallway and I said, "That is very JFK Jr." He just laughed. He was going to this important meeting in corporate and he wanted to look the part. John didn't walk around looking in the mirror, but he was always trying to tame his hair. He'd use Kiehl's Silk Groom and put a hat on. He loved weird funky hats.

In the beginning, I didn't know who he *really* knew or who he'd want to talk to and who he didn't. Anytime Carolyn called, he took the call. His family called a lot—Bobby Shriver, Tim Shriver, they called all the time. Maria Shriver once in a while. Bobby Kennedy. Caroline called a lot. He always took her call, and every couple weeks he would go over for dinner and Marta would cook one of his favorite dishes. Her son, Jack, was little, three or four. He used to take Tatiana and Rose to Knicks games. He would find them in Central Park when they were sledding on snow days, visit them on birthdays. Caroline came up a few times—they were always laughing. Their inside jokes.

When his cousin Kerry called, she would say, "It's Kerry Kennedy Cuomo." I would give him his messages. He always liked hearing from her. The third or fourth time he asks, "Why do you write that?" I said, "That's what she says." And he's like, "I know who she is. Why does she have to say Kerry Kennedy Cuomo?" His door was open a little bit, and he called her back and goes, "Hey, Kerry, it's John. Do you really say Kerry Kennedy Cuomo every time you call? That's a mouthful." I was just like, *Oh my God, I can't believe he just said that to her.*

We had subscriptions to every single magazine. I had the magazines on my desk, and *New York* magazine was there and the cover was a photo of Bobby that said "The Kennedy Who Matters." John picked it up and he looked at me and goes, "To who?" It was a joke. . . .

He brought his demented German shepherd rescue, Sam, to the office every day. Sam would growl and snap, and he bit the intern. He'd go for my lunch, so I'd walk out of the office and let him have it.

Zach Haberman, Nancy's son and a *George* intern

Sam was my desk mate—I had a little closet office. The only people that the dog liked were John and me. And if anybody came by, the conversations were short because that dog was a beast.

Joe Armstrong

John had the advantage of people wanting to work with him. There was so much curiosity. I mean, Norman Mailer—he wouldn't wanna work for a start-up magazine or little magazine. He wrote a couple of pieces. John could get in to talk to anybody—who wouldn't make time for John?

Steve Gillon

He had access to anyone and he gave writers freedom. But he wasn't just going to be a figurehead. John actually was an editor—he was hands-on.

Lisa DePaulo, *George* contributor

When he interviewed former vice president Dan Quayle, he asked us to come up with the cover line. People are throwing out ideas, and then John pokes his head in and says, "Dumb and Dumber; John Kennedy interviews Dan Quayle." Oh my God. It was fucking brilliant!

Dick Morris was a senior advisor to Clinton, and he got run out of town because he was sucking a prostitute's toes on the balcony of the Jefferson Hotel and the press got photographs. Dick was trying to make a comeback. I was going to do an exclusive interview for *George*. The night before, Dick chickened out. I called John and said, "What am I going to fucking do? He says he can't do it because he's in a twelve-step program for sex addiction and he doesn't think it's good to be near a young woman."

John said, "What step is he on?" I said, "I think step four." John said, "Tell him that if he gets through this, he can get to step five." I called and said, "Dick, this is an opportunity for you. You can get to the next step."

He's like, "Do you really think so?" He said, "I'll see you in the morning." I called John back and said, "He's going to do it!" John's laughing and he says, "Don't wear sandals."

Sasha Issenberg, *George* intern

I was fifteen years old, nerdy about politics, and looking for something to do over the summer. My aunt called Gary Ginsberg, a friend. I came into the office one afternoon, and we have a nice chat and I walk out to make my way back to Grand Central to go home and Gary is running out behind me and says, "You can start working." Gary told me later that John had seen me walking out of his office and said, "Gary, is that your son?" And Gary said, "No, it's some kid that asked me to work here." And then John, because he thought it was funny, he said, "Well, he looks like your son, you have to hire him."

Matt Berman

John had a bunch of people in the office that were young and new. He could have hired anybody, the sharpest of the sharp, the famous. And he didn't—he had all unknown people that he clicked with personally. We had nothing to model the magazine after because we hadn't come from anywhere, really. . . . Looking back, I don't know if I would've hired me and Rose. But if he had a personal connection with you, then it worked because there was this trust.

RoseMarie Terenzio

We'd have an editorial meeting every other day. John ran the meetings. People got annoyed because they went too long—it felt like people just wanted to stay in the room with John. Everyone contributed, from the interns to the executive editor. He was sometimes too democratic, to the point that Matt Berman started calling him "Robin Hood."

Matt Cowen, *George* assistant editor

We'd all sort of cram into his office. Whenever the youngest person in the room came up with an idea, he loved to make them feel good. He was inclusive before inclusive was a thing.

Mike Showalter, head of facilities at Hachette

John was the best—I don't lie. He didn't care what people had or didn't have, he was just down-to-earth. One day he called me up at my desk and said, "Mike, come down. I got a surprise for you." Because he knew I was a boxing fan. He told me to bring the maintenance guys I work with. I got down there, I'm like, "This is Muhammad Ali!" I was shocked. I loved it. But that's just how good John was. I called my boys Stanley, Leonza, and Carl. I said, "Come on, man, you got to come. Muhammad Ali is here." I've got the picture still in my room of me, Ali, and the other guys from maintenance. I keep it on the wall.

Sean Neary, *George* fact-checker and later editor

He was better friends with the maintenance staff than the fancy people at *Elle Decor* who worked down the hall.

RoseMarie Terenzio

He liked to ride his bike or take the subway if he could. One day we were on the subway, there were three Black men, and they were looking at him. One of the guys said, "Are you him?" He just kind of smiled and said, "Yeah, I'm him. Nice to meet you." And one guy said, "Can I ask you a question? How come you never put Black people on the cover of your magazine?" And he said, "Well, I've tried. I've asked Michael Jordan, Prince . . ." He named a few people and they had told him no. He said, "And to be honest, the numbers I get from my publisher, Black people don't sell on magazine covers." People actually said things like that back then. The guy said, "You could change that." John took out his business card and said, "Here's my card. Why don't you send me your ideas? I'd love to hear them."

John loved giving out his cards. Because it wasn't him answering the phones! Once a week I'd get a call and they'd ask, "Is this John Kennedy's office? He gave me his card and he told me to call him." And I'm like, "No more business cards for you, John."

Matt Berman

There were similarities between a lot of the people who worked at the office. It was like people who had just had tough childhoods—he noticed people who were a little bit damaged. I think he identified with those kinds of people. It was like a trauma bonding kind of thing. . . . I guess traumatized people are interesting. They usually have a good sense of humor—like half the comics in the world had weird childhoods. He collected strays, but he saw things in us we didn't see in ourselves.

RoseMarie Terenzio

I didn't come from a pedigreed background. I think some of the editors assumed I wasn't very smart—they saw me as a secretary who kept the calendar. Eventually, they came to realize I was more of a right hand or chief of staff, which some editors didn't like. They treated me like a secretary who shouldn't have an opinion on the magazine.

There was an editor who wanted John to go to breakfast with the head of PBS. I asked John and he said, "I don't know anything about it." I told the editor, "John wants to know why he's going to breakfast with the head of PBS." And the editor said, "Do you even know what PBS is?"

I told John because it really hurt my feelings. John marched right down the hall—"Don't ever talk to her like that! That is outta line." The editor said, "I was joking." John said, "Well, your joke wasn't funny." The editor apologized to me, and we ended up becoming friends.

Another time, five or six editors all went to lunch. John asked, "Where is everybody?" I told him and he was like, "You could have gone to lunch with them." I said, "They didn't invite me. I'm not an editor." He says, "We're going to lunch." He said, "Where did they go?" I told him Broadway Grill. We walked into Broadway Grill and they plopped us right in the middle of the room. He never said a word. We went back to the office and let's just say it was a bit of a different tune. Things started to change because they started to see that John trusted me.

He would have short bursts where he would lash out—that's how John dealt with guilt. I'm not a psychoanalyst, but there was something about making him feel bad about something that would trigger his temper. When the first issue was sent to the office, the staff went into John's office and he showed them the magazine. I didn't know it had come in and I had worked something like forty-five days straight without a day off to help them get it out. I was really upset that I wasn't included. When they came out, I was like, "What is that?" And they're like, "Oh, it's the first issue."

John could see I was upset and said, "What's wrong?" I said, "I can't believe you showed everybody else the magazine before you showed it to me, or didn't ask me to come in." And he said a "Oh, come on, don't get upset, it's no big deal" kind of thing. And then I started crying at my desk and he came out and said, "If this is the way you're going to behave all day, then you can just go home now."

I went to the bathroom and composed myself and we went through the rest of the day. Carolyn called and she could hear that I was upset. She said, "What's wrong?" I'm like, "Nothing," and I told her—I think I might've gone to the pay phone because I didn't want him to see me crying again. I said, "Please don't say anything." The next day, he came in and I acted like business as usual. He said, "Come into my office." And I was like, *Here we go. He's going to fire me.* He said, "I'm really sorry. It was insensitive—I should have showed you the magazine first. Here it is. Let's go through it. You should be so proud."

I talked to Carolyn and said, "You said something, didn't you?" And she's like, "Of course I said something. Are you kidding me? As soon as he walked in the door, and went in the shower, I walked in the bathroom and said, 'So you made Rosie cry? She doesn't cry. Are you kidding me? What did you do?'" And the next morning he came in with his tail between his legs.

Elephants in the room

Lisa Dallos, *George* publicist

The first time I met John I came up to the office. I was working at MSNBC. I thought, *I'm gonna meet with probably one of the most famous humans on the planet and not be able to speak.* My fear evaporated—he was very gentle. I remember his father's briefcase, an old black briefcase with the initials *JFK*, was leaning on the left side of his desk and that got me nervous again when I realized, *Oh my God, the president of the United States' briefcase, what am I doing here?*

RoseMarie Terenzio

I think the *George* office was the only place, other than home, where he felt like he could exhale and be himself. His office was beautiful, with these huge windows overlooking Central Park. And then Carolyn got him a nice mid-century couch and a coffee table. On the wall, he had really cool artwork by Art Spellings. A canvas with just a red round sort of paint swirl. . . . To the right there was a handwritten letter from Abraham Lincoln. And then there was a picture of him and his father at the White House—he's in white shorts standing on a bench and his dad is sitting on the bench in a suit. His dad is looking up at him and smiling.

To the left there was this giant portrait, probably three feet long, and it had sketches of every president on cream-colored parchment paper in a beautiful gold frame. Every president from George Washington to his father, along with their original signatures. He told me that Lyndon Johnson had given it to his mother when they left the White House. Like, *Here's a little something.* What the hell?

Steve Gillon

He said that after his father died, Johnson took it off the wall of the White House and gave it to him. The first time I saw it in his bedroom back in the mid-eighties, I said, "John, why is this hanging in your bedroom? It should be in the National Archives." He mumbled something like "He gave it to me. I think it's mine."

Lisa DePaulo

The day I first met him to write for *George*, there was a blizzard and I'm like, *Come hell or high water, I'm making this appointment.* . . . He was wonderful. He's like, "I just love your work and I want you to be part of the *George* family." There was this picture of him and his father on the bookshelf. I didn't acknowledge it. He said, "So where are you from?" And I said Scranton, Pennsylvania. He said, "Scranton is very important to me because my father's last stop in his campaign for president was in Scranton." And that's how he took the elephant out of the room.

Biz Mitchell

He used to come into my office with things that he had come across or someone had sent, all related to the history of his family. One time he came with this picture of him being carried into the White House as a baby, and there's media and staff on the steps. Like him marveling that this was the way his life began.

He was interested in being able to learn more about his family and his past through the interviews he did. He would assign a lot of stories that took place around the time of the Kennedy administration.

Gary Ginsberg

He absolutely had a curiosity to understand his father in a much more "first person" way than he ever had before, and *George* was in part that instrument to do it. I think one of the areas he wanted to explore were the people and the issues that were in opposition to his father's presidency. He had to figure it out for himself.

John picked George Wallace for the first interview because he was this larger-than-life racist Southern governor who had literally stood in the doorway of the University of Alabama to keep two Black students from enrolling there in 1963. He became the symbol of racial hatred and bigotry, and that moment at the door was the catalyst for the president to finally put the full weight of the federal government behind the fight for civil rights. JFK sent in the National Guard to enforce a federal court order.

In '72 there was an assassination attempt on Wallace that left him paralyzed from the waist down. He had this late-in-life conversion where he recognized that his views on race were outdated and wrong. John was always interested in redemption stories. I think with Wallace, where other people had just written him off as this racist, John wanted to see if there was humanity to the man. That happened in John's personal life, too—he was always befriending people who other people would've shunned. He always wanted to give second chances.

So John and I go down to Montgomery. Wallace lived in perennial pain after his assassination attempt and was heavily medicated at our first interview. We had set aside three days of interviews, knowing he was really frail. Turns out he could barely hear or speak and was in far worse pain than we imagined. At one point, I was shouting questions into his ear. By the third day, he was so sick he had taken to his bed—a hospital bed in the middle of his living room. He's going in and out of consciousness. We were trying to make sense of what he was saying, but it was all incoherent.

Getting on that plane home was like, *Whoa, this is the centerpiece of our inaugural issue and we have no idea if we have anything usable.* We were petrified. I said, "John, we got some holes in this thing." When we got back the transcript, it was even worse. So we went back down to Montgomery and got more material to put it together.

Steve Gillon

John wanted to interview all these antagonists of his father. Fidel Castro was the main antagonist other than Khrushchev. Castro is also wrapped up in all these conspiracy theories about his father's assassination—that Castro was behind it because he was seeking retribution for American efforts to kill him.

John arrives in Cuba and Castro strings him along for three days. John calls at one point and says, "I'm leaving." That's when he gets a call from Castro's people to come over. They put him in a minivan with the windows covered and bring him to the presidential palace for dinner. But now he's told no interview and no photographer.

Castro holds forth for five hours, haranguing him with the standard Marxist spiel about the evils of capitalism. Before John left, Castro wanted to have a private moment. He says, "I just want you to know Oswald applied for citizenship here and we turned him down." And John interpreted that as his way of saying, "I had nothing to do with your father's death."

Matt Berman

Because our first cover was such a hit, we kept doing it. John said, "Let's do it again," and I was like, really? So we did Robert De Niro posing with George Washington's sword. John had George Washington's personal sword and that's what we used on the cover. I said to John, "This should be at the Smithsonian. . . ."

Then we started to branch out. I had a big stack of books of these American icons that we wanted to do for the covers. The Statue of Liberty, Rosie the Riveter, Lincoln—and as we would book each celeb, I'd talk to the publicist and we'd discuss who they wanted to play. Streisand chose Betsy Ross and Julia Roberts chose Susan B. Anthony and Harrison Ford chose Lincoln.

Julia Roberts

For the Susan B. Anthony cover, we did this photo shoot and they painted me silver and my hair silver. I was shooting a movie and I had to work the next day. This stuff was supposed to just all wash off after the shoot, and it didn't. I remember being on the phone with John saying, "I don't know what to do. My hair is all full of this silver stuff!" And he was like, *Oh my god, how can I help?* I think somebody who worked for him said, "What about Dawn dish soap? It's supposed to cut grease." The paint was petroleum-based. So we ended up using what felt like gallons of Dawn dish soap to get the silver out of my hair. It was fun—but the effects were pretty long-lasting!

RoseMarie Terenzio

John had this idea of having Madonna pose on the cover as his mom. We would dress her in a suit, her signature sunglasses, and a pillbox hat sitting on a stack of books as a nod to her being an editor. He sent a fax asking her to do it and she replied via fax. I still have it.

> *Dear Johnny Boy,*
>
> *Thanks for asking me to be your mother but I'm afraid I could never do her justice. My eyebrows aren't thick enough for one. . . . When you want me to portray Eva Braun or Pamela Harriman, I might say yes.*
>
> *Hope you're well,*
>
> *Love,*
>
> *Madonna*

Matt Berman

It was like a crazy thing because it was so daring. I mean, things didn't faze him. We loved trying new things.

We had Dustin Hoffman and Robert De Niro—it was to promote their political satire *Wag the Dog*—in formfitting Savile Row jackets made out of camouflage material. Dustin was getting agitated. It didn't fit him the way he liked. De Niro let him wear his jacket because it was a little bigger. John said, "Matt, they're actors. You're supposed to just go up and tell them what to do. That's their job. Don't let them intimidate you."

For the June 1996 cover, Demi Moore had this doll idea. She wanted to be an early American doll that she had at home that an artist friend made. She posed in a Revolutionary War costume, and her corset was body-painted onto her. John called me at the shoot. At that moment, she had her arms straight up in the air and her bodice was being body-painted onto her nude torso. I mumbled, "You're not going to believe this—she's buck naked." He laughed and said, "You're kidding me, can she talk?" I had to hold the phone up to her ear while they chatted.

Demi Moore

We had met before, very briefly, in Sun Valley over a ski holiday. He was with Carolyn and came to my house. He reached out to ask if I would be interested in doing a cover. It was post my body-painting and pregnancy covers for *Vanity Fair*. There was something for me about things that are provocative—I really liked what he was setting out to do. He was extremely charismatic and had a very kind of quiet strength and intelligence. I thought this would be really a lot of fun. He had such a strong, clear vision—that was very exciting and intoxicating.

RoseMarie Terenzio

Demi called a lot. She came to the office with a teddy bear backpack and seemed like she didn't want to leave. She came two or three times and she stayed until seven o'clock at night. "Can we order food?" John got a kick out of her and finally had to say, "Listen, we gotta go home." He loved that she was so into the cover and making it her own.

Demi Moore

I think I was arriving at the office feeling nervous, uncertain, probably a little insecure. As I did often, I couldn't believe I was being asked.

Matt Berman

After the issue came out, she called and said how much she didn't like the cover. The assistant said, "Demi Moore's on the phone and she sounds really mad." I couldn't figure it out. She said, "Well, it printed really red." I was like, "You know, John really loves the cover, so now I feel funny because I have to go into his office and tell him you're really mad." That was such a John move on my part. . . . She started to backpedal; she changed completely.

Demi Moore

If I didn't like it, I'm sure it was coming out of my own insecurity and maybe feeling like it was a little bit more exposed of my body than I was expecting?

Whoopi Goldberg posed as Rosa Parks for a feature titled "Rebels & Revolutionaries."

Whoopi Goldberg

I remember being really honored to get the ask because I knew that it came from JFK Jr. Like most women, I thought he was cute. And lo and behold, while I'm posing and looking like Rosa Parks sitting in a bus for the shoot, in walked this really great-looking man. I kinda felt guilty because when people talk about him, they talk about him as a national treasure, and here I was just being a lustful woman. He was sweet and he thanked me. I really wanted to say, "Thank me? Thank *you*, John."

John called Pamela Anderson to ask her to be on the cover. She posed draped only in an American flag.

Pamela Anderson, actor

Oh, gosh. It was way over my head. I just giggled. I don't even know what sounds came out of my mouth. It was so embarrassing. But yeah, he was very charming. I mean, a man like that. I just was speechless. Yeah, I was goofy. Not sexy for sure. I was completely embarrassed.

RoseMarie Terenzio

For the December 1998 issue, we shot Sean Penn for the cover. He was promoting his new movie *The Thin Red Line*. He and John had dinner after the photo shoot.

A friend

They had some history. . . . John said they addressed it. He said that he'd transgressed, but he told Sean he never knew Madonna in the biblical sense.

Still, morally he felt there was no justification. He said he took the elephant out of the room and then they became friends. They shook hands.

Sean Penn

It was a fantastic conversation. It was sort of, you know, you've gone a decade with some thorn in your side with each other, and it all comes out on the table and you realize how silly it was in the first place. We had a really lovely dinner.

Biz Mitchell

Sometimes John had ideas I thought were a little cockamamie. The William Wegman dog on the cover dressed as George Washington. This is not gonna sell—nobody's gonna buy the dog cover. And it really did badly. John just was into his dog at the time and Wegman was doing an exhibit, so he's like, *Let's do a cover.* But I mean, they *were* the most beautiful covers.

RoseMarie Terenzio

Tons of people turned him down. Princess Diana, Michael Jordan, Prince, Hillary Clinton, Bill Clinton.

Gary Ginsberg

When people said no to John, he never took it particularly well.

Biz Mitchell

John would mime opening up this "Book of Grudges," as he called it, and writing a name in it. That was his joke around the office. Tommy Lee Jones, who was Vice President Al Gore's roommate in college, said he wanted to interview Gore if we could set it up. John went through all kinds of hoops to make it happen. After all that, Tommy Lee said he didn't feel comfortable doing it. John opened the big book of grudges for Tommy Lee Jones.

Steve Gillon

Early on, Hachette wanted to make it a John Kennedy Fan Club magazine—they wanted John on the cover, and they saw the magazine as a way of giving readers access to John's life. John, on the other hand, planned to stay in the background and allow the magazine to speak for him.

Matt Berman

At some point I was begging John and Carolyn to do *American Gothic* as the cover. It was after they were married. Can't you just picture it? I said, "Carolyn doesn't even have to change her hairstyle." He would've had a pitchfork, we could have had a designer do a fashion version of that prim dress. He said, "Oh, that'll look good, Matt. Now I'm down to whoring out me and my wife on the cover for sales."

RoseMarie Terenzio

After years of turning down requests, John agreed to several interviews to promote *George*. I listened to the *Howard Stern Show* every morning at my desk. I was beyond a fan. At first, he'd walk by and say, "Oh no, you're listening to Howard again?" And then he'd catch something Howard said that was funny and start laughing. One day I said, "If you ever do Howard Stern, I'm coming with you." He said, "That's never going to happen." Howard was the ultimate shock jock and you never know what he would ask. Totally unpredictable.

I'd been pushing for Howard to be the cover: "He has six million listeners." Unfortunately, Howard Stern's audience didn't buy magazines. . . . I said, "We'll get tons of publicity." Matt sketched all these amazing ideas. One was Howard as George Washington crossing the Delaware with strippers in a boat. John was like, "We're not doing that." Matt came up with Howard as a bad boy George Washington chopping down the cherry tree.

We shot Howard as George at the studio. I helped spray-paint these little cherries onto these tree twigs. John came by on his bike to say hi. Later he said, "It's only fair that I go on his show. He did the cover." So I called his executive producer and said, "John wants to do the show." He said, "Are you fucking kidding me?" He couldn't believe it. There wasn't anything Howard couldn't ask—John never imposed rules on what questions he could or couldn't be asked.

Before the interview he said, "Tell me what to do. You listen to the show every day." I'm like, "Anytime you're uncomfortable, just defer to Robin— Howard's cohost Robin Quivers. She's obsessed with you and she's going to get all giggly, and Howard's going to go in on her for kowtowing to you. Just say, 'Hey, Robin, want to help me out here?'" If you listen to the interview, that's exactly what he does, he says, "Robin, I thought you were supposed to help me out here." And what's funny is that she is so fucking head over heels, she goes crazy when he walks in.

Howard always said about John, "All he does is bang chicks and rollerblade." When he said it to John on air, John just laughed and said, "Well, I do rollerblade a lot." The best was when Howard said to him, "When did you know?" John says, "Know what?" "When did you know, 'I'm JFK Jr.'?" And John goes, "Pretty early on."

Carolyn and I got up at six o'clock that morning and we were on the phone, listening together. We were howling. She loved every minute of it. After that, she had the biggest crush on Howard, because he's like, "You got the hottest chick on the planet. Give her the ring, give her the dog. What are you doing? If that was my girlfriend, I'd give her whatever she wanted. I'd have taken my clothes off and run down the street naked. What are you doing? Why are you fighting with her? She's the hottest chick ever." After the interview, John was laughing and he said, "You told me to defer to Robin—but it didn't work!"

On May 14, 1998, John appeared along with Jerry Seinfeld on The Tonight Show with Jay Leno. *The show was to mark* Seinfeld's *final episode.*

Dave Berg, co-producer of *The Tonight Show with Jay Leno*

Of course, one of *Seinfeld*'s most popular episodes, "Master of My Domain," focused on JFK Jr. John wasn't on the show, but he was a big part of it. It was about who could go the longest without masturbating—they never used that word. Elaine happened to see JFK Jr. at the gym, and she was enamored. Of course, she dropped out of the contest first. John told this incredibly self-effacing story about what happened the day after the episode aired.

Jay Leno: Now . . . you weren't on Seinfeld, *but you were portrayed, right?*

John: My elbow, I think it was. . . . It was funny because I hadn't seen the episode, and I come out of my house in the morning, and everyone is yelling across the street, and I'm walking to work. I was a district attorney then. And people are driving by in their cars and honking. And I'm going, "What? What? What the hell is going on here?"

So, I walk in, and as people start to say, "Oh, I saw you last night. Were you on Seinfeld?*" I said, "No, no. What was everyone talking about?" So they explained it. And then I had a trial, and I walk into the court, and the defendant is sitting there . . . and he goes, "You were on* Seinfeld." *And I was like, "No, no, I wasn't on* Seinfeld." *And he leans over to his lawyer, and he goes, "Guy is an actor too. No wonder he failed the bar exam."*

Dave Berg

Before the show he'd told me, "I am really nervous." He wasn't sure that anyone would have any interest in him. I still can't get over that. When he walked out of the dressing room to go onstage, he made the sign of the cross. The audience didn't know John was going to be on. I worked there more than twenty years and had never seen a reaction like this. He got this incredible standing ovation when he walked in, and they wouldn't stop.

He and Jerry had perfect chemistry. They could banter. Jay asked out of the blue, "John, do you have any tips for Jerry?" John said, "Yeah, there's this great restaurant that serves soup in New York. The guy that runs it is a little bit testy."

After the show, he said, "Do you think that was okay?" *Do I think that was okay?* Jay was thrilled. He was our favorite guest because it was the best segment we ever had.

Jay Leno

When John walked out and I shook his hand, I'm not sure if I had a tear in my eye, but boy, it was pretty close. It was just like a huge kind of emotional moment.

I was thirteen years old when I heard Kennedy had been shot, and I remember the funeral was on TV and my mother . . . when your mother's hysterical, you're like, what do I do here? When little John-John saluted the casket, I remember her going, "Poor little boy. He lost his father, what's he gonna do?" I'm sitting there going, "It will be okay, Mom." Fast-forward thirty-five years. I said, "My next guest, the son of a president of the United States, John Kennedy Jr. . . ."

He was very nice and self-effacing. Him being nervous made him nicer. I thought, "Hey, Mom, the kid's all right."

"Very human, he was"

RoseMarie Terenzio

John liked interviewing people for *George*. He did one every other month or so—"the John Kennedy interview." They usually weren't covers. It was more following his curiosity. When he went to interview the Dalai Lama in Dharamsala he took the train, the rickety train. I'm like, "There's a flight you could take. It's a private plane." And he's like, "I can't go interview the Dalai Lama on a private plane. That's so hypocritical." It's a sixteen-hour train ride from Delhi. He said, "I finally fall asleep and these guys come knocking on my door. All they said was 'Excuse me, you're our son of Kennedy. We have come to look at you.'" And he's like, "You know, it was just so honest."

In September 1996, John interviewed President Gerald Ford, the last surviving member of the Warren Commission.

Susan Ford Bales, Gerald Ford's daughter

My dad told us that after they finished the interview, he said, "John, is there anything you would like to know about your dad? His office was across the hall from mine for years." He said to John, "I'm the last living member of the War-ren Commission." Until the day he died, he believed in the Warren Commis-sion. He said, "I believe Oswald acted alone." He wanted John to know that.

RoseMarie Terenzio

Sometimes I would clean up John's interviews for him and do some light edits. I remember after the Ford interview I asked if he wanted me to delete that line about Oswald, where Ford addressed him directly: "The truth is, John . . . there is no doubt in my mind that Lee Harvey Oswald commit-ted the assassination." Since any mention of the assassination in relation to John would make news. He said, "Leave it in." I think he wanted it in to show he didn't believe in the conspiracy theories about his father's death.

Gary Hart, 1988 presidential candidate

I liked John very much . . . he was so personable and persuasive. The part of the interview I did not like very much . . . I was working very hard to put an incident behind me. My experience in '87 changed American politics because, up to that time, a politician's personal life was private. And my expe-rience broke that rule. Everything was fair game.

I stepped out of politics in '87—that's why I probably pushed back a lit-tle bit on resurrecting a very brief unhappy experience. That's what he wanted to talk about, and I just wanted to move on. There was a lot of irony in it, obviously, given his father's history and stories about it. Certainly, by the delicacy of his questions, I could tell he felt a bit awkward about it.

I felt that he was very supportive after that terrible experience that my family and I had had. And he could identify with that since obviously his whole life was in the public eye. He was public property all of his life.

Why did he mean so much to America? The question answers itself—he's his father's son. His father, a tragic figure, had totally changed my gen-eration. He was a transforming figure, and his uncle as well. They brought idealism to American politics—not often experienced.

I don't recall talking with John about his father, but it was almost as if President Kennedy was in the room. Unspoken.

Garth Brooks, singer-songwriter

We did the interview for *George* in Nashville over at the studio. I agreed to do it as long as I could interview him at the same time. I had three children and, at that point, they're seven, five, and three. So my big question for him was, what advice would he give me that would help me raise my three girls?

I don't know about you, but I learned parenting very early from my parents. The three main things were "No, hell no, and are you crazy, we can't afford that." And then God, with his wicked sense of humor, now all of a sudden our kids can afford what they want and you have to come up with another reason why they need to work for it.

John said being the child of a celebrity, no matter how hard you work, how much you outwork everybody else, people are always gonna say it's handed to you. And the only person that matters—that knows that you earned it—is you. I've used it a million times with my kids. My three little girls, they understood work ethic from day one because of that. That changed my parenting philosophy.

Gary Ginsberg

John wanted to interview Gerry Adams, the leader of the IRA's Sinn Féin. The conventional wisdom was he's a terrorist. I think John was fascinated by him.

RoseMarie Terenzio

Gerry Adams felt like he was fighting for a cause, freedom for his people. John wanted to explore that for himself.

Gerry Adams, president of Sinn Féin

I was surprised when he said he was gonna come to Ireland. I often say to people, get under the skin of the place and form your own judgment. John came as it so happened when a Republican prisoner, a man called Paddy Kelly, had died in jail in Britain. . . . There was a lot of outrage in Ireland that he had been denied basic medical treatment. John agreed to see me at the funeral. An Irish funeral can be particularly poignant—there were pipes playing lamentations. Later on we did our interview back at the Sinn Féin office in Dublin. Things were a bit precarious at the time in terms of the peace process. He never made any judgmental remarks. He was pleased to know that his uncle Teddy and his aunt Jean had such a pivotal role in terms of persuading the White House and the president of the day, President Clinton, and advising them at different times in the peace process.

I'd invited him to come to West Belfast. So we arranged that Chrissy and Richard McAuley, my assistant, would pick him up.

Chrissy McAuley, Sinn Féin council member

My husband said, "We're going to be meeting somebody tomorrow. John Kennedy Jr." I went, "No, you're having a laugh." And he says, "We're gonna let him see what it's like for himself." John came up on the early-morning train. We packed him into the small car—his two knees were nearly up around his chin. When we got to the first set of traffic lights, a British army foot patrol came across the front of the car. They always train these automatic rifles, and they're always fully loaded and ready to fire. They trained the rifle straight in the window at John's face. He tried to get down. And I went, "Welcome to British-occupied Belfast." Very human, he was. He challenged us, how violence isn't really the answer.

"You read it under the covers with a flashlight"

Gary Ginsberg

We knew these guardians of conventional political journalism were going to hate *George*. And right on cue, one after another, the great columnists with acid pens came out and trashed us from the get-go. That we were dumbing down politics. But John was trying to appeal to people whose views wouldn't depend on whether it got the approval of the *New York Times* or a *Washington Post* columnist. He knew he wasn't going to get the thirty-year-old new bride in Topeka, Kansas, to pick up a political magazine if he had a turgid story about Medicare reform on the cover. And that's who he wanted to appeal to—a whole new class of readers.

Jonathan Alter

It was about politics and entertainment, and so by definition, it's gonna be a little bit superficial.

RoseMarie Terenzio

I don't know if the Clintons took *George* seriously. I remember in '95, Clinton's advisor George Stephanopoulos—I don't know if it was in the *Washington Post*—said, like, "*George* magazine: you read it, but you read it under the covers with a flashlight." They asked John about it, and he said, "I don't care where you read it, as long as you're reading it."

Gary Ginsberg

Let me just be very clear. The high temples of publishing at the time were watching the launch with a combination of mockery and fear, rooting for our quick demise.

Sasha Chermayeff

His own family condescended to what he was doing. I think his sister was maybe struggling with the lack of acknowledgment for what *she* was doing, her books and so on. I mean, *George* was kind of made fun of: "Oh, what's this half-assed celebrity shit?" I remember a lot of nasty interpretations of the magazine, at least in the beginning.

Steve Gillon

John was at a dinner with some friends and his sister and Ed when he told them he was starting *George*, and Ed was sitting there and just turned the other way and started a private conversation while John's making this big announcement about what he's doing with his life.

RoseMarie Terenzio

When Ed came up to the office, John showed him the art room. He didn't have a reaction. They went to John's office. Ed just said, "Nice view." The whole issue, the layout, was posted on the wall. Afterwards John said, "Can you believe it? All he said was 'Nice view.'" I later asked him, "What does Ed do for a living? What does his company do?" He said, "Rosie, when you figure that out, you let me know."

Sasha Chermayeff

Ed wanted to be taken seriously among New York City players. And John didn't need to do that—he'd already landed on the top of the pile, and they were just climbing up to him.

RoseMarie Terenzio

To mark President Clinton's fiftieth birthday, John had the idea to have someone dressed as Marilyn Monroe singing "Happy Birthday, Mr. President" on the cover. I don't think anyone else would have had the nerve to bring it up. His thing was, why is it okay for everyone to play with my family's iconography and not me? Barbra Streisand was the first choice to be Marilyn because of her relationship with the Clintons. When John asked her, she said she thought it was in poor taste.

Drew Barrymore said yes. As you can imagine, women had unpredictable reactions to John, including some of the most famous women in the world. What's so funny is that John thought Drew Barrymore was gonna be wild and crazy and calling the office all the time with all kinds of ideas but she said yes to the cover and didn't seem to have much of a reaction to John and that was it. She was in L.A., so they didn't even end up meeting.

Drew Barrymore

John called me and said, "I'm creating a magazine, and this particular issue is extremely personal . . . I would love for you to pose as Marilyn Monroe." In my brain I'm like, *Oh god, I don't look anything like Marilyn Monroe.* He explained that it would be the Marilyn who sang his dad "Happy Birthday." I said, "The see-through, flesh-colored dress?" And he said, "Yeah." He's like, "I really want to get the dress right. I really want to get the hair right." I didn't want to get caught up in anything scandalous, but I could just tell that everything about this cover was with a wink and a smile. He said something like he wanted me to do it because he was coming at it with playfulness, and he felt that I was playful. I got that he wasn't out to hurt anyone, and that's what make me feel really inclined to do it. I was like, "I am so in."

Matt Berman

We made a replica of that famous Marilyn dress—I have it somewhere in storage. John knew we were going to do her the night she sang "Happy Birthday"—he green-lighted that. Drew was excited. She said she was watching Marilyn Monroe movies all day before the shoot.

Drew Barrymore

The dress was perfect—fit like a glove. The wig was really good. I was terrified to be Marilyn Monroe. I mean, hello! But I just tried to channel her and think about John during the shoot. *Am I going to get this right for him?* I remember watching him my whole life in total admiration—his wink, his smile, his energy, the way he carried himself. There was just such a delight to it. I was like, *I need to make this perfect for him.* The magazine came out and I loved it.

Nancy Haberman

John brought me into the art room to show me the cover before it was out and he smiled and said, "I guess I'm working out my demons one by one."

He went on *Oprah* to promote the issue. We didn't know they would show footage of Marilyn singing "Happy Birthday" to his father. Afterwards he said, "Did you know that was coming?" I said, "Of course I didn't know." He said, "Well, I guess we kind of asked for it."

RoseMarie Terenzio

Caroline didn't like that he did that cover—not only that, she was pissed he never gave her a heads-up. John said, "Caroline's upset. . . ." I told him I thought she was right to be upset because it directly affected her. I said, "It's her family, too." And he just looked at me like, *You got a point.*

Gary Ginsberg

His mom's passing may have allowed him to do things like start *George* or take certain liberties with it that he probably wouldn't otherwise have taken. Would he have done the Marilyn Monroe cover with his mom alive? Probably not.

Joe Armstrong

I didn't understand the Marilyn Monroe cover—a woman who's thought to have been involved with his dad. I loved his mother, and I was very upset about it. Obviously, there were contradictions in John. I just often thought, *Well, maybe it's like a kid playing with matches.*

CHAPTER 17

Meet Me at the Carlyle

"The two most famous people on the planet"

In December 1995, John met Princess Diana at the Carlyle Hotel in New York City. Separated from Prince Charles since 1992, Diana was thirty-four and at the height of her celebrity: she had done her bombshell interview with the BBC—the sit-down where she alluded to her husband's affair with Camilla Parker Bowles ("There were three of us in this marriage")—just a month before.

RoseMarie Terenzio

John wanted to ask Princess Diana to be on the cover of *George*, to dress up as an American historical figure—we hadn't decided who yet. He wrote her a letter. She was going to be in New York, staying at the Carlyle, and her private secretary, Patrick Jephson, and I arranged for them to meet on a weekday afternoon. There was all this worry: Should he go in the front door? Should he wear a disguise, because won't there be rumors that he's having an affair with her? John decided to just have Effie drive us over in John's Saab. John said, "Rosie, come with me. If I go in by myself and I leave by myself, if any-one sees me, there's gonna be all kinds of speculation. You know, *They were caught at the Carlyle.*" They were the two most famous people on the planet.

He wore a navy-blue suit. Nothing extravagant, not full-tilt-boogie JFK Jr., but on the cusp. I waited in the lobby. He entered through the front door because all the paparazzi were waiting at the side door for Diana. He went right in without being noticed.

Patrick Jephson, private secretary and equerry to Princess Diana

My recollection is that John wrote to me and it was obviously all based around *George*.

I showed that to Diana and she was keen on the idea of meeting him, or interested anyway.

We discussed the magazine cover, and my suggestion was that she should not do it because it would look kind of un-classy. It would look as if she was endorsing the project. There were, at the time, quite a few magazines, sort of start-ups . . . and magazines are pretty dodgy territory. So if *George* is a huge success, it shouldn't be because of who John has on the cover—it should be because it's a really good magazine. That was why we thought she would do the twentieth or the fiftieth or the hundredth issue or something. But the message was clear: you make a good job of the magazine, and I'll think about it.

We were to be in New York anyway for the Humanitarian of the Year award. I think it was the United Cerebral Palsy charity of New York. And this was a big bash at the Hilton where Henry Kissinger and Colin Powell and Rupert Murdoch and every kind of supermodel you can imagine were attending. We agreed that she would find time in her program in New York to meet him. Nobody wanted it to be public.

It was never made public, so that made it quite fun, actually. Diana wanted it to be discreet because it had all the makings of a great gossip story, didn't it? World's most eligible bachelor, wasn't he at the time? And she had just got unmarried or was in the process of getting unmarried. It would've been a rather intriguing thing to dream about. She didn't want that, but she was curious to meet him. Partly, I think, because Sarah Ferguson had the hots for him and Diana wanted to, I think, do one up on her.

So anyway, I was hanging around the lobby of the Carlyle at the agreed time, and we actually met outside Bemelmans Bar in a rather dark passageway that goes through to the front foyer.

He dressed up for the occasion, you know, he was smart. And she was smart. It was a working meeting. Business attire.

We introduced ourselves, and I took him up in the elevator to the penthouse, and we sat down and I think had tea and/or champagne. He was quite in awe of her. . . . Not uncomfortable, but he certainly seemed to be on his best behavior. He rather sat on the edge of his chair and looked nervously at her.

She was not nervous at all to meet him. She was very cool—and jolly, you know, and smiley and welcoming. And he did his pitch. He showed her some mock-ups and she gave me a look and said, "Well, you know, this is all very nice, John. Thank you. But I hope you'll forgive me if I don't take up the opportunity this time, but would love to maybe for your fiftieth or your hundredth issue or something." He accepted that without fuss. And then, as I recall, we continued chatting about various other things . . . probably the award dinner.

Once it seemed that the time was up, this was a pretty well-practiced thing that she and I had—we would've agreed beforehand how long we would give it. And I would say something like, "Sorry to interrupt, but we've got to get ready for the next thing." And John then got up and I escorted him downstairs and that was it. They shook hands. He called her "Your Royal Highness" and "ma'am."

After the meeting she said words to the effect of "That went well, and it was the right thing to do." She didn't say "what a hunk" or "beefcake" or anything like that.

I can't remember the words, but there was a degree of sympathy. I think she might have spoken about the famous picture of him as a little boy. And she had sympathy for him growing up with the name and being the object of public fascination. These were things that she could relate to. I definitely picked up a sense of sympathy, of concern, for him.

She didn't see him as the rest of the world saw him. As this big, famous, handsome guy. She saw him, I think, as rather vulnerable because he had grown up in public.

She would often say that about people. Sometimes to my surprise, she would see a vulnerability in them or she would see where their lives were difficult when most other people would only have seen privilege and opportunity. It was an attempt to see the challenges that they had overcome, difficulties that the world didn't see.

I would probably say that this would've been in her mind when she was talking of John, that he was always having to be careful—people taking advantage of him. As people were often trying to take advantage of her. And indeed, on this occasion, he *was* trying to take advantage of her, but in a nice way. I think she saw in him a fellow victim, if you can put it that way, of life in the public eye and difficulty of knowing who to trust. And I think that that did create a connection between them. I wouldn't call it a bond, but an affinity, a recognition of each other's unusual hardships and difficulties.

She didn't comment on his looks, which is probably an indication of how she very much saw the inner person. She was used to being judged by her looks and therefore didn't have much time for it.

The fact that she wrote to him afterwards, I think, confirms the fact that she did feel a connection and an empathy for what the media were like for him.

Matt Berman

We sent him over with a bunch of covers. I would draw sketches—Magic Marker on tracing paper. I did one of her in a limousine with paparazzi flash bulbs—it was her in the back with the windows half up. How weird is that? They were both not gonna be around in the next few years. Who would've called that one?

Gary Ginsberg

I remember he came back and I was giving him shit . . . because at that point everybody knew that she and Charles didn't have a relationship. I just remember making fun of the fact that it was the princess and the prince having their first sit-down together.

RoseMarie Terenzio

Afterwards, I remember him saying, "She's much taller than I thought—and she's got great legs." And that she was "very shy, very polite, but she said no." On the way back to the office, I asked if he got lucky and he started laughing and said, "Shut up, Rosie."

They stayed in touch and he asked her again for an interview. On February 3, 1997, she wrote John a note from Kensington Palace. I still have a copy of it.

She thanked him for his letter and a few copies of *George* he had sent over. She said "regrettably" she must decline his offer and that she would get back in touch when the time was right. At the end, she wrote, "I hope"—and she underlined "hope"—"the media are leaving both you and Carolyn alone. I know how difficult it is, but believe it or not, the worst paparazzi are here in Europe!"

CHAPTER 18

"The only gift we could actually give them is their privacy"

RoseMarie Terenzio

By the time the 1996 Democratic convention came around, we had the first year of *George* under our belt. From John's perspective, we should really put on the dog, as he used to say. The way that *Vanity Fair* owns the Oscars, we should own this. We hosted a big party—probably a thousand people—at the Chicago Art Institute, and he was like, *Let it rip. We wanna be the hottest ticket in town.* I walked in with Kevin Costner, and you couldn't even move. I was wearing a strappy dress, and the next morning I had bruises on my back from people shoving me, trying to get a picture of John. Hillary and Oprah got a photo with John—they had just gotten there—and right behind them were fire marshals coming in to shut it down. We were violating a fire code. Then John left the party, and it was like Elvis has left the building.

Sean Neary

John was so inclusive—Carl Robbins and I were junior staff at *George* but we got to be there for the party. There we were in line next to Chelsea Clinton trying to get in. . . .

RoseMarie Terenzio

John and Carolyn's wedding was just a month away. But almost no one knew that—they were keeping it so secret. It was very low-key. No wedding planner. We never really had a conversation like "Oh, we're planning the wedding." It just started to be private conversations where Carolyn would ask, "Where are we going to get married?" I remember Caroline said, "Well, why don't you just announce it in the *New York Times*?" Like she did. And Carolyn was like, "No fucking way. My life will be hell if I do that. Are you kidding me? By the time the wedding happens, we'll be stalked every minute."

I started to go down to the apartment and we would talk through where to have the wedding. I remember saying, "What about Nova Scotia?" Because everyone always says Nova Scotia's really beautiful. There won't be paparazzi. They went to Nova Scotia and Carolyn called me from there and she was like, "Honey, this is the most depressing place ever. I'm not getting married here." It felt like *We are just going somewhere that's remote just to be remote.* They wanted to be somewhere that had some kind of connection to them—a place that had meaning.

There was even talk about "Should we do it at the house in Hyannis? Should we do it on the Vineyard?" And then John came up with the idea of Cumberland Island off of Georgia.

Gogo Ferguson, owner of the Greyfield Inn on Cumberland Island

When John was with Christina Haag they came down together, and then after that, he kept coming down with friends. We kept in touch with John because he adored Cumberland Island. Cumberland was a place where he could be carefree. And then we'd see each other either in New York or summer on the Vineyard.

RoseMarie Terenzio

They went to visit and Carolyn fell in love with it, too. John asked Gogo if they could get married there.

Gogo Ferguson

He was reticent to ask me to have the wedding here. He knew my family was very under the radar. Quiet. Our island—there are only like thirty-some-odd people who live here. My family opened their home as an inn—the Greyfield Inn. Finally, one night, John asked me. We were in Martha's Vineyard and Carolyn and I were hanging out. . . . I thought she was utterly breathtaking and she was a lot of fun.

John said, "Go, we're getting married—but I have to ask you, could we maybe do it on Cumberland Island?" My husband Dave and I talked about it, and we said, this is the only gift that we could actually give them is their privacy. He'd been looking everywhere, and they couldn't find a place that they could get people to without being noticed.

Dave is a pilot—John used to fly with him all the time. So Dave knew that logistically once they got on Cumberland, there may not be any paparazzi because we've donated 90 percent of the island to create a national park. So it's just my family within a national park. We finally said, "Yes, but here's how it's gonna go. You're not telling anyone in your family. No one. And we're not telling anyone in our family." I booked the inn. I had to buy a couple of guests out that had booked a year in advance.

John was adamant on getting married at the First African Baptist Church. One of my cousins had told him a story that when Robert Kennedy was shot, Beulah Alberty, who was the deacon of the church, came racing down to tell everyone around the island. And the entire island gathered, and they had a service in that church for Bobby. That really meant something to him. That's why, when I was like, "Couldn't you just get married on the dunes or at the Greyfield compound?" he insisted on the church.

Charles O'Byrne, family friend who officiated the wedding

When he asked me to officiate his wedding, that was a total surprise to me. I was sworn to secrecy obviously, and we were sitting at a picnic table at his house in Hyannis Port with Carolyn. He asked me if I would do it, and at the time I was a deacon, I wasn't a priest yet, but I was allowed to do marriages. I said I'd be honored. I'd love to.

To be married in the Catholic Church, you need to have a series of meetings and conversations with the priest or deacon that was going to be doing the ceremony. So the three of us had several meetings, I think all but one over dinner at their apartment. Those conversations are largely private, but you know, what I can share is that there was real joy and love between the two of them. They were both very excited about this and they wanted as much of the ceremony as possible to reflect them. From the readings that were selected to the prayers that were said to the setting. They wanted it to be their moment, so privacy was very important. And they wanted their vows to reflect that. I thought it was very reflective of the bonds that had developed between the two of them.

RoseMarie Terenzio

Once Gogo said yes, it was this whole logistical thing of—there's really nothing there. There's the Greyfield Inn, but there's not a hotel or a restaurant. Only thirty people and wild Spanish horses. So we started planning, and I remember Gordon Henderson had a friend who owned a restaurant in SoHo. It was Gogo who did most of it, with me and Gordon and Carolyn helping out. And through Gordon's friend, we were getting the plates shipped and the wine and the booze and all of that, because everything had to come over by ferry.

I think there might be only two ferries a day that go to Cumberland. It's not a Martha's Vineyard or a Nantucket where there's five or six ferries a day and you can bring a car over. There are no cars. Gogo and her family have pickup trucks.

Carolyn flew down a few times. She went with her mom once or twice. I think John went once. Gogo really had to do it all. It wasn't like you could go down there and meet with the caterer. You had to do it all remotely and then get it all down there.

We used to refer to it as "Nicole Miller's wedding." Gogo knew Nicole. And I was so paranoid about anyone overhearing us that whenever Gogo and I talked about the planning, we would just say "Nicole Miller's wedding." I think Nicole was getting married at the same time or something. And so we were always planning "Nicole's wedding."

Carolyn had an idea of what she wanted for her dress. There was a meeting with Narciso Rodriguez, who was her close friend, at Cerruti. Gordon designed John's dark navy-blue suit. It was perfect. Gordon had a friend who was a tailor and they worked together to make it. The circle was kept very tight.

Carolyn flew to Paris to meet with Narciso. Her dress was a combination of things that she liked. I think she had seen a bias-cut dress of John Galliano—she wanted something definitely bias-cut. Carolyn was always about simplicity. Something that wouldn't look dated. She didn't like a lot of adornments. And when you look like that, you don't need it.

She went to Paris for one or two fittings. And then the dress had to be shipped, and it was like, "Where should we ship it?" If I remember correctly, they shipped it to the *George* office, and then I sent it to her mother because I was thinking, *I don't want this thing here.* It was like hot potato. And then her mom brought it to 20 North Moore. It couldn't be sent there because there was no doorman. It was this giant box that somebody had to be there to receive. It wasn't like you could leave it at the front door. We didn't want anyone to see a big box from Cerruti. If it came to the office, we could say it's a costume for a cover shoot.

George Kyriakos

We did tests on Carolyn's hairstyle for the wedding in New York at my apartment. We wanted something classic and of the time, and that's what we came up with—the twist. And she could take it down later at night and it'll look great down.

Gogo Ferguson

On the island we took over as many family houses as we could. I had a jewelry store in Martha's Vineyard, and I can't tell you how many times I would disappear—fly from the Vineyard with Carolyn and Effie and one or two times with Carolyn's mother and go down to the island undercover to look at the church and talk about all the logistics.

Carolyn wanted white Ecuadorian roses for the reception, and we had to have a barge to bring the tent over. About a week before, I had every one of the staff sign a confidentiality statement so they would not take a picture, talk about it, or anything. After the wedding these guys were offered hundreds of thousands of dollars for anything. They all honored it.

They wanted someone to sing a capella. I went all over the county interviewing singers. I finally found this young man [David R. Davis, to sing "Amazing Grace"]. I said, "Okay, this is for a wedding over in Cumberland." He had no idea who it was for. Everyone we hired outside had to stay on the island until Monday so they wouldn't talk. And the young man comes over on the boat and he comes in to meet John and Carolyn and I thought he was gonna have a heart attack. He had no idea.

RoseMarie Terenzio

It took five or six months to pull everything together. Carolyn didn't seem nervous. She was focused on the logistics—the marriage part of it was the easy part. It was more like, "Where are we going to print the programs?" We couldn't go to a printer because we were afraid that somebody would leak it. Carolyn had this pale gray paper from Crane's that she really liked. We had to do it at night. I called her and said, "Okay, everybody's gone." She came up to the office. We smoked a couple of cigarettes, we giggled, and then we started printing the programs. The first time, the paper got stuck in the printer because it was too thick. So we had to get different paper. We had to come back again at eleven o'clock the next night. And it worked because the paper was a little bit thinner. She went right home with them. This was not even a week beforehand. That was kind of crazy because she had to bring a lot of things to her own wedding. Everything was DIY.

The big heavy stuff like the booze and the dishes and all that was shipped. But the programs, anything that was paper, that she could take with her, she took. You couldn't really hire people to do any of this stuff because we were afraid it would get leaked.

Even the photographer was her dear friend, Jacky Marshall—it wasn't some famous photographer. Denis Reggie—Teddy's wife Victoria's brother—also took photos.

They both had a plain gold wedding band. Hers was very thin, his a little bit thicker. After they got married, Carolyn rarely wore her engagement ring. She really only wore the plain gold band.

She saved her engagement ring for special occasions. She would always wear something that John gave her from his mom whenever she would go to something related to her. She wore Jackie's charm bracelet to the Municipal Art Society gala at Grand Central in 1998. I think it was at American Ballet Theatre, there was this necklace that Jackie had, with a charm on it that had a bird in a cage. It was amazing. And I think she wore that to their gala. She wore the swimming ring from Jackie to the Whitney Museum gala.

It wasn't like Carolyn had a ton of jewelry from his mom. She had five or six special pieces and she would wear them for special occasions. I think there was one time when they were going to be at an event with Carolina Herrera. She knew that John's mom and Carolina Herrera knew one another, so she wore something of Jackie's.

There were no wedding invitations. John and Carolyn let only a few people know. I think with his family members, it was more like a save the date. They had their annual family trustees meeting every year, where they go over charity donations, and I think John said, "I want to have the trustees meeting at the Vineyard this year on this date. Make sure you're available." I told John to tell each friend they were the only friend that's been invited so that they wouldn't talk to each other about it. No one had any idea who was and wasn't invited.

John Perry Barlow

John called me up and he said, "Listen, Barlow, I'm gonna tell you this and I know you've got a big mouth, but you can't tell anybody. You gotta promise me and if you won't promise me then I'm not gonna tell you." I don't break promises and he knew that. I said, "Okay. I promise you." Then he said, "We're gonna get married." I said, "Well, I knew that." I knew when they started talking baby talk to one another, if they weren't married, they would be shortly.

RoseMarie Terenzio

John didn't talk about the wedding that much—he was more focused on planning his honeymoon trip to Turkey. John just thought, "As long as it's on Cumberland, it's going to be amazing."

Narciso also made Carolyn's dress for the rehearsal dinner. It was a version of her wedding gown—a nude-color slip dress, embellished with crystals. Honestly, it was the most beautiful slip dress. A bias-cut tank dress with very subtle beading all over it. And the shoes were Manolo. They were just plain white strappy sandals. One thin strap across the toes with a slingback.

Sasha Chermayeff

Only a few family members were invited. Caroline and her family, one family member representing each of his father's siblings—Bobby Jr. and his wife, Mary Richardson; Tim Shriver; William Kennedy Smith. . . . His cousin Anthony was his best man, but Lee Radziwill wasn't invited. How did he resolve that? *Anthony's my best man, but his mom is not coming to my wedding.* I think if his mother had been alive, I think out of respect for how that would have looked, he would have asked his mom what she wanted him to do. But without his mom there, he clearly didn't give a shit. Carolyn did say to him, "Are you sure? Is this crazy not to invite her?" And the answer was, I'm not inviting her.

She never referred to herself as his aunt. It's *Lee Radziwill.* He was wonderfully not in that world. Lee was not around John much.

I think that John's mother was acutely aware of the fact that Anthony didn't get proper mothering, either. And she tried to make up for it when Anthony was going through his cancer the first time. And then Mrs. O found him a doctor when he was diagnosed with testicular cancer. She took a lot of responsibility for him.

Lee was not loving, caring, drop everything, my son has a very painful kind of cancer. She was just absent. And I don't think John liked her for that. She was more "I have a plane to catch, I have parties to go to, and I need new clothing from Yves Saint Laurent. I have a couture fitting. . . ." Not there. That colored John's perspective. That's why she wasn't at the wedding, that's why she was never there on the Vineyard. She was never a part of their life, from my perspective. Maybe she was at some of the Christmas parties. Not day-to-day.

RoseMarie Terenzio

I think part of the reason why John didn't invite Lee to the wedding was because he didn't trust that she would keep the confidence—that's what he said. He knew she would not abide by their wishes, and that would blow the whole thing. And the funny thing is, that Christmas after the wedding, they exchanged gifts, Carolyn and Lee at their apartment. Carolyn gave her a Hermès blanket and Carolyn opened her gift from Lee and it was a box of clips from Duane Reade. Scrunchies and hair clips from Duane Reade—like Goody hair clips. Carolyn said, "I actually think this is hysterical." She was like, "You know what that was, don't you, honey? That was like 'Fuck you for not inviting me to your wedding. How dare you." Because I'm sure Lee, who was all about appearances, was embarrassed that she wasn't invited to John's wedding.

On September 20, the day before the ceremony, I went to the apartment, and we were going over last-minute details. I said goodbye and Carolyn said to me, "I feel really bad—I feel like we're leaving you behind." I laughed and said I don't want to go. They had invited me, but I knew there was going to be a media frenzy and I needed to stay in New York to deal with it, not be on a remote island with no Wi-Fi or cell phones. They started laughing. They had gotten tickets to Paris, for me and a friend, to thank me, and I could leave a few days after the wedding. After the press died down. Little did we know.

George Kyriakos

When we got to the island they gave us these coins—these buffalo nickels to carry around—because there was so much security at the wedding and we'd have to show them to get around. I still have mine. They were from a rare year and everybody had them.

Gogo Ferguson

We had a wonderful cookout on the beach after guests started to arrive. Then the rehearsal dinner was on the upstairs porch of the Greyfield Inn. It was absolutely beautiful, and the speeches were incredible. Dave and I got up and welcomed everyone. When Teddy got up and said, "John, your parents would be so proud of you for choosing this place to be married," it was so moving.

Sasha Chermayeff

It felt small enough to have this really fun, intimate feeling from the minute we all got there until the minute we all left.

The rehearsal dinner night, Carolyn was in a very good mood. John put me next to him at the table. And he whispered to me, "This is where my mother would've sat." The dinner was set up on this beautiful big porch. I remember giving a toast and talking about my seeing Carolyn for the first time and just being so blown away by her and I had such a strong feeling that she would be the one that he would be in love with.

I told the story how, at my own wedding, John kept saying to me, "How did you know Phil was the one?" He was asking me over and over. "How do I know?" I said. "I just know that he's my man. I can't tell you why, but I do. I'm just sure in my bones." And I remember John was so excited that such a possibility could happen to him—that he would have somebody. I felt like Carolyn was that woman. I loved her—I thought she was so great because she just wasn't going to crumble under the pressure. I mean, who knew. . . . It got complicated.

Carolyn was nervous, and then the next day, the day of the wedding, she was out of sight. We were playing on the beach—Carolyn was not there, but we were all very warm, friendly, very comfortable, just messing around and playing with John's nieces.

George Kyriakos

John slept in my then-wife Jackie's and my room the night before the wedding on a cot. Which is crazy—there was this huge mansion where everybody had rooms and John was sleeping on a cot in our room. It was the whole don't-sleep-with-the-bride-the-night-before-the-wedding thing.

Robbie Littell

I remember seeing all three of them together at Carolyn and John's wedding—the Bessette sisters. They were like the Fates. And the mom was a toughie. She was like a herd rider. She was the toughest thing out there. The dad, not so much in the picture. But they were a force of nature, the Bessettes.

"She looked like a calla lily"

RoseMarie Terenzio

I think Carolyn did her own makeup for the wedding. She never wore that much makeup—a sheer moisturizer foundation and probably a little eyeliner and mascara and her favorite Bobbi Brown Ruby Stain lip color. She always did her makeup—I never remember having her hair or her makeup done for events.

Gogo Ferguson

On the day of the wedding, we had our pickup trucks, and you know, everyone's decked out. John wanted to be married in the First African Baptist Church on the north end of the island. This island is almost twenty miles long. I had everyone in my family driving people. We had a cargo line of trucks going up the beach at low tide with everyone dressed up, sitting in the back. We had to put all the Chippendale dining room chairs in the back of these pickup trucks so they wouldn't have to sit on the truck floor. We drove sixteen miles in pickup trucks because he wanted to get married in that church.

The night or two before, I called the Candler family—they founded the Coca-Cola Company and they have a property on the north end of the island. And I asked Mary Warren [Candler] if John and Carolyn could change in one of the houses beforehand. Getting that dress on took an hour because it was so cut on the bias and so fitted. It was like pouring cream over her body. She looked like a calla lily. Narciso was trying to sort of sew her into the dress. We were all in such a hurry 'cause we were so late to get to the church. I didn't sense that she was nervous at all—she was excited.

RoseMarie Terenzio

The neckline was too tight to get over her head, so Narciso had to open it and then re-close it. She had gone for two fittings. But I think the dress wasn't fully made yet and then when they put the finishing touches on, Carolyn was thinking, "It'll be fine." She wasn't going to fly back to Paris for another fitting. But that's what took so long. And then when she got dressed that day, they put a scarf over her head to slip the dress on. To not mess up her hair and not get makeup on the dress.

George Kyriakos

I was doing her hair and everything. We were in the room with Carolyn's friend Jules and Carolyn, and her sister was working on the dress, and we were just all hanging out on the bed and talking and stuff. That was really beautiful. Nothing really made Carolyn sweat—she was not nervous at all. Her mother was there and I think that that was a little tense. But any mother can make a daughter tense. She was super happy.

We got ready at this house that wasn't part of the hotel. There was a woman who worked there, a domestic worker for the family that let us use the house. She was dressed in a white uniform. She is like, "Mr. Kennedy, it's so nice to meet you. You and your family have done so much for my people." John's like, "You wanna come to the wedding?" And she's like, *What?* He invited her and she sat in the front row. But he didn't invite the family that let us use the house, which I thought was so funny.

Gogo Ferguson

We finally get her dressed and John's forgotten his dad's cuff links. So Dave's driving, God knows how fast, down the beach to try to find those at the inn. We finally get it together and I get Carolyn in my pickup truck and she's in the back seat on her knees with her hands on the front seat, so she doesn't sit down and wrinkle the dress at all. And we're bouncing down this road to the church.

George Kyriakos

The crazy thing when we were driving, there was a reporter who had tried to sneak onto the island, but he was literally going through alligator-infested swamps, and he just surrendered. He put his hands up and he surrendered because he was so fucked-up from going through the swamp. He just said, "Please just arrest me. I need to get outta here."

Gogo Ferguson

Everyone's been waiting like an hour and a half for the ceremony to start. . . . Finally, we got to the church and it was just the most beautiful ceremony.

Carolyn had tiny beautiful Bibles on all the seats that had the date of the wedding. I still have mine and a little straw fan. It was very hot, so she had little straw fans for everyone.

We lit the church with all the candles and flashlights we had because by the time we got her in her dress and I drove her down the road in my truck, it was getting dark. There was no electricity in the church. It was beautiful. I mean that one photograph of them standing at the altar—so beautiful. Everyone was very quiet inside the church. We were all in the moment and just joyous at the end. We all applauded after they said their vows, and I think we all sang along to "When the Saints Go Marching In."

The day before, word had started to spread and paparazzi started trying to pay people who had boats to get them to the island. There were helicopters and reporters and photographers paying loads of money to get over on a boat and then off-load into the marsh. But no one ever got a picture.

I just remember when it was over, driving down the beach, Maurice Tempelsman was just saying, "This place is exquisite." By then, the sheriff's department was notified. I think they drove John and Carolyn back into the inn compound. The entire compound was lit with white paper sandbags with candles, and just driving in, it was one of those moments that you just want to hold on to for the rest of your life. Just the whole idea that we actually pulled the whole thing off.

We were sort of in a hurry to get down to the inn for the reception. . . . So I think everyone sort of rushed into pickup trucks and to get there before the tide came in. I do remember that there was incredible heat, and lightning just pulsating, and everyone was just in awe of how beautiful it was driving down the beach at dusk.

At the reception, we had a DJ. I remember my little stepdaughter trying to teach Teddy the Macarena—it was pretty funny.

Sasha Chermayeff

And then when we were all eating dinner and cutting the cake, Carolyn let her hair down, which was a classic thing with her. It was literal with her. Her hair was either up or down. And it had a lot of relationship to how she was feeling. I remember her nervousness, and when the whole thing was done, we were clapping our hands together, like a pair of high fives. "Wow!" They had just tied the knot.

One thing was strange. I didn't feel like her circle was very well represented. It was just kind of a weirdly John-centric wedding.

RoseMarie Terenzio

Carolyn's circle of friends was small, and it was a group that she trusted. Most of them she had come up with through Calvin. She didn't have as big of a circle as John—because he was John Kennedy.

Carole Radziwill

Ed made a toast and he said, "Politics plus fashion equals passion." He had a T-shirt made that said that on it and he showed it to everyone. Carolyn's mom also gave a toast at the rehearsal dinner and it was sort of a cautionary tale. Something like, I hope my daughter has the strength to handle all of this.

Gogo Ferguson

John and Carolyn stayed at our house that night after the wedding. Someone had the great idea of putting rose petals all the way up our driveway and into our bedroom, which ended up a complete mess. They decided that was gonna be the honeymoon suite. We kicked someone out of the guest room so we could have a place to sleep. It was hysterical. And then pretty much everyone left the next day, but I do remember Carolyn, John, Dave, myself, and Christiane Amanpour sitting watching CNN the next morning and, of course, the phones were ringing off the hook. Our cell phones, because we don't even have real phones down there, trying to find out where Christiane was, 'cause they thought she was on Cumberland Island. And Mike Wallace was calling me saying, "Gogo, pick up the phone right now and tell me what's going on." None of us called anyone [back].

They were thrilled that they pulled it off. It was such a complete shock. I remember my cousin and Dave flew John and Carolyn to Tampa instead of Miami because there were thunderstorms, and then they had to find their way to Miami to leave for Istanbul. I remember John standing in the doorway of the plane and he just said, "This was absolutely extraordinary."

Robbie Littell

I will never understand why he gave us underwear as a gift—boxer shorts. I thought that he put his initials on them so that we would wear 'em to bed with our wives. But in fact, it was our initials. But still, it's a weird thing. Little skimpy silk underpants.

RoseMarie Terenzio

I'm guessing that was Carolyn's idea.

Robbie Littell

Mine didn't fit so good. Two sizes too small. It was probably an insult on purpose.

RoseMarie Terenzio

The next morning, we were working to finalize the press release. The plan was to release it after they left the island for the honeymoon. I was connected to Melody Miller and Jeannie Kedas, who both worked for Teddy. Teddy's office was doing the press release. There was no press office for John—or for Carolyn. I was the press office. So, the next morning, Jeannie and I were on the phone finalizing everything. I think it was seven o'clock in the morning and we were going over last-minute additions.

But before we could get the press release out, Patrick Kennedy breaks the news at a press conference he's at around ten o'clock. And he says, "For those of you who were wondering, my cousin John did tie the knot yesterday. . . ." We wanted to make sure that they had left the island before news got out, and then Patrick blabbed and Jeannie called me and we were like, "Fuck, I can't believe he opened his mouth." And then she was scrambling to get out the release. As soon as I hung up with her, my phone just exploded.

Later that morning, they were still on Cumberland. Carolyn and I were giggling on the phone and she was saying, "Oh my God, this is so crazy." And then we talked about the photo. They were asking me which photo to release. Carolyn said, "Denis Reggie's going to send you options for the photo. What do you think?" They were kind of similar, but she said, "Well, I trust you. Whichever one you pick is fine." John didn't know Patrick had blabbed and I didn't mention it. The photo—I mean, it's ridiculously perfect. Carolyn coming down the steps looking at John while he's kissing her hand, the quaint church behind them . . . They look so happy, like a prince and a princess in a fairy tale.

And then John got on the phone and he was like, "I'm married now. You are going to have to listen to me. I'm a mister now—you call me mister from now on. . . ." And I said, "Oh God, shut up. No one even cares about you." He just started laughing.

After that, it was just nonstop. People, friends, reporters calling me and leaving messages on my home answering machine. And I just didn't pick up the phone. And then I finally went out with a friend, and I said, "John got married. . . ." And she was like, "What?" Because I told no one. Not my family, not my friends, not a soul.

Gogo Ferguson

He called us from Istanbul, and he said, "I don't know why I ever left Cumberland Island." Because it was very secure and private.

RoseMarie Terenzio

Back in New York the next week, I put out gifts John had left for the staff. A bottle of champagne for the women and a cigar for the guys. I put them out at around seven o'clock in the morning. Along with a note he wrote:

> *Well, while you were all here toiling away, I went and got myself married. I guess you'll all have to call me Mister now.*
> *As you guys can imagine, we had to keep it a secret, but thank you for all your hard work, and all that.*

Then the morning when he came back from the honeymoon, we had coffee and tea and juice and muffins and bagels and congratulations. John was on cloud nine, wearing his gold wedding band. He was so grown-up. I told him, "You look so old now. . . ."

Jon Macks, comedy writer for *The Tonight Show with Jay Leno*

Not long after John and Carolyn got married my friend Paul Begala said, "John Kennedy is giving a big speech to a bunch of advertisers for

George." There was a Nike connection. "He needs an opening joke or two—can he call you?" John called, we chatted, I probably sent him ten or fifteen jokes. He started his speech by saying, "You might've read that I got married recently." He said, "And this was a big decision in my life. Obviously I waited a while and . . . I needed a sign. So, I looked out the window of my hotel, and right outside was a huge billboard. A Nike ad that said, 'Just do it.' I said, 'Okay!' And that was it."

Gogo Ferguson

Caroline had a celebration dinner party for them at her apartment after they got back from their honeymoon. We flew up with the top of the wedding cake in our laps because they left it in the freezer at the Greyfield Inn and they wanted to have it for the dinner.

Jack Merrill

The dinner was mostly for friends who were not invited to the wedding. It was a classic Park Avenue dinner party with everyone seated in certain seats at round tables.

RoseMarie Terenzio

Caroline had given a nice toast. It was chill and relaxed. John and Carolyn were very casual. She wore a Prada black tank dress and a pearl necklace from John.

It was a sit-down dinner and there were maybe ten round tables. I went with my friend Frank Giordano. And I remember Caroline's son, Jack—he was three or four maybe—he was kind of running around and a little restless and Carolyn had taken him in her arms and went downstairs with him into the lobby, and there were paparazzi outside and they were taking pictures. She just took him downstairs, and I think Caroline was upset because she thought that Carolyn was being irresponsible. But she didn't go outside the lobby—she went down the elevator and then back up.

And Carolyn was shocked that Caroline would think that she would go downstairs intentionally and expose Jack to that. She was like, "I would never do something like that—I would never take him outside in front of the paparazzi." And that was a bit of a contentious thing. There were like three doormen and security in the front of the building—there was no way a photographer was gonna get inside that lobby. And Carolyn said, "It's not like I took him outside. I took him down the elevator and back up. I wasn't parading around the lobby with him." She was surprised at the reaction. It was tense.

We were shocked by the amount of paparazzi gathered outside. John and Carolyn thought once they were married, it would be—they're a married couple now. No big deal. He thought he was much more interesting as a bachelor, you know, who's he dating, who's he breaking up with? He thought it would die down, that it wouldn't be the same intensity.

Jack Merrill

I walked out with John and Carolyn that night and there were hordes of photographers out front—it looked like there were a hundred, and the lights flashing were blinding, and we couldn't see. Everything changed when John got married. The attention was way more intense. We were all surprised by it, John included. For the rest of us, we could choose not to be with John, but she couldn't choose and now it was directed at her. She wasn't just another girlfriend. She was stylish and beautiful and funny. And now she was Mrs. Kennedy.

CHAPTER 19

"It just escalated and escalated"

RoseMarie Terenzio

There was so much going on between '96 and '99. Carolyn left her job in the spring of '96—they would have expected her to wear Calvin Klein for red-carpet events with John, and *George*'s other advertisers wouldn't have been happy. She wore Yohji Yamamoto a lot because Yohji didn't advertise anywhere. Also, she was so busy planning the wedding and traveling with John for interviews, for advertisers. . . . He wanted her to go with him; they wanted to be together. And then her thing was "You want me to go out and get another job, but then I get dragged into 'Oh, we have to go to Milan because we have to meet with *George* advertisers, or we have to go to La Scala for the Biennale.'"

There was gonna be a lot of media and scrutiny over whatever she did next and she wanted to be sure it would be the right thing. She had to be careful it wasn't a job that was using her for the media attention. She had talked about doing documentary films.

She didn't know what she was going to do next, but it was not going to be fashion. After Calvin, she did not go to fashion shows. *Been there, done that.* And she was never one to order clothes off the runway. She was very high-low—there's a photo of her and John and she's wearing these brown corduroy flares from Cheap Jack's, the thrift store downtown, but her sweater was Prada.

She would still come by the office from time to time. She would huddle with Matt and they would go through ideas for how to style and shoot *George* covers.

A few of John's former girlfriends were still calling the office. He was still friends with Julie Baker. Carolyn knew that they were in touch. I mean, I don't know if he told her every single time Julie called the office.

Carolyn loved to tease John about being a heartthrob. One Valentine's Day—it might have been the first one after they were married—all of a sudden these flowers were delivered to the office, maybe seven bouquets. The notes were from all these beautiful women. "I love you. You're the best." From Pamela Anderson, and then bouquets from Amber Valletta, Claudia Schiffer, Cindy Crawford. . . . The office was full of roses, all different colors, all ordered by Carolyn. He thought it was hilarious.

Sasha Chermayeff

It looked from the outside that once she married John, Carolyn's own life disappeared. She's this fabulous girl. New York, Calvin Klein—the girl John had been waiting for. This whole downtown *I have my own life* kind of thing. . . . A woman who can handle his life. John took for granted that she understood. But her identity completely changed. She went from being the coolest girl in her circle but not famous, to being completely famous and subject to the whims and insults slung by the tabloid media.

She got off a plane after her wedding and was harassed by photographers. Everybody thought, "Get your shit together, girl. Look good and show up with a smile." She needed somebody to help her.

RoseMarie Terenzio

Carolyn never had a second to exhale after they got married. Even on their honeymoon in Turkey, photographers found them—they could never completely escape. Before John, she was not on society pages or photographed for magazines—she wasn't interested in it. She was private, and while she knew things would change when she marrried him, I don't think she expected it to be so aggressive.

Jim Rutenberg, New York *Daily News* staff writer

Right after the wedding I was asked by my editor to record a day in the life of the newlyweds. My colleague Virginia Breen and I are there bright and early waiting for Carolyn and John to come out. They walked to Bodega in Tribeca for breakfast and we followed them and decided it would be wise to hide behind this van. We both felt bad. We had the quote, unquote exclusive on their first breakfast, but who gives a shit? We also feel kind of silly hiding. It's one thing to stake out a dirty cop or a politician. This is two nice people trying to live their lives.

John walks out, and it's not clear at first what's happening. *Where's he going? Holy shit! He's coming to talk to us.* He comes and says, "Listen, you guys, I totally get you have a job to do. This is how my life is, but Carolyn has not lived with this and it's very upsetting to her. She's having a hard time. Just really do me a solid. Please, can you just tell your editors that you can't do it?" We are both like, *He is so right. We are so sorry.* We go to what then was a pay phone and call our editor and say, "This is wrong and we really shouldn't be doing this." And the answer was "What the fuck?! Get back there and stay on them." We're both sort of young and not gonna defy our bosses. We followed them to Square Diner. Then we realize that Carolyn has slipped out the back door. I run, and John's there on his bike and starts riding and then goes into the subway with his bike. We just let him go so we could say honestly that they had slipped us. I think the biggest scoop we got is they had scrambled eggs.

Gustavo Paredes

The paparazzi would always be in front of John and Carolyn's apartment. Monday through Friday was one van, Saturday and Sunday there were two vans. Usually between five and eight people on a normal day, up to twenty on the weekends.

RoseMarie Terenzio

It was so much worse than it had been with his other girlfriends—I mean, Daryl Hannah didn't marry the world's most eligible bachelor and take him off the market.

If the paparazzi saw her leave the house, she would be followed the whole day, and that freaked her out—that she had a tail on her. If she left by eight in the morning, she'd be okay. She'd call me and say, "I'm going out in the field today, honey, wish me luck."

One Christmas, she was out shopping and she's in a taxi and the driver said, "I'm letting you out here, too much traffic." She had all these shopping bags and she was like, "I'm not getting out." Carolyn Bessette Kennedy standing on the street with all her bags, trying to get another cab—can you imagine? He said, "Are you kidding me?" and she said, "No. Are you kidding *me*?" She locked the doors and said, "Just so you know, I have nowhere to be, so I can sit here all day," and he's like, "Lady, okay, I'll take you, I'll take you. . . ."

Steve Gillon

The paparazzi treated Carolyn horribly and she took a lot of her frustration out on John. He could have done more to help her. Why couldn't he hire someone to help handle the media and try to corral them in some way? He was brilliant in the deep end, so he thought Carolyn could do the same.

RoseMarie Terenzio

John never had security, neither did his mom when she lived in New York. Carolyn did not want to walk around with bodyguards, either. That would attract even more attention—that was so not her. She would have seen it as a further invasion of her privacy.

But her experience with the paparazzi was entirely different than John's. She wasn't a man. When she was alone, the paparazzi would bait her, get really close and say things like, "Carolyn, are you pregnant yet? Are you getting divorced?" They would shout, "Bitch," or worse to get a reaction for a photo. They would also get very close to her or walk backwards in front of her to try to stop her from walking so they could get a photo. She had worked in PR and was used to handling the media, but that was a controlled environment—paparazzi weren't chasing Calvin Klein down the street.

They'd never do any of that when John was around. He didn't see it. It was almost gaslighting.

Everyone kept saying, "If you just give one interview it will stop." That was ridiculous—it would have garnered more questions and more scrutiny. I remember Carolyn telling me that she saw Barbara Walters at an event and Barbara told her never to give an interview.

Sasha Chermayeff

John had the perspective of *It's not a big deal.*

RoseMarie Terenzio

He just didn't let that enter into his personal day-to-day. His birthright was all the privilege and the fame and the money, but the price for that . . . It had to be overwhelming and sometimes really hard. I think he chose to say, "I'm going to live my life on my terms, and whatever happens I'll deal with."

Jack Merrill

Before he met Carolyn, we were in his apartment downtown one day. Everyone had answering machines back then, there were no cell phones. And his phone rang. He would listen to who it was before he picked up. The machine started beeping as if someone were pressing the numbers on the phone. I said, "What's happening?" He said, "Oh, they're trying to break into my answering machine." It was an early scrambler that was being used to try to break in. He just unplugged the phone.

Another time a woman came by Naked Angels and said, "John is in grave danger and you have to tell him and I'm a psychic. If you don't tell him, then it's gonna be on your hands." I didn't want to tell him that some crazy woman stopped by, but if I didn't tell him, what if something happens? So I told him. He said, "It happens all the time. Just ignore it."

Shirtless Frisbee in Central Park with friend
Robbie Littell (left), June 6, 1997.

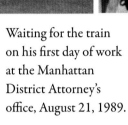

1

Waiting for the train
on his first day of work
at the Manhattan
District Attorney's
office, August 21, 1989.

John and friend Barbara
Vaughn on a white-water
rafting trip in Maine,
September 1989.

4

With
girlfriend
Christina
Haag in
1986.

3

Dancing with friend John Mosley at the
after-party for Robbie Littell's wedding,
April 13, 1991.

5

6

7

With friend Sasha Chermayeff, ca. 1991.

Prepping the kayaks with cousin Robert F. Kennedy Jr. on August 24, 1997, Hyannis Port.

8

9

With girlfriend Daryl Hannah at a holiday party in New York City, December 19, 1992.

Outside his Tribeca apartment on October 22, 1996.

Skiing with girlfriend
Julie Baker in Aspen,
ca. 1992.

In D.C. with his uncle Ted
Kennedy, May 4, 1994.

11

Taking a walk with his
dog Sam in Hyannis
Port after the death of
his grandmother Rose
Kennedy, January 1995.

Leaning in: with Caroline in 1977 (top) and 1995;
together with their mom in 1993.

13

14

15

With local fishermen in Ha Long Bay, Vietnam, 1998.

"Ladies and gentlemen, meet *George*": John strains to hear a question at the heavily attended press conference announcing the launch of his magazine, New York City, September 7, 1995.

A visit to Mount Rushmore, May 12, 1999.

Halloween 1995: channeling George Washington with friend Jack Merrill as his footman.

20

John and Carolyn arrive at the Kennedy Library for the Profile in Courage Award ceremony, 1998.

21

Dancing to Prince with RoseMarie Terenzio at *George*'s Christmas party, 1999.

With Carolyn off Martha's Vineyard, 1997.

22

23

At the *Vanity Fair* party after the White House Correspondents' Dinner, May 1, 1999.

John and Carolyn's wedding on September 21, 1996, on remote Cumberland Island, Georgia. Described as "the most iconic wedding image ever," this photograph by Denis Reggie is in the permanent collection at the Smithsonian's National Museum of American History.

Only one wedding photo was planned for release, but John was drawn to Denis Reggie's photograph of the exchanging of vows and included it in his editor's letter in *George*.

With Carolyn in Manhattan, 1996.

27

28

RoseMarie Terenzio

John did have boundaries when it came to the paparazzi, and he would enforce those boundaries in a very definitive way. Once, on a private beach in Hyannis, I think it was, there was a photographer who waited until John went into the water to swim, and then he came up to Carolyn on the beach and started harassing her. And John was like, "That's not cool. I walk away and so you go after my wife," or my girlfriend, whatever she was at the time. "If I'm walking down the street in New York City and you're a paparazzo, yeah, I'm fair game, but I'm on a private beach."

Eric Hyman, friend of John and Carolyn

I remember sailing with all of them in Hyannis Port. Eunice Kennedy Shriver was on the rudder. Carolyn was standing on the ship's deck, pulling ropes and moving sails with her long legs, wearing tan Levi's corduroys. John unceremoniously dove off the boat as it was cutting through the waves at considerable speed. I was shocked and I turned to everyone and said, "Man overboard, John just jumped off the ship!" Everyone just laughed and said, "Yeah he does that, he'll swim back to the beach to avoid the paparazzi." It seemed like we were miles from the shore. When I turned to look back a few seconds later, he was barely a small dot behind us, three hundred yards away.

RoseMarie Terenzio

I think she just wanted him to frickin' cop to it: "I'm not crazy, just give me the satisfaction of saying I'm right. They are out of control." But John felt responsible for it, so he was defensive. He'd say, "Get over it." I think he didn't want to feed into it. And that would frustrate her. She was hoping he would hold her hand, and that wasn't John.

Her friends were still partying and single and flying around and doing drugs; she was married and had a different life. I don't think she had someone she could call up and say, "I'm having a really hard time with this."

Sasha Chermayeff

John thought some of her fashion world friends were cretins. She almost never had a friend to the Vineyard. . . .

RoseMarie Terenzio

Fortunately, and unfortunately, the friend she could complain to became me. It was tough because I wasn't going to pick a side. I was just trying to get her and John to communicate.

Sasha Chermayeff

She genuinely felt she was in danger. The paranoia set in when she kind of let her mind spin off—*What if somebody wants to kidnap me?* After they got married, it just escalated and escalated and escalated. Every time she went out with their dog Friday, she was preoccupied with being followed. Either they were coming at her with the telephoto lens or they were right in her face. I knew the paparazzi that were outside of North Moore because I had been going there forever. I'd say hi to someone I'd known for twenty years and she was saying, "You can't talk to them—they're ruining my life."

John was five years older. And being followed, it's very different for a two-hundred-pound man than for a woman alone. He didn't have fears connected with being abducted. He didn't have paranoia that could go wild. By then she was thinking, *They're spying on me. They're stalking me. Now my life is being afraid. And now even cleaning up after my dog is going to be on the front page of the newspaper, and that's meant to be humiliating.*

Shortly after their marriage, maybe the following winter, she started to get really reclusive. John wanted me to get her out of the house. When we did go out alone, she was talking about her relationship problems. "How do you keep the fires going?" I said, "Why are you worried about that? You're probably still really hot and heavy. You've got a decade before your relationship transfers into something less hormonally driven." But what she was saying was *I am worried about it. I'm losing my connection to him.* . . .

How could I have missed that? I was so blinded by the side of me that just thought, who wouldn't be in love with John? And Carolyn is gorgeous, strong, interesting, funny. The best thing that ever happened to him. And then it crumbled.

Jack Merrill

All of a sudden, she couldn't leave the house. John was upset and he would try to get me to go out with her. One night he asked me to take her to a movie. We ended up having dinner at home. I always felt the tragedy with Carolyn was that she knew how to deflect that kind of attention when it was aimed at John, but she couldn't deflect it when it was aimed at her.

RoseMarie Terenzio

Toward the end, she *was* staying home a lot more during the day, and John was frustrated by that. They didn't have call-waiting, so he would try to reach her and the phone would be busy, so he knew she was home, talking on the phone. This caused tension because he wanted her to have a job or be doing something that would give her a purpose and get her out. She would call me sometimes to make sure I gave her a heads-up when he was on his way home, so he wouldn't notice that she was home all day. It became kind of a joke with us. "Honey, is he leaving soon? I gotta get my shit together because I don't want to get busted." We would laugh about it. I think he knew we were in cahoots sometimes.

That said, the whole thing about her never leaving the house is ridiculous. She went to all kinds of big events with John, she went to Hyannis or Martha's Vineyard every weekend, and I went out to dinner with her at least every other week.

"If she wasn't Jacqueline Kennedy Onassis, one could hardly blame her for that"

John Perry Barlow

The celebrity came quickly for Carolyn. It was much slower for Jackie, but it was a different kind of celebrity, too, because people were inclined to be favorably disposed to Jackie. For some reason, the press had decided they were not going to be favorably disposed to Carolyn. They were beating up on her without having any idea of who she was. If somebody was gonna steal our prince, they wanted her to be some kind of entirely unblemished princess.

Paul Begala

The one time I saw John lose his temper—I remember this very distinctly. I think while he was on his honeymoon, Maureen Dowd wrote a column which, as my memory serves, basically said John's late mother wouldn't have liked his new wife. I have reason to believe John knew his mother better than Maureen did! I talked to him on the phone and he was yelling. I can't remember the words but it was anger and f-bombs and *how dare she?* I think Maureen had sort of diminished Carolyn.

John Perry Barlow

Carolyn was magical and special. It didn't seem to matter. She was just somebody for them to chew up. The more she hid, the more valuable she would become and the more they would run a Wallis Simpson on her—they would just create this character. . . . It was cruel. It was heartless.

The woman you read about was crazy. The woman you read about wasn't kind—and she was. The homeless guy that made a shelter across the street from their place on North Moore, she always made sure he had food. People were trained to dismiss her as being a lightweight, and she was by no means a lightweight. I remember her as somebody that I turned my daughters over to to emulate, as an example of how to be a woman. She taught them a lot about fashion and design and style. And if she wasn't Jacqueline Kennedy Onassis, one could hardly blame her for that.

It was getting harder and harder [on their marriage]. How could it not? John started trying to get me to come around as often as possible just to have another person to talk to. She was a very bright but fragile person. Hell, nobody could tolerate that. I mean, John and Caroline could, but they've been raised by the best. I want people to know that Carolyn was poorly treated, undeservingly. . . . She was so quirky and imaginative and surprising, kind of eccentric. She was her own self. That was part of what made the press so ravenous to have at her. She wasn't gonna play anybody's game.

Amelia Barlow

It's hard for me to describe Carolyn to you. . . . When my sisters, Leah and Anna, and I were small, like seven or eight years old, my dad would just send us in a taxi, write the address of the apartment on our hands, and send us to Carolyn. We would order all this Chinese food and then we'd go down onto the street after we had eaten, and we would give the rest of it to the homeless people who she said were our guardian angels.

She had very specific people that lived on particular corners—those people were her protectors. We would give them food and look them in the eye and thank them for keeping us safe in New York. Those people were basically her security detail. And she was extending that web of protection to us girls. She taught us if you connect with them as people, they'll protect you and they'll be your allies when you need it the most.

Anna Barlow

When we were older she would take us to Bloomingdale's. I mean, it was just like totally stepping into this miraculous, beautiful New York experience that can't be more exciting as a thirteen-year-old girl. I remember we went to Kiehl's, and I was like, "I want to smell like you." And so she bought me her mixture. It was cucumber scent and something else. . . . I just loved it. I still sometimes get the cucumber scent from Kiehl's.

She was the first person to pluck my eyebrows. She was like, "Oh, honey, we are getting rid of this." But in a way that was so . . . If any other person did that, you might be like, "Did I not look okay before?"

We went home with clothes, makeup. I mean, as a young girl living in Wyoming, you're like, "Did I just meet a fairy person?"

Sean Penn

I met Carolyn at the White House Correspondents' Dinner in 1998 when I was *George*'s guest. One had heard a lot of claims of stridency and so on. And I just found her to be very warm. . . . I remember telling people after that night what a light Carolyn was. So alive and really authentic. I absolutely understood why he was crazy about this girl. And that's not what I had been told about her.

When people say Carolyn knew what she was getting into—if you fully understand what you're getting into, that means you've fully given up your innocence, which is not a fair expectation on anyone. It's what people who have not experienced it say, and it's what envious people say.

RoseMarie Terenzio

John's cousin Anthony had an aggressive form of cancer that started with a diagnosis of testicular cancer in the 1980s. By 1998, whenever he was in the hospital, whether in New York or D.C.—when he was at NIH—Carolyn would go and be there with him and his wife, Carole Radziwill. She'd go to one of his favorite restaurants, Il Cantinori on 10th Street, and bring him his favorite dishes. She took Carole on. *I have to get Carole through this. . . .*

Maybe it was a distraction. She had a way of taking on other people's problems—and that also meant not having to make a decision about her own life. What to do next.

Sasha Chermayeff

One thing about Carolyn, she knew the answers. This is how you look good in New York. This is what you say to a guy when he's being a dick. This is what you tell your boss. But she could not bring all of that wisdom and point it at herself, to deal with her fears.

CHAPTER 20

Under Pressure

"There were missteps"

RoseMarie Terenzio

In 1997, John's thirty-nine-year-old cousin Michael Kennedy was involved in this scandal with the family's fourteen-year-old babysitter. John was furious. He called me down to his apartment on a Saturday, because we knew Monday morning it was gonna be on the front page of every paper. He was like, "What the fuck, Rosie, can you believe this?" He was really mad. Just kind of like, *Here we go again.* Another cousin, Michael's oldest brother, Joe, had recently filed to annul his marriage to his wife, Sheila Rauch—after thirteen years. John wrote an editor's letter: "Two members of my family chased an idealized alternative to their life. One left behind an embittered wife, and another, in what looked to be a hedge against mortality, fell in love with youth and surrendered his judgment in the process. Both became poster boys for bad behavior. . . ."

The cover was Kate Moss as Eve, in the Garden of Eden, and Kate was naked. John thought for his editor's letter, what if he appeared as Adam?

Matt Berman

He was in his underwear pretending to be naked. It was just from the waist up, it wasn't anything risqué. We hung an apple down in front of him. That was his sense of humor.

The film went missing—we ended up having to publish the Polaroids of the shoot. I actually worked with the photographer, Mario Sorrenti, again a few years ago and I asked if they'd ever found it and he said, "We never figured it out." It's still a mystery.

RoseMarie Terenzio

It looks like John's naked in the picture. That was the first headline: "JFK Jr. Naked..."

Keith Kelly, media columnist

I was at the *Daily News* at the time and I wrote that he was nude and it was in bad taste. He sent me a handwritten note back and it said, "Dear Keith, Nude is nude. That was not nude. Perhaps you spent too much time in Catholic School." He signed it John Kennedy and in parentheses, "Not John-John." The *Daily News* always referred to him as "John-John."

Steve Gillon

The editor's letter was a jumble of convoluted thoughts that really made sense only to John. He expressed frustration with his cousins' transgressions, but the real villain in his eyes was the media and its "ferocious condemnation of their excursions beyond the bounds of acceptable behavior." His point was that the world rewards rule following and stifles the passions that make us human—a problematic position considering that an affair with a fourteen-year-old is statutory rape.

The letter was so unclear that the firestorm of criticism he received was not for having defended his family members, but for calling them out. The *Guardian* called it "a vicious attack on the conduct of two of his cousins."

RoseMarie Terenzio

His cousins took the letter as a shot. Joe was on the front page of the tabloids saying, "Ask not what you can do for your cousins, but what you can do for your magazine." They were on the phone yelling—I could hear them. I'm sure half his family was pissed off at him on the RFK side.

Gustavo Paredes

A week later, we're all at the Cape together. Joe came through those gates looking for John—I was like, "Oh, I know what *he's* here for." And then Joe has got a temper. They talked outside. John apologized. He realized he should have navigated [the whole thing] better. But John also said he had to address it. He said, perhaps I should have worded some things differently. "I know we're family, but I had to write about it." But Joe remained seething for another year. And yes, it was a big deal.

Biz Mitchell

There were a lot of things that John just didn't want to touch in the magazine, and I argued with him. The biggest one: the death of Princess Diana.

RoseMarie Terenzio

After Diana died, the *George* editors were thinking, *We should take the whole issue apart*. John disagreed. *We're a monthly, so it's not like we were gonna break news*. And there was a hesitation—he felt it would become about him and the paparazzi. "Do you think you're next? Are you and Carolyn afraid?" She was saying to John, "See, I'm not blowing this out of proportion. They're dangerous."

Celebrities were going on TV and talking about the stalkerazzi, bemoaning their plight, but he found that disingenuous. John felt that the more scrum you had around you—security guards, a publicist, a manager—that created some of that momentum of being pursued. Instead of talking about Diana with the editors, he started cleaning out his office files, throwing them into a big dumpster. I think he thought, *This is going to push my wife over the edge even more.*

Steve Gillon

Her death exposed the kinds of unique tensions he faced as an editor. One of his colleagues said he had an emotional reaction to it. It was an important story to cover, but John hesitated.

Biz Mitchell

I told him you can't just completely ignore it. He was mad at me for pushing it. In a fury, essentially. I said, "It's a major story." And he's like, "I don't think it matters." Matt ended up doing a photo essay.

Seamus McKeon

We were in Hyannis Port the day of Princess Diana's funeral. John did not say much. He just kept playing the Rolling Stones, "You Can't Always Get What You Want." Carolyn, let's just say she was in a world of her own. The two of them seemed to be on different wavelengths.

Kathy McKeon

John always played the Rolling Stones over and over—"You Can't Always Get What You Want." I always wondered, why does he play that? Because he got everything he wants. But that's how he felt.

John put me at the top of the table that weekend, that's where Madam sat, and asked, "Kath, could you tell my wife how my mom took care of the photographers? All she did was go out the gate and give them a nice smile, and they left her alone. Carolyn, do you hear that? That's what you're supposed to be doing." He said, "Carolyn, you're treating them all wrong." She said, "I'm terrified of them."

Seamus McKeon

She told a story about them cornering her and chasing her to the building and she said, "They were right on top of me." John was very much like, "Get on with it."

Biz Mitchell

In 1998, John didn't want to cover Bill Clinton and Monica Lewinsky. He thought the whole thing was being blown out of proportion. It's an affair, like, so what? He was straight-out mad about it. He felt that if you're going to take away politicians' private lives . . . He didn't want to give it more air.

Steve Gillon

When President Clinton was getting impeached, he was furious. He would say things like "What about Clinton's record in office?" I think there was some transference going on—it was exactly how he'd always felt about the way people used his father's personal failings to attack him politically. The editors could tell that John was uncomfortable. There was a lot of uncertainty about how to deal with the impeachment, and how to approach John. It was awkward that *George* was not dealing with it at all.

RoseMarie Terenzio

He told me that if he covered that story, it would become about him because of his father's reputation. He said the details made public by the prosecution in the *Starr Report* were in bad taste and it really read like a salacious novel rather than an examination of the facts. We got a lot of criticism for not covering that.

Lisa DePaulo

Right after the scandal, I had this idea because there were rumors that Bill Clinton had a fling with [former vice president Walter Mondale's daughter]

Eleanor Mondale. The idea was that she would've been the perfect mistress: she grew up in politics, she knew not to talk, but she was also really hot. My editor said, "Are you kidding? John would lose all respect for me." But John and I had a meeting scheduled, so I told him my idea. He said, "I love it! Do it." As I was walking out of his office, he said, "By the way, you might encounter some of my cousins in your research."

RoseMarie Terenzio

We were being criticized all the time. *George* was called "the political magazine for people who don't understand politics." *Spy* described it as "scrambling for celebrities 'with tits' as often as possible to put on the cover and then trying to figure out what that person had to do with politics."

Keith Kelly wrote a piece for the *New York Post* with the headline "Mag Run by Hunk Now in a Funk" about declining ad dollars. One day John told me, "You can't be famous and good-looking and smart. I can't do anything about being famous and good-looking, so I guess smart had to go."

Joe Armstrong

He was definitely disappointed as the hoopla went down.

Abigail Pogrebin, journalist

I came up to the *George* office to interview John for *Brill's Content*, a magazine that covered the media. There was always this narrative of whether he was really smart or he was being propped up by his legacy. His answers were fluid and nuanced and he had a command of the vision for the magazine. It was clear that he was running the show.

The *Brill's Content* piece took him seriously, but there was always . . . Obviously the press needs the angle, and the angle I really remember with *George* was: Is this fluffy? Is this substantive? Does he really know what he's doing?

Peter Kiernan

At the time I was running the media and communications group at Goldman Sachs and I was working on *George*. There were missteps with the magazine, but for every misstep, there's a visit to interview Fidel Castro. My God, genius. What they had with John was lightning in a bottle.

John was aware that the magazine was not fully living up to expectations after the first couple of issues. So much of the pressure and the weight were on him. He was frustrated, but he was very determined to make it work. No matter how convivial and sort of goofy he was on the outside, he was a serious man.

He was doing so many jobs that were an obscene waste of his time—he was getting sucked into the minutiae. He was not completely comfortable negotiating budgets. . . . I remember coming in to see him a couple of times, one time where he'd been up most of the night, and of course I'd slept well and I looked like hell, and he looked fabulous and he'd had no sleep.

Steve Gillon

Carolyn, because she had no other outlet, would come over to *George* and start getting involved. Michael Berman was upset that she was making creative decisions that John had hired a professional staff to make decisions about. He felt that John was deferring too much to Carolyn—there were two partners, not three. Michael would say, "I don't bring my wife to work, I don't have her chime in on what she likes about the cover. So why should he?" I don't think he did anything to hide his disdain for Carolyn. And John deeply resented Berman's effort to control him.

RoseMarie Terenzio

John and Michael had this idea to do a *George* TV show similar to *Politically Incorrect*. Initially, the TV execs they were speaking to assumed John would host. That was never gonna happen. They started to look for other hosts. John was on board with that, but then he quashed the idea entirely—I don't know why—and he didn't discuss it with Michael. When Michael found out, he felt betrayed and he was pissed. That added to the strain. In Michael's vision, *George* would become a media company with a TV show, a website ... more than a magazine. John felt like he had to make the magazine a success before he could even go there.

Steve Gillon

The battle between Carolyn and Michael kept escalating. She was calling Michael and shouting, saying he had no idea how stressful life was with John and that the magazine was keeping him away from home. The calls became more frantic and more heated, and at one point she yelled at Michael, saying that John would be more successful without him. By early 1997, things had grown so tense that Michael and John had a loud shouting match over the TV deal—one of many fights they'd had in recent months. They ended their partnership and John bought out Michael's 25 percent stake in the magazine.

"He was so close with his sister, and then they were not speaking"

Steve Gillon

From the beginning, John felt that Caroline didn't like the fact that he was involved with this magazine. But the real tension was with Ed. The first issue between them was the auction of their mother's goods after she died. They needed to pay taxes—a lot of money—on Martha's Vineyard, so they needed to sell a lot of items. John wanted a private auction—he didn't want the media attention of a public auction. Ed thought a public auction would raise more money, and rightly so. What John resented was that Ed was making the decision—he believed that he and Caroline were the only people who should make decisions related to the family. And he resented that Caroline delegated some of that responsibility to Ed.

Joe Armstrong

I remember John asked me how I felt about the auction, and I said, "It's the opposite of who Jackie was." He said, "I'm leaving the country when that happens."

RoseMarie Terenzio

The few conversations John and I had about the auction were *It's what his mom had wanted*; he and Caroline had already picked out what they wanted. But he didn't want to deal with the media hype: *Why are you selling your mother's furniture?*

Caroline was kind of annoyed because it was hard to pin him down to make decisions. She was handling most of the details, attending the meetings at Sotheby's, and he kind of left it to her. He was doing his best to ignore the whole thing.

I think they both left town. John went to Europe for *George*—it was deliberate. Before he left, he dropped an envelope in my purse. I didn't find it until I got home that night. The note read, "Thanks for all your help. . . . Don't get used to it. It's not every day that we sell Mummy's shoes." It was a bonus—$1,000. That was a lot of money.

Sasha Chermayeff

The whole story about John and Ed really starting to not get along at all . . . Problems got worse after the inheritance, even down to redecorating. What if you don't want to redecorate your mom's house on the Vineyard? You don't want Ed Schlossberg posters taking the place of the Thomas Hart Benton? That was the feeling.

Steve Gillon

The other issue between John and Ed was this HBO documentary—Ed told them that John would narrate it, and John just flipped out over that.

RoseMarie Terenzio

Ed had made some sort of deal with HBO executive vice president Richard Plepler to be an executive producer. The documentary was planned around the anniversary of the assassination—John and Caroline never did anything around the anniversary of the assassination. . . . John was mad because they had basically proposed him as the narrator. Without asking him. Not only would he never have done it, he certainly never would've done it with Ed as the executive producer. I think I still have the note from John to Plepler. It was like, "Who the fuck is *Ed* to decide? It's my father. He doesn't get to decide."

He met with Caroline and Ed and blasted her. He said to me, "I didn't even look at him. I directed everything at her as if he wasn't even in the room." He said, "If you wanna give your father's legacy over to him, that's your business. But it's my father, too. And Ed doesn't get to decide what I do and when I do it." That was the big fight.

Steve Gillon

I was in the office one time when he was screaming at her on the phone. I heard him say, "You wouldn't do this if Mummy were still alive."

Robbie Littell

John saw Ed as the milkman—milking the family name. I know that HBO thing drove him crazy; he kept bringing it up. I never said anything back. Because that is the rule: someone tells you something bad about their sibling, it's their right to say something, but you're not allowed to say anything bad about them.

I think his sister saw the name as a brand more. Because she was very much like, "Don't use the name." And why did she say that? Because *she* wanted to use the name.

RoseMarie Terenzio

Ed wasn't very friendly. He was cold and dismissive. I remember John telling me that he went to some sort of book party for the literary agent Esther Newberg. Ed ignored him. John went to say hello to him, and he walked away.

Jack Merrill

Ed Schlossberg blew me off on the street once and John used to make me act it out because it made him laugh. Caroline and Ed had come to a Naked Angels benefit and I was talking to Ed. The next day, I was walking to the gym and ran into him. So I said, "Hey, Ed, Jack from Naked Angels last night. I want to thank you for the donation and for coming to the benefit." He blew me off like he was some big star and just says, "Yeah, nice to see you," like I was bothering him. John would say, "Remember when you saw Ed on the street? Do that again." He thought it was hilarious.

Sasha Chermayeff

John thought Ed was entitled, and he was driving a wedge between him and his sister. John was so close with his sister, and then they were not speaking. Up until that point, nobody drove a wedge between John and his sister, and John resented the hell out of that. Carolyn was like, *Fuck them. They belittle you, they boss you around.* She was going to amp that up, because her thing was protection.

John was sticking with Carolyn. Caroline was sticking with Ed. The rift was a deep wound.

RoseMarie Terenzio

Around 1999, John and Caroline were splitting up the furniture from the Hyannis house, their parents' house. That was considered John's house—he spent most of his summer in Hyannis. There were two highboys that belonged to his father and she wanted both, I think. Caroline was say-

ing she wanted almost all of her mother and father's stuff. John felt that
was unfair.

Christiane Amanpour

I spent a lot of time around both John and Caroline. They had a really profound and important existential bond between them. There was a deep, deep
love. Which does not mean that, like any siblings, they didn't have their dis-
agreements, their arguments. I'm sure Caroline thought he was a pain in the
ass a lot. You know, John could always be late. But deep down, when it matters, they were very, very close.

"In the shadow of death"

Jack Merrill

Billy Way. Billy Wayward, that's what I used to call him. That's when we all
ran around. Later he was completely broke. He became a drug addict.

RoseMarie Terenzio

John's Brown friend Billy Way was one of those people who called the office
all the time. John would play tennis with him at Town Tennis—Billy was a
star tennis player from a prominent family in Bermuda. I didn't have a sense
of Billy's issues at first. I just remember one day John telling me that he was
arrested, I wanna say in Puerto Rico for possession of marijuana, and he was
in prison. Teddy's office helped find an attorney in Puerto Rico to get him
out of jail.

Robbie Littell

Billy's lifestyle pushed a lot of people away. Sometime in '96 we had an intervention for him. It was an absolute disaster. John brought Bobby Jr. in. It
took him forty-five minutes to tell all these horror stories—you know, he
was supposed to be the intervention expert. He told his stories, we're all sit-

ting there with our jaws on the ground, going, "Oh my God, how is that man alive?" Billy said, "See, I'm fine. *I* don't have a problem." We ended up going out for a beer.

Sasha Chermayeff

I don't know what exactly Billy Way was hooked on. John did try to help him get to rehab. Billy wasn't the only one, there were other people in John's life who were falling apart, that were really getting fucked-up with drugs and alcohol. People John really cared about. Then he gave up, because you can't cure somebody else's addictions.

RoseMarie Terenzio

I got a call from Robbie. John was at his therapy appointment. Robbie said, "Where's John? Billy was hit by a cab last night and he died." I panicked because I was afraid that if John came out of the appointment some photographer or reporter would run up and tell him. I called the shrink's office and said, "Please don't let him leave without calling me." John called. I said, "You need to come back right away." I didn't want to tell him on the phone, but he kept asking. I said, "Billy Way died."

He didn't come back right away. He went and identified the body. Then he went to Billy's apartment, and my guess is that he went because the police were gonna go in and he wanted to make sure there was nothing sensitive or anything that would hurt Billy's reputation. If his parents came to the apartment, he didn't want them to see anything that would upset them. The electricity had been shut off because Billy hadn't paid the bills and it was in complete disarray.

Robbie Littell

John was totally freaked out, just distraught. Because he was the one who identified Billy along with another friend. Just didn't look like his friend—he saw a monster. Billy had enough head trauma to create a monster.

I always felt bad that he did that. But he had a little distance from it, too. That distance was protective. It was like, *God, I saw this strange thing.*

Steve Gillon

In his brief life, John experienced more death than most people ever do. He was incredibly resilient through all the deaths he had lived through. The guy grew up in the shadow of death.

On December 31, 1997, John's cousin Michael Kennedy died in a skiing accident in Aspen.

Sasha Chermayeff

Michael's death—such a horrible death. So stupid. Can't you just go skiing, you have to play competitive football while you're downhill skiing at high speeds? Bobby was throwing the football and Michael was going to catch it, and he smashed into the tree and died on impact.

Bobby said that was the most horrific thing he'd ever been through. He's been through a lot of traumas. He was fourteen when his father was assassinated. Two years later, he was into hard drugs. Mary, his wife at the time, told me that Ethel would only say one thing to the kids after the assassination: "Move a muscle, change a thought." The kids were taught, do not let yourself sit around and weep. You move a muscle, and you change a thought. That was the mantra. Michael was married, there was an affair—there were a lot of damaged goods. And John was just somehow removed from that.

RoseMarie Terenzio

I also think John's mother wasn't going around saying, "Move a muscle, change a thought."

Sasha Chermayeff

And then Michael's death had come on the heels of the poster boys for bad behavior letter John had written for *George*. John was getting shit for having done that.

RoseMarie Terenzio

Both he and Carolyn were really upset. Michael had young kids and so much was left unresolved between him and his wife, his family, his kids.

Sasha Chermayeff

I remember John and Carolyn just going, *Oh my God, it's bleak*. I remember people saying, *Another tragedy*. But the worst was yet to come.

Gary Ginsberg

After Michael died, John and I had this conversation. In just the last four years, he had lost his mom, a really close friend, and now his cousin. I was like, "Man, you take death better than anybody I know. How do you do it?" And he said something like "Because we have suffered so much death, I learned. I trained myself to never wallow." I think that's why he never commemorated anniversaries of assassinations or deaths. Only birthdays. His constant mantra on death was *I cannot let it get to me*. And he didn't.

RoseMarie Terenzio

When my best friend Frank Giordano died, John said, "When you lose someone like that, there's a growth in the loss and you just have to hang on to that little nub of green that's gonna grow into the next phase of your life."

Frank died of an accidental overdose in 1998. We were all friends. John was away the week Frank died. When he got back, he came straight to my office and closed the door. I started to cry and he was hugging me. I told him the whole story. Frank was HIV positive and constantly wondering when he would get sick. He'd been partying a lot, but I was not aware that his drug use was so out of control.

John said, "He's your Billy Way." John had this thing—you don't banish people because they're not doing the right thing. He'd tried not to judge Billy. I didn't judge Frank, I just tried to love him. He also told me, "Don't glamorize him. Don't glamorize the dead." Remember them for who they were—the good and the bad. If you glamorize them, you're not really remembering the whole person.

Carolyn came over to my apartment and just hugged me, and then the next day she drove me to Bronxville to Frank's mom's. She also drove me to Frank's funeral. She met my family. She was sitting on the steps with my sister Anita, outside the funeral home. Carolyn said to me, "God, I love your sister. Her skin is amazing. But boy, she could talk your legs off your body...."

That Christmas, Carolyn came to my apartment and gave me this little gold band from Tiffany. I still have it. It had a teardrop with little diamonds that dangled off of it. And she gave me this note. This is from December 20, 1998.

Dear RoseMarie,

I wanted you to have something that helps you rejoice in your friendship with Frank. The diamonds are the tears you will cry forever in his absence.

"There is nothing lost that can't be found if sought." Shakespeare.

Look for love. Open your heart and you will see miracles everywhere.

RoseMarie, you are loved. So very much. XOX CBK and JFK.

CHAPTER 21

Off-Hours

"Anything could happen"

Jack Merrill

Whenever John called and said, "What are you doing tomorrow night?" you knew it would be something great. He would call me often at the last minute. "Can you go to the Knicks tomorrow night?"

It was April 1998 and we were sitting in John's courtside seats. As soon as we sat down, there was a commotion behind us and someone's calling out, "John, John," and he says to me, "Who is that? Would you look over your shoulder?" I look over and it's Donald Trump, and John is like, *Oh God*. He ignored him.

At halftime, the guy sitting to John's right disappeared. Trump then sat in his seat and all of a sudden photographers showed up. He was trying to talk to John. John was very well-mannered, so he spoke to him for a short while, and then Trump left. When the other guy came back to his seat, he told us that Donald Trump paid him $2,000 cash so he could sit in that seat during halftime to get photos with John.

Another time he said, "We're going to a fight in Atlantic City." He had chartered this little plane to fly us forty minutes to Atlantic City. There was a town car on the tarmac in Atlantic City that took us to a Trump hotel. We got out of the car and there were all these guys, you know, gold chains, Jersey tough guys and rappers. John loved it. These guys in their New Jersey accent are yelling, "Jaaahn Kennedy, hiya!"

John's seats were midway up the arena, deep in the middle of everyone, which is exactly where he liked to be. He liked to be *in it*—no special treatment. He was so present and so unafraid of being thrown in the crowd that the crowd would always respond in a positive way. We're in with the guys and they're calling out, "Hey, Kennedy! How ya doing?" One of them yells, "Hey, Kennedy, my sister wants to fuck ya!" We just laughed.

All of a sudden, a guy worked his way down the row and said, "Mr. Trump would like to offer you seats ringside." We looked down and there's Donald Trump and Marla Maples. John looked at me as if to say, *Do you want to go?* and we knew we didn't want to. So he turns to the guy and says, "No, but thank you very much." The guys sitting around us are going crazy saying, "What, are you kidding me? Trump wants to give you ringside seats. Go sit with him!" So we get up and they take us all the way down to the front. Trump was off to the side doing something with Marla Maples. They sent waitresses over to get drinks for us.

Trump is now coming towards us with a whole gang of photographers. The crowd sort of surges in our direction and the waitress trips and the whole tray of drinks flies up in the air. John looks at me and goes, "You ready?" I said, "Let's go." We ran back to our seats and the lights are going down and the fight starts. Well, that was one of the shortest fights in history. I think it lasted less than sixty seconds. Riddick Bowe hit the other guy under the belt and the whole fight was called off. Everybody's screaming. We flew all the way to New Jersey! So everybody's mad, people are streaming out and we just sat there waiting for the crowd to move, and John's like, "Uh-oh." Donald Trump and Marla Maples have spotted us and they start heading up the aisle.

We run to the exits. We had about three hours to kill before we're flown back. So we went to the casino and neither one of us were big gamblers. We were just playing slots, and all of a sudden here comes Donald Trump and Marla Maples *again*, and they're waving and yelling, "Hey, you guys, wait up." We took off and hid. Rolling around and hiding behind slot machines. We got down under an abandoned card table that wasn't being used and they passed by us. I felt like we were in junior high.

RoseMarie Terenzio

John thought Trump was kind of funny and like a character, but he always had him at arm's length.

John was a boxing fan. He went to the Mike Tyson–Evander Holyfield fight in Las Vegas in 1997—the one where Tyson bit off Holyfield's ear and was disqualified from the match. The fight was huge front-page news. Afterwards, John sent Mike this very heartfelt note. I typed it up. I still have a copy.

John wrote, "The only absolute truth is that no amount of bad press matters. . . . They crucify saints and anoint fools as kings." He wanted Mike to know that the only thing that matters is that the people who know you best respect and love you. And that everyone has flaws. "The people who hold the greatest fascination for the public are not the relentlessly good, but rather those who in their best efforts and worst failures show themselves to be human. That despite all they have, they still struggle. That's why, 35 years after his death, my father (and his family) still sell books, miniseries, magazines, etc. . . ."

Brian Steel

You always felt with John that anything could happen at any time. He had this sense of adventure, and he was able to execute it unlike anyone I had ever met.

In the fall of 1996, I was a little down in the dumps. To John this was as good a reason as any to pull out his two kayaks, get in a little exercise, and discuss next steps. On the kayak and the plane, you were disconnected.

As we were passing the Battery Park marina, John spotted the *Honey Fitz* docked in the marina. The *Honey Fitz* was the presidential yacht that his father used—the yacht itself predated the president, but JFK renamed it after his mother's father. John wanted to circle the *Honey Fitz* in our kayaks. So we paddled down toward the stern and crossed over by the back of the boat. As we headed up toward the bow a woman peeked over the side and saw us in our kayaks. As was often the case with John, there was a quizzical look followed by sheer excitement. She waved and we waved back. Then the woman disappeared and I could hear her yelling to somebody. A minute later, after John had already turned at the front of the boat and was out of sight, a man peered over the side at me and said, "Hey there." I waved. The man looked at me and I could hear him say to the woman: "That is *not* John-John." I caught up with John and we both chuckled at what we thought was the ensuing conversation.

Another time we flew into Bar Harbor, Maine, and landed about 10:00 p.m. I started talking to the woman at the Hertz counter to see if they had any rental cars, and John came up. Right away she recognizes John, but he doesn't want to say anything. Before she got his driver's license, she had already given us a brand-new Bronco with no mileage on it and said we could return it anytime.

On those trips we would talk a lot and he would do a pretty good imitation of Teddy. He would say in Teddy's Boston/Kennedy accent, "My brothaaaaa Bob. . . ." By the way, he loved his uncle Ted—probably more than anyone in the world.

RoseMarie Terenzio

John was a great mimic. He LOVED the song "Pretty Fly for a White Guy" by the Offspring—he would sing along in the same accent as the singer. *All the girlies say I'm pretty fly for a white guy. . . .*

He loved to mimic Arnold Schwarzenegger. He would do his accent perfectly, and loud. There was a girl who worked at *George* named Heather Tuma, and every single time she would walk by or her name came up, he would imitate Arnold in *Kindergarten Cop*: "IT'S NOT A TUMOR!"

John Perry Barlow

There was one time when we went to a Prince concert at Radio City Music Hall. You are not supposed to dance at Radio City, which was pretty silly, especially at a Prince concert. The audience, they are sort of swaying like kelp in a mild swell. John turns to me and says, "I'll bet if we started to dance, everybody else would join us." I said, "There is also a chance we would set off a hideous feeding frenzy as soon as they realize who you are." He said, "That is a chance I am willing to take." We started to dance like crazy, and everybody got up to dance like crazy. That concert was so much more fun after that.

Sasha Chermayeff

John and I both used marijuana—this connection was part of our friendship. It's a significant part of John Kennedy that nobody wants to talk about probably, or maybe now they can be okay with it since Western medicine now understands the pros of cannabis and some other psychedelic substances.

John used it every single day of his life, and I'm not exaggerating, from fifteen onward. He probably didn't when he was in Kuala Lumpur, where it carries the death sentence. Cannabis frees you from self-obsession. And that was medicine for him, because he came from a place where your fucking family, they're brilliant. They're writing books. They're intellectuals. They're not lying around on a couch thinking about how beautiful the tip of this plant with a water droplet on it is.

He wasn't a big stoner—he didn't get stoned all day long. You take a couple of hits at the end of the day. You stop ruminating. It's great if you want to let go of your day's troubles and absorb some nice music or a beautiful walk or a nice conversation where you're not striving. There's nothing to achieve. It was a medicine that he took to chill out. He didn't become an alcoholic—he did some recreational drugs. He did coke in the eighties and nineties, eighties more. I guess it was nineties, too, sometimes. He had a friend who was a coke addict. John wasn't. But he did use marijuana every day.

Jewell Wooten, hostess at El Teddy's restaurant

I saw John-John at least once or twice a week. I always called him John-John, I don't know why. You know, he never wanted special treatment. I loved that about him.

The thing that was funny was watching him walking around the courtyard, trying to find a cigarette. He was asking people sitting at the tables at El Teddy's. And I'm like, "What are you doing?" He said, "I'm trying to get a cigarette." I said, "Would you go sit down? I'll get you a cigarette. All you're doing is drawing attention to yourself." I knew both my bartenders smoked. I would go to my bartender and say, "Gimme another John-John." He knew what I meant as soon as I said it—John was always begging for cigarettes. I guess he never bought packs because he wasn't a real smoker. When you drink alcohol, even if you don't smoke, you tend to want a cigarette. He drank margaritas. I mean, come on now—El Teddy's made the best margaritas in the city. There was nothing John wouldn't eat in that restaurant, but the smoked chicken and goat cheese quesadillas were his favorite.

Dr. William Ebenstein

One time I was meeting John for dinner at Shun Lee, the so-called best Chinese restaurant in Manhattan, to talk about our projects. John comes in and he's got paint all over his hands. I go, "John, what's with the paint?" He says that he's just come from his sister Caroline's house and he was playing with Tatiana and Rose on the floor with finger paints. It was just typical John—so happy on the floor with his nieces, playing with paint. But also, he didn't go wash it off. He just comes to the restaurant with child's paint all over his hands.

Robert Curran, photographer and friend

In 1998, we traveled to Vietnam with our mutual friend Kenan Siegal and some other friends to interview General Giap for *George* magazine. [During the Vietnam War, General Giap was minister of defense of North Vietnam.] After two days in Hanoi, we took off to tour the countryside. Eventually we made our way to Ha Long Bay, to kayak amongst the two thousand limestone spires jutting out of the bay. We arrived in the afternoon and put our kayaks together and John of course wanted to set off right away, but the sun was already beginning to set, and we convinced him to get a hotel and set off in the morning. This was a good idea, as we discovered there weren't too many places to land the kayaks, as the islands had sheer cliffs of limestone with very sparse beachheads that became submerged with the high tide.

The next morning, after three hours kayaking in the hot sun, our good friend Kyle Horst went back and got an old Vietnamese junk on which we lived for the next few days. One day we were swimming about an hour from our boat with John and Kenan and we noticed the tide was rushing into this cave on one of the limestone spires. We peered inside and the sight line went black after about ten feet. We were back-swimming casually, as the current was pulling us into the black cave. It didn't look at all hospitable.

Suddenly, John just stopped back-swimming and drifted into the black cave backwards, looking at us as he disappeared. I stared into the darkness, really hoping after a few seconds he would reappear, but unfortunately that was not the case. After about five seconds, Kenan and I looked at each other and went in as well. The current brought us through this bending long black cave. We eventually had a little bit of light at the end and the cave opened into kind of a small lake in the middle of this huge mountain. We found John standing on a shallow ledge on the side of the cave. There was a small waterfall. We made our way onto the ledge and stopped there for a while and just kind of looked around.

It started getting cold and we tried to swim our way back. John and Kenan were very good swimmers and made it out in one stride. I wasn't, so it took me a good forty-five minutes to get out of there, stopping every twenty yards to catch my breath, clinging on to the side of the cave and getting cuts on my legs from the open razor clams that didn't like my presence.

On a quiet Sunday afternoon, John and I came back to Hanoi and went to General Giap's home. Giap made a remark that has stayed with me all these years, both in words and the moment between two men. "If that unfortunate event—the death of your father—had not taken place," he said, "things would have been different."

Kerry Kennedy

One Thanksgiving, John went sailing on a sailfish (essentially a surfboard with a sail, known as "the ironing board of the ocean") in Nantucket Sound. All was well until the wind came up, the waves grew, the boat capsized and headed towards Ireland. John, a strong swimmer, miraculously made it to shore. Freezing cold, he stumbled to the closest house and knocked on the door. When no one answered, he tried the handle, which was open. He surmised they had headed south for the winter and, shivering, he walked in, found a washroom, and immersed himself in lifesaving warm water. All was well until the couple returned from the grocery store and found him in the bathtub. After a bit of explanation and calming of nerves, they had a good laugh and cheerfully brought him home.

Betsy Siegel, friend

The first time I met John, it was supposed to be him and Carolyn, my then-boyfriend Kenan and me, and another friend ice climbing. I'm from Florida, so I had no idea what ice climbing was. I didn't find out that Carolyn wasn't going until I got there. I was the only girl. She canceled at the last second because she was still working at Calvin then and she said it was work, but I think probably she didn't wanna go.

It was a nightmare. You climb up and then you gotta rappel off backwards from the top of the mountain—absolutely terrifying. I don't know what temperature it was—it felt like zero, but it was probably in the teens. Had I known what ice climbing was, I would have said, yeah, I'm good, you guys go. I got pneumonia and I couldn't stop coughing. John always had to do these extreme adventure sports.

I remember he would always hang his head out the window of any car like a dog because he was always so hot—he ran like 103 degrees. Even if it was freezing cold or raining or snowing, it didn't matter, he'd always have his head out the window to cool down. But I think he just liked to feel the weather, you know?

Sasha Chermayeff

John wanted to go to fucking Afghanistan—he said the hiking is amazing. I said, "You want to go to Afghanistan? Where they're beheading people and you are John Kennedy?" He had to choose one of the most dangerous places that an American could go. I said, "Why do you have to be in danger? You can't just jump in the waves, you've got to swim eight miles. Why do you have to go to the Arctic, don't you just want to go out to dinner in Paris? Have a nice glass of wine on some Greek terrace or the Amalfi Coast? But no, you have to jump out of a helicopter to go skiing in a glacier, where if you take a wrong turn, you're dead."

How come he needed to go to such extremes? Because he had a particularly extreme experience of life. Why did he tell me "You never get over it" when we were talking about his dad's death? Because he hadn't. He was trying to: If you're constantly reliving the past, how do you stop being obsessed? By being present in something incredibly challenging.

Maybe the extreme activities John would take part in were connected to his trauma. I see it as reaching for something because of a deep loss—the extreme of one thing that helps you understand the extreme of the other.

RoseMarie Terenzio

He went to Mount Rushmore to promote *250 Ways to Make America Better*, the first in a series of *George* books. He thought it would be really cool to go to the top and rappel off, but they said it was against park rules. I still have the message pad from his office calls, where a Parks and Recreation woman called to say, "No rappelling." He was bummed.

Mike Pflaum, National Park Service ranger

At the time, I was the chief park ranger at Mount Rushmore National Memorial. That was an instant "No" from the park superintendent. It's just illegal activity. It just wouldn't have been a good fit for that park. The visual, the unlikely but potential damage on the sculpture, the unlikely but potential risk to humans. Who is allowed to do that? The maintenance crew. What did I think? I thought no way is this gonna fly.

Steve Gillon

I drove in a car with John—I knew how reckless he could be. There's a story about how he went mountain climbing. They were on the side of a mountain that was sheer ice. John had never mountain climbed before. These experienced guys were like, "We have to go back, it's too dangerous," and John just flipped out on them and said, "We have to keep going."

While writing my book about John I tried to figure out, where does this come from? I met with a psychologist at Columbia who specializes in trauma. Think about the trauma John had—it's not just his father's assassination, five years later it's his uncle who became like a father figure, and shortly after that it's Onassis who also became his stepfather. All by the time he's fourteen. The trauma is compounded by the fact that they were moving all the time. John leaves the only house he knew, the White House. They moved to one place in Washington, another place in Washington, and then to New York. A year after his father's assassination, John lived in four different houses. And then the Secret Service themselves are a constant reminder of what happened to his father—and that his own life might be in danger.

The psychologist said one of the ways that people respond to that type of trauma is to seek out danger. They are thrill seekers because they realize life could be snuffed out at any moment, so they want to live their life to the fullest. But also, they're like a moth to a candle. They're drawn to danger and the possibility of further trauma.

I'm not psychoanalyzing John, but it makes sense to me.

"In the air, no one sees you"

RoseMarie Terenzio

John started taking flying lessons again after he and Carolyn got married—in 1997 or '98. He was trying to get his pilot's license. He had taken lessons before, but other things came up and he paused before he completed his training. He started going to the flight safety school in Vero Beach, Florida. They rented a house for ten days so he wouldn't have to keep starting and stopping his lessons.

Carolyn never seemed scared about flying with John—she didn't seem to have much of a concern. I don't think she was thrilled about staying in Vero Beach for ten days. . . .

Biz Mitchell

At the time that he wanted to go take flying lessons, he asked me permission because it would mean that he'd be out of the office a lot. And I would have to basically kind of run things. I was saying to him, I don't know if it's such a great idea because you're a terrible driver. And he said, "You know, I've loved it since I was a kid."

Nick Chinlund

John was crazy about flying. He used to have this little pedal plane—it's a go-kart version of a plane, the Buckeye powered parachute. He's three hundred feet in the air. Dude, it doesn't matter if you're three hundred or three thousand, if that falls, man, you're done. He had no fear when it came to flying.

Robbie Littell

That was some of the happiest times he ever had. Floating around with the buzzards in his Buckeye. Because that melded with that observer side of him. And that observer, it's a protective place. It's a safe place.

He loved flying. It was the freedom. But most of all, it was getting away. Flying made him super happy. Free spirit, in control, doing something, you know . . . a James Bondian endeavor. Playing James Bond.

William Cohan

I believe his love of flying was related to his desire to be free of the pressures that he felt on the ground. I think every part of his life, whether it was his personal life, his married life, his social life, his professional life—the guy was under a lot of pressure. He did do a lot of crazy things, but I don't think he had a death wish. I think he thought he was invincible, which is pretty crazy given his father and uncle were assassinated. Here's the thing: Name the topic, I think the regular rules never applied to him. They never did.

Rachel Horovitz

I knew when he took up flying that that was it. I'd been in car accidents with him—I'd be shaking and he'd be laughing. There were never any consequences for him. I remember driving with him in a blizzard and he ran us off the road into a snowbank. When the cops came and asked for his license, they waved it off and helped us get the car out. The car reeked of weed. Maybe he got away with too much.

Mike Tyson

He flew that cheap creepy plane. I was saying, "Hey, listen man, leave that alone. Why don't you get a private jet? I can get a private jet, man, I know they'll give you one." That plane that he had—I could lift that plane up. I said, "You need a G4, G5." And he said, "No, that's not me. I like my little prop plane. You have to imagine how I feel. It feeds me up there."

Chris Benway, flight instructor at FlightSafety International in Vero Beach

In 1998, the school assigned me to John. I had a lot of experience teaching primary training, which means beginners. I taught him to get his private pilot's license. He was an easy student. He would probe to make sure he understood something. He was a very good pilot. Carolyn went on one lesson—John wanted to take her up. She sat in the back while we did a lesson.

When John got his private license, he bought the Cessna 182. I'm like, "John, learn how to fly. Don't buy anything faster or bigger, no fancy autopilots, just get a Cessna 182," which was similar to the plane he learned on. "Fly conservative, you're still learning."

In aviation, you have to stay conservative after you get your private pilot's license. There's no room for error—it's not like if you're driving your car on the highway and you run out of gas or something breaks and you pull over. Flying is unforgiving. We called certain airplanes "doctor killers" because doctors would get their private airplane rating, they'd go buy a high-performance airplane, and they'd go kill themselves. Doctors are some of the worst students, not because of their capabilities but because of their arrogance in the cockpit.

John bought his Cessna 182 and says, "All right, we're gonna bring this plane up to Caldwell [in New Jersey]." We flew up the East Coast and he did great, great flying. VFR—visual flight rules. We had a couple stops. One of 'em was in Washington, D.C. He says, "Okay, can we stop at Washington National?" I'm like, "Washington National, the commercial airport downtown?" I'm like . . . "It's gonna cost money." He's like, "Yeah, but can we do it?" He was an adventurous type. I feel the waters a little bit before I jump in, but John was like, "Why can't we do that? Let's go."

I left FlightSafety in May or June of '99 to go to Continental Express. My last flight with him was doing some instrument training at FlightSafety. When he finished his primary flight instruction for his private license, he was a very good private pilot.

John got a lot of fun out of flying because it was a challenge, and it gave him a sense of freedom. When you're up in the air, you're the only person responsible for you. You're focused on that and nothing else, and it gives you clarity. It's exhilarating. You are alive and you are in the moment.

If someone else is flying, you're just watching a movie—if you are flying, you *are* the movie. John is walking down the street, people are gonna see him and be like, "Hey, that's JFK Jr." In the air, no one sees you.

Gary Ginsberg

He said, "It's the only place I can go where no one is bothering me. I have complete silence, and no one can get to me except the air traffic controllers." I was always struck by that because he never struck me as being terribly bothered by the attention on land. But I think for him, it was just a solace. Maybe that gives you insight into what he was really dealing with on the ground. He wasn't a complainer, but I think this was the antidote to it.

Sasha Chermayeff

Ed Hill told me that John had seen a psychic in France who told him that he wouldn't live past forty. It wasn't like Nancy Reagan—I mean, he wasn't looking for psychics. He did not worry that his life was going to end just because a psychic said he was going to be short-lived. I would say it's in the minds of both Bobby Kennedy and John that the world is crazy, and your life can end at any moment.

Barry Stott

Once, we were waiting for John outside my hangar. I said something to Carolyn like, "Oh, you should be flying with John in his plane." She said, "I'm always nervous about flying with John. I'm happier to fly with you guys," or something like that. It was one of those casual asides.

RoseMarie Terenzio

When he got his plane, the Cessna, you have to have a tail number and he wanted 529 because that was his dad's birthday—May 29. When he went to reserve that number to register it with the FAA, that one was taken. They had to track it down. He ended up buying the number from the person who had it. The tail number on both of John's planes was N529JK

Lisa Dallos

My mom has a home on Martha's Vineyard and at one point John said to me, "Hey, do you ever want a ride up?" Here my boss is offering me a ride in a Cessna, single-engine, four-seat plane. I said, "Sure," thinking, *Why did I say yes?* But I'm not gonna offend him.

The day before we were supposed to go, the forecast was rain and he told me he was going to delay the flight. I thought, *Thank God I don't have to fly*. He said, "I'll give you a ride home on Sunday." I said okay, never thinking he would call. He called on Sunday morning. He said, "I'd love to give you a ride." We met at the airport. The plane was bigger than my mother's Honda, but small—it was just him and the four seats.

There was not a cloud in the sky. We took off and I was really nervous, not because of him, but more because I thought, *Oh my God, now am I gonna have the psychotic episode I always thought I was gonna have on a plane?* The sun was setting just as we were turning into Rhode Island. We landed at Caldwell, and he goes, "That's the first time I've ever flown at night."

CHAPTER 22

"How do you become your own person . . . when you almost belong to everybody?"

RoseMarie Terenzio

John invited New York senator Alfonse D'Amato to a lunch meeting at *George* with his staff in '98 or '99 to discuss New York City's upcoming mayoral election—just a casual get-together. D'Amato kept pointing to John. "If John ran for mayor, it wouldn't even be an election. It would be a coronation." Embarrassed, John just shook his head. After he returned to his office, I asked, "Why wouldn't you run for mayor?" John said, "Rosie, how many mayors do you know that have become president?"

Ed Hill

I used to kind of clumsily inquire about the whisperings in his ear by prominent figures in the Democratic Party. That was a conversation he was very resistant to. He didn't want people, especially close friends, to start assuming him to be the presumptive heir to his father's legacy. But it was irresistible. Everyone had the expectation virus with John.

Jeffrey A. Sachs

One time we were up in Hyannis Port before his mom died—she would have a great picnic for the whole clan. Jackie was sitting all by herself. I sat down next to her, and we started to talk, and I said, "John, he's doing so well. He's been giving these great speeches. . . ." She goes, "I'm not that interested in him being in politics." And she got up and walked away. I guess she thought I was bringing him into that realm and John was drawn to it.

Gustavo Paredes

Entering politics, well, it was on his mind. We were walking on the beach in Hyannis Port, talking about that, having to raise money constantly, losing your sense of privacy. He had finally built up a very good sort of bubble, but he realized he would have to give that all up. He was thinking of running for governor. . . . Absolutely, he felt it was expected that he run for president someday. He was trying to figure out the road to get there. When he came up with the idea for *George*, it gave him a reprieve. John matured late and all those expectations came early. He felt he needed to earn things. He had to build his gravitas.

Dan Samson, friend

John once told me he wanted to live his life like Thomas Jefferson—gain a breadth of experience in different arenas and then put it all together and begin a life of public service. We both smiled broadly when conjuring up how great it was going to be when he'd be able to have a helicopter fly in provisions next time we fell short on one of our hikes.

I don't doubt that would have happened. He was a modest (believe it or not), thoughtful, sympathetic, engaging, energetic, bright, funny, confident, loyal, sensitive, serious, and boldly adventurous person. John might have flunked the bar a few times, but he was smart in matters that mattered.

Christiane Amanpour

I think he struggled also with the projection of what he should be in life. Clearly everybody wanted to know whether he would be a politician. . . . There was a lot of pressure. . . . I think the pressure sort of fell off him when he founded *George*, because on the one hand, he obviously had the professional pressure of making that a success. But I think he had found what suited him at that time. I've always thought *George* was—maybe he knew it, maybe he didn't know it—dipping his toe into what the future would hold. Whether it was being a journalist, running for office, becoming a philanthropist, an activist. The divisions and the fake poisonous political dysfunction and the hate that our whole world is consumed by right now—I think he would've had the desire, the ability, and the credibility to forge a different path. He's somebody who could really, really work across an aisle. Because I remember in college he would be very, very open to all sorts of different ideas but, you know, clearly, he was a proud Democrat.

Steve Gillon

John would talk about his cousins who went into politics and how miserable they were, and that's not the life he wanted for himself. But he was dropping breadcrumbs. . . . He wanted to run for governor of New York, but his ultimate goal was to return to the White House. No doubt.

When I first met him at Brown, we would have these conversations about his father. He always referred to him as President Kennedy, as if he was out *there*—as if John wanted to keep himself separate from who that person was. As time went on, he would refer to him as "my father." And at least once in those last couple of years, he called him daddy: "my daddy."

I think he was going through this process of figuring out who he was. He was more willing to embrace his father because there was no need to keep a distance from him. He used to say, "I don't want to do what people expect me to do," and I think over a series of years of doing things that were different from what people expected him to do, John discovered that what he really wanted to do is what people expected him to do. And as he became more comfortable with his identity as someone who wanted to be in politics, he was more willing to embrace his father, and his father's memory.

He had spent his whole life trying to figure out who he was and what he wanted to do. John did not want to enter politics because of his last name. And what he discovered in those last couple of years was that politics was a part of his DNA. This was his calling. And he was ready to answer that call.

Sasha Chermayeff

People always wanted to know, would he have ended up in the White House, and yes, of course he would. I used to say that to him: "When I come down to look at the National Gallery, I expect my bedroom to be ready." He kind of knew it was a joke, but it wasn't really a joke.

Mike Tyson

I asked him to go into politics. He said, "You think I'll be good?" I said, "It's in your bloodline. You know you wanna do it. You have to run for office. And people look up to you."

He came to the prison—it was world news that he came to see me. And I have to tell you this, something that no one knows. He came to see me and I'm in isolation. So, they have other guys that are isolated and they're with me and these guys, their mothers—they were freaking out. I said, "Go ahead, hug him. He's a real person. He's a good man." Everybody in the visiting room was hugging him and stuff. They were moms and they were crying on their knees like he was the pope. And that's the biggest pleasure I got—more than him coming to see me. How people loved him. He made people happy. You had to see this shit—I wish we had cameras.

He said the only reason you're in here is because you're Black. He just felt I've been done wrong—that's what he believed. And I didn't want to tell him, well, I struck two people in the face and knocked one of the guy's teeth out. I didn't wanna tell him that, but I knew I wasn't there because I was Black—I was there because I was really violent. And I might have been drinking while I was driving, too. It's never been because of my treatment by the cops—most of my experiences with cops have been pretty respectful and kind. They arrested me because I was being, you know, stupid.

I remember he was fighting with his family when he came. He said, "They all told me not to come visit you. Everybody says I'm making a big mistake." I guess it was his image they were worried about, you know. But he came and hung out with me.

He wanted to be his own person. But how do you become your own person . . . when you almost belong to everybody? That's why everybody felt a common bond with him.

I think that's the reason that he was being so familiar with the people and loving the people—cuz he was setting up for office. He just wanted to get confidence from the people around him. "You think so? You think I should?" He wanted to stay humble. But I said, "Listen, your father didn't become president by being humble." He fought for his presidency. I noticed that John needs the people to inspire him, tell him great things about himself. He really never had what we call a hype man now—you need Flavor Flav. Oh man. Can you imagine? What the hell you care about a Rockefeller, a Rothschild? You John F. Kennedy Jr., baby. Ain't nobody like you, you need a hype man to know who you are, baby. I know you're humble, but listen, you gotta recognize your preeminence.

RoseMarie Terenzio

I asked why he was going to visit Mike Tyson. Tyson was serving time for a road rage incident. John said, "Because no one else will. Nobody else will put out a hand for this guy." He *wanted* media at the prison. I remember him saying, "I wanna make a case in the media that this guy is human."

Steve Gillon

John did not always think deeply about things. I think that Mike Tyson was another person—like members of his family—who he felt had been treated poorly or misunderstood, and he empathized with those people. I think he blocked out everything else. If he had been thinking then about running for office . . . If he had gone a step further and thought about how this would make people perceive him, I think he might have approached it differently.

If John was campaigning for office, people were going to see the real John and not that John Fitzgerald Kennedy Jr. image they have in their minds. I do wonder if they would have been disappointed. John wasn't his father. He wasn't as sharp; he wasn't as articulate. So I don't know how that would've played out. John had the skill, the intuition, the intelligence to be a very good president—I think the road getting there would've been very difficult.

RoseMarie Terenzio

Carolyn had no qualms about John running for office. We talked about it as though it was inevitable. The only thing she was concerned about was having a kid in the city because she was afraid that it wouldn't be safe, being chased by paparazzi. She wanted a place outside of the city. But she would have read everything, learned everything about the office, the opponent, the laws of the state if he was running for governor. She would have been fantastic at campaigning for him.

"He's as ready as he's ever going to be"

Steve Gillon

John had been talking about having a family since they got married and Carolyn refused. She had a point. She said, "Look at my life. How can we possibly bring children up in this world?" With Anthony, she would say, "Your best friend is dying, the paparazzi are following us everywhere we go, this is not the time to start."

Sasha Chermayeff

She used to say things like, "I'm not ready. John's not ready, either." But John *was* ready. He used to tell me how much he wanted children. He was willing to wait because she was younger. He loved, loved children. So did Carolyn. They were always holding our kids. Always tumbling the kids in their arms, carrying them, getting in the kayak with them. "Pass the babies over."

Robbie Littell

After they got married, if you went over to their house, it was pictures of all our kids they had around.

Amelia Barlow

Carolyn was sort of my heroine, role model, mom. My dad would always plan our trips for when John was out of town so that my sisters and I could go live with Carolyn. I would sleep with her—she would always say, "Okay, you're gonna be right here with me." They had that huge bed in the master bedroom. It felt like an ocean because I was so little—I'd never seen a California King bed before. Here's this bed and it's like an entire room. The bathtub was a swimming pool. It was awesome. We would get in bed and she would get up and get a banana in the middle of the night and I would chase her back over to the other side and she'd say, "I've never quite had anybody chase me around a bed before."

I would call her on the phone from Wyoming. Often when I would have these emotional fluctuations I would wanna go to her because she understood. One of my best friends was a bully and I called Carolyn and I was in tears. She said, "When I was your age, I was very similar. I was very sensitive and a lot of people didn't understand me. And I was being bullied." She said, "The best thing I ended up realizing is that I am unique and these girls are gonna stay in this town forever, but I'm going to be able to leave because I am different. So the best thing you could possibly do is tell them that they're little bitches and walk away." I told them to fuck off, and they stopped bullying me.

Sasha Chermayeff

John was Phinnie's godfather—he asked if he could be. He wanted that. And Phinnie loved John and Carolyn. There was a crazy love between them.

Phineas Howie, son of Sasha Chermayeff and Philip Howie

We would go to the beach on the Vineyard. Carolyn was super sweet, super affectionate with us. John was running around—he wasn't one to sit down too much. I remember Carolyn as more of a sensation. She was squeezing and hugging us a lot. So affectionate that it drove me crazy a little bit. I was like, *Gee* . . .

My dad wouldn't just get us a toy if we asked him out of the blue, but she spoiled us. I remember a plastic bumblebee on a stick that would spin in the wind. My sister, Livi, and I each got a different color. Carolyn's long, long blond hair was sort of wispy and it would blow around. . . .

I learned the concept of what fame was. My mom explained it to me, how it worked with John. She was like, "Well, so many people know who John is, but he doesn't know who they are." It didn't make sense. Paparazzi would sometimes fly tiny planes over the beach to try to take pictures. We were out in a sailboat and then John jumped off to swim around another cove to avoid them.

He was definitely sort of a super figure to us. He was my godfather, an uncle that I really loved—a magical person for sure. We went every summer, but then it just suddenly stopped and then we never went back.

Sasha Chermayeff

John loved his sister's kids. In particular, Rose—there's something about her that connected to John. He would show me pictures and say, "Have you seen how much she looks like my mother?" There was a certain pride.

He liked the name Flynn. Robbie and Frannie's kids were Coco and Tate, we had Phinnie and Livi. Coco and Phinnie would snuggle. John watched this little lovefest continue in the next generation.

Andrew Kandel

I remember I had just had my second kid. He was asking me a lot of questions—"Oh, you have two kids, what's that like? How do you balance life and work and kids? When do you go to the gym?"

Sasha Chermayeff

Carolyn said he wasn't ready. I remember looking at her and thinking, *I don't know, gal. He's as ready as he's ever going to be.*

CHAPTER 23

1999

"The last year was just bad"

Sasha Chermayeff

John was always saying to me, "Carolyn could do anything she wants. Suck it up. Get your shit together." He said to me at North Moore in the kitchen, "If you were married to me, wouldn't there be all kinds of stuff you'd want to just do with your life? You're just going to sit around kvetching and being too neurotic to go outside?" He wasn't so graceful about it—he did lack compassion when it came to that.

RoseMarie Terenzio

Carolyn had taken scuba diving lessons so she could go on trips with him. She went ice climbing with him in New Hampshire or Maine and she said it was fucking scary. She said, "I'm never doing it again." She felt he took it all for granted. She was looking for him to say, *Hey, you gave it a shot.* And that was the crux of their problems. *I gave up my whole life and have tried to assimilate to your lifestyle*—and it was like, *Yeah, so?* Like it was never enough. She'd say, "There is no money in the bank with John."

Sasha Chermayeff

And then the tool that she had was withholding intimacy.

Michael Bergin, a former Calvin Klein model who once dated Carolyn, claimed in his 2004 book The Other Man *that their relationship had continued after John and Carolyn married. According to Bergin, he and Carolyn met up several times during the course of the marriage up until the spring of 1998. "I tried to get her to open up but she didn't feel like talking," he wrote about a visit they had at the Days Inn on Sunset Boulevard in the fall of 1997. "She seemed lost deep inside herself and I didn't say much either. I really didn't need to ask her what was wrong. She was having an affair. People don't have affairs unless they are unhappy in their marriages."*

RoseMarie Terenzio

Michael Bergin and Carolyn dated in the early nineties. She didn't talk about him much. One time in the late nineties, we were at a place called Embassy, and he was there. It was a cool Tribeca place, a big fashion hangout. She introduced me to Michael and it was really casual. John came by and said hello to everyone, including Michael. No big deal.

There was a time in '99 when Carolyn's friend Gordon was visiting his mom in Seattle and he asked Carolyn to go with him. On the way back, they stopped in L.A.—Gordon had some job interview and I think Michael was living in L.A. at the time. Gordon and Michael were good friends and they all saw each other in L.A. I don't know if Carolyn and Michael actually slept together that night—no one does. But they were not involved during the marriage. Paparazzi followed her everywhere—if she and Michael saw each other in New York, how come they never got a photo of her coming out of his apartment?

Sasha Chermayeff

I knew nothing about relationships with other people during their lifetimes. I don't think Michael Bergin just fabricated what he wrote in his book. . . .

I knew John and Carolyn were having intimacy issues, sexual intimacy issues, that last year. She had a lot of anger, but so did he. They were in a painful period.

Steve Gillon

Carolyn felt trapped. It wouldn't have been easy for her to have a career, she was overshadowed so much by John, the media were hounding her, and the relationship had not turned out the way either one of them had hoped. John was just lost. He was so good at analyzing people's situations, at finding that common ground with people, but he couldn't find that common ground with his wife. He could not figure out how to help her.

Sasha Chermayeff

The last year was just bad. John and his sister were in this terrible way. *George* was falling apart. Anthony was dying. John and Carolyn were estranged a lot of the time, even though John was still really wanting—they both were—to work through something.

RoseMarie Terenzio

People always want to know, *Were they going to get divorced?* And my answer to that is always to ask Richard Burton and Liz Taylor.

They were looking for a bigger place in Tribeca. They also started looking for a second place in Snedens Landing, New York. It was close to the water, and he could kayak across the Hudson to get to a train to get to the office.

John was starting to form a relationship with Carolyn's sisters, especially with Lauren. Lauren had just moved back from Hong Kong and bought an apartment on White Street in Tribeca, around the corner from John and Carolyn, a big loft. She was dating Bobby Shriver—it was a long-distance thing because Bobby was in L.A. She was a VP at Morgan Stanley—her office was across the street from *George.* We were around the same age, and we became friends. We'd go out for drinks, and when people would ask, "What do you do?" she'd answer, "I work at a bank." I asked, "Why do you say it like you're a teller?"

Carolyn was happy they were in the same neighborhood. She introduced her to all of her friends and Lauren just became part of Carolyn's circle.

John was also in the process of buying his mom's Martha's Vineyard property from Caroline, who spent her summers in the Hamptons, in Sagaponack. She wanted to sell off some of that property because she felt like they didn't use it and it was a lot to maintain. John did not want any of that property sold, he wanted it left intact—he was adamant. He said it's one of the last pieces of property in the country that has that much acreage on the ocean, like three hundred acres. His mother loved that place. The paperwork was drawn up for the sale to him.

Neither John nor Carolyn wanted to end their relationship—their goal was to fix what was broken. They went to a security company partly so that it would give Carolyn some peace of mind.

Michael Cherkasky

I went to work at a place called Kroll, one of the biggest security companies in the world. I was CFO. John comes in with Bob Viteretti, who had worked with us at the DA—I had hired Bob. He brought John in because of the paparazzi issue—he wanted to discuss the security concerns in his apartment, in Hyannis Port, when he traveled. He said, "I'm about to start a family with my wife and I want to think about how I'm gonna protect them." He said in Hyannis "there are people always waiting for us." It was just, *Are we gonna do this with Secret Service type hires? How do I make it so my child is raised in the most normal of circumstances?*

He wanted an assessment of risks and how we would handle it. We did that for a number of very famous people.

Bob Viteretti

To my recollection, we put in this very elaborate but passive security system that was not intrusive because they didn't wanna walk around with bodyguards. I believe the only monitor was in their apartment. On at least one occasion—maybe they were just going on vacation—they had what you could think of as bodyguards. No one knew about it. We were there in the event something were to happen. John was trying to address his wife's concerns.

Leroy Frazer

At some point in '99 he and Carolyn came in to file a complaint. Morgie [DA Robert Morgenthau] came and sat in on the meeting because we were planning an investigation into paparazzi harassing Carolyn. She had come out of the apartment and one of the photographers was following her and she hopped in a cab, thinking it was all over by the time she got to Midtown near Sixth Avenue. As she was just jumping out of the cab, all of a sudden the photographer jumped out in front of her. She was startled and a car almost hit her. They were very upset. We agreed that we were going to put something in place to, bottom line, see whether or not it rolls to the level of criminality, aggravated harassment. Both were very concerned.

John knew that it was time for things to change from the way he had been living. He said something like, "I've had to deal with this, but . . . we plan to have a family one day and we can't have this sort of thing going on if Carolyn has a baby in her arms." We were going to put together an investigative plan.

RoseMarie Terenzio

It was full-tilt boogie for John the last year. My Week-at-a-Glance January calendar that year included: meetings in L.A. about a possible *George* TV show—as long as he didn't have to host it. Then back to New York, then down to D.C., where he has breakfast at Teddy's office, then meets Clinton's press secretary. Here's a date for coffee with Henry Kissinger on January 27 at 11:00, then Switzerland, to the World Economic Forum, then South Korea, to meet with the CEO of Hyundai about advertising in *George*. . . .

The night of February 10, he went to Caroline's. It says "CBK," that's how he referred to her—Caroline Bouvier Kennedy Schlossberg. Same initials as Carolyn—I know, it's crazy, right? And then he went skiing in Alta for a few days. That's what was his life was like.

On May 1, he and Carolyn went to the White House Correspondents'

Dinner. Larry Flynt and Sean Penn were his guests. John had interviewed Larry for *George* and they stayed in touch, so John invited him to the dinner.

Joe Armstrong

I was speechless—I didn't understand it at all. What Larry did to John's mother by getting these photographs of her nude on a private beach, on a secluded island in Greece—he [published them in *Hustler*] and made millions off of that. Maybe it goes back to "I don't want to do what people expect me to do" with John. . . .

RoseMarie Terenzio

Teddy Kennedy sent a fax afterwards about how upset and disappointed he was—that it was embarrassing to have Larry Flynt there.

John sent him back a note and it said, "After all the indiscretions in this family, I think me having Larry Flynt at my table at the White House Correspondents' Dinner for *George* kind of pales in comparison. Kind of like 'the pot calling the kettle . . .'" John was really offended.

It was resolved. I think Teddy still thought it was in bad taste. But I think he understood John's point of view. Like, *I'm a grown man, I know what I'm doing.*

Brian Steel

The last time I saw John and Carolyn was at the White House Correspondents' Dinner that year. We were at I think the Russian Embassy and Carolyn comes and sits on my lap. John and I were super competitive, like brothers, always kind of fighting over things. I said to her, "Carolyn, I don't know what you're up to, but get off of my lap and go over to him." She was trying to piss him off—it wasn't sexual, it was just her being manipulative, but it pissed him off.

Joe Armstrong

At that dinner John came up to me with Carolyn and said, "Carolyn never knew Mummy. Is there any chance that sometime you would have lunch or dinner with us and just talk about Mummy?" I was touched and elated because his mother had done that for him—asked people to talk to him and his sister about their father. And here was John asking me to do the same thing with his wife. We were going to do it a few weeks later.

Steve Gillon

That spring John had traded his Cessna for a Piper Saratoga, which was faster and more complex.

Munir Hussain, New Jersey businessman and pilot

John used to fly from Caldwell Airport and so did I. One day he said, "I saw your plane and I really like it. I wanted to see inside." So I give him a whole tour. My plane was a Saratoga and he used to fly a Cessna 182. Saratoga was a much sharper, much faster, much more advanced plane. He starts asking me how fast this goes and what's the ceiling—meaning how high he can go. I give him all the information. Then a few weeks later he said, "Munir, if you buy a new plane, I would like to buy your Saratoga." Before I sold it to him, I sent for inspection. I make sure everything is perfect. Plane was really almost brand-new.

I remember I said, "Hey, this plane is much, much faster than your old plane, so make sure you are really trained well and all that."

Jeffrey A. Sachs

I was going to be his first solo passenger on the Piper Saratoga, although I didn't know it at the time.

I got him to do a commencement speech in Maryland at George Washington College. President Kennedy was supposed to speak there before he was assassinated. He never gave the speech. John was asked if he'd come and speak and he agreed.

So he flew from Teterboro in New Jersey, picked me up in East Hampton, and we're going to fly to Maryland together. He starts jabbering over the radio with some pilot that's landing, and this voice goes, "John, is that you?" And John says, "Jay?" Turned out to be Jay Biederman, his regular flight instructor, who just happened to be there with another client. Jay says, "It's going to be kind of rough weather tonight. Why don't you fly with me back to Teterboro and then I'll fly down to Maryland with you guys."

So we get back into the plane to Teterboro and I close the door and we take off, and I noticed the door is open a crack. I go, "John, the door's open," and he says, "Well, open and close it." So I open it, now it won't close at all. I'm looking down, I see the beach. John says to Jay, "Jeffrey's door won't close." And Jay said, "Just leave it alone, the air pressure will never let it open. Don't worry about it." So I'm holding on to the door and we land in Teterboro.

Then we take off for Maryland and we run into some not great weather. The next morning, we get up and John says, "Sometimes I think God is watching over me." I said, "What makes you say that?" He said, "What are the odds of running into Jay at East Hampton? We ran into that bad weather, and it was just great having him there." And I said, "What makes you think God isn't watching over *me*?"

"Politics is what I know"

Ed Hill

I met up with with John at Moondance Diner downtown near his apartment on May 9—Mother's Day of 1999. He had to go up to Hyannis that day to meet with Caroline because they had to talk about the apportionment of some of the furnishings. John was not looking forward to that trip because it was one of the semi-contentious sibling-division-of-the-estate-type encounters. He also had the sense at that point that whether *George* was long for the world, he probably wasn't long for *George*. And that was hanging over his head.

So, it was a morning of preoccupation. When we got to the diner, he was pretty candid. And in talking about maybe shuttering *George*, he talked about the next step in his career, which was politics. He said to me, "I don't know what to think about, Eddie. Politics is what I know." We talked about the Senate. I was thinking, *Let me do some political math here. In 2008, I predict I'm going to be voting for a fellow of my age for president. . . .* And that's exactly what happened. But it was the other guy.

Gary Ginsberg

He spent that spring thinking about running for the Senate. Had Hillary not decided to jump in, he probably would've.

RoseMarie Terenzio

On May 19 he was interviewed by Katie Couric on the *Today* show—it was for the tenth anniversary of the Profile in Courage Award, to honor his dad. Katie showed a clip from an interview where JFK talked about hoping his kids would go into public service in some way.

Katie Couric: When you hear him talk about that do you ever feel like your choice not to pursue a career in public service might have disappointed him?

JFK Jr.: No . . . You know, he always said that he thought everyone should run for office. Listen, there's a lot of time in life to do all sorts of things. . . . There are other ways to contribute to the public discourse. . . . And I think everyone has to find their way into politics or any other professions on their own. Do it on their own speed, and then in their own way.

Katie Couric: That sure sounds like you haven't given up the notion of maybe going into politics.

JFK Jr.: Maybe, maybe not.

Sasha Chermayeff

When they showed him footage of his father talking about his children— there was this beautiful expression on John's face as he watched that. A tender expression. He barely remembered his dad. But whenever he did talk about him there was this pride that came out—being proud of his father and comfortable with being, in a way, the next one.

Katie Couric

In retrospect, that's a very poignant interview. The last television interview. Like most women in America, I had a mad crush on John. He was so handsome, but he emanated humility. I remember he rode his bike to the *Today* show. And I was a little, what is the word? Dumbstruck? I was kind of nervous around him, believe it or not. He came by himself, and did I mention I had a crush on him? He also wrote me a nice note when [her first husband] Jay died, something about people dying young. He was just so charming.

That evening, John and Carolyn appeared at the second annual Newman's Own George Awards, which John and Paul Newman had set up to honor companies for their philanthropy.

Tim Hotchner, *George* colleague and son of A. E. Hotchner, Paul Newman's best friend and partner in Newman's Own

I remember saying to John when I first got to *George*, "You haven't met Paul Newman?" Paul was very politically active, and he was always kind of tickled by John and *George* magazine. I just felt this kindred spirit between the two of them. How they approached the world and fame, didn't take themselves too seriously, both liked to be at the bar with a beer in their hand. And they both had a mischievous sense of humor. I said, "Guys, you have to talk." The idea that came out of that was the Newman's Own George Award. Paul was giving away all his money through Newman's Own and he and John did the award together for two years, '98 and '99.

Before the '99 event, we wanted to make a video of the two of them and Paul said, "What if we do St. John and St. Paul as fallen angels? We've come back from the heavens to present these awards." Paul's humor. I got the angel wings from the Broadway show *Angels in America*. One morning my phone rings and it's John. He says, "Tim, I'm not doing the angel wings." I had made really crappy halos out of wire and tinfoil, so they both did the halo. We filmed it at Paul and Joanne's apartment. It was a crappy little video. The two of them, St. Paul and St. John, came down as fallen angels.

Before the event that night we all met at Paul and Joanne's in the city. John and Paul went out on the balcony, overlooking the reservoir between 93rd and 94th Streets; I was off to the side. Paul said, "You know, your mother is responsible for this. It's what Joanne and I look out at every day. This would be overrun with buildings here—it was your mother that saved this reservoir." John got a little emotional . . . which he didn't do too often.

They leaned out over the balcony and stopped speaking. Paul lost his son when he was probably about the age John was at that time—Scott died of an overdose. That left a huge hole in Paul's heart. There was something in that moment—if you ever look up a photo of Scott Newman, he was tall and handsome like John, and had this big life ahead of him.

It took a lot to impress John, but he had a deep respect for Newman, who was very involved in politics and had been with Martin Luther King and part of the civil rights movement. And Paul took great pride in someone like John who could go forward and be a good man.

Two years before, we were at a party at Pravda, the vodka bar in SoHo. I remember everybody was looking at Carolyn. Every time I moved an inch, she would take me by the collar and pull me back. She said to me four times, "Don't move, don't go that far away from me." And to see her two years later . . .

I remember the two of them walking into that second Newman's Own George event. That's when she came into her own. It was wow! I felt she was starting to really embrace the role. He was starting to embrace his role, and potentially life beyond *George*, and all of that was finally coming together. It did have that kind of royal feel to it.

"Anthony doesn't want to talk about dying"

John Perry Barlow

John had this really crazy flying parasail. Once we were out on the Vineyard and he'd taken off and it was starting to come on sunset. He'd fly around up there, and Carolyn said, "Look at him. He's alone and yet he knows he has us." She was standing on the ground next to me in Martha's Vineyard at his mother's place. It's a lovely image.

Robbie Littell

He crashed the stupid Ultra Light—[the Buckeye]—into a bush on Memorial Day weekend. It was super dumb.

Sasha Chermayeff

He broke his ankle. He was lying on the floor with his leg up on the couch. I lay down next to him and put my feet up on the couch and we lay back on the floor face-to-face and held hands, entwining our fingers. He was incredibly emotional. Tender. He was squeezing my hand really hard. Carolyn walked by and looked at us and there was this look between them. She said, "I'll be with the kids," and then she left. It felt as if she should be where I am and I should be where she is. She was furious with him, as if he'd made a stupid mistake.

RoseMarie Terenzio

I honestly think it was *Now it's all about you again.* Everybody's like, *Oh, poor John.* If it's not Anthony it's *George,* and if it's not *George,* it's your broken ankle. Carolyn was feeling lonely. And then it was *Everything we do is in service of something about you. Whether it's* George *or your cousins, your family's charity, another time I have to walk a fucking red carpet. And I just want to go out and have martinis with my friends and get drunk and be silly.*

Sasha Chermayeff

What I remember the most from that weekend is John saying, "She's so shut down." Emotionally they were so disconnected. *You ruined my life. I can't walk down the street anymore,* is her perspective. His is *Why are you shutting me out?* He had been talking to a friend about them not having sex—they hadn't been sleeping together for a while. They were at a very important crux

334 ROSEMARIE TERENZIO *and* LIZ McNEIL

in their relationship. A moment where you're either going to see the other person's perspective and be able to forgive or the feeling is, this relationship is making my life harder. John felt really hurt by her. His heart was breaking, and I think hers was, too. A lot of it did come down to pressure from the outside world. John was on this pedestal and she's supposed to show that she's good enough. Think about the way the press would talk about her. "Is she up for the job?" "Are you good enough or not?"

One thing about John—he did not distance emotionally. John would get on a helicopter and go skiing alone, confronting nature—that gave him sustenance. But he didn't emotionally distance from people when he was upset.

There was that moment where he realized, *Oh my God, I'm going to be stuck here with my broken ankle.* If he couldn't hike Mount Kilimanjaro and risk his life heli-skiing somewhere, he was going to go nuts. Exercise was a crucial balancing out for the stress.

Anthony's death was looming. And when we were holding hands, he said, "Because of this, I'll just be with Anthony. I won't be able to get up and bike twenty miles and come in for five minutes. Anthony won't be able to go anywhere. I'll just sit with him. I'll give him the time he needs before he dies. We'll be two grumpy old men. We'll just do this together." I saw a wise person. I did not see John crying a lot. There were tears welling up in his eyes. And he was suffering.

RoseMarie Terenzio

Anthony had just been going for more treatment and more treatment to remove tumors and there was no "Okay, the reality is that he's probably not going to make it another year." John was frustrated that they just kept going through with these rigorous treatments. It was like *Groundhog Day.*

Sasha Chermayeff

John told me, "He doesn't want to talk about it. He wants to pretend that he's not dying." Anthony was just like, *The cancer spread here, take it out, the cancer spread here, take it out.* And John would say to me, "How am I supposed to say, 'Dude, you can't take out your heart'?" Where's the person who's going to say that to you? Where's Elisabeth Kübler-Ross when you need her?

Gustavo Paredes

Part of John just thought that Anthony was still going to be able to make it one way or another. There's an inevitable end, but he didn't want to deal with it till then because I think it would've taken away time being present with Anthony.

Steve Gillon

The weekend after Memorial Day, they were going to the beach and John's limping along and Anthony's in front. Anthony takes his shirt off before they reach the water's edge and for the first time, John saw his entire back was marked by scars from all the surgeries. And John just put his head into his hands and sobbed uncontrollably.

He thinks they have to tell Anthony that he's dying. He was reading a book about the stages of death, telling Carole, "We need to have that conversation with him," and Carole just said, "No. Anthony doesn't want to talk about dying. He wants to talk about living."

"The writing was on the wall"

Steve Gillon

By that spring Hachette was disappointed about the sales numbers—the numbers weren't what they expected them to be.

RoseMarie Terenzio

There was more pressure to meet advertisers, more dinners. John had to meet advertisers one-on-one and he was seeing their ads in other magazines. He felt he was being used to sell ads for all the Hachette titles and not investing in *George*. The writing was on the wall.

Steve Gillon

He was deeply suspicious that they were using him to raise money for other magazines. That was Carolyn's big issue with John and something I witnessed firsthand.

One evening, it must have been June, he and I went to Odeon for dinner. He seemed down. Near the end, he said, "Would you come back to the apartment? I want to show you a letter, I need to get an objective pair of eyes on it." It was only a few blocks. I went up into the apartment and Carolyn came from the living room. She was wearing an oversized sweatshirt and smoking a cigarette. John handed me the letter. It was from Hachette. I can't remember exactly what was in it, something about his failures. But I remember saying, "John, I think what this means is that they're coming after you. They are putting you on notice that they will attack you personally and blame you for the failure of the magazine."

He and Carolyn were passing a cigarette back and forth and she just erupted at him. I had never heard so many F-bombs in a sentence. "They're fucking you, John, everybody fucks you. You let people fuck you, John. You've got to start fucking people back." It was uncomfortable. John was flustered. He said, "I'm going to walk you out."

We went down the elevator. We got outside and he went left, and I went right. I turned around. He walked down this dark street, almost no streetlights, and sort of hunched over, his hands in his pockets, and I'm just thinking, *Poor guy.* I saw the two major dysfunctions in his life, his marriage and his magazine. They were intersecting, and I caught a glimpse of what was going on in his private life—and had been for a while.

RoseMarie Terenzio

They did marriage counseling. It was right at the end—three or four sessions. They both had their own shit going on. *You don't understand what I'm going through. You're not considering that I'm trying to run a business.* And they both were confiding in me.

Sasha Chermayeff

Things were very rocky. He still had the cast on during the Fourth of July weekend on the Vineyard, and Santina and me and Robbie, we all felt it: the reason we are all here is because they can't be by themselves. He said, "I'm proud that I'm facing my demons. I'm seeing who I am." He was talking about the dark sides of being human, the shadow sides—anger, jealousy, resentment, feelings you're not comfortable with. Processing the darker things. He wanted to know himself in a deeper way, face his own contradictions.

John used to say, "I want to be with my family—not my *family*." We *were* his family, but our being there also was a way to not confront what he and Carolyn needed to confront.

Robbie Littell

We had two wonderful weekends, Memorial Day and July Fourth. He and Carolyn were good together when we were all together. But he had actually stopped talking to me about her about six months before because I was always big on fidelity. Make a decision and stick with it. Stop looking. Carolyn was living on the other side of the house for a while. I think she stepped out of line first.

Sasha Chermayeff

We had dinner in New York on July 8 at David Kuhn's apartment with Jenny Christian, John's old girlfriend from way back. Jenny knew David, who was an editor at the *New Yorker* then, from Harvard. Jenny was visiting me in New York. She and John always loved being together—I was always kind of mischievously putting them together. We were all good friends. But I don't know really if there was anything other than just teenage love between them. I said, "Wasn't Carolyn supposed to be here?" He said, "She doesn't feel like coming." Carolyn was not there, conspicuously not there. So part of me was thinking, *Well, who wants to go out with your husband's first love anyway?*

John was wearing these gorgeous yellow lightweight pants. This beautiful lemon color. We were having a really intense conversation about the difficult time he was having writing Anthony's eulogy. We were on the terrace. I said to him, "Those are such great pants. Those are beauties—they fit you like Romeo Gigli just tailored them on you." He leaned in and said, "They're my father's pants." There's a photo of JFK wearing those yellow pants holding John's hand, crossing the street in Hyannis.

He was going to be spending the following weekend with Christiane Amanpour and her husband, Jamie Rubin. He said it's going to be an interrogation. That was a red flag. He didn't feel like answering a lot of questions. And then I realized everything is coming up dread for John right now.

The very last thing was he had his arms around us, with his cast, and he was kissing my head, and he was kissing Jenny's head, and he was singing, "Oh, my two best girls, my two best girls." And then when he got into a cab, we said goodbye and Jenny turned to me and said, "I just don't feel like I had enough time with him."

Christiane Amanpour

I have totally joyful memories of the last weekend we spent together on the Vineyard. The only sadness, and it was a profound sadness, was that Anthony was clearly at the end of his life. He was so thin. We were doing our best to be there for him and to cheer him up and to try to have a normal weekend amongst friends.

Carolyn gave me two pairs of Jackie's distinctive leather sandals and I have them to this day, and I wear them. She said, "Kissy, I really want you to have these, and I'm sure John's mother would've wanted you to have these." John and Carolyn were totally playful and affectionate that weekend and I have a beautiful picture of Carolyn sitting on his lap.

Then they drove Jamie and I to the Martha's Vineyard airport. We were going back to Washington. I remember them waving us off and seeing John going to his plane—he was flying to Toronto to drum up business for *George*. That was weighing on his mind that weekend.

Keith Stein, Canadian business executive

On July 13 John flew into our hangar and I was waiting for him. When people fly in privately, their planes are pretty substantial. I guess I was taken aback to see it was a pretty small plane—a bit of a puddle jumper. His copilot was this very young guy who looked like a kid. Then he came off the plane and he had his foot in that boot.

He hopped in my car, and he was like a little kid in some ways. It was a nice summer day, and he was sticking his head out the window, like the way a dog sticks his head out the window, just taking it all in.

I said, "You know, you're approaching forty. Do you ever think about getting older?" He said, "I don't worry about what I can't control." I asked him, "You're John Kennedy, you could meet with anyone, all sorts of people with money and investors, why come up to Toronto?" He said, "I like to operate off the radar." He was trying to find a new financial partner and I guess maybe it was uncomfortable. It's not an easy thing looking for money. Even if you're John Kennedy.

He thought that he had a great property in *George*, and that he could make it into what he always hoped with capital. He seemed very committed—laser-focused on *George*. The publication business was scary to me then, but I thought part of the investment opportunity was the relationship with John. There aren't many opportunities to develop a relationship with one of the most famous people on the planet. He was going to provide me with financial information and more intel. He asked me if I wanted to go for a spin on his plane. I declined.

"Just too stressful"

John and Carolyn's relationship hit a low point during the week of July 12. Though accounts vary, John spent at least one night that week at the Stanhope Hotel, away from their downtown loft. And Carolyn was refusing to go to his cousin Rory Kennedy's wedding in Hyannis Port that weekend.

Carole Radziwill

John called me every day that week. He was struggling to write Anthony's eulogy and he said he decided to stay at the Stanhope because he wanted to be alone to focus on it. He called me from the Stanhope. He was distraught having to write it and he was asking me questions and running things by me.

Sasha Chermayeff

They were spiting each other. Maybe Carolyn was trying to make him worry. *Well, I'm just not going to come home*—he didn't know where she was. So then he did it the next night. It was really fucking immature. He was not with her those last two nights.

The Stanhope thing was tricky. I think he went there to meet Julie Baker. If he really did seek out that liaison . . . it's really sad. Everybody always asks me, what do I think would've happened? Anything was possible. He never talked about divorce with me.

Steve Gillon

When she told him she wasn't going to the wedding, he told a friend, "If she's done, I'm done." He went to the Stanhope on Fifth Avenue. In the last couple of days he said that he was going to separate from Carolyn and they were going to need to make changes, otherwise the marriage was going to be over. John was with Julie Baker that Wednesday. He told her he was afraid of being alone. It's striking how lonely John was at the end of his life. This guy we see as this celebrity who everyone wants to be with, is in a hotel talking to a former girlfriend about how lonely he is.

Julie Baker

I spoke to John for the last time the night before he passed. There is a rumor going around that I was with him at the Stanhope [that night]. This is not true. He was at a baseball game and wanted me to meet up with him and his friend after to grab a drink. I was away so I couldn't. I did however grab a quick lunch with him (which we often did) at the Stanhope a few days before the accident.

RoseMarie Terenzio

John and Carolyn had a bad week. There was Anthony, John was working late on the close of the magazine. They were screaming at each other and not being heard. But you're going to tell me that doesn't happen in every single marriage? Especially after three, four years? Then you better bottle that shit and sell it.

They were not living apart. Regardless of what other people say. There were two houses they were going to go look at that following week in Snedens Landing. When people say they were living apart, all of that was still going on. It wasn't like, *We're canceling it*. I was at their apartment the night they died, I packed everything up for the next month. All of her stuff was there and so was his.

Gary Ginsberg

John called me Wednesday night and he said, "I have a chance to get my cast off tomorrow morning. Are you okay if I miss your son's bris?" He said, "If I get my cast off, I can fly—I don't have to fly with an instructor." He was psyched. I said, "Yeah, of course." He was a guy who loved to challenge himself physically, mentally, professionally, personally, and thrill-seeking was kind of part of all that. He was an outdoorsman and adventurer. And sometimes that involved taking risks some would consider okay and others might describe as batshit crazy.

Jeffrey A. Sachs

We'd made plans to fly to Hyannis together on Friday night. I get the stomach virus. I was in Long Island, and I decided I didn't want to come to the city. I remember calling John, I think it was Thursday, saying, "Can you come pick me up on the way like what you did last time?" He goes, "No, we're leaving too late, but you should call Jay Biederman. You could charter a plane for four hundred dollars and come back with us." I called Jay and arranged for this charter on Saturday morning.

Sasha Chermayeff

I always wanted to paint a beautiful picture. I did not want to admit this, but the last thing John said to me about Ed Schlossberg was "God, Ed's such a prick." John saw Ed as the problem between him and his sister. They hadn't spoken for months. Everything was coming to a crunch, and he said, "I'm going to make amends with my sister." It was just too stressful to have this toxic thing going on with her. He called her before leaving for the wedding . . . because he missed her. Thank God. They had that one phone call.

Steve Gillon

On Thursday, John called Caroline. They agreed they needed to do a better job of staying in touch. John warned her that things with Carolyn were really bad and there would probably be some bad press. At that point he thought Carolyn wasn't coming to the wedding. . . . He and Caroline loved each other. I think they both probably always thought they had time to work it out.

RoseMarie Terenzio

He called his sister from my desk. They picked up where they left off and acknowledged that they needed to get together and talk things through. It was sort of a let's-stop-the-nonsense call. Then she called back, and he went into his office to talk.

I had a conversation with Carolyn Thursday, the day before the flight. I said, "The problem here is that you and John are both fucking acting like adolescents who are just trying to get their way and stomping and screaming about each other. You need to stop this." She was crying, saying, "He's so selfish," and I said, "It'll be a spectacle if you don't go to the wedding."

Steve Gillon

I read the Michael Bergin book, which I found very credible. But the fact that Carolyn went to the wedding in the end, that was a sign that she was trying. If it's over and she's given up, then she wouldn't go. A close friend of theirs said, "Anyone tells you they know what was going to happen in that relationship, they're lying, because John and Carolyn didn't know what was going to happen."

John and Caroline were talking about making an effort to be closer, and he was talking to other people about ways to turn *George* into an online magazine. So, he's fighting to turn around his life. And there's hope with his wife, there's hope with his sister, there's hope with *George*. John never gives up. The only aspect of his life he can't turn around is Anthony dying.

"What do I do with George*?"*

RoseMarie Terenzio

John got his cast off on Thursday the fifteenth and then he had lunch with Jack Kliger, the Hachette CEO.

Gary Ginsberg

That night we went to a Yankees game. He'd had a very unsettling meeting that afternoon with Jack Kliger. It was clear that the funding was no longer guaranteed, and that if *George* was going to survive, he was going to have to either find new funding or new partnership, or leave it. He goes up to Kliger's office. He said, "This is when I knew it was over. I put my water bottle down and Kliger's so nervous he picks up *my* water bottle and starts drinking it. That's how I knew he's going to cut the cord on me. *I was fucked.*"

It was not a good last night for John. I think his most immediate concern was "What do I do with *George*?" It was an unsettling period. There were a lot of unknowns in his personal and professional life. But what he was talking about that night was running for governor. Against Pataki.

344 ROSEMARIE TERENZIO *and* LIZ McNEIL

There was a lot of uncertainty. He didn't want to get divorced. When one of his cousins was getting divorced a few years earlier, before he married Carolyn, John turned to me—we were on a plane, I remember—and he said, "I never want to get divorced." He was a sticker, not someone who looked to get out of things. He looked at his sister's marriage and saw how happy it was and wanted the same for himself. So I'm thinking, *In a perfect world, it all works out.*

CHAPTER 24

"John's not coming back"

About two weeks before he died, we talked about a bunch of things. At one point, I said, "Do you remember that conversation you and I had back when you were in college about you becoming a good man?" He said, "I think about that conversation frequently." I said, "Well good, because I just wanted to let you know that . . . you've become that person I aspired that you would be. . . .

"I know how hard it has been. I know how much bullshit you had to suffer whether [from] your cousins or the public or the press, and you've been graceful and kind and good. And I just want to let you know how I honor and respect you." And there was a long pause and he said, "I am very proud you are proud of me."

I told him, I am a pilot. I said, "You have now enough hours to be dangerous . . . just enough time to be overconfident. And moreover, I know that you are definitely going to fly yourself into conditions that you are not up to, and the reason for that is that you are always late. I wouldn't set my watch by either one of us . . . it takes us a long time to tear ourselves away from the moment. You need to learn how to be prepared for different visual conditions and ones that you will be flying into. All I am asking you, and this is a really important thing . . . if you can't see the horizon, don't look for it because it is not possible to find it from inside the cockpit."

—John Perry Barlow

RoseMarie Terenzio

Friday, July 16 was one of those pea soup, humid New York City days. Carolyn still wasn't sure that she was going to go to the wedding that morning—we talked a few times. She was crying and very upset and not feeling like she wanted to put on a brave face. She just wanted John to pay more attention—and that would get him to pay more attention. And he was upset because he really didn't wanna be in a position of having to explain to his entire family why she wasn't there.

I said there would be all these questions about why you're not there, and that will bother you more than going, and then you'll be more upset. I said they could talk things through when they got back. I think she and John talked. That would happen with them—they would have passionate arguments and patch it up the next day. She said, "I don't have anything to wear." I told her it's Hyannis, it's not black tie. She got a dress that day and she asked me to call her a car to the airport.

Lisa DePaulo

I was in L.A. interviewing Rob Lowe for the cover story. John had said to me, "Could you drop everything and do this? He's going to talk for the first time about the sex tape he was accused of making in his hotel suite in 1988, while he was in Atlanta for the Democratic convention. And how he's trying to restart his life with *The West Wing*. And I need it fast." I said I'd love to. I spent all this time with Rob, and I told John it was going great, and he was thrilled.

I took a red-eye back Thursday night—I was supposed to meet with John Friday to tell him more about what I got. Rose called me and said, "Please don't come in. He has to fly to Rory's wedding, and if you come, he'll get talking and he won't leave on time." And I said, "Well, I'm supposed to hand this into him right away, Monday." And Rose said, "He'll give you a few days."

RoseMarie Terenzio

It was a typical day, a little more activity than usual for a Friday because he was meeting with Peter Kiernan, his friend who was a partner at Goldman Sachs, at ten o'clock, and they were talking about a business plan and funding for *George* and finding another investor. And then there was a staff meeting.

Peter Kiernan

We developed a more profound relationship when I was running Media at Goldman Sachs and advising him on his challenges at *George*. John was on to something transformational, but fighting and articulating this battle was not a strength. On the afternoon of his death, we talked about his life and his frustrations and his aspirations and his family, in ways that we never had before. He talked about his sister, Caroline, about how important she was to him. He didn't feel like the rest of the family were as embracing of Carolyn as you would've hoped. The family business of politics—the awareness just wasn't in Carolyn, it's just not how she operated. She was just not the classic Kennedy wife who was immersed in all this stuff, and that caused some tension.

He wanted to repair his relationship with Bobby, like, *I've gotta strengthen our relationship. Bobby's smart and he's forceful and he's just got these demons, and we all have demons.* He was incredibly complimentary of Caroline, how righteous, how capable, how much he cared about her. Bobby was important, but Caroline was *really* important. He said something like, "It's the two of us left and she's a part of me, I'm a part of her." The kind of thing any sister would love to have her brother say.

We're both Irish Catholics. We joked about how his aunt Eunice used to always refer to the "Blessed Mothah," with the Boston accent. I wrote a letter to Caroline afterwards to say, *He was incredibly loving and caring about you.*

Matt Cowen

I remember him talking to the staff at the last editorial meeting, and it was an unusual tone for him. He said something like, "I know I've seemed distracted or haven't been around as much, but there have been things going on that I've had to deal with." I think he was talking about his cousin Anthony and the magazine's struggles.

RoseMarie Terenzio

I was on the phone all morning trying to get someone to fix my air conditioner. John was kind of annoyed because we had stuff to do to get him out the door. He said, "No one's coming to fix your air conditioner. It's Friday. Why don't you just stay at our apartment? If Carolyn knew I was gonna let you sit in your apartment and swelter, she'd kill me." And then he said, "Don't sniff my underwear." His way of teasing me. When I told Carolyn that, she said to him, "Oh, honey, Rose is the last person on the planet that gives a shit about your underwear."

He talked to Bob Merena, one of his flight instructors, and said that he didn't need him. Maybe Bob was on standby to fly with him or he called and said if John needed him, he was available. It wasn't unusual for him to say he was gonna fly alone. He had made that flight before alone. I don't know if in that plane. There were two or three flight instructors that John flew with regularly and Bob Merena was the instructor based at Caldwell Airport in New Jersey, where John kept his plane.

I talked to Carolyn once more, just details on me staying at the apartment and that John was meeting Lauren in the lobby at six o'clock. She asked me to get her a car. She said she'd call me on the weekend. She was meeting them at the airport.

The plan was that John and Carolyn would drop Lauren off on Martha's Vineyard, where she was staying with friends for the weekend, and then they would fly on to Hyannis for Rory's wedding. I have a note in the datebook, "Lauren to ride to Vineyard and Dan Samson arrives Boston, flight 02." Dan was one of John's closest friends. He was coming to Hyannis to talk about a business idea that John had, and he was supposed to pick John up at the airport.

I asked John if I could borrow some cash. I had none, as usual on a Friday, and he told me to get some for us both. I went to the cash machine. This was around four o'clock. I saw him walking out. He said, "I'm going to the gym for an hour." I said, "You have to meet Lauren in the lobby at six o'clock." I gave him $60 and kept $100 and he's like, "How is it my card and you get more?" I said, "I'll pay you back." He said, "Have a good weekend." We hugged, which was not the norm. There was just a lot going on—it was an emotional few weeks.

We had both just gotten flip phones. It was his first cell phone—not many people at *George* had them yet. I left it in the box with a sticky note saying, "This is your cell phone." I left a pink sticky note on the table. "Meet Lauren in the lobby at 6:00." And that was it.

Gustavo Paredes

I was going to fly to the Cape with John that day. I flew with him many times. I was always impressed about how careful he was about flying. I was like, wow—he really is meticulous and thorough. He checks the wings, the tires, all of this.

He was planning to leave around five thirty or six o'clock. But then I said I'm not going to be able to make it, I'm running late. And he says, "You're always running late." And I said, "No, you always run late." Who runs late more? And that was at four. The weather report showed that it was clear.

RoseMarie Terenzio

He always checked the pilot brief ahead of time. It's a federal aviation website where you check the weather.

Munir Hussain

That afternoon I flew from Poughkeepsie to Caldwell. I landed around four or five o'clock and I saw my previous plane, the Saratoga, getting fueled. So I knew John is flying. My friend wanted to meet him, so I asked the guy who used to maintain his plane, "Hey, what time John is flying?" And he said, "Maybe seven o'clock." I told my friend, "Let's have dinner and be back at seven to say hello." I said to the guy, "Just so you know, the weather is really,

really bad. I hope he's not flying alone." He said, "No, no, no, he must be fly-ing with an instructor."

Mike Showalter

I talked to him that night before he left. He told me he was going to Martha's Vineyard. I said, "The weather is pretty bad." He said, "Yeah, I won't have a problem." I said, "Okay, good luck, man."

Gustavo Paredes

John was trying to wrap up some stuff at *George* and then Carolyn was trying to coordinate with her sister, so everybody was running late. And then there was horrible traffic and it took them two hours to get to Essex. So by the time they took off, the weather had shifted. And John didn't get an update. And he'd gotten this new plane—it's like going between, say, a Lexus and a Formula One car, a lot more instruments, and he had not enough hours in that plane.

William Cohan

They were all late to get to the airport in New Jersey. John was running late and he had a very difficult day at *George* trying to convince Hachette to pro-vide more financing. And he had just gotten his cast off.

I was told that the flight instructor offered to go with him. John was not certified for instrument flying. He was only certified for visual flying. And the plane was several magnitudes more powerful than he really was comfort-able in. So the instructor offered to go with him, but John said, "No, you don't have to. It's gonna be late." The flight instructor had a wife and family. "Go home to your wife and kids." I mean, this is the way John was. *I can handle this. I'm gonna be a good guy. We'll be fine.* So that's what I was told happened. It got later and later and hazier and hazier.

Barry Stott

I had made multiple trips to and from the Vineyard that afternoon and evening, back and forth to New York and New Jersey and from Block Island or maybe Fishers Island, south and west. It was clear as a bell until sunset. But that evening a complete haze developed. It was sort of like fog all the way up to eleven thousand feet. The visibility was very, very poor. I remember making instrument approaches into the Vineyard on every flight that night. But legally it was probably still VFR [visual flight rules].

David Clarke

I was living in Amagansett, on Long Island, at the time. I distinctly remember that night because I had my single-engine Beechcraft parked out at East Hampton airport. Pilots are always looking at the weather. As we walked onto the deck—the sun was setting and the backyard lights were on—the temperature dropped and instantaneously the yard lights became sort of filled with droplets of water, like cigarette smoke at a disco. I turned to my wife, Sue, and said, "Boy, this would not be a good night to be landing in East Hampton."

Munir Hussain

When my friend and I were done with the dinner it was after seven, I thought, *Oh, John already took off.* So we didn't go back to say hello. If I knew John was leaving later than planned I would have gone back. I could have said, "The weather is really bad. You come with me, I drop you there," or something like that. I regret that basically my whole life.

"Where are they?"

Dan Samson

John had hoped to arrive in Hyannis around 8:00 p.m. But he called from Teterboro to say they were running late and he now estimated they would be in Hyannis around 10:00. Provi and the gentleman who had just refinished the house's hardwood floors—I can't recall his name—were also waiting on John. Provi took great delight in preparing all of John's favorite dishes. On this night it was a chicken casserole that would never be served.

Adam Budd, intern at Martha's Vineyard Airport

It was around 9:00 p.m. and most everyone had left the airport by then. John's was the last flight coming in on the manifest. The weather wasn't great, but it wasn't terrible. A couple who were friends of theirs had come to pick up their friend [Lauren]. They waited around for about half an hour and asked me what I thought and why he hadn't arrived. I asked them what time he left, and I said he should be here by now or he landed somewhere else. I couldn't get access to the flight plan because they're private and I didn't have clearance. At about 10:30, it didn't seem like he was coming, so I left.

Dan Samson

At around 9:30, the gentleman who had refinished the floors offered to pick up John and Carolyn from the Hyannis airport [for me]. John, and now John and Carolyn, were always late, so when he wasn't back at 10:30 I wasn't too concerned. But when he returned without them around 11:15, I lost my appetite. By around 11:30 I was worried and started making phone calls.

When I called the Vineyard house, Carole Radziwill just assumed they were running late. But I knew too much. John had called me right before they were leaving—I would have heard from him again if they weren't taking off. All I could think was there's a lot of water out there, so I told Carole we should call the Coast Guard. We each contacted the unit in our area. She also asked me to contact John's cousin Joe. Joe asked me to inform Senator Kennedy personally, so I knocked on his door around 1:00 a.m. and within moments the search was on in earnest.

RoseMarie Terenzio

I got to John and Carolyn's apartment where I was staying until my air-conditioning got fixed. I don't know why, I just had a weird feeling tht night. I got back at 9:30 or 10:00. I had a beer and I called Matt Berman. This was probably 10:30 and we talked for about an hour. He was leaving the next day to shoot Rob Lowe for the cover.

They had two phones in the apartment—one in the kitchen, and then a fax machine at the other end of the apartment. Only three or four people had the fax number. The fax line was ringing—they didn't have call-waiting. I said to Matt, "I think they're trying to call me."

I picked up the fax phone and it was Carole. She said, "Oh thank God you're there." I said, "Carole? It's Rose." She said, "Where are they?" I was like, "What do you mean where are they?" She said, "They didn't land in the Vineyard." I said, "Maybe they went to Hyannis first?" And she said, "No, I called. They're not there. They were supposed to land an hour and a half ago. No one's heard from them. I called the Coast Guard." I was like, *Are you crazy?* Because I was thinking, *If there's a big crazy story—if they called the Coast Guard because the idiot couldn't find his way, or he didn't tell people where he was going—he's gonna kill me.*

I called Hyannis. Provi and John's friend Dan Samson were there. No one knew where John was. I called Caldwell in New Jersey, where he'd left from, and said, "Did the plane take off?" They said yes. My next question was "Did somebody see them take off?" It's midnight, one o'clock in the morning. I asked, "Who was there?" It was Bob Merena. They said he's sleeping, I said wake him up. He called me back and said the flight took off at 8:39. That's when I panicked.

I called Carole. Then Ann Freeman, Carolyn and Lauren's mom, called. She said, "Rose, what is going on? What is happening?" At that point it was one or two in the morning, and they had been getting phone calls. I just kept saying, "We don't know anything yet. I'm calling the airport, I'm calling Teddy." I was trying to give her a play-by-play of what was happening. She was panic-stricken. I said, "Don't think the worst." She said something like, "I told him never to take two of my girls up at the same time." She was angry. Crying. It was panic, shock. It was a hysterical time—everybody was scrambling to figure out how the fuck did this happen. Disbelief.

I called Teddy's house. I couldn't reach Caroline because they were on a whitewater-rafting trip. Teddy's housekeeper, Dolores, answered and said, "He's sleeping." I said, "Wake him up. We can't find John. The flight took off at 8:39." Teddy called and left a message first because I was on the other line. I heard his voice, "John, it's Uncle Teddy. Are you there? Can you call me?"

I ran down and said, "Senator, it's RoseMarie." I told him what happened, and he was like, "Okay, all right. Stay put, I'll call you back." I called John's regular flight instructor, Jay Biederman. I found him in Switzerland late at night. He said, "He hugs the coastline the whole way, there's no way he could have crashed."

There was banging on the door—this was like two in the morning. "First Precinct. Police. Open up." I was like, " 'Police open up'? What the fuck is 'police open up'?" They said, "You have to leave." I said, "Are you crazy? I'm not leaving." Initially when Carole started calling, I wasn't at the apartment yet and she thought, *What if they're in the apartment and they're dead, God forbid?* When she wasn't getting an answer, she wanted the cops to check the apartment to see if they were still there. I was this random person in these famous people's apartment, which could be a crime scene, so the police wanted me out. I explained who I was and why I was there and they understood.

And then—I just remember the phone started ringing off the fucking hook. I guess that's when it hit the news. Probably 5:00, 6:00 in the morning. I was terrified—I didn't know what was happening. I called Carolyn's friend Jessica and said, "You need to come down here right now." It felt like two seconds later she was at the door in her pajamas. I called the gym, Pat Manocchia, because that was the last place John went. I was hoping maybe he said something to Pat, that he had changed his plans and was gonna go to Nantucket. It was just chaotic. One call after another. Narciso had heard the news and was flying in from Italy or Paris. Matt Berman wasn't picking up. He was leaving to go to L.A. that morning to shoot Rob Lowe. At 8:00 a.m., I finally reached Matt and said, "They can't find John's plane." He didn't say anything for thirty seconds, and then he said, "This is gonna be terrible."

It was such a blur. Caroline didn't know yet that I was at their apartment. Sometime that weekend she called my apartment and left a message. "Hi, it's Caroline. I'm so sorry. I know how close you were, and I know it's probably really hard for you, too." I think Anthony was able to find them at the hotel where they were staying on their trip. Cell phones weren't widely used then.

Barbara Walters called and said, "Will you ever forgive me for calling you at a time like this?" I said, "No." Because ABC was the first to put the dates up: *1960 to 1999*. She said, "I'm going on air tonight and if there's any way you would . . ." I said, "Absolutely not." She said, "I'm going on air anyway with a story, so if anybody . . ." I said, "Anybody who talks to you tonight didn't know them well, so do whatever you need to do."

Sasha Chermayeff

The phone kept ringing at our house in Catskill. I thought it was my father, because he would do annoying things, like call at six in the morning, so I said, "Don't answer." It kept ringing and ringing and Phil went downstairs and it was David Kuhn, who had been watching the AP. He said, "John's plane is missing." Phil told me the plane was missing and I said, "With him in it?" And he said, "Yeah, with him in it." I shot out of bed and called David. He said, "It was John and Carolyn and Lauren." I said, "And the copilot." And he said, "No, John and Carolyn and Lauren." I said, "John didn't fly without that copilot. John and Carolyn and Lauren and the copilot." And he said, "No, Sasha, they're just saying that the plane took off with three people: John and Carolyn and Lauren." As far as I knew, John didn't fly out without a copilot on the Piper. It was the first day of his cast getting off. I didn't understand.

I just remember going into that catatonic state, lying on the couch all of a sudden, no idea where I am. No idea what time it is, what time of year. I went outside. The kids were still asleep. I stood in the yard, and I had to figure it out. It's not winter, it's warm, it's not spring because the leaves are pretty big, it's not fall, they're not orange. . . . It must be summer. I had to deduce that. Just unbearable agony—and shock.

John Perry Barlow woke up to find an email from John, sent before he left the office for Essex airport, expressing his condolences on the recent death of Barlow's mother.

John Perry Barlow

I got up, found out that his plane was missing. I went to my mother's funeral. I came home and there was that email sitting in my inbox, taking note that my mother had died and that this would be a great time for us to hang out and reflect. My first thought was *Oh thank God, he is alive, maybe he has gone off some place. . . .* Which we joked about over the years—go somewhere and get a little plastic surgery and not have to be John F. Kennedy Jr. Possibly they had done something really cool and engineered their permanent disappearance and would never be seen again.

Jeffrey A. Sachs

The phone rings at 5:30 in the morning, and it's my brother, he's out fishing. He says I've been hearing this on the ship-to-shore, your friend's plane is missing and they're asking us to keep an eye out, all boaters. And then you put on CNN, by 9:00, 10:00, the reports started coming in. I flew up and it was supposed to be Rory's wedding, and the tent was set up for the wedding. It was just a very dark, dark period. I ended up staying with a friend because I was supposed to stay with John at his house. But then Provi says, "Jeffrey, I'm so sorry, but Caroline says nobody can stay here now." It was pretty clear that he was gone.

And so—I caught the lifesaving flu. Because I would've been on the plane for sure. Always weird. Especially given our conversation we had the last time. *How do you know God's not watching over* me. . . .

Julie Baker

I was with a guy that I was dating at his house in the Hamptons, and he had it on the TV in the morning and I ran home and had three of my best friends there. We just sat there, and it was horrible, horrible, horrible.

Gogo Ferguson

I was on the Vineyard. It was so strange because my husband, Dave, and I had gone to New Bedford and we flew our plane over. It wasn't foggy on Cape Cod. Whereas where John lived on the Vineyard, it gets really foggy. I remember looking around at Woods Hole and the Cape and it was clear, and I remember Dave had to circle around while approaching for landing on the Vineyard because a jet was coming in faster. We landed and he looked at me and he said, "That was the most uncomfortable flight I've ever had in my life." Because of the fog.

We got up at 6:00 the next morning and it was all over the news. I think it was probably ten or fifteen minutes after they went down that we were landing on Martha's Vineyard.

When the Coast Guard was searching for the plane right off the coast, we all just gathered and watched the television in utter shock. You wanted to crawl out of your skin. I was so inundated with paparazzi at my store on the Vineyard that I closed it down and I put a beautiful wedding photograph of them coming out of the church in the window.

Tim Hotchner

About an hour after the official word came that John and Carolyn had died, my phone rang early in the morning. It was Paul [Newman]. He was really upset because now he had this connection with John. He said, "Where are those photos?" He said, "Destroy them." I said, "I'll lock them in a safe and they're never gonna get out." He was so flipped out that two or three months earlier he has a zany idea to be fallen angels with the halos—and now John's dead. It was too bizarre and painful. He said, "I just did that as a lark. And now he's gone. And now if those photos get out?" He was just apoplectic. I had never heard him like that—Paul would rarely be alarmed or panic.

He was devastated—the loss of John really rattled him to his core. They didn't spend that much time together. . . . It was a strange thing—alchemy. Paul did things quietly and John did as well. They were going to get together the weekend after. It was not a business thing. It was *We need to spend time together*, and that was on the calendar.

Paul Kirby

It was the most beautiful day you've ever seen in your entire life. We'd cut down through the compound to go to the beach. And the anticipation of the wedding on such a beautiful day was just palpable. Everybody was in a great mood in the morning. People were flying in still, cars were coming, driving in and *Hey, how you doing? I haven't seen you in a long time.* It was this group of three hundred people that were the happiest people on the planet. And it just deteriorated like a cloud storm coming over. *Where's John? He hasn't shown up.* And then after, as I remember it was by noon or so, the mood went from the highest you could possibly see, by degrees, getting darker and darker and darker. Certain members of the family went into the house and shut the doors. Word got around something's wrong. And the mood went to really quiet.

People just started leaving. The crowd started thinning out, and it was just obvious that something bad had happened. The family got the story that radar had been lost or whatever first indication that they had that it was really, really serious. And it just sort of dissipated. It's just like this beautiful group of people that were incredibly happy on an incredibly beautiful day, just kind of dissipated out into the miasma. . . . What an incredible contrast. Crazy. You could feel it in the air. I mean, it was still a beautiful day, but it just, the air was different.

Clint Hill

The first thing that went through my mind was exactly what I once heard Mrs. Kennedy say to me, "I think he's going to be a pilot and fly airplanes someday." I was glad she wasn't around to see this. The president, Bobby, some of Bobby's kids, now John. The only one left was Caroline.

Sasha Issenberg

I just went right into the office. There was part of me that was like—not that he would've faked his own disappearance like some caper, but there were a million John things that I imagine could have happened. Happy to be off the grid.

Matt Cowen

I got a phone call from a friend who said, "You need to put the TV on. John Kennedy is missing." It was wall-to-wall coverage. I wandered into the office. I remember someone saying, "It's John. I'm sure he is swimming."

Lisa Dallos

When I got to the office, there were ten reporters in the lobby already. The press calls were coming in hundreds an hour, from every publication, every TV. There was the Katie Couric call, the Barbara Walters call, and the Diane Sawyer call. They all had their people call. It was both somber and chaotic. Saturday and Sunday we were all there all day into the night.

Lisa DePaulo

Rob Lowe called early Saturday and he's like, "Oh my God, I'm devastated. Oh, can this please not be true? Can this please not be true?" We cried a lot on the phone. I just couldn't . . . I just couldn't get my head around it.

Joe Armstrong

I was walking on the beach in St. Martin, where Jackie took her children— La Samanna, which was one of the first luxury resorts in the Caribbean. She had told me about it. A man walked up to me and said, "Kennedy is dead." And I flashed back to November of '63 because I just didn't understand what he meant. It's a beautiful day, you're in the Caribbean, and some guy walks up and says, "Kennedy's dead." That's what people said thirty-five years ago.

Kathy McKeon

I said, "He'll show up." I thought, *He is going to show up somewhere.* Because I could see him coming through the seagrass and crawling up there and sneaking in.

Seamus McKeon

You thought he was Aquaman.

Kathy McKeon

I did not think he was gone.

Seamus McKeon

For a little while, we thought that he might have pulled what he pulled at the wedding, a little bit of a decoy. The next day, I was resigned to the fact that it was over with, but Kathy kept hope.

Kathy McKeon

Provi had the same idea as me—he'd show up somewhere. He's coming. And Provi had dinner ready for him that night. When they found pieces of luggage on the beach and someone's medication, that's when I realized he was down in the ocean.

John Beyer

It was just horrible. I talked to Barry Clifford, we initially talked about bringing the dive boat to help search, and we both said, *Kennedy's not gonna die out there. He's a survivor.* But that wasn't the case.

We realized it was crazy to bring the dive boat—the government search was not gonna allow us in that area. I still remember the weather the night it happened, you know? The sea is the same as the sky. You can't tell where the sky ends and the sea begins. I just wish he'd turned around. He could have landed in Providence. Probably would've been fine.

Barry Clifford

His cousins called me up, I think Max and Bobby, and they asked me if I wanted to go look for it, the plane, and I couldn't do it. I was too upset. There's no way I could see him like that.

Chris Oberbeck

I had just taken my son Conrad to hockey practice. I came back late morning and my wife just grabbed me by the arm and took me to the TV. I'm looking at the constant image of the ocean. . . .

I went to play in a tennis match and it was a distraction because I kind of knew, but I didn't wanna believe it, so I played tennis. Then, in between games, a friend of mine came up and said they found luggage washed up.

Mark Rafael, friend from Brown

It seemed so impossible. But also, so horrific to be absolutely blind in an airplane and not have any visibility. It must have been terrifying.

Brian Steel

I was a senior advisor to Vice President Al Gore at the time. I was in my apartment and Mike Feldman, who was Gore's traveling chief of staff, called me from Air Force Two at about 6:30 in the morning. The vice president got briefed that John Kennedy Jr.'s plane was missing.

I knew the second that Mike called me that he was dead. Having flown into several very quiet airports with John late at night, people instantly knew he was there. John Kennedy Jr. can't disappear like that.

Christiane Amanpour

I was in Washington, and it was a Saturday morning, and someone from the foreign desk at CNN called me just to give me a heads-up. They knew I knew John. I can't even talk about it. . . .

He told me that he wanted me to know before it was all over the press that the plane was missing. I just turned on the television and I sat there, numbed for days. I mean literally for days until it was clear that he was no longer alive. I didn't even come close to wanting to cover this. All my instincts as a journalist flew out the window.

The only two things I agreed to do was that weekend, *Larry King* and *60 Minutes*, because I wanted to believe that he might still be alive. I wanted to let people know what a phenomenal person he was, beyond the Sexiest Man Alive, beyond the salute at his father's passing, I wanted them to know what he was as a young man and how much of a void his death would leave, and did, and has.

Cheryl Gould

I remember being in the office all day that Saturday. As a newsperson, you have to hold it all together, but because it was so personal, I just had a lump in my throat the whole time. Once John died, I knew it wouldn't be long before Anthony went. He didn't want to hold on anymore.

And to all of us who cared about John, it was just, *Ugh, why did he have to be so stupid? Why did he have to do that?* He was so carefree and careless.

Santina Goodman

Phone call from my business partner, "John's plane is missing"
First call to Martha's Vineyard (spoke with Carole Radziwill)
Next call to Hyannis (spoke with dear friend Dan "Pinky" Samson)
Next call to John's apartment (spoke with RoseMarie Terenzio)
Fell to my knees "Oh God . . . No . . . Oh please, God . . . No"
Called to comfort Rob Littell, who was crying, "I lost my brother"

After missing one day, I knew John and Carolyn were gone. If still alive, they would have called me so I wouldn't worry. Walking up Broadway and seeing their faces on every newsstand. Lost it, on the verge of fainting, hailed gypsy cab. Decided to cab it to and from work. From work jumped in cab, driver says, "They found their bodies."

Mike Tyson

I was in Los Angeles and my wife at the time called me and said we can't find John Jr. And then she called me back and said she thinks he's crashed. Everything stopped.

RoseMarie Terenzio

I was talking to Teddy's office every hour. On Sunday, Teddy's office said, "The Coast Guard is switching their mission from search and rescue to search and recovery." I asked what that meant, and they said, "It means they don't expect to find them alive."

That night there was someone at the door, and it was Richie Notar, the manager and partner at Nobu, across the street. He came up with bags of food. He said, "I figured you were holding a vigil and I thought I could bring some food." I couldn't take the constant news reports. We put on Chris Rock's *Bring the Pain* special. I think I watched it five times in a row. That morning, Sunday, the newspapers were on the doorstep. Every single newspaper had "Missing" and the dates: 1960–1999.

Sunday night, Carole came, and Lisa, Carolyn's sister. We did not say not much. We were glued to the TV. Bobby's wife, Mary [Richardson], called. She said, "Bobby hasn't spoken in two days." She said, "He's just been painting. That's all he does." I think somebody told him I was still saying, *Maybe they're gonna find him*. I was sitting on the bed and Bobby got on the phone and he said, "I know this is really hard, but RoseMarie, John's not coming back."

One day kind of bled into the next and I just remember the flowers. The entire front of the apartment was a memorial—it spilled from the stoop to the sidewalk almost to the street. It was halfway down the block. The flowers, notes, candles. The line of people who came to mourn for days was incredible. There were police barricades down the entire block because people were lined up.

Everyone was just confused. In shock. Ed Hill flew in. He came to the apartment. So it was Ed and Brian Steel, Kevin Hynes from the DA's office, Matt. I slept at the apartment for several nights. I mean, I didn't sleep. Everyone came back the next day. Carolyn's friends Gordon and Jessica and Danny were there. It was like a vigil, waiting to hear. I don't think I ever had that many phone calls in my life. Friends. Family, *George* people. The lawyers, the National Transportation Safety Board—NTSB—which began their investigation right away. Mrs. Freeman. I spoke to her a bunch of times. She was really angry at John. She was really mad. It was just terrifying. Like the earth cracked open. And he wasn't there to guide me.

Sasha Chermayeff

That Sunday, the phone rang. It was Mary Richardson. She said, "Bobby can't speak. He is sitting in this room and painting watercolors." Then the phone clicked and he came on. He said, "I'm painting a wave." I said, "You're doing watercolors. Well, we're like-minded people." I thought, *This guy is really wrecked right now. He's as bad as I am.*

John's close friend Kevin Ruf called when the suitcase was washed up. It must have been Sunday afternoon. We were both crying. He said they found luggage tags . . . and I said does that mean they're all dead? Because we were still clinging. I just remember Kevin saying yes, probably, and then I put the phone down. I hung up on him. Then Monday, the bodies were found.

President Bill Clinton

When his plane went down on that fateful night, I told a frustrated Coast Guard to stay on the water until they found him, Carolyn, and her sister. I had hoped so much that the son and nephew of two slain heroes would live and work for many decades, using his amazing combination of curiosity, good instincts, good heart, and winning personality to make our union more perfect. I believe he would have truly come into his own in the twenty-first century, finding new ways to cross boundaries and bridge divides, a living embodiment of the better angels of our nature. Now all we can do is remember him fondly, accept the raw truth that too often the good die young, and keep the flame of hope for a better world burning.

Bob Shrum

I think Teddy had a very clear sense that it was hopeless, and this was before they found the bodies. He called me and said, "You need to start writing the eulogy."

He was sad. He just didn't talk about it. He had borne so much loss in his life—just another unspeakable tragedy. And the way he dealt with it was to keep trying to move forward.

I was very sad when working on it, but I knew it had to get done. When I reread it after I had finished drafting it, I knew it would have a pretty profound effect on the audience.

That family had too much practice at this—you know, someone dies or is lost and the funeral, the eulogy. All of the surrounding events, that's all you can do. You can't bring the person back.

I did too many eulogies for Teddy, but this one was different. Rose Kennedy had lived a full life—there was no sense that she had been lost too soon. And Jackie, we knew she was sick for a while. John was particularly poignant because it came out of the blue. And there was a real sense of a loss of enormous potential. Teddy read it. He liked it. He said, "I just have to make sure I can get through it."

CHAPTER 25

"A dark night"

The National Transportation Safety Board determimes the probable cause(s) of this accident to be: the pilot's failure to maintain control of the airplane during a descent over water at night, which was a result of spatial disorientation. Factors in the accident were haze and the dark night.

—NTSB Aviation Investigation Final Report

Chris Benway

He was still in the middle of his instrument training. He was struggling with it, but everybody struggled with IFR training—it's like someone put a white sheet over the airplane and now you're expected to get to your destination.

So unfortunately, he was similar to those doctors I trained—they had the money to go buy the higher-performance airplane and they're gonna get themselves into trouble.

Was he reckless? Reckless is the wrong term. No, adventuresome. That's why it's a tragedy, because the way he died has happened to other pilots.

It's extremely sad. But I was really upset at him after he died. Like what the f— did you do that for?

Jeff Guzzetti, NTSB investigator, Office of Aviation Safety

If I were sitting down with a friend and they asked what happened to JFK Jr., here's what I'd say. He took off just after sunset from New Jersey. I don't think he intended on taking off at night, but it just worked out that way. He followed the Connecticut and Rhode Island coastline and then he turned out to sea to head towards Martha's Vineyard. And since it was dark and it was over the ocean, he probably had no horizon.

The weather conditions were technically visual flight rules (VFR), even though it was hazy—he had enough visibility in miles to make the flight legally. But as soon as he turned out to the black ocean with three to five miles of visibility in haze, it might as well be instrument flight rules (IFR)—meaning you must scan your instruments and that tells you whether your wings are level or if you are climbing or descending. However, he was not trained for instrument flying. He was trained to look outside to get his visual cues. There were no visual cues.

I believe he was on autopilot as he flew along the coast because the altitude remained incredibly consistent and so did the heading. But when he turned out towards Martha's Vineyard, my view was the autopilot was not engaged. He may have accidentally disconnected it, or purposely disconnnected it so that he could "hand fly" the airplane on its approach to Martha's Vineyard. We just don't know, because small airplanes like this do not have "black boxes." As a VFR pilot he likely did not have a great familiarity with the use of the autopilot. We ruled out any kind of autopilot malfunction after a detailed examination of the equipment and also a flight test during our investigation.

The last thirty miles, he starts to wander as he begins his descent to Martha's Vineyard. His flight path into the water is indicative of something called spatial disorientation. His inner ears were playing tricks with his sense of orientation. Your inner ear says you're turning to the left and you're actually not. So you correct to the right, thinking that you're leveling the airplane. His flight path into the water is consistent with what is known as a graveyard spiral. The airplane makes a spiral nose-down, down, down to the grave, kind of like going down a drain. The plane went into one final turn and it stayed in that turn pretty much all the way down to the ocean. It plunged into the Atlantic Ocean in a steep nose-down inverted attitude. He went in seven miles from Martha's Vineyard.

Munir Hussain

When I used to fly that Saratoga in bad weather, I always used the autopilot. If he had kept it going, he could have taken the plane down to two hundred, three hundred feet, until he saw the runway, and then disconnected the autopilot and landed. He must have disconnected earlier, then very quickly lost control of the plane. Nobody knows why the autopilot was not engaged.

Jeff Guzzetti

He was flying just fine over the coast, where you have lights. He was close. If he just would've flown straight and level and not done the maneuvering, he would've been over Martha's Vineyard in three to five minutes.

Flight-testing did not reveal any pre-impact malfunctions or deficiencies. Nor was there any evidence of a nefarious act or an explosion on board the airplane or any kind of fire. The fact that he had gotten his cast off the day before played no role. We had a medical doctor on staff at the NTSB and he looked at that thoroughly. The evidence suggests he had full range of his foot to be able to do what he needed to do for that flight.

In my personal opinion, I don't think the passengers knew what was happening to them. I'm sure they sensed something was changing, but perhaps it was *Oh, I guess we're getting ready to land soon.* It was seventeen seconds from the time they began to divert from their flight path to the time they impacted the ocean. They might've felt a little g-force pushing them down in their seats, like, "This feels a little bit weird." You would've heard the rush of air over the fuselage accelerate or get louder, during the final fatal plunge. Perhaps feel yourself accelerating a little bit. But whether or not a non-pilot's brain would pick up on a problem, I don't know. And then they hit the surface of the water and it's over. Boom.

Now, the pilot is different. The pilot's gonna pick up on those cues. You see your airspeed go up and you don't quite know where you're at. I would expect that the pilot would be very confused and perhaps a little frightened because the instruments may have not been matching up with how he was feeling. We'll never know whether JFK Jr. articulated any of this to the ladies who were seated behind him. We don't have a cockpit voice recording.

Examination of the seat structure revealed that they were wearing their seat belts at impact. The impact forces were tremendous. Due to the sensitivity about what was actually seen at the crash site at the bottom of the ocean, I was not privy to the video of the recovery. The NTSB typically doesn't get into gory details. There was so much secrecy and sensitivity about glimpses of the wreckage or glimpses of the bodies at the time that we were pretty tight-lipped about what we were seeing or what the navy saw. The wreckage had a twenty-four-hour guard because a newspaper—the *National Enquirer*, I think—was reportedly offering a $250,000 reward for any photographs of it. So we would take our pictures and then we'd take our film canisters out of our cameras and we'd give them to the investigator in charge, who would lock them up in a safe. I've been involved in many major airline accidents. I still haven't seen an accident that drew that much press attention.

The NTSB interviewed all of his flight instructors. One of them said that on the day of the accident, he called JFK Jr. and said, "Listen, you're gonna be making this flight at night, and there's haze out there. Are you sure you want to go alone? Because I'll go with you." And JFK Jr. told him, "No, I wanna do this alone." Maybe he could have used some better judgment and said, "You know what? It's getting late. It's too risky, I'm just not gonna do it. Flight instructor, you come with me just to make sure."

The NTSB interviewed an instructor who flew with John between that May and July. He said the pilot had some training flying the airplane on instruments without a visible horizon, but he had difficulty performing additional tasks under such conditions. He also stated that the pilot was not ready for an instrument rating evaluation as of July 1 and needed additional training. He said that he would not have felt comfortable with the pilot conducting night flight operations on a route similar to the one flown and in weather conditions similar to those that existed on the night of the accident.

That is one flight instructor's opinion. What does that tell me? It tells me that perhaps JFK Jr. was overconfident in his abilities for that particular flight, or he didn't recognize the additional hazards of flying over the ocean at night in a haze by himself, which is often the case with pilots. They don't conduct an adequate or accurate risk assessment.

The instructors said he had issues with doing multiple things at once, which is very typical when you're at the beginning stage of your instrument rating. To fly an airplane safely, especially under adverse weather conditions, you need to be able to multitask.

JFK Jr., who by all measures was a good pilot, who was progressing in his training, was not ready for that flight that evening. It was a dark night, the moon wasn't well lit, there was haze. A couple of other pilots who flew that night reported to the NTSB that they decided not to make the flight because of those conditions.

He was likely in over his head. He could have made better decisions, but I don't think that's reckless. The safety board didn't either in their analysis. Pilots don't intend to launch into IFR conditions, but things happen. So reckless, no. Less than good judgment, yes.

In the end, it's a cautionary tale for any private pilot to understand your own personal limitations.

David Clarke

Fog and darkness are tough—you've got to really be good to do that.

There's this thing in flying called get-home-itis. Where you just press on and press on and press on when you really shouldn't. He pressed on, and he wasn't skilled enough to do it. Oh God. Terrible.

Steve Gillon

There's no such thing as a Kennedy curse. They take risks that most other people would not take. John's uncle Joe took on what was a suicide mission in World War II. His aunt Kathleen flew into a thunderstorm. His father rejected the advice of the Secret Service and refused to put a bubble top on his car. Robert, without any Secret Service protection, plunged into crowds during the sixties when there are already three leaders assassinated, including his brother. John was a risk-taker.

John is solely responsible for the death of his wife and her sister. He bears the responsibilities of his recklessness that night—it was his poor judgment. Was that easy for me to say? No. But my responsibilities as a historian supersede my responsibilities as a friend. The historical truth is what it is.

He should not have gone up that night. The first sign of danger, he should have done what a lot of pilots did that night: flown inland. Spent a night somewhere and then picked up the next morning. He was reckless. He had been reckless his whole life.

John had escaped death and danger so many times. Christina Haag talks about how they were kayaking and were coming in over these rocks and they thought for sure they were going to die. He almost died in that little contraption that he loved flying around, the flying lawn mower. I think John always believed something was going to save him. But it just didn't that night.

CHAPTER 26

"A nightmare week"

RoseMarie Terenzio

When I came in on Monday, the pilot brief website was still up on John's computer, where he checked the weather before flying. It was the last thing he looked at on the computer.

I had to start cleaning out the office. I was concerned that there was all of that valuable artwork and the flag from the moon landing, the framed sketch of former presidents. . . . Trying to protect him still and make sure that none of his personal things were mishandled.

Ed Hill and some of John's friends came and helped pack. Then the guys on the staff helped put everything in boxes and shipped it off. Certain boxes were going to Caroline's house, the paintings and other boxes were going to the JPK [Joseph P. Kennedy] family office, and his personal things, his files and his *George* files, went to his apartment. There were drafts of editor's letters, articles with his comments, his Rolodex, address books and his Filofax, the crazy knit hats he always wore. The random things that you stick in a drawer.

We cleaned out his closet—his suit, shorts, T-shirts he would rollerblade in, sneakers, bike helmets, his ties. I always kept his calendar on my desk. At first, I couldn't look at it. When I did, I remember thinking I didn't have to call anyone to cancel because the whole world knew. On July 19, he was supposed to meet Paul Newman. On July 21, lunch with Larry Flynt . . . and then on the twenty-ninth he had Bruce Springsteen tickets.

We couldn't unbolt the computer, so the entire desk went to the JPK office and then was returned. Ed Hill was trying to be strong for me. He understood what I was about to take on between cleaning out their apartment, the office, the barrage of media and people wanting information—it was monumental.

Mike Showalter

We put the locks on the door. We didn't want nobody to go in that office. The friends took the pictures off the walls the whole night. Then we shipped it all out. We sent his desk, but we got the desk back. We didn't give it to nobody to use after that.

Lisa Dallos

I had seen John at the end of the day on Friday throwing a football with interns in the hallway; now his friends were pushing the trolley out with all of his boxes. His office was about to be sealed. I thought, *Yes, he was very famous, but he was still just a human being playing with his staff on a Friday afternoon.* And on Monday there was nothing left in his office. I can still see those two men pushing the cart down the hallway.

RoseMarie Terenzio

The NTSB was calling. Monday morning, I called John's attorneys and asked, "What do I do?" They said, "You can talk to them." I did. They just kept calling. *What time did you see him last? What did he say? Was he nervous? Was he in a good mood? A bad mood? Who did he talk to?* It was like they were trying to re-create the entire day. It was just like being cross-examined, you know? In hindsight, I understand because it was so high-profile. They had to make sure they had every single detail and there wasn't foul play.

A week later, I got a big brown box from the mail room. I think it was from the NTSB. There was his wallet. It was all water-damaged and warped. And one crutch. I sent it to Caroline. I just cried.

I was speaking to Caroline a few times a day. A lot of logistics about the funeral, making sure that all of his valuables were in a safe place, that everyone on the staff was okay. And then there was also the whole thing—what do we do with the last issue? *What would John want us to do?* We had this meeting in the conference room. We were all crying and trying to figure it out. John wouldn't want us to make a whole issue about him. That would make him cringe. A photo of him on the cover of *George* would be the worst thing we could do. He never wanted *George* to be about him—he wanted it to stand on its own.

Matt came up with this idea of a flag—John was a part of American history. Most of the issue we left intact. Those pages were probably the last things that he looked at and edited. We included a letter from the whole staff—it was our tribute to John and our tribute to *George*. We wanted so much for the magazine to live on. That would have been the ultimate tribute.

Hachette CEO Jack Kliger came down to our conference room that day and said, "I know this is difficult. I don't know what's going to happen to the magazine. At the end of the day we still have a business to run." He later called me up to his office and I remember sitting across from his desk. It's not like I had a job lined up. I didn't know what my position was anymore. He gave his condolences. He said he didn't know what was gonna happen with *George.* I wouldn't say he was the most comforting. He had just started, and he was probably not equipped for that. I mean, who would be?

I didn't know what to do with the grief. You're grieving with the staff, with his friends, and then my own grief and the whole world is grieving. And then Carolyn's friends and Carolyn and Lauren's family, and that was a whole different set of grief. A mom lost two daughters and a sister lost two sisters. Lauren wasn't a public figure, and she was obscured by the magnitude of John and Carolyn's fame. She was so beautiful and so smart and so funny. The loss of those two women is more than any family should have to bear. I was the central command for everybody for information, updates. I was trying to do what I would have done if he was still there. But I didn't have them to call and say, "What should I do on your behalf?"

Sasha Issenberg

I didn't even want to talk to my parents. I didn't feel I could talk with anybody because it would be a violation of whatever unspoken code. The staff went to our regular place, Café Loup, twice that week and we're basically there for a wake, but we can't really acknowledge why we're there because it would end up on Page Six. The whole country is grieving about the same thing and I'm experiencing it and being less public than some rando on the 1 or the 9 train.

I boxed stuff up. That made me feel like I was contributing in some way.

RoseMarie Terenzio

St. Thomas More, the church where the funeral was going to be held, could only hold 350 people. So it was a lot of figuring out who needed to be there. Caroline said I could pick five from the *George* staff and I said that that was unacceptable. He spent ten hours a day with them for five years. She said okay. I made sure that every single person from *George*, all forty, were invited because those were John's people.

Teddy wanted John to be buried in the family plot in Brookline, Massachusetts. I think there was a plot for John and Carolyn, but there wasn't one for Lauren. Because Lauren wasn't a Kennedy, she couldn't be buried there. Carolyn's mom did not want them separated. "I don't want the girls separated. I want them together." Caroline called me and asked how Catholic John was—she wanted to be sure cremating and spreading the ashes would be the right thing. I said, "Caroline, I think you should cremate them, and they should all stay together. I think John would want that. . . ." She wanted to honor her brother.

There was a meeting about the funeral with Carolyn's family. Teddy and Caroline did not go. They sent Ed Schlossberg and Ted's wife, Vicki Reggie. I think that Carolyn's family felt that was disrespectful, that Caroline should have been there. Vicki was trying to convince them to bury John and Carolyn in Brookline. She was inserting herself in a situation and being very dramatic and histrionic about why John had to be buried in Brookline. It wasn't taking into consideration the tragic way they had died. John was piloting a plane and Mrs. Freeman's two daughters had died in the plane crash that killed all three of them. They died together and they were sisters. In the end, they decided on a burial at sea.

"Such palpable grief"

I really don't know why it is that all of us are so committed to the sea,
except I think it's because in addition to the fact that the sea changes, and
the light changes, and ships change, it's because we all came from the sea.
And it is an interesting biological fact that all of us have, in our veins,
the exact same percentage of salt in our blood that exists in the ocean,
and, therefore, we have salt in our blood, in our sweat, in our tears. We
are tied to the ocean. And when we go back to the sea—whether it is to
sail or to watch it—we are going back from whence we came.

—John F. Kennedy, remarks in Newport at the Australian
Ambassador's Dinner for the America's Cup crews,
September 14, 1962

On July 22, a U.S. Navy destroyer, the USS Briscoe, *brought members of the Kennedy and Bessette families to the waters off Martha's Vineyard to scatter the ashes.*

Louis Iasiello, navy chaplain

The only controversial thing was whether or not anyone was entitled to a burial at sea from a naval vessel. But President Clinton quickly put an end to that discussion. When the commander in chief says this is what's going to happen, that's exactly what happens.

What I remember vividly that day was the way that Senator Kennedy went from family member to family member, a fatherly figure ministering to the family. His way of touching them, giving them reassurance that they were all together as a family and as friends.

There were hymns sung, including "Eternal Father," the navy hymn. It was very moving.

William Petruska, navy chaplain

There were only seventeen members of the Kennedy, Bessette, and Freeman families who came aboard. Of the Kennedy clan, I only recognized the senator, Ted; Caroline Kennedy and her husband, Ed; William Kennedy Smith, Bobby Kennedy, Maria Shriver, and others I knew were Kennedy children but could not identify.

Barry C. Black, navy chaplain

I had the privilege of carrying the urns with John's ashes and Carolyn's ashes that day. A Roman Catholic priest, one of my dear friends, carried the other urn, with Lauren's ashes.

I'm a navy chaplain. I've officiated at over a hundred funerals—I know grief. I have not seen such palpable grief anywhere else in my life.

When the little barge—the boat with the families—came to the USS *Briscoe*, there were a lot of photographers everywhere. Helicopters were hovering. We wanted to get away from the tabloids, and we finally did.

It took a while for the actual services to begin—I had an opportunity to fellowship with the families. Senator Kennedy was looking out into the water. There's a verse in Isaiah 53 that refers to our Lord; it says, "He was a man of sorrow and acquainted with grief." And that is what you sensed with this great family: that they were acquainted with grief. So much so that saying goodbye and having the public grieving with them was a norm. I walked over to him. I was very nervous—I didn't know him at all. I said, "Senator, Romans 8:28 says, 'In everything, God is working for the good of those who love him, who have been called according to his purpose.' " He looked at me. There was such an intensity in his eyes. And he said, "Would you repeat that?" I said, "It's Romans 8:28, Senator. 'In everything, God is working for the good of those who love him.' " He said, "Everything?" I said, "Yes, sir. There is no circumstance, Senator, where God is not in it." And then he repeated the text. "Romans 8:28," he said. "I'll have to remember that."

They had gone through so much. They had given so much.

I was able to be with Mrs. Freeman for probably an hour. I shared with her the fact that I had lost my mom. Not that there was equivalence, but I shared with her my anger at God and the fact that God is big enough to handle our rage. I had been talking with her, but there was no response—she was just listening. As she was leaving, Mrs. Freeman embraced me. She put her lips next to my ear, and she whispered, "What you said back there is the first thing that has made any sense since this whole horrible ordeal." That He can handle our rage.

When it came time to put the ashes into the water, I first led the Bessettes down. It's almost a ladder—we call it the stairs. They go down into the water. I'd done burials at sea . . . but the ashes clumped. And then, like someone from Harry Potter touching it with a wand, the clump just disappeared.

I led Caroline down and Caroline clutched the urn as if, given what she had just seen, *There's no way in the world I am going to lose my brother this way. He's not going so instantaneously.* I calmed her, and we went down. I mean, oh my God. Contorted with grief is not even an adequate description. I can still see her. She put the ashes in. As the ashes were pouring, she reached her hand into the water to put some water back on her. *I'm not going to let go of his hand.*

William Petruska

I guess the most poignant image for me was seeing Teddy take Caroline in his arms after she came back up from the water. They embraced for a good long while and I had a clear view of his face. He squeezed his eyes shut and clenched his jaw. It was such a grimace of pain.

We had taken three beautiful wreaths with us: red and white carnations with red roses. They were never used. One of the family members had a canvas bag with wild flowers. They each took some and threw them over the side as the ashes were scattered. I noticed that members of the Bessette family threw envelopes into the water as well.

Barry C. Black

They dropped flowers as the ship was sailing. They embraced one another as if that human closeness would somehow mitigate the ache.

William Petruska

Bobby, Robert's son, said to me, "No one will ever know how good John was."

RoseMarie Terenzio

The funeral at St. Thomas More the next day was a formal private funeral for John and Carolyn. Many of John's closest friends were left out because of space, and people were rightfully hurt they were not included. There are people to this day who feel cheated that they didn't get to say goodbye. I understand.

President Clinton was there. He had done so much to help find them. He had deployed the U.S. Navy and the Coast Guard. There had been backlash because they were private citizens and because of the time it took to find their bodies, five days. At one point Clinton said, "Because of the role of the Kennedy family in our national life and because of the enormous losses they have sustained in our lifetimes, I thought it was appropriate."

Muhammad Ali was there. He was John's hero. Rosey Grier was there. John loved Rosey. They talked about once a week.

Sean Neary

The *George* staff wanted to walk into the funeral all together, so we gathered at Sarabeth's Kitchen on the Upper East Side, near St. Thomas More. I remember going through security and someone saying, "Who are these folks?"

Sasha Chermayeff

My dad let me use his apartment on 81st and Lex for everybody to gather, so me and Robbie and Ed Hill, the best friends who were coming in from all over the place and a bunch of stragglers, we were all so broken that we had this weird gathering, like camping out in high school. Jenny Christian came up from North Carolina. I called Caroline and Ed the night before and said, "Can Jenny please come?" Jenny and our friend Kevin Ruf and I went through the police barricade together. New York is closed off. It's eerily quiet. Just helicopters. The whole city was shut from Lexington to Fifth.

RoseMarie Terenzio

I went to the funeral with Negi Vafa, the creative services director at *George*. We were in a cab going uptown on Park Avenue and couldn't get past a certain point. A cop said, "You can't go any further." Negi said, "We're going to John Kennedy's funeral," and he just said, "Get in." He took us to the funeral in the cop car.

There were no other cars on the street. We were saying, "Why are all the streets closed?" And he said, "Because of the funeral. The whole city is in mourning." It made me feel empty and sad and mad. Mad because it wasn't fair—it just seemed like a rip-off that he was gone. I was scared. He was my friend, my mentor, and my boss. I felt so lost.

Sasha Chermayeff

Teddy's eulogy was intense. Me and my husband, Philip, we were just shaking. Philip was convulsing—just a stream of tears. Teddy's choking up—he could barely get the words out. It was such a noble job. The hardest thing probably he ever did. Even with his brothers.

Senator Edward Kennedy eulogy, July 23, 1999

Once, when they asked John what he would do if he went into politics and was elected president, he said: "I guess the first thing is call up Uncle Teddy and gloat." I loved that. It was so like his father.

From the first day of his life, John seemed to belong not only to our family, but to the American family.

The whole world knew his name before he did.

A famous photograph showed John racing across the lawn as his father landed in the White House helicopter and swept up John in his arms. When my brother saw that photo, he exclaimed, "Every mother in the United States is saying, 'Isn't it wonderful to see that love between a son and his father, the way that John races to be with his father.' Little do they know—that son would have raced right by his father to get to that helicopter."

But John was so much more than those long ago images emblazoned in our minds. He was a boy who grew into a man with a zest for life and a love of adventure. He was a pied piper who brought us all along. He was blessed with a father and mother who never thought anything mattered more than their children.

When they left the White House, Jackie's soft and gentle voice and unbreakable strength of spirit guided him surely and securely to the future. He had a legacy, and he learned to treasure it. He was part of a legend, and he learned to live with it. Above all, Jackie gave him a place to be himself, to grow up, to laugh and cry, to dream and strive on his own.

John learned that lesson well. He had amazing grace. He accepted who he was, but he cared more about what he could and should become. He saw things that could be lost in the glare of the spotlight. And he could laugh at the absurdity of too much pomp and circumstance.

He loved to travel across this city by subway, bicycle and roller-blade. He lived as if he were unrecognizable—although he was known by everyone he encountered. He always introduced himself, rather than take anything for granted. He drove his own car and flew his own plane, which is how he wanted it. He was the king of his domain.

He thought politics should be an integral part of our popular culture and that popular culture should be an integral part of politics. He transformed that belief into the creation of George. *John shaped and honed a fresh, often irreverent journal. His new political magazine attracted a new generation, many of whom had never read about politics before.*

John also brought to George *a wit that was quick and sure. The premier issue of* George *caused a stir with a cover photograph of Cindy Crawford dressed as George Washington with a bare belly button.*

The "Reliable Source" in The Washington Post *printed a mock cover of* George *showing not Cindy Crawford, but me dressed as George Washington, with my belly button exposed. I suggested to John that perhaps I should have been the model for the first cover of his magazine. Without missing a beat, John told me that he stood by his original editorial decision.*

John brought this same playful wit to other aspects of his life. He campaigned for me during my 1994 election and always caused a stir when he arrived in Massachusetts. Before one of his trips to Boston, John told the campaign he was bringing along a companion, but would need only one hotel room.

Interested, but discreet, a senior campaign worker picked John up at the airport and prepared to handle any media barrage that might accompany John's arrival with his mystery companion. John landed with the companion all right—an enormous German shepherd dog named Sam he had just rescued from the pound.

He loved to talk about the expression on the campaign worker's face and the reaction of the clerk at the Charles Hotel when John and Sam checked in.

I think now not only of these wonderful adventures, but of the kind of person John was. He was the son who quietly gave extraordinary time and ideas to the Institute of Politics at Harvard that bears his father's name. He brought to the institute his distinctive insight that politics could have a broader appeal, that it was not just about elections, but about the larger forces that shape our whole society.

John was also the son who was once protected by his mother. He went on to become her pride—and then her protector in her final days. He was the Kennedy who loved us all, but who especially cherished his sister, Caroline, celebrated her brilliance and took strength and joy from their lifelong mutual admiration society.

And for a thousand days, he was a husband who adored the wife who became his perfect soul mate. John's father taught us all to reach for the moon and the stars. John did that in all he did—and he found his shining star when he married Carolyn Bessette.

How often our family will think of the two of them, cuddling affectionately on a boat, surrounded by family—aunts, uncles, Caroline and Ed and their children, Rose, Tatiana, and Jack—Kennedy cousins, Radziwill cousins, Shriver cousins, Smith cousins, Lawford cousins—as we sailed Nantucket Sound.

Then we would come home—and before dinner, on the lawn where his father had played, John would lead a spirited game of touch football. And his beautiful young wife—the new pride of the Kennedys—would cheer for John's team and delight her nieces and nephews with her somersaults.

We loved Carolyn. She and her sister, Lauren, were young, extra-ordinary women of high accomplishment—and their own limitless possibilities. We mourn their loss and honor their lives. The Bessette and Freeman families will always be part of ours.

John was a serious man who brightened our lives with his smile and his grace. He was a son of privilege who founded a program called Reaching Up to train better caregivers for the mentally disabled.

He joined Wall Street executives on the Robin Hood Foundation to help the city's impoverished children. And he did it all so quietly, without ever calling attention to himself.

John was one of Jackie's two miracles. He was still becoming the person he would be, and doing it by the beat of his own drummer. He had only just begun. There was in him a great promise of things to come.

The Irish ambassador recited a poem to John's father and mother soon after John was born. I can hear it again now, at this different and difficult moment:

We wish to the new child A heart that can be beguiled By a flower That the wind lifts As it passes. If the storms break for him May the trees shake for him Their blossoms down.

In the night that he is troubled May a friend wake for him So that his time may be doubled, And at the end of all loving and love, May the Man above Give him a crown.

We thank the millions who have rained blossoms down on John's memory. He and his bride have gone to be with his mother and father, where there will never be an end to love. He was lost on that troubled night—but we will always wake for him, so that his time, which was not doubled, but cut in half, will live forever in our memory, and in our beguiled and broken hearts.

We dared to think, in that other Irish phrase, that this John Kennedy would live to comb gray hair, with his beloved Carolyn by his side. But like his father, he had every gift but length of years.

We who have loved him from the day he was born, and watched the remarkable man he became, now bid him farewell.

God bless you, John and Carolyn. We love you and we always will.

RoseMarie Terenzio

People were sobbing. Teddy's voice cracked. Part of me was thinking, *Why are all these people here and John's not?* At the end, Wyclef Jean sang "Many Rivers to Cross" and everyone burst into tears. It was so beautiful and emotional. The idea of many rivers to cross—it was like John was going on a journey, but we were not going with him.

Wyclef Jean, musician

Bobby Shriver told Jimmy Iovine they're looking for someone who can sing, who could compose a piece for the event. Jimmy says, "Just call this kid, whatever you want, he can put it together." I wanted to sing something that can uplift us. Where I come from, we don't really mourn death—death is a transition. Maybe I could start with Jimmy Cliff's "Many Rivers to Cross." A moment of transition and not easy to get there. At the end of this song, I was like, *Okay, what can I mash up and catch a vibe?* I picked it up with [the hymn] *Because He lives, I could face tomorrow,* just to raise the hope for those that are still in this life.

I recorded it in twenty-four hours. And then they had to get the whole family together and play this demo. And that was it. I showed up.

They could have called anybody. So why call a kid from slums of the ghettos of Croix-des-Bouquets, that small village in Haiti where I was born? If John was to pick someone to sing, he wouldn't be looking for the fanciest singer or the pop chart killer. He would be looking for me, just a straight-up viber, the slumdog millionaire that can show up and then people feel something.

I could feel John in my soul. There was a spiritual energy, a John energy moving through that room. Like, *I'm going to be okay.* All I did was channel that wave.

When I told my mom I would sing at John's funeral, she prayed with me. And my mom says, "Make sure you move them." I never sang it again. That was a gift that can't be duplicated.

RoseMarie Terenzio

Anthony was there, walking with a cane. He was so frail. His suit was hanging off of him. No one expected John to die before Anthony. You could see the toll of John's death in that moment.

Gustavo Paredes

Anthony was devastated. He became completely deflated—he dissipated after.

Santina Goodman

I had to read the first "Prayer of Intercession" (worried I'd fuck up). Walked to the altar, stood in front of the microphone to speak. Realized the reverend had not completed his "Homily." I just took a few steps back and waited until Reverend was done. Stepped to the microphone again and said, "Sorry." All I could hear was a little "chuckle" from everyone. At that moment I just knew John was "laughing his ass off." Reverend O'Byrne says, "You're doing fine. . . . You're moving us along." Looked up and focused on the people right in front of my eyesight. Smiling at me were the Kennedy family and Bill and Hillary Clinton. When I sat, I could feel how proud John was of me ("That's my girl").

Paul Begala

One of Carolyn's relatives read a poem and it said something like, *She's not gone, she's just away. She's in the next room.* I thought that was really comforting. I was sitting with John Kenneth Galbraith, President Kennedy's ambassador in India. Galbraith says, in too loud a voice because he's 90 and hard of hearing, "A tad optimistic, it seems to me."

Sasha Chermayeff

I was asked to speak. I didn't have the nerve to say I'm going to say something different. I'm not religious. I don't like using words like "blessed" and stuff. So, I just made up my own version. I came up with it the night before, unable to sleep. I just said their names. "John and Carolyn, you live inside of me. You live in all of us." When we went outside, Ann Freeman put her arms around me and whispered, "You were the only one that made me cry." My heart broke for her. All I could think of was "I was the only one?" What about Teddy? But I hadn't lost two of my children due to a certain amount of negligence on the part of John. In all honesty, I was glad that I was there to help her cry. Maybe because I said their names with such love. I was pleading to somehow just keep them alive in me, alive in us.

The John-centric-ness of the whole thing—I don't know if I really noticed it enough at the time. As much as I love John, if two of my beloved girls got killed in a car wreck with Brad Pitt, and all I heard about was Brad Pitt, I'd be fucking out of my mind. The John-centric-ness of the world's response to the death of three people . . . What happened to Ann Freeman is so unspeakable. Apparently, she had felt bullied by the Kennedys in terms of the funeral arrangements and where they were going to be buried—I remember Bobby saying stuff about it. People had so much anger around the accident—the stupidity, the fact that it could have easily been prevented.

RoseMarie Terenzio

There was a reception after at the Convent of the Sacred Heart school, where Caroline went. Teddy was being the Irish storyteller—he understood he had to bring everybody to a place of hope, and he turned it into a celebration of John's life. It was unlike anything I had ever seen. Life is for the living—Teddy embodies that. There is no other human being on the planet who could have brought everybody together. Unimaginable grief to now, camaraderie and celebration. He was the great comforter. He had an unbelievable gift to give hope. Everyone formed a circle around him. I will always be thankful to him for that.

Sasha Chermayeff

At the reception, Caroline had no expression. It was scary to me. No tears. That was when I realized how traumatized she really was. I just thought, *Oh my God, she's lost so much.*

After the reception, there was a memorial get-together hosted by a friend of John's. I was in such a trance. I had not slept for seven days.

I remember looking around this crowd going, *Who the fuck are all these people and why are they dressed like it's a cocktail party?* Marci Klein, Calvin Klein's daughter, she was wearing strappy black heels. I felt like Mary Tyler Moore in *Ordinary People*, the scene when she is correcting Donald Sutherland's choice of outfit and then he breaks down later in therapy and says, "I was going to my son's funeral."

John's dead. People were partying. There were women who were dressed to the nines. I just felt so separate.

Many people were really angry. Angry that he killed them all by flying. Angry that in a stress-related bad decision, he had gone without a copilot and he had gone at night when he didn't have non-visibility experience or even certification. Ed Hill, the men, were all furious. I think the anger was also to cover up their pain.

Between the disappearance of the plane and that party, my week was lying on a couch with my little children, who wondered why I wouldn't get up. I can't imagine how it was for the families, negotiating burial sites—it was a horrible kind of argumentative week, a nightmare week.

On July 24, a memorial for Carolyn and Lauren was held at Christ Church in Greenwich, Connecticut.

RoseMarie Terenzio

Matt Berman and Pat Manocchia and I went together. Mrs. Freeman was so determined to make sure that Lauren and Caryoln were the focus, and so many of Lauren's friends and colleagues were there and spoke about her with such love. Carole Radziwill read from *The Portrait of a Lady*. I believe Bobby gave the eulogy for Carolyn. Ann Freeman's brother Jack gave Lauren's eulogy, and two of Lauren's friends spoke. It was time to focus on Lauren—the person she was—and Carolyn. Not Carolyn as John's wife.

Sasha Chermayeff

I went to Greenwich for the memorial for Carolyn and Lauren. I bonded with Ted Jr. John and I had been talking about him maybe a month before.

John was saying, "My cousin Teddy is such a sweet guy." I said, "John, out of the blue, just told me he really loved you." I wanted him to know.

I became friends with Bobby Jr. after John died. It's like nobody else can understand what you're going through. I remember even Bobby said to me there's nobody I can talk to. Everybody else just is "Oh, that's so sad. It's time to move on. . . ." It's like you're clinging on to something and you go to the people who are sort of clinging to the same thing.

RoseMarie Terenzio

A week or so later, I began cleaning out their place. Caroline asked me if I would mind packing some things up. So, drawer by drawer, closet by closet, I packed everything up in these big moving boxes. It was devastating to pack up their lives. In some ways, it felt like I was violating their privacy. Packing up socks and underwear and clothes and all of his ties and all of her shoes.

The hardest part was the nightstands because it was their little books, things they were reading, and their drawers, private things that no one would ever want someone to rifle through. And the photographs—the Herb Ritts photo of the two of them on the weekend of their engagement. They looked so in love. And the photo I gave them for their anniversary, she's sitting on his lap laughing. I had it framed. And then the photographs of their friends' kids. Beautiful old Tiffany silver frames with treasured photographs. They were all put in a box.

Packing the closet felt awful. All of John's suits were on one side and all of Carolyn's clothes and shoes were on the other. Everything was very organized. Her clothes were so classic and minimalist. Almost everything was black, white, navy, or gray. That was her mantra. John hated black—at the *George* Christmas party he had one rule: no black, but of course Carolyn wore black just to mess with him.

John had this massive amount of ties. Carolyn had tons of shoes, fifty or more pairs. She would shop for spring, fall, and summer, but she did not have a huge amount of clothes. She expressed her more whimsical side in shoes— that's how her personality came through.

Carolyn's sister Lisa came over and helped with her things. That was a week or so later. It was me and Lisa and Jessica that went through her clothes. I remember she had this Comme des Garçons skirt, a fishtail black skirt. She had loaned it to me for some event. I remember saying to Lisa, "That's the skirt and jacket I wore. . . ." She gave it to me. We were just trying to be task-focused so Lisa could get through it, you know?

David Clarke

Caroline called Sacred Heart and asked my wife's sister, who worked there, to take John's belongings and scatter them to the wind. In other words, nothing that left John's apartment was flagged as belonging to John F. Kennedy Jr. It was all given away anonymously because it would've caused such an icky thing. *I've got John Kennedy's overcoat*, then eBay. That's an amazing thing, his entire wardrobe, everything, all went to Sacred Heart, and all went out and nobody was the wiser. It's kind of fitting, there's some homeless guy walking around in John F. Kennedy Jr.'s tuxedo jacket.

Samantha Schmidt, David Clarke's sister-in-law

I went to Sacred Heart, as did John's sister. I ran sort of the facilities for Sacred Heart School and got called in by Sister Salisbury. She said, "We're gonna get these boxes of things and you have to hang on to them for three to four months and then donate them to Little Sisters. But you can't let anybody look in the boxes." And then she told me why. It was brilliant because otherwise it would've ended up being sold. Little Sisters of the Assumption—it's a charity that Sacred Heart worked closely with. They didn't want anyone making money off of it or to make a scene. So I thought it was a very dignified way to handle everything.

"Trying to hold on to the person . . ."

RoseMarie Terenzio

There was a back-and-forth with Caroline about these lacquered nightstands that they had next to their beds that were Mrs. Onassis's. Carolyn loved them. I think Lisa and her mom hoped to keep them. They were going back and forth with Caroline because she wanted them back. I think I was on a call with Caroline and she said, "Well, those were my mother's—those were Mummy's end tables." At one point there was discussion of, they can keep one of them. And just back-and-forth nonsense. I honestly don't remember what the outcome was. It's like, *Really?* It happens in every family. Trying to hold on to the person . . . and any connection you can find.

I don't remember specifically what happened with the jewelry. I think at one point Caroline felt like the jewelry that was Jackie's that John had given Carolyn, she should have back because it was her mother's. I wasn't privy to what happened. Carolyn's family were saying it was given to Carolyn by John. Some was in a jewelry box on Carolyn's dresser. I remember one piece, a necklace, and it had this charm, a cage with a bird in it. It was beautiful. And there was this purse, a black satin clutch. The clip to close the purse was jade with some jewels on it. I don't know if it was rubies and diamonds—it was phenomenal. I tried to stay neutral because it really wasn't any of my business. I don't remember who took what and how it eventually all got distributed. It's just sad that it comes down to possessions when it was really about the unimaginable loss.

Caroline came down a week after the funeral. Marta Sgubin, the long-time nanny and chef who worked for Mrs. Kennedy, came with her and went through the kitchen, whatever was left, dishes and glasses. Caroline was stoic, but I think she was still in shock and trying to process. Now this whole thing is thrust upon her to deal with.

The Freemans came to pick up a few final things, including a beautiful portrait of John and Carolyn. Ann came with her husband, Dick. I got the sense they just wanted to get out as quickly as they could. Carolyn wasn't there anymore. And they were still in shock. I put things aside that she had wanted. I can't imagine how hard it was for them and for Lisa. She was trying to spare her mom from all of that.

The last day at their place was a month or two later. It was horrible. I didn't go to Tribeca for years. It just felt so empty walking out of the there, alone. Even now, there are too many memories.

Not long after the funeral, I met with Caroline. We went out for breakfast. It was good to see her. She was funny and warm. We were joking and she was like, "He was a Republican, right?" I'm like, "Yeah, he was. . . ." She's like, "Oh, he was totally a Republican." We were laughing about that. She has a great sense of humor.

Hachette laid me off a few weeks later. They said there was no role for me—and they were going to withhold my bonus because I had not worked the entire year. Matt Berman went to the head boss at Hachette and said, "Her boss died, what are you talking about?" I don't think I said goodbye to anybody. I just left.

He's not supposed to die. He's supposed to be this superhero to all of us. What do you do when your boss dies? I didn't know where I belonged anymore. That was my identity.

I stayed in touch with Carolyn's family for a few years. At first, our conversations were more like *I'm just trying to cope. Just trying to survive day-to-day*. Seeing how they were, them seeing how I was. It was beyond sadness. Ann wanted to set up some sort of foundation in Carolyn's name, and we talked about a scholarship for at-risk kids. . . . I don't know if it ever happened. I think she was overwhelmed by all of it.

When Lisa would come into town, we would have lunch, drinks. Me and Jessica. It was also comforting 'cause we could all kind of bond together over the loss and keep the connection to Carolyn. We felt safe with each other. We would tell funny stories about Carolyn. Lisa also had to deal with Lauren's apartment and cleaning that out. I helped her a little bit. Lauren had just moved into her new apartment. Everything was still in boxes.

Lisa was just trying to cope. There were times when she would cry, and times when she was being a rock for her family. There was the media, her mother, her family, her friends. It wasn't like she had time in those first six months to process. We stayed in touch for a few years and then, eventually, people go back to their lives and it was too painful for Carolyn's mom and for Lisa to stay in touch. In a way maybe me and the other friends were a reminder of the loss. I think of them every day. For that family, I think there's no such thing as moving on.

Maybe two years later, John's friends and some *George* colleagues started talking about doing something to remember him. Someone asked Caroline if we could do something to honor him, maybe in Sheep Meadow. It was a shithole that he loved. It wasn't maintained back then, it was uneven, but he loved it. That's where they always played football. Maybe try to get Sheep Meadow named after him. We needed her support because we weren't gonna get it done without her input. She said no. Whatever her reasons were, they were private. We also thought about a bench. I don't know if we ever pursued the bench because it was like *Really, a bench?* Only time he sat on a bench was to take his Rollerblades off.

I wish there was a place for John to be remembered in the city he loved. Matt had the idea to do a book of *George* covers along with his editor's letter for each issue, with outtakes from the cover shoots. Caroline asked for a proposal, which we sent, but she didn't want to do it.

Other than my mother's death, it was the worst finality I ever experienced. I didn't have an identity anymore. It was hard to figure out what to do next. They were always this beacon. I think Santina said it also. *As long as John's in the world, you're gonna be okay.* What can happen to you? If you get arrested, John will figure it out. If you don't have money, he'll get you a place to live—at least give you the basics. Jack Merrill said it, too. *Our get-of-jail-free card.*

A year or more later, Marta Sgubin invited me over—we stayed in touch. She adored John and Caroline. Marta was telling me about all the changes Ed was making to the Martha's Vineyard house. She said he tore down the tower. That was John's place at the house. He was erasing John's presence, and she was upset about it.

Santina Goodman

For years after John passed away, I had many "John Dreams." One dream, I was standing in a balcony area and there was a lower-floor area. John walked onto the balcony and was talking with people. He walked over to me, and I remember we were laughing and having a great time. Then he suddenly said, "I have to go." I remember saying, "Please, John, don't go." He started walking to the lower-balcony area and I followed him. He turned around and said, "T, you can't go with me."

Roberto DiPelesi

Santina adopted their cat after he and Carolyn died, and when the cat died, I think that was like her last connection to John. Then one day years later, she told me she'd found an alphabet cube in the snow with the letter "T" on it. She said, "This is a signal from John. Nobody called me T but John." I think for her, that was like *John's calling me, and I've made the decision anyway.* And then she took her own life.

Sasha Chermayeff

Everybody was so lost . . . Santina was very fragile. She became more and more isolated, more lonely. She needed help, but I didn't realize how much.

John's people, we weren't in touch anymore in the same way after he was gone. But when I had breast cancer in 2006 and I was in the ICU after surgery, I heard Robbie's voice in the waiting room. He's not allowed in the ICU and he had a bouquet of flowers, also not allowed in the ICU. I hadn't seen him in five years.

John helped create these deep, trusting relationships. And I realized we have this John tree, this kind of sacred thing.

I do feel like John and Carolyn's incredibly untimely loss served in this very sad way to make life so precious. The fleetingness of it—that sense of the beauty, the brevity. They gave it to us.

Coda

"How could you not cry?"

Neal Gabler

People say, "Well, who was he? He really didn't do anything." They don't understand what JFK Jr. meant spiritually to America.

Ted Kennedy returned to the Senate after John's death and the burial, and he spoke at the weekly prayer breakfast, and he was emotionally naked in a way that he almost never was. He was a very guarded person. But he came to that prayer breakfast, and he just basically cried, and he talked about the loss and what it meant.

I think he understood what we kind of all understood, which is: it's over. Carrying the Kennedy legacy meant being the voice for the voiceless, the power for the powerless, the conscience of the country, the force that would do right when all the wind in this country was blowing against doing those things. JFK was a president of whom we could say, "He made us better." We hate every president now, that's just a given. The country loved John Kennedy.

I think Ted felt that John was the prince; he was the individual who is going to carry on the legacy. These other Kennedy kids, whatever one thinks of them, they don't have what John had—the combination of gravitas and unpretentiousness, the sensitivity to how to live within that narrative. They screw up the narrative. And I think Ted, who'd screwed up the narrative himself so many times, absolutely understood. It's over. Nobody else is going to carry that "fallen standard," to use the words he used after Bobby had died. Well, JFK Jr. was going to pick up the fallen standard. Now he was gone, and nobody was there to pick it up.

Sasha Chermayeff

I used to say to him, "It isn't just that you're famous, handsome John Kennedy. My kids don't know anything about that and they follow you around. It's more." The pied piper thing, it was really true.

I'm sixty-four now. John's been dead for almost twenty-five years. . . . My daughter, Livi, was staying with me, and we were sleeping in the same bed in our little cabin. I woke up crying, just saying to her, "Oh God, I've just been missing him for so long." And my daughter was saying, "I know, Mom, I know."

Missing John has been this huge part of my life. I felt, goddamn it, even though the dream was beautiful, and we were laughing, and I was loving him. I was saying to him in my dream, "It's not only that you've been such a superstar, but it's also been so much fun. Hasn't it been so much fun?" And we were smiling at each other and then I woke up thinking, *It's so strange how much he's affected my life.*

Ed Hill

I was really mad at John. I was so disappointed in the way he lost his life.

But I really cannot muster an ill word about that guy. Okay, he left shit in taxicabs. God knows how many bicycles that guy owned and lost, God knows how many cars were stolen or wound up in impoundment or that sort of absent-minded thing that was a big part of him. Not that those things aren't substantial. But where the rubber hit the road in terms of the way John treated other people, in terms of what John was willing to do for other people, I mean, he was as good a man as I've ever known.

Christiane Amanpour

I miss his incredible friendship and his generosity and his fun and his warmth. And, you know, being treated a bit like his sister. I relied on his friendship for years.

I'm heartbroken that he never got to meet my son, whose middle name is John for John Kennedy, my friend. I'm sorry that we weren't able to grow as journalists together, because I'm sure that *George* would've gone on in some form or fashion. I was actually quite envious about all those people he was interviewing. He wasn't a dilettante, and I want the world to know that.

Narendra Taneja

I was angry with God that he took him away. He was so full of life. In my culture, we would go to temple and protest to God. "How could you do that?" In our religion, we have the right to protest. We ask this question to God.

I do know one thing—that if you happen to meet wonderful people in life, like I met John, that's thanks to God, that you meet—and that you remember.

Garth Brooks

The older you get, you start to realize that there are people that wear their story when you see them—in their face, their actions. Most of us are trying to put on a front to make you think we're better than we are. He was very casual and very relaxed, the way he carried himself. . . .

His whole life was public from the first second. But he just seemed to wear his life right in front of you.

Sean Penn

Oh God, this country thought they owned him from the time he was born. I don't think there's anything comparable to it, not even the Beatles. It was so invasive and so scrutinizing. How do you breathe?

I've thought about him often. I definitely had the sense [when we met] that this guy is as impressive as I had wanted him to be. He was the top of the American wedding cake—tall, dark, handsome, and charming as fuck. But I didn't expect his gravitas. His death is one of those things where you wanna roll the tape back—just let me hear that did not happen.

I just really dug him. We were looking at doing a coast drive in California together in the next couple of months . . . and just as I was feeling I had a new friend, it was over.

Mike Tyson

How could you not cry? You gotta be the hardest person, the downest person in the world, if you can't cry over a person that we're not gonna see his lights again. He was just special. He's almost like God sent him and God says, "Hey, that's enough for y'all. I gotta take him away now." He's just a young kid. . . . I wish he had kids. I'm very grateful that I could spend time with him.

This is what I learned from John. He said he met a lot of great men, but all the great men he met, they were not good men. That changed my life. You have no idea, man.

John Perry Barlow

Of course the whole world had him, but all that was this *thing*. It was this nation's balloon that it tugged overhead. It was "John-John" that floated overhead. All they had were the magazine covers. It was not him at all. It was a cartoon series. And the bigger the cartoon series got, the further away it was from the person he was. We had the person he was.

Steve Gillon

He was fascinated by my working-class Irish Catholic family in Philly. I would tell him how we grew up in this neighborhood. People were fighting all the time, there's gangs. And he used to love this story: When I was in eighth grade, I got mugged by a gang of twelve guys who were five, six years older than me. My brother Franny finds out who each of them were and beats each of them up. I had nothing to offer John, really, but what I had was life experiences that were different from his.

I think a lot of people, especially family members, want to paint a fairly simplistic view of John. They don't want there to be any complexity, and that's not the John I knew.

Jack Merrill

He used to live in a great apartment on Hudson and he had the whole top floor. We were hanging out and he asks, "Do you want to go work out?" I didn't have any workout clothes, so he gives me some shorts and a jersey and they're way too big and we get on our bikes and go to the Downtown Athletic Club. We come into the lobby and there's like ten dudes standing there in their Wall Street suits. Perfect, well-bred East Coast guys. I look like a clown and we're laughing, and I looked at them and they all looked at him and then they look at me like *What's he doing with you?* And I thought, *That's why I love him. He's with me and he's supposed to be with you guys.*

RoseMarie Terenzio

We would bicker like two old ladies. He'd say, "It's not Halloween. Take that fright wig off," when my hair was curly and not blown out.

I kept all the special notes from him and Carolyn. Just like I keep my mom's, in a special box. This one was after the first Newman's Own George Awards in 1998. He left me a check for $5,000. Carolyn had gotten me a kitten, for no reason other than I should have a pet. It was an Abyssinian—that cat had a tiny head. So, he wrote on the card:

> *Rose, many thanks for doing such a typically first-rate job on the Newman's Own George Awards. Go buy a cat with the right size head.*
> *With gratitude,*
> *John*

Hans Hageman

I was walking on Park Avenue. I heard somebody calling my name and I turned around—it was a guy on a bicycle and it was John. The last time I saw him. He mentioned that he had nominated me for an award, I think it was the Astor Foundation. He said, "The good news, you were a semifinalist and you were going to move into the finalist round. But then they decided that you've got a lot of years ahead of you, so they moved some other people to the final round."

And then he laughed and said, "But you and me, we've got a lot of years ahead of us."

RoseMarie Terenzio

I remember one time, years ago, we were walking to lunch on 51st Street between Broadway and Eighth. A bunch of construction workers saw him and they yelled, "Hey, John-John, I love your magazine." And he said, "Thanks, guys—but it's one John." We laughed.

There really *was* only one John.

David Clarke

He was a wacky little kid, but he could have been president. God only knows where we'd be right now. If that little butterfly effect had gone a different way, the world might be a different place.

Dan Samson

Every once in a while I'll tell my kids how much different this world would be if my friend John was still alive. Perhaps joking, but really not, I tell them how John's life plan might have synched up perfectly to run for president in 2016. Trump would've had no chance against John—none, zippo, nada! My kids give me a look like I might be a bit wacked, but I know I'm not. We'd be living in a better world today if John Kennedy and Carolyn Bessette Kennedy were still among us. That possibility is gone, but a tiny bit of their spirit lives within each of us.

RoseMarie Terenzio

When I was cleaning out John and Carolyn's apartment at the end, I found this book on his nightstand. It's called *Knowledge That Leads to Everlasting Life*, with excerpts from the Bible. It's a Jehovah's Witnesses book. I kept it—*I* was certainly looking for answers. There was a sticky note on chapter 9, "What Happens to Our Dead Loved Ones." The book is inscribed, "To John, from Todd Roy."

> *To John,*
> *Losing a loved one is never easy. Especially when you are reminded of it regularly. True happiness and peace of mind comes when you have a hope as we do. Read chapter 9 first, then the rest of the book. If you have any questions, please feel free to call.*
> *Your friend,*
> *Todd Roy*

John was always searching, and not always where you'd expect. Maybe he was thinking about death right then because Anthony was so sick, or maybe something to do with the loss of his mother. Who knows? I wouldn't be surprised if he gave Todd a call.

Robbie Littell

What do I miss? Our camaraderie. Just laughing it up. You miss him, but on a level that it's not so much about you. You put yourself in your friend's shoes and you miss *for* him.

I've heard they cut a tree down in Irish culture when someone dies young, because they only lived half of their life. And I like to say, here's a guy who lived twice as hard as anyone else. Twice as *well* as anyone else. So in his almost forty years, he lived two lifetimes. But now you look back and you're like, poor guy. I think of the loss, not so much my loss, but his loss—of not being able to experience life, which he loved so much.

I get mad. That's my defense. The loss was going to come when the stories faded—and I didn't want to lose the stories. I used to say the first half of life is for making them so the second half, you start telling 'em. But it actually makes sense to make 'em as long as you can.

When you can't remember a person's face or something slips your memory, that's when it hurts. It was something that was there every day for a long time. . . . You don't wanna obsess about it, either. I think the best way you can handle a loss is *What would they want me to do? How would they want me to be?* Laugh. Have fun. Enjoy life. Nothing more.

That was nice from his sister at the memorial service—she told me, "He really loved you." And that was it. That was mutual.

Acknowledgments

Thank you to all of our contributors—John's friends, colleagues, schoolmates, and relatives who so graciously shared their memories of him. We are especially thankful for the generosity and guidance of the friends we interviewed time and again: Joe Armstrong, Jason Beghe, Sasha Chermayeff, Gary Ginsberg, Jack Merrill, and Steven M. Gillon, whose biography of John, *America's Reluctant Prince*, was also an invaluable resource.

We are sorry that three contributors—Santina Goodman, Paul Eckstein, and David Clarke—are no longer with us to see how their stories enriched the book.

We would like to thank the team at Gallery Books/Simon & Schuster for giving us the opportunity to bring this book to fruition and for the idea that John would be well served by an oral biography: editor Pamela Cannon along with Jen Bergstrom, Aimee Bell, Sierra Fang-Horvath, Hanna Preston, Jen Robinson, Sally Marvin, Kell Wilson, Caroline Pallotta, Stephen Breslin, Jaime Putorti, and John Vairo.

Special thanks to our agent, Steve Troha at Folio Literary Agency, for his support and good counsel throughout the process.

We appreciate the assistance of the following organizations: Wesleyan University Library, Special Collections & Archives for their help with the William Manchester Papers, and the John F. Kennedy Library.

We would also like to thank Yvette Manessis Corporon, Mara Buxbaum,

Marcy Engelman, Jo Mignano, Nancy Seltzer, Jill Fritzo, and Melanie A. Bonvicino for their support of our project. A special thank you to Anne-Marie Fox.

We were fortunate to have such a hard-working team at our sides: Olivia Weeks, Annie Mattix, our transcriber David Chiu, fact-checker Sabrina Ford, and photo researcher Brenna Britton.

We are deeply indebted to Martin Torgoff for his creativity, his early critiques of the manuscript and ideas for interview subjects, and for always saying, "Why not?"

We are extremely grateful to one of the finest editors in the business, Kim Hubbard, for her meticulousness, rigor, insight, humor and—always!—her follow-up questions. She was instrumental in shaping the book from start to finish.

RoseMarie Terenzio

I am grateful for the opportunity this book provided to celebrate and remember John through the voices of those who knew and loved him. His spirit certainly lives on in each and every one of them. It was insightful to hear their stories and get to know them and John in a more profound way.

The support of my family, friends, and colleagues made the book possible.

Thank you to my husband, David Mazzella, for always lifting the corners of my mouth and for taking care of me throughout.

Special thanks to my family for their enthusiasm and encouragement: Marion and Anthony Terenzio, now gone; Anita and Raymond Perillo; Andrea and Rino Rizzi; Dr. Amelia Schreibman; Maria Perillo and Alex Salta; Christina Perillo and Rafael Lopez; my stepdaughter, Julia Mazzella; and my mother-in-law, Mary Ann Mazzella, now gone.

I'm indebted to my dear friends Matt Berman (AKA 234), Tricia Viola, Roger Woody, Michele Ammon, Charley Tucker, Jessica Weinstein, Jennifer Zweben, Jennifer Simpson, and Roland Foster, who were always available to listen, laugh, and encourage. The guidance and advice of my colleagues Maureen Dowd, Eric Herman, Kent Holland, and Alex Spiro was invaluable.

Liz McNeil

When I first began work on this project, I was impressed by how deeply John's friendship marked those close to him. As the book progressed, I saw that of course it went both ways: the people he loved—an astonishing array of delightful characters—had a profound impact on him as well. It's been a pleasure getting to know them.

I thank my colleagues at *People* magazine, especially Wendy Naugle and Alex Brez, for their support of this project and for the incredible opportunities my job has allowed.

I could not have written the book without the help of family and dear friends. I'm grateful to Firoozeh Dumas and Pamela Keough for their wisdom and encouragement, and especially to Clint Hill and Lisa McCubbin Hill. I began the project with an interview with Clint, now ninety-two, and he and Lisa remain examplars of how to tell a story with honesty and integrity. Special thanks to my parents, Ray and Bettina McNeil, now gone, and my sisters, Pam, Lynne, Jennifer, Loretta, and Leslie, for their support and kindness.

My husband, Michael Thomas, and our son, Maxwell, provided much love and understanding. Mike helped me structure the book from the beginning, helping me see how the voices of John's friends could be in conversation with one another on the page, and he took care of me in the 101 ways that any writer struggling to author a book requires.

Contributors

Adams, Gerry: Irish Republic politician; president of the Sinn Féin party from 1983 to 2018

Alter, Jonathan: Author; political columnist

Amanpour, Christiane: College housemate; Chief International Anchor for CNN

Anderson, Pamela: Author; actor; activist

Armstrong, Joe: Friend of Jackie's; magazine publisher; philanthropist

Auchincloss, Janet Lee Bouvier: Jackie's mother (died 1989)

Awodey, Lou: Kenya branch director, National Outdoor Leadership School

Baker, Julie: Girlfriend; jewelry designer

Bales, Susan Ford: Daughter of President Gerald Ford and Betty Ford

Balfour, Victoria: New York correspondent for *People* magazine, 1988–91; author of *Rock Wives*

Barlow, Amelia: Daughter of John Perry Barlow; founder/director at Color Outside the Lines

Barlow, Anna: Daughter of John Perry Barlow

Barlow, John Perry: Wyoming rancher; Grateful Dead lyricist; cofounder of the Electronic Frontier Foundation; author (died 2018)

Barrymore, Drew: Actor; producer; host of *The Drew Barrymore Show*

Bartlett, Martha: Wife of D.C. columnist and JFK confidant Charles Bartlett; John's godmother

Begala, Paul: Former counselor to President Bill Clinton; political consultant and commentator; author

Beghe, Jason: Collegiate classmate; actor

Benway, Chris: Main flight instructor at FlightSafety International, Vero Beach, Florida; pilot

Berg, Dave: Co-producer, *The Tonight Show with Jay Leno*; author

Berman, Matt: Creative director, *George* magazine

Beyer, John: Underwater explorer; commercial fisherman; retired mortgage broker

Black, Barry C.: 62nd Chaplain of the U.S. Senate; former Chief of Chaplains of the United States Navy

Boyer, Greg: Trombonist with Parliament-Funkadelic; former trombonist with the Chuck Brown Band

Bradlee, Ben: *Washington Post* managing editor and then executive editor, 1965–91 (died 2014)

Bradlee, Tony: Wife of Ben Bradlee, artist (died 2011)

Brooks, Garth: American singer-songwriter

Bruce, Preston: White House doorman, 1952–77 (died 1994)

Budd, Adam: Former intern at Martha's Vineyard Airport; senior analyst Delta Airlines

Cherkasky, Michael: Former Chief of the Investigations Division, Manhattan DA's office; former president and CEO of Kroll; cofounder and board member of Exiger

Chermayeff, Sasha: Phillips Academy Andover classmate; artist; yoga instructor; grandmother of three

Childers, Kathryn: Secret Service agent, Kennedy Children's Detail; author; television producer

Chinlund, Nick: Brown classmate; actor

Clarke, David: Collegiate schoolmate; media and IT specialist (died 2023)

Clifford, Barry: Diver; underwater archaeological explorer who found the pirate ship the *Whydah* in 1984; founder of the Whydah Pirate Museums

Clinton, Bill: Forty-second president of the United States

Cohan, William: Andover schoolmate; former banker; novelist; author of *Four Friends: Promising Lives Cut Short*

Couric, Katie: Journalist; former co-anchor of the *Today* show; founder of Katie Couric Media

Cowen, Matt: Assistant editor, *George*; owner of Cram Content, Ltd.

Cramer, Bob: Collegiate classmate; advisor to and investor in pre-seed and seed stage companies

Curran, Robert: Traveler; explorer; photographer

Cushing, Richard Cardinal: Archbishop of Boston, 1944–70 (died 1970)

Dallos, Lisa: Director of communications, *George*; CEO of High 10 Media

D'Angelo, Joe: English and social studies teacher and karate instructor at Collegiate (retired); educational consultant

DePaulo, Lisa: Writer, *George*; journalist

DiPelesi, Roberto: Neighbor and friend of Santina Goodman; operatic tenor

Duchovny, David: Collegiate classmate; actor

Duffy, Karen "Duff": Former MTV veejay; author of *Wise Up: Irreverent Enlightenment from a Mother Who's Been Through It*

Ebenstein, William, Dr.: Executive director of the John F. Kennedy Jr. Institute for Worker Education (formerly Reaching Up)

Eckstein, Paul: Founding member of Naked Angels theater company; actor; television writer and producer (died 2023)

Emigh, John: Professor emeritus, Theater, Speech & Dance Department, Brown University

Fee, Gayle: "Inside Track" columnist for the *Boston Herald*, 1991–2017; now golfer and grandmother

Fekkai, Frédéric: Celebrity hairstylist

Ferguson, Gogo: Wedding host/owner of the Greyfield Inn, Cumberland Island; jewelry designer

Frazer, Leroy: Former deputy bureau chief of the Special Prosecutions Bureau, Manhattan DA's office; president of Leroy Frazer Jr. Consulting Inc.

Gabler, Neal: Cultural critic and author of the Edward M. Kennedy biographies *Catching the Wind* and *Against the Wind*

Gaines, Jim: Managing editor, *People* magazine, 1987–90; managing editor, *Life* magazine, 1990–92; managing editor, *Time* magazine, 1992–96; author, most recently, of *The Fifties: An Underground History*

Gillon, Steve: Brown University teaching assistant, history department; author of *America's Reluctant Prince: The Life of John F. Kennedy Jr.*; historian

Ginsberg, Gary: Brown University classmate; senior editor and counsel, *George*; Clinton administration official; media executive; author of *First Friends*

Goldberg, Whoopi: Actor and comedian

Goodman, Santina: Brown University classmate (died 2019)

Gould, Cheryl: Former executive producer of *NBC Nightly News with Tom Brokaw*

Grier, Rosey: Professional football player; bodyguard for RFK during 1968 presidential campaign

Guzzetti, Jeff: Former air safety investigator, National Transportation Safety Board; president of Guzzetti Aviation Risk Discovery, LLC

Haberman, Nancy: Public relations consultant for *George*; media director, EVP, Rubenstein Communications

Haberman, Zach: Intern at *George*; journalist, NBC News, *New York Post*; account director, BerlinRosen

Hageman, Hans: Collegiate schoolmate; former Executive Director of the Tutwiler Community Education Center in the Mississippi Delta; educator

Hannan, Philip M.: Auxiliary bishop of the Archdiocese of Washington, 1956–65 (died 2011)

Hart, Gary: U.S. senator from Colorado, 1975–87; 1988 Democratic presidential candidate

Hart, Jim: Former husband of Carly Simon; author of *Lucky Jim*

Hay, R. Couri: Gossip and society columnist; CEO, R. Couri Hay, Creative Public Relations

Heffernan, Paul: Former Boston juvenile court probation officer; judge

Hertz, Randy: NYU Law School professor, vice dean for Curriculum at NYU Law

Hill, Clint: U.S. Secret Service Agent who served five presidents: Eisenhower, Kennedy, Johnson, Nixon, and Ford

Hill, Ed: Andover classmate; attorney

Horovitz, Rachael: Andover classmate; film producer; writer

Hotchner, Tim: *George* magazine assistant; writer and film producer

Howie, Phineas: Son of Sasha Chermayeff and Philip Howie

Hussain, Munir: New Jersey businessman and private pilot

Hyman, Erik: Partner of Herb Ritts; Paul Hastings partner and global co-chair of Entertainment and Media

Iasiello, Louis: 23rd Chief of Navy Chaplains; rear admiral; Franciscan Scholar in Residence, Siena College

Issenberg, Sasha: Intern, contributing editor, *George*; author; journalist

Jean, Wyclef: Founding member and guitarist for the Fugees; Grammy Award–winning artist and producer

Jephson, Patrick: The private secretary and equerry to Diana, Princess of Wales; British-American television presenter; journalist; author

Kandel, Andrew: Former assistant DA at the Manhattan District Attorney's office; Global Chief Compliance Officer, Senior Legal Counsel, and Senior Managing Director at Cerberus Capital Management

Kelly, Keith: Former New York *Daily News* columnist; former *New York Post* "Media Ink" columnist; now editor-in-chief of *OurTown/The Spirit/Chelsea News*

Kennedy, Edward: Uncle; U.S. senator from Massachussets, 1962–2009 (died 2009)

Kennedy, Kerry: Cousin; lawyer; president of Robert F. Kennedy Human Rights organization

Kiernan, Peter D. III: Former partner at Goldman Sachs; Board of Directors, the Robin Hood Foundation; author; CEO of Kiernan Ventures

King, Charlie: Brown classmate; attorney; politician; partner at Mercury Public Affairs

King, Martin Luther, III: Eldest son of Martin Luther King Jr. and Coretta Scott King; human rights activist; chairman of the Drum Major Institute

Kirby, Paul: Hyannis Port friend

Kyriakos, George: Fashion hair stylist

Leggett, Christopher J.W.B.: Andover classmate; FACC interventional cardiologist

Leno, Jay: Comedian; host of *The Tonight Show with Jay Leno*

Lieber, Janno: NYU Law schoolmate; chair and CEO of the Metropolitan Transportation Authority in New York

Littell, Robbie: Brown University roommate; author of *The Men We Became*; founder of Revotop, LLC

Macks, Jon: Top writer for *The Tonight Show with Jay Leno*; producer of live television; author; president of Wild Bronco Productions

Maglione, Massimo: European and world history teacher at Collegiate (retired)

Maier, Thomas: Author of *The Kennedys: America's Emerald Kings*

Manocchia, Pat: Brown classmate; owner, founder, and director of La Palestra Center for Preventative Medicine

McCray, Wilson: Collegiate and Andover classmate; artist

McKeon, Kathy: Live-in housekeeper and personal assistant to Jacqueline Kennedy Onassis; author of *Jackie's Girl*

McKeon, Seamus: Husband of Kathy McKeon; general contractor who also helped John and Mrs. Kennedy with repairs in Hyannis

McMullen, Cabot: Hyannis Port neighbor; production designer for film and television

Merrill, Jack: Actor; co-founder of the Naked Angels theater company

Mitchell, Elizabeth "Biz": Executive editor at *George*; journalist; author; editor

Molloy, Joanna: "Rush & Molloy" columnist for the New York *Daily News*; coauthor of *The Greatest Beer Run Ever*

Moore, Demi: Actor

Mosley, John: Running back for Notre Dame; public-relations executive; director of college football development for the New York Yankees

Moutsatsos, Kiki Feroudi: Aristotle Onassis's private secretary; owner of La Perla Villas in Santorini; author of *The Onassis Women*

Murphy, Todd: Diver; Green Beret (retired); systems engineer/software developer

Neary, Sean: Associate editor, *George*; managing director, Edelman Smithfield

Neu, Charles: History professor emeritus, Brown University

Oberbeck, Chris: Brown University housemate; chairman of the board, chief executive officer, and president of Saratoga Investment Corp

O'Byrne, Charles: Former priest; executive vice president for policy, Related Companies

Paredes, Gustavo: Son of Jackie's personal assistant Providencia Paredes; Principal at GAP Strategies

Petruska, William M.: Captain, Chaplain Corps, U.S. Navy (retired)

Penn, Sean: Actor; director; filmmaker; cofounder and chairperson of the board of CORE

Pflaum, Mike: National Park Service ranger (retired)

Pitzer, Hilli: Art director for *People* magazine, 1983–2004; art director, *Daily Front Row*; creative department designer, Mount Sinai Hospital

Pogrebin, Abigail: American writer; journalist; podcast host

Radziwill, Carole: Television news producer; wife of Anthony Radziwill; author of *What Remains*

Rafael, Mark: Brown classmate; actor; professor emeritus at the University of San Francisco College of Arts and Sciences

Raposa, Laura: Former "Inside Track" columnist for the *Boston Herald*; now cook, baker, owner of the Foodsmith, Duxbury, Massachusetts

Richards, Cordelia: Brown University housemate; actor; writer

Roberts, Julia: Actor

Rush, George: Former "Rush & Malloy" columnist for the New York *Daily News*; co-author *Scandal: A Manual*

Rutenberg, Jim: Former New York *Daily News* staff writer, media columnist, White House reporter; now writer at large for the *New York Times*

Ryan, Fred: Assistant to the president and director of presidential appointments and scheduling for President Ronald Reagan; chief of staff to former president Reagan; former publisher and CEO of the *Washington Post*; founding CEO of Politico; chairman of the board of trustees of the Ronald Reagan Presidential Foundation & Institute

Sachs, Jeffrey A.: CEO of the Sachs Policy Group advising health care leaders on state and federal health care policy, trends and business strategy

Samson, Dan: Friend from college days; CEO of Lovin' Brands

Schmidt, Samantha: Convent of the Sacred Heart alumna; owner of Sophisticated Animal Minding

Seymore, Jim: *People* magazine executive editor, 1987–90; *Entertainment Weekly* managing editor, 1990–2002

Shaw, Maud: White House nanny to John and Caroline, 1957–63 (died 1988)

Sheehan, Michael: Corporate and political communications trainer and strategist; president, Sheehan Associates

Shields, Brooke: Model, actor, founder of Beginning Is Now

Shields, Lisa: Girlfriend; former ABC News editorial producer; strategic communications executive

Showalter, Mike: Head of facilities, Hachette Filipacchi Magazines

Shrum, Bob: Political strategist and speechwriter

Siegel, Betsy: Wife of John's Brown classmate and friend Kenan Siegel

Simon, Carly: Singer-songwriter; friend of Jackie's

Spiegel, Jeremy: Former intern and associate producer, *A Current Affair*; executive producer, *EXTRA!*

Steel, Brian: Former assistant DA at the Manhattan District Attorney's office; now managing director, Strategic Communications at Vista Equity Partners

Stein, Keith: Canadian business executive

Stone, Oliver: Film director; producer; screenwriter

Stott, Barry: Pilot; ran the Martha's Vineyard charter airline Air New England

Styron, Rose: Author; journalist; human rights activist; wife of writer William Styron

Taneja, Narendra: Chairman, Independent Energy Policy Institute, New Delhi

Teodorescu, Radu: Celebrity fitness trainer

Terenzio, RoseMarie: John's executive assistant at *George*; strategic communications professional and author of the *New York Times* bestseller *Fairy Tale Interrupted*

Tyson, Mike: Former world heavyweight boxing champion; friend; entertainer; entrepreneur

Vaughn, Barbara: Photographic artist

Viteretti, Bob: Former acting bureau chief, Organized Crime Unit, Manhattan DA's office; investigative and intelligence consultant; CEO of RJV Associates

Wells, Tom: Secret Service Agent, 1959–81

Warnecke, Fred: Son of Jack Warnecke, architect who designed JFK's memorial at Arlington National Cemetery

Worrell, Geoffrey: Collegiate classmate; former appellate attorney; high school English teacher in New York City

Photo Credits

6. Photo by Stephen Rose/Getty Images

7. Photo by Sasha Chermayeff

8. Photo by Jon Naso/NY *Daily News* Archive via Getty Images

9. © Barbara Vaughn

10. Photo courtesy of Julie Baker

11. Photo by Jeffrey Markowitz/Sygma via Getty Images

12. Photo by Stephen Rose/Getty Images

13. Photo by Ulrike Welsch/Photo Researchers History/Getty Images

14. Photo by Brooks Kraft LLC/Sygma via Getty Images

15. Photo by Brooks Kraft LLC/Sygma via Getty Images

16. Bob Strong/AFP via Getty Images

17. Robert Curran Photography

18. National Park Service

19. Photo courtesy of Jack Merrill

20. Kevin Wisniewski/Shutterstock

21. Photo courtesy of RoseMarie Terenzio

22. Kevin Wisniewski/Shutterstock

23. Photo by Tyler Mallory/Liaison

24. Photo by Denis Reggie

25. Photo by Denis Reggie

26. Photo by Jon Naso/NY *Daily News* Archive via Getty Images

27. *Boston Herald*/Shutterstock

28. Everett/Shutterstock

About the Authors

RoseMarie Terenzio is the *New York Times* bestselling author of *Fairy Tale Interrupted* and the former executive assistant to John F. Kennedy Jr. She served as JFK Jr.'s chief of staff at *George* magazine and oversaw his public relations and philanthropic causes until his death in 1999. Terenzio is the executive producer of Paramount Network's *I Am JFK, Jr.* She is from New York City, where she lives and works as a strategic communications professional.

Liz McNeil is an editor-at-large at *People* magazine. She was an executive producer of the Discovery+ documentary *Rebuilding Hope: The Children of 9/11* and the writer, narrator, and executive producer of *People*'s podcast *Cover-Up*. She lives in Hastings-on-Hudson, New York.